THE GENTLEMAN FROM GEORGIA

THE GENTLEMAN

THE BIOGRAPHY OF

FROM GEORGIA

NEWT GINGRICH

By Mel Steely

MERCER UNIVERSITY PRESS

MACON, GEORGIA

2000

ISBN 0-86554-671-1
MUP/H500

Mercer University Press
6316 Peake Road
Macon, Georgia 31210-3960
©2000
All rights reserved

First Edition.

∞The paper used in this publication meets the minimum requirements of
American National Standard for Information Sciences—Permanence of Paper
for Printed Library Materials, ANSI Z39.48-1984.

Library of Congress Cataloging-in-Publication Data

Steely, Mel.
      The gentleman from Georgia: the biography of Newt Gingrich / by
Mel Steely. —1st ed.
      p. cm.
  Includes bibliographical references and index.
  ISBN 0-86554-671-1 (alk. paper)
    1.   Gingrich, Newt. 2. Legislators—United States—Biography. 3.
      United States. Congress. House—Speaker—Biography. I. Title.

E840.8.G5 S74 2000
328.73'092—dc21
[B]   99-052465

CONTENTS

Preface

By the time I met Newt Gingrich he had already led a fairly unusual and interesting life. Born in Pennsylvania in 1943, his first formative years were spent with an essentially single mother and being raised by an extended family. Adopted when he was three he grew up in a military family following his father's postings around the country and to France and Germany. As he grew into his teens he experienced the Cold War at first hand. It was apparent early on that he was bright and inquisitive. At ease with adults, he seemed mature beyond his years.

In high school in Columbus, Georgia, Newt made new friends who would be close to him for years to come. He excelled in academics, played football, got involved in politics, and courted his math teacher, marrying her shortly after graduation. He entered college, had a baby, worked a variety of jobs to make ends meet and became a Baptist. He expanded his political activities into state politics and dropped out school for a semester to run a congressional campaign. He entered graduate school in New Orleans, worked on the Nelson Rockefeller presidential campaign, had a second child, and began teaching. He spent a year in Belgium with his family working on his doctoral dissertation and in 1970 came to West Georgia College where I met him.

I was on the committee that hired Newt to teach history at West Georgia College and was impressed and intrigued by his span of reading and his approach to teaching. He moved to a house on Howell Road just across from the campus and on a late summer morning he walked over to the Social Sciences building where I was preparing for the upcoming quarter. He stuck his head in and introduced himself. We did not discuss politics but we did begin a friendship that has lasted three decades.

Jimmy Carter was about to be elected Governor and I had worked for his primary opponent, Carl Sanders. Newt was interested in the details of the Carter campaign. I had been interested in politics since my father let me help him in the 1946 Gene Talmadge campaign and that meshed with Newt's political interests and ambitions. I got involved with his first campaign in 1974 and we began saving campaign materials almost from the start. We wanted to use the 1974 materials for the next campaign but also with an eye toward future scholars. It did not seem presumptuous to us because we thought Newt would be successful in his quest for a seat in Congress and that he would have a sizable influence on political history. He was successful in 1978 on his third try and I worked in his campaigns and as a congressional aide through 1992. I became curator of his papers after he agreed to donate them to the West Georgia College archives.

In the fall of 1994, when it became clear that he would be Speaker, I decided to write a biography that would show Newt as I knew him instead of the caricature being presented in the press at that time. While hardly perfect he was not the evil Grinch stealing Christmas. During a drive to the airport in Nashville following a speech he made at Opryland, I told him I was going to write the book and asked if he wanted to be involved. He told me to go ahead but that he was much too busy to be involved and for me to write it as I remembered it. This proved to be true. Getting his time during the four years of his speakership proved to be a daunting task. I worked mostly from my own papers collected from campaigns and my congressional work and from some of the Gingrich Papers in the University of West Georgia (UWG) Archives. Most of his papers, over 600 boxes, have yet to be processed and catalogued. I also interviewed numerous aides, friends, and colleagues who had worked with Newt and they were generous with their time and memories. These mostly taped interviews are now part of the Gingrich Papers or the Georgia's Political Heritage Program which is also housed in the UWG Archives.

I want to thank Myron House, the UWG archivist, for invaluable help in working with the Gingrich documents and Charles Beard and the staff of the Ingram Library for their help and kindness while I worked on the book. My colleagues in the history department were generous in allowing me occasional released time for writing. Dr. Marc Jolley and the editors at Mercer University Press were both patient and helpful with their time and assistance.

I owe a great debt to my wife, Nancy. She not only offered support and encouragement, but spent many hours reading the various chapters and suggesting needed revisions. Finally, I want to thank my grandchildren for their forbearance and understanding as I spent time on the book instead of spending it with them.

TO HENRY T. STEELY
Who introduced me to politics and
taught me the love of the game.

THE GENTLEMAN FROM GEORGIA

1

PREPARATION

Newton Leroy Gingrich, named after his two grandfathers, was born after a long labor on 17 June 1943 in Harrisburg, Pennsylvania of Scotch-Irish stock to Kathleen "Kit" Daugherty and Newton McPhearson, a farm boy from Fiddler's Elbo, Pennsylvania. They had married in Middletown, Pennsylvania in 1942 and Newt was their first child. Kit's father had been killed in an auto accident prior to her marriage to Newt. They lived first in an apartment beside her mother and then with his parents in Middletown. The marriage was not happy for very long. One morning, while Kit was pregnant with Newt, her husband hit her and drew down his father's wrath. The elder McPhearson told his son that he could never again enter his house if he hit her once more. Newt joined the Merchant Marine shortly after that and was not present when his son was born in June. He came home on leave in August and Kit began divorce proceedings.[1]

While Kit worked as a "junior mechanic," servicing machines for the war effort, Newt was doted on by a supportive and loving extended family. "He was a beautiful little boy." Those closest to him, besides his mother, were his grandmother Ethel Daugherty and his Aunt Loma and Uncle Calvin McPhearson. Kit and little Newt lived with her mother who helped Newt develop a desire for learning. Ethel and Loma read to Newt a great deal and instilled a love of books and reading that would stay with him.

---

[1] Robert and Kathleen Gingrich, interview by author, tape recording, 22 March 1992, Gingrich Papers, State University of West Georgia Archives, Carrollton.

Spending time with Loma and Calvin was heaven for Newt and he credits them with being his earliest teachers and two who had an exceptionally strong influence on his life. Uncle Cal taught him early on that "the world was tough—a stoic world where you did your duty and endured."[2]

In 1946 Kit married Bob Gingrich who had worked on the Reading Railroad before joining the Army. Shortly after the marriage Bob adopted Newt and changed his name to Gingrich. From that time on Newt led the nomadic life of an "army brat." After graduating from Gettysburg College in 1951 Bob was sent to Korea as a combat infantry officer and Newt spent a good part of the summers of 1951 and 1952 with Aunt Loma playing on wagons in the orchard and breaking his arm while trying to be like Burt Lancaster flipping up to a tree limb.

That same summer of 1952 Newt saw John Wayne in the *Sands of Iwo Jima* and was so impressed by the characters' sense of devotion and stoicism that he watched it three times in one day. The fact that his father was in combat in Korea at that time made it an especially relevant film for Newt. Films played an important role in Newt's life whether they were Lancaster adventure epics or John Wayne war and western movies. These films carried a message for the young Newt that this is how men are supposed to act and that message was reinforced by the men around him, "Big Newt," Bob Gingrich and his Uncle Cal. The concepts of duty and devotion to that duty were made real by these experiences.[3]

After Bob Gingrich returned from Korea he was transferred to Fort Riley, Kansas. Kansas remains vivid in Newt's mind. There he received a first-hand introduction to the old west. He saw General George Custer's horse (stuffed) and viewed signs noting this site was the eastern-most site of Comanche Indian raids.

He loved animals, collected snakes and had a Doberman Pinscher named Captain's Pride of Riley, "Pride" for short. Later, when Newt was fourteen, he would venture into frozen waters to rescue Pride after the dog broke through ice on a frozen pond. A friend drove the shivering pair home. His compassion for animals came out again when his mother, no lover of snakes, ordered him to release one and take it

---

[2] Newt Gingrich, interview by author, tape recording, 13 January 1993, Gingrich Papers, State University of West Georgia Archives, Carrollton.

[3] Ibid.

out of the house. He objected, noting that it was cold and the snake would freeze. Kit was insistent. He removed the snake from the house, dug a hole for the creature's warmth, and came back in with tears in his eyes because he feared the snake would die.[4]

Newt was not the average school child. At Fort Riley he was ahead of his class and the teachers, noting his interest in and knowledge of animals, gave him a projector and slides on animals. He would go from class to class talking about the animals to the other students. He also developed an interest in filmmaking when his father took him out with an aggressor unit training at Fort Riley. He watched "The Big Picture," a television program sponsored by the Defense Department, as it was being filmed and spent time with the cameramen. His teacher called Kit one day to let her know that Newt wanted to write to Hollywood to check out the cost of a movie camera to see if he could purchase it and make movies. This desire, though unrealized due to cost, was reflective of his fascination with movies.[5]

In Kansas Newt also learned to appreciate the company of adults. He was knowledgeable beyond his age due to an inquisitive nature and an insatiable desire for reading. At Fort Riley he was taken under the wing of Colonel Lucius Clay, then the intelligence commanding officer at the school at Fort Riley. Clay and his wife took Newt into their home for long talks about the art of war and peace and gave him a chance as a young teenager to experience and participate in adult conversation. They took his questions and comments seriously and did not treat him as a child but with respect. Clay also helped guide Newt's reading and taught him an invaluable skill he had picked up in China—how to go to sleep instantly, an ability he later found especially useful while on the campaign trail and in Congress.

Newt returned frequently to Pennsylvania in the summers to stay with Aunt Loma or with Aunt Louise and Uncle Bruce in Harrisburg, "Big Newt" in Steelton and other relatives in Royalton. He had a large extended family in a twenty-mile radius around Harrisburg. Kit and Bob felt it was important for Newt to know and be close to the McPhearsons. This enabled him to grow up within a family community, indeed the person he was closest to, other than his mother, was Loma

---

[4] Bob and Kit Gingrich, interview, 1992.

[5] Ibid.; Newt Gingrich, interview, 93.

McPhearson who gave him both love and affection as well as a desire for learning.

The future professor spent much of his time at the library in Harrisburg, traveled to Hershey, visited relatives and followed up on his interest in fossils and dinosaurs which he had acquired in Kansas. He was thirteen at the time and worked for an archeologist named John Wittoft who was associated with the University of Pennsylvania. It was during this period that Newt met Paul Walker, editor of the Harrisburg *Home Star*, a shopper's newspaper.

During the summer of 1953 Newt came to believe that Harrisburg should have a zoo. He went to city hall and talked to the mayor, Nolan Ziegler, about it. Ziegler passed him on to his friend Paul Walker. "Paul, there is a young kid that's been bothering me over here for the past week about establishing a zoo in Harrisburg and it is taking up too much time and I don't have an answer for him. You're running a newspaper and you want news and this kid is news so I'm going to send him over to you." Shortly after that Newt met with Walker.[6]

Walker took an instant liking to this brash young man who did not realize he was being brash. Newt was "neat, spoke slowly, was polite and listened." Walker thought Newt exhibited real salesmanship. "I told him there was a typewriter...write it up after you've got a statement from the mayor and then ask some people on the street. Then write an article and I'll print it." The article appeared on the front page. From that point on Newt dropped by the newspaper office when he was in Harrisburg, mostly in the summers, and helped take ads, check on circulation and be a general "boy Friday" for Walker.

Newt credits Walker with training him but Walker insisted he "didn't exactly train him, I encouraged him to write and suggested books at the library that would help in his career." He told him to read *Walden* and "Civil Disobedience" by Thoreau to teach him to think and introduced him to Frank Canton, a conservative Pennsylvania writer. He took his young helper to Davenport's Restaurant for lunch to repay him for his help at the newspaper and to have him listen to lawyers, bankers, merchants and newspaper people. Newt would usually voice an opinion, "quietly expressed, very gentlemanly, not arrogant. He was practical and curious, trying to find the truth." Newt and Walker

---

6 Paul Walker, interview by author, 15 June 1984, Gingrich Papers 086, State University of West Georgia Archives, Carrollton.

talked at length about politics and argued good-naturedly about the 1956 presidential campaign with Walker for Stevenson and Newt for Eisenhower. In 1960 Walker, a solid Democrat, supported Kennedy and Newt was for Nixon. Walker remembered Newt being interested in Nixon early on. Newt was not interested in local or state politics. "I'm not surprised that he went to Congress...he had his eye on Washington back then. We didn't clash but exchanged ideas on politics...our ideas bumped around and made sparks."

While working at the State Museum, Wittoft informed Newt that the museum would be closed for renovation. Newt leaked this information to Walker and they crusaded successfully, along with a paper in York, to keep the museum open. Newt wanted to continue pushing for a zoo and had other ideas he wanted published, but Walker's motto was "all the news that fits we'll print." Newt's articles were taking up space that could go for ads. Walker decided to introduce Newt to John Price, the news director at WHP radio hoping Price would let Newt air his ideas on radio. "Give Newt a contact and he'll know how to handle it," said Walker.

At WHP Newt was able to gain experience "doing radio shows, reading commentary and reading stuff off the wires." Walker noted, "John got a kick out of Newt, like I did." Walker, a very patriotic man, a naturalist and lover of the outdoors, told Newt stories about his favorite president, Teddy Roosevelt, whom he had met and shook hands with as a boy, and stirred Newt's interest in rock collecting. He advised Newt to "read all you can, ask questions, be curious and don't be too sure of anything until you check it out."[7]

In 1956 Bob Gingrich was sent to France and took his family, Kit, Newt, and daughters Susan and Robbie with him. Newt had been accepted by kids in Pennsylvania because of his family contacts and his repeated appearances there in the summer. He had been "fig Newton" or "Noodle soup" to them playing ball, going to amusement parks and so on. The summers were fun for Newt but he made few close or lasting friendships among playmates his age. Adults now made up a large part of his world. Being mature beyond his years was both a curse and a blessing for the "army brat." Newt's friends would come and go as their fathers were transferred and he learned to accept that fact of life and not to establish very close relationships.

---

[7] Ibid. Newt Gingrich, interview, GIN087, 1993.

The first few months in France the Gingrichs lived in a one-bedroom hotel room in Orleans where Newt attended the eight and ninth grades at the American high school. He learned discipline from a tough retired Marine officer who taught there and became close friends with a boy his own age, Billy Wilson, with whom he built rockets and played war games. Wilson's father was transferred after nine or ten months and Newt once again turned to adults for companionship.

After a few months Bob rented the first floor of a chateau in Beaugency south of Orleans. With a live-in maid and a gardener for the three acre garden, the Gingrichs lived comfortably off the economy. Newt had his dog, Pride, and purchased a ten-speed bike with his bingo winnings. He often rode the bus into Orleans to seek adventure. Once he and a friend told their parents they would be sleeping at the other's house and then went into Orleans to stay out all night in violation of the curfew. Early in the morning as exhaustion set in, the pair went to an MP office. The MPs called Bob, who later had to answer to his commanding officer for his son's indiscretion, and then brought Newt home. "Dad picked me up off the floor and slammed me against the wall threatening me with bodily harm if I ever did that again...he was furious." Bob said Newt took it because "it is hard to be belligerent when your feet aren't touching the ground. I think that was the last time I ever laid a hand on him." When Newt talks about the experience it is clear that his stepfather would never have occasion to repeat the incident.[8]

Newt learned enough French to survive and frequently he and the other students would trade at PX for goods to swap for champagne with local residents. The economy being what it was the American dollar was highly valued and good deals could be had on a regular basis. American influence was growing in Europe at the time and Newt remembers drifting down a dusty walk in a small French carnival listening to Little Richard sing "Lucille" over a loud speaker—rock and roll was in. He thought as a fourteen year old, "This is what it meant to be an American...we are going to dominate the planet. After all, American kids were not walking around listening to French songs." He pursued his interest in fossils and had some of them confiscated by the French government when he attempted to mail them home.

---

[8] Newt Gingrich interview with author, 1993; Bob and Kit Gingrich interview with author, 1992.

Living in Europe offered the opportunity for travel and the Gingrichs took full advantage of it. In the summer of 1957 they went to Barcelona, Spain for a few weeks. There they attended bullfights, listened to Spanish music and absorbed local color. There Newt also fell madly in love with an older Spanish woman in her early twenties whose uncle owned the campground where they stayed. She would bring Newt American papers each morning but otherwise totally ignored him. Newt loved Barcelona and still has great affection for that region today.

Driving back through the Pyrenees Mountains and through the length of France, Newt gained a heightened appreciation for the history of the area that excited the naturalist in him. In the spring of 1958 they went to the Brussels World's Fair and spent time in Belgium—a place Newt would visit later while working on his doctoral dissertation. His strongest memory of the World's Fair is one of being impressed by the number of national pavilions, and especially the Soviet Union pavilion. "I must have collected 600 pamphlets there to take home and study for the next few weeks." His interest in the Cold War and a desire to know the enemy caused him to study the literature carefully for hours.[9]

One trip made an impression on Newt that was to have major lasting effect. In 1957 the Gingrichs visited old friends, Darvin and Sue Patrick, in the historic town of Verdun. Sue had been a schoolmate of Bob's in Hummelstown and both were Army families, Darvin having been a POW of the Japanese during the World War II. They stayed with the Patricks and Newt slept in a storage room filled with war memorabilia. He was surrounded by the tools of war and felt as though he was sleeping among icons.

Battle damage from World War I was still evident in Verdun as Darvin pointed out to Newt. During the three days they stayed with the Patricks, Newt listened to the two soldiers swap war stories about World War II and Korea. He walked the streets of the battle-scarred city of 20,000 and absorbed the cold reality of the impact of war. The two families went to visit the great World War I battlefield just outside the city. The costs of war were becoming more and more evident to young Newt.

After visiting the fortifications and seeing where so many had fought and died, the two families passed through a tourist building

---

9 Newt Gingrich, interview with author, 1993.

which contained an ossuary holding the bones of thousands of French soldiers who had died during the great battle. The bones were clearly visible through windows and filled the room. Seeing these bones caused Newt to come face to face with the futility of war and he decided that he would do what he could to prevent such a reoccurrence. Even today he views this moment as a genuine turning point in his life. "That last day was probably the most stunning event of my life. It was a sense of coming face to face with an unavoidable reality."[10]

Seeing John Wayne assault Iwo Jima in the movies was mythic. Seeing the ossuary was real. The damage he had seen at Verdun was real. The damage from Patton's tanks in Orleans was still visible and real. One of his French friends had lost his father in World War II and his loss was real. Watching the paratroopers challenge DeGaulle's republic was real. Past history was past reality. The daily grind of the US Army in France preparing for a hot instead of a cold war was real and ever present in Newt's life.

In the summer of 1958 the Gingrichs were transferred to Stuttgart, Germany where they lived in officers quarters instead of a chateau. Here they were part of an American enclave instead of living among the locals as they had in France where they had lived on the economy. They arrived on the day the US landed troops in Lebanon as part of the Eisenhower Doctrine. Newt remembers his father reading the announcement in *Stars and Stripes*, move back from the table saying, "I'll be back later," and reporting for duty. They had no idea whether he would be going to Lebanon or when "later" would be. Newt remembers the "vividness of the reality of the Cold War and of the imminence of potential combat that was absolutely part of our world."[11]

Though living inside the Army enclave and being bussed in an armored bus to school, he did manage to involve himself in typical teenage pastimes. He went to the zoo, attended dances, played second string tackle on the school football team, attended the Protestant chapel where he was acolyte to a Methodist minister (Newt had been raised Lutheran), and worked in the post library. He earned money while setting pins at the bowling alley and as a gardener for a base housing project. This latter job gave him time for reflection while working outdoors. It was while he was putting in sod that he decided to do

---

[10] Ibid.
[11] Ibid.

something with his life to help "stop" the Soviet Empire and to protect freedom as the other men in his family had done. It was clear that he could not contribute in a military capacity due to his poor eyesight and flat feet so he decided to focus on public policy. His study of history and political science had shown him the importance of political decisions in the great issues of war and peace. He also remembered the discussion his father and Darvin Patrick had following their visit to the Verdun battlefield wherein they observed the real responsibility for the carnage at Verdun rested on the politicians who sent the soldiers off to die. He decided he would focus on politics and government.

Newt pulled at society's restraints and wanted to go beyond the limits when possible. He wanted to join the University of Maryland's campus abroad program as an eighth grader but his father refused. He had studied stock investing and economics and wanted to invest the money he had earned if for no other reason than as a learning experience. Again, his father refused. Newt did not agree with either decision but now feels both were correct.

Though his parents were strict and army life placed restrictions on him, he received an astonishing amount of freedom for a fifteen-year old. On a trip to Paris with his mother and sisters, Newt served as navigator and elder male. After convincing his mother, he was even allowed to stay up all night and wander Paris. He loved the city and ended up in the early hours of the morning in the great market sleeping on a park bench and being awakened by a beggar trying to pick his pocket. "The world is large, interesting, constantly changing and full of amazing interesting things. Why wouldn't you be sort of happy and amused and wander around learning when given the opportunity?"[12]

Despite the romance and adventure around him, Newt still remembered Verdun. He remembered thinking at the time that "life is real and Auschwitz is real and the Nazis were real and we were faced in our lifetime by an enemy equally as dangerous and that while life could be very sweet it could be equally dangerous." President Ronald Reagan's designation of the Soviet Union as an "evil empire" resonated with Newt because of those teen years in France and Germany three decades earlier.

---

[12] Ibid.

He read material on politics and politicians, especially books and articles about Richard Nixon. He went to his sophomore English teacher, Nando Amabile, who was teaching in the US Army High School in Stuttgart and would later teach Newt history. He sought permission from Amabile to write a major paper on the balance of naval power between Russia, Great Britain and the United States. Because Newt was the best student he had Amabile agreed. Newt spent the most of the year researching and writing this paper. Though a poor typist he turned out ten pages a day and eventually handed in 200 pages. "Newt was an unusual student who would stand out no matter what. Just imagine, 200 pages single spaced and have it make sense...as a sophomore. The truth is that I didn't teach Newt a whole hell of a lot. What I did was recognize a talent and let it run loose. He was not a great speller but if detail was important he would be thorough. He didn't have much interest in grades...he was interested in learning."[13]

The practical Newt emerged early in his first political experiences.[14] Amabile tells of the time Newt was running for a school office and stood up to make a speech about why they should vote for him. He had his notes prepared but when he stood to speak, he looked at Amabile, smiled, wadded the notes and threw them into a wastebasket. He then joked with the students, used humor and talked to them instead of making a speech. "He was a born politician. He used humor instead of logic because that is what students were interested in and what would work."

The teacher noted that Newt associated well with other students, but that he could also talk to adults and was treated as an equal. "Newt was better read in history, politics, and government than I was. He had a keen mind, a very good analytical mind." Amabile's assessment of Newt would be confirmed during the 1960 presidential election. During the early stages of the campaign Newt told Amabile, "[T]here is no way Kennedy can possibly lose [the nomination]." Amabile supported Governor Robert B. Meyner of New Jersey as a dark horse. Amabile's opinion of Newt grew, however, as Meyner's chances for nomination faded and Kennedy became the Democratic candidate.

---

[13] Nando Amabile, interview by author, tape recording, 16 June 1984, Gingrich Papers, University of West Georgia Archives, Carrollton.
[14] Ibid.

Amabile was impressed with Newt in other ways as well. "He told me when his dad got to [Fort Benning,] Georgia that he was going to join the Republican Party, that he was going to go to college in Georgia and that he was going to earn his Ph.D. and teach college and that he was going to run for Congress by the time he was twenty-nine years old. I believed him. Newt didn't reject ideas just because they came from the left He looked at them. He was a man-boy. He recognized that he was still in a learning situation and approached life and school as something that was giving to him…balanced by what he took out of it."

In Stuttgart Newt led a more Americanized life than in France. He played football badly (second string tackle and third string fullback) but loved it. He read military doctrine manuals, was active in student government and church groups, went to Munich for Oktoberfest and had his first alcoholic drink with his father who systematically inebriated him as a lesson on drinking. He took dance lessons and went on trips, but always had the bomb damage from World War II in Stuttgart to bring him back to reality. He listened to Armed Forces Radio, read the *Stars and Stripes*, the *Herald Tribune*, *Time* and *Newsweek* but was not really in touch with America. He did not dine in fast food restaurants, or learn how to drive a car, watch drive-in movies or experience other aspects of American teenage life.

Newt differed from stateside teens in another sense. His mother always kept a footlocker filled with things they would take with them if they had a twenty-four hour alert and were leaving the country. Kit had an escape route to Switzerland planned and had gone over it with the children. During the late 1950s, the Berlin crisis and Castro's takeover in Cuba as well as the Lebanon incident and Sputnik greatly raised international tensions. The year before Newt arrived in Europe the Soviets had brutally crushed the Hungarian freedom revolution. The young Gingrich felt the Cold War palpably and daily. "When you are awakened at 3:00 A.M. by an alert and watch your dad and the 7th Army HQ go into the field, there is a real sense that you are a hostage in a way," he remembered. The Cold War was very real to him, but there was no alternative for a soldier's family.

In late January 1960 Kit and the children left Bremerhaven on a US transport ship and spent six days crossing back to New York. During the crossing Newt walked the decks and spent time looking at sky and sea considering both the past and the future. The stoic views of his stepfather and Uncle Cal influenced him—the idea that the infantry will take casualties, endure privation, remain until the objective was taken was important in shaping his thinking about his own future. Newt began to view serious politicians much like soldiers. To him there was a mission involved that was more than just solving the constituent problems of those who elected him, though that was a vital responsibility. Newt remembers thinking, "This will absorb my life. I could be an active participant in the process of shaping public policy in order to preserve freedom by containing and defeating the Soviet Union." It seemed to him that this was a direct extension of his stepfather's career. "It was the most effective thing I could do to ensure that the US would remain free. When I arrived in New York I embarked on a thirty-two [now almost forty] year odyssey."[15]

---

[15] Newt Gingrich, interview, 1993.

2

APPRENTICESHIP

Newt, his mother, and two sisters joined Major Gingrich at Fort Benning in Columbus, Georgia. They lived off post for a few months before moving into officers quarters and Newt entered Baker High School. His two years at Baker had a great impact on the young Gingrich. He came at a time when the relatively new principal, Dr. Fred Kirby, was building a first rate academic institution. He had built an excellent faculty, including four individuals who would influence Newt for years to come: Foster Watkins, the assistant principal and coach; James "Bubba" Ball, the head coach; Dr. Katrina Yielding, a government teacher and teacher of the accelerated class; and Jackie Battley, Newt's math teacher and future wife.[1]

In addition to the teachers who would influence him Newt also met two other "army brats," Jim Tilton and Calvin Rausch. Tilton would quickly become his best friend, until his untimely death from cancer in 1993. Rausch, who was very bright and a leader in ROTC, was also close to Newt and Jim at Baker High but he too died at an early age, in his early thirties. The closeness between Newt and Tilton was deep and lasting and approached that of brothers.

Living and traveling with a military family had stimulated Newt and opened him to new ideas and experiences. He had learned to make friends quickly and to jump into the middle of almost any intellectually challenging situation. Tilton remembered first meeting Newt in an accelerated group government class taught by Nancy Armstrong, the

---

[1] Foster Watkins, interview by author, tape recording,. 9 February 1993, Newt Gingrich Papers State University of West Georgia Archives, Carrollton.

most feared and respected government teacher. Newt sat on the first row "with that huge head and lots of hair." During the course of the lecture Newt interrupted and challenged her on the first day. His boldness shocked and interested the other students and the fact that he survived with a draw further impressed them. Tilton thought he was worth helping and decided to take him under his wing to explain how things worked and to "show him the ropes." The next class they sat on the back row and "that was the start of a good friendship, a friendship that has meant a lot more to me than anybody could know."[2]

Newt was very friendly and loaded with information and ideas. He was not desperate to fit in but did want to know the rules. He had a panoramic view of history and was very eager, knowledgeable, and confident. "I can't imagine anyone who knew him more than a day or so really thinking he was arrogant," said Tilton. Watkins, Ball, and Yielding also deny any arrogance but note that some might mistake a sure knowledge of his topic of conversation as arrogance.[3]

Newt was a Merit Scholar semi-finalist, won essay contests, the Time Magazine Current Events Award and was in debate, and the Thespian Society. According to his teachers, he believed in the great liberal arts tradition, generalization was better than specialization. Newt and Tilton were debate partners and did very well most of the time. Tilton was the presenter and Newt had great rebuttal skills. Early in their junior year, they debated two girls from Little Doe Run High School and joked about Big Baker versus Little Doe Run. They did not research nor prepare well and lost the debate. Though a humiliating experience, the lesson was a good one: prepare and take nothing for granted.[4]

Newt very quickly focused on the math and geometry teacher, Jackie Battley, a good friend of Nancy Armstrong. His interest in her led him to get involved in the Junior Class Talent Show and the Thespian Society because Battley was the sponsor. Newt loved comedy. He, Tilton, and Rausch would often do routines from the

---

[2] Jim Tilton, interview by author, tape recording, 26 March 1992, Gingrich Papers, State University of West Georgia Archives.

[3] Ibid.; Watkins, interview, 1993; James Ball and Katrina Yielding, interview by author, tape recording, 11 February 1993, Gingrich Papers, State University of West Georgia Archives.

[4] Tilton, interview, 1992; Ball and Yielding, interview, 1993; Watkins, interview, 1993.

movies—frequently around Tilton's mother's kitchen table. They selected a scene from "The Apartment" to do for the talent show. Newt also served as the master of ceremonies for the show and failed to practice his timing. As a result his jokes were flat and he was dying on stage. Seeing every situation as an opportunity he told the audience, "If you are not going to laugh, at least throw money." The audience loved it and threw pennies. Newt collected thirty-two cents and he and Tilton went next door for ice cream.

Newt loved to read and usually carried a big bulky brief case full of books and papers with him. He would read while he walked and during his spare time at work. He worked at libraries at Fort Benning, Emory University, and at the Atlanta Public Library to make money. Tilton would substitute for him at the Fort Benning library when necessary. He also loved movies, especially comedies and heroic epics such as *The Magnificent Seven*, *El Cid*, and *Khartoum*. Indeed, almost anything with Charlton Heston or John Wayne would draw these young men to the theater. Brave men doing their duty with vision, facing impossible odds never failed to impress them. These movies became almost a metaphor for life and an extension of life's reality as they knew it.

The two also talked a great deal about religion. Newt had been raised a Lutheran and Tilton was just a regular, Army-issue Protestant. Both took religion seriously and talked about God, revealed wisdom, the importance of responsibility, and other issues. "Newt was a seriously God-fearing person, one who felt the responsibility. He was a good person but not a goody-goody. Church was very important to him. He became a Baptist after marrying Jackie, who was a staunch Baptist, and eventually became a deacon in the Baptist church."[5]

Along with church, Newt loved football. He came out for football in spite of the fact that he could not see well and was not fast. He was put on the defensive line as a tackle. He enjoyed hitting and getting hit. He would come out of a scrimmage absolutely elated, "happy as a clam." He earned the admiration and respect of the football players and brought humor to the team. This sport suited him well and gave him some of his greatest lessons. He was not a great athlete but he persevered. Coaches Foster Watkins and "Bubba" Ball taught him to get up quickly no matter how hard he was hit and he learned the

---

[5] Tilton, interview, 1992; Ibid, 26 March 1992.

lesson well. He would bounce up and be "cheerfully in your face" on the next play. "That's the kind of spirit people can't ignore." He also worked to encourage his teammates after a bad play.[6]

Newt considered coaches to be warriors, field generals worthy of emulation. To Newt, Vince Lombardi, Paul "Bear" Bryant and Joe Paterno were all examples of leadership and skill. While he admired many coaches, he was personally influenced most by Coach Ball at Baker High and Coach Charlie Grisham at Carrollton High, where Newt's daughters attended school and with whom Newt attended church. Coach Ball, for whom Newt had the greatest respect and affection, had him cut his hair to a crew cut in order to fit the helmet. About Ball, Newt said, "A great coach. I learned a lot of what kept me going when I ran for Congress from Coach Ball. He was a coach, not a teacher. He knew how to inspire and get the best out of you." "Coach Ball taught me that will, persistence and courage matter. This is what life is like. You stick it out or you don't. You just do the best you can. That is the basis of small business and of my political career. I think he genuinely shaped me in the best sense."

"Charlie Grisham was a wonderful, wonderful experience. [He was] the greatest coach I've ever personally known. Great coaches don't coach sports, they coach people. I would sit on the sidelines during practice and in church and ask questions, how do you think about a team, how do you think about a particular student, how do you lead? How does he do it [win state championships] and what is his philosophy of football and life? Charlie Grisham had it about as good as anybody I've ever talked to. I asked him what he tried to accomplish this year, how do you measure success, how do you handle problem kids, etc. I think of myself as a coach for Congress, not a teacher. Teachers grade down and coaches train up. Newt also noted that this sort of leadership is not limited to athletics and used the Carrollton High band leader, Don Hall, as an example of someone who had the same philosophy and success. "Hall was leader of the band, not of music but of people."[7]

Coach Foster Watkins also greatly impressed Newt. A line coach, Watkins had played for Bobby Dodd at Georgia Tech, a coach Newt very much admired. Watkins was also blind in one eye and never let

---

[6] Ibid., 26 March 1992.

[7] Newt Gingrich, interviewed by the author, tape recording, 13 January 1993, Gingrich Papers, State University of Georgia Archives, Carrollton.

that stop him. "Watkins was a very human person, a great human being."[8]

Newt had played football in Germany and had risen to be a possible starter in Stuttgart. When he came to Baker he was in for some shock. Having been in an integrated military school he was now in a segregated school. The only Blacks at Baker were from Egypt, Panama, or some other country, no American blacks were enrolled. The average player here was also larger than in Stuttgart. Newt weighed 195 pounds and was up against two tackles weighing 220 and 250 pounds. During the course of the football season Newt began to have problems with his left eye. The doctor told him that a vein in the eye expanded under pressure, and could burst and blind him. The decision to stop playing was a difficult one and he often wondered if he should not have sought a second opinion.[9]

Newt finished his first year at Baker with high grades and new and lasting friends. During the summer of 1960 he returned to Harrisburg for a month or so and renewed his relationship with Paul Walker, working in the Pennsylvania State Museum and appearing from time to time on local radio and television shows. He also sought to establish a personal relationship with the Republican Party. While in Harrisburg he sought out GOP leaders who could give him an introduction to Republicans in Georgia figuring that a high school student might not be taken seriously without such an introduction. He wanted to get active in the campaign.

Upon returning to Columbus, Georgia at the end of the summer he talked it over with Jim Tilton and the two decided to work in the Nixon-Lodge campaign in Muscogee County. He had his letter of introduction to Jim Briggs, the Muscogee County GOP chairman and since neither had a car, he and Tilton walked across Columbus, a rather spread-out city, to meet Briggs. When they arrived at Briggs' home they were told that he was in Europe for at least a month, neither having thought to call ahead for an appointment. They then walked all the way back across Columbus.[10]

Newt and Jim were active around GOP headquarters licking envelopes, sweeping out and answering the phone. At school they

---

[8]Ibid.

[9] Ibid.

[10] Tilton, interview, 1992.

organized debates and got Kirby's agreement that students should be involved in the election. Newt presented the GOP foreign policy position and Jim the agricultural position. They also got Kirby to agree to let students with cars get out of school to participate in a Republican motorcade. They then used getting out of school as bait to drum up a rather large contingent of Baker High students.[11]

All of their efforts were to no avail. "One of the longest nights of my life was sitting by the radio listening to Nixon lose in November 1960," said Newt. Following the defeat the two then assessed the campaign and wrote an article on the future of the Republican Party in the South. This article essentially outlined what would become Nixon's famous "southern strategy" in 1968. They sent the article to the *New York Times* but it was rejected.[12]

Their senior year Newt talked Kirby into letting the top eight or ten students at Baker High set up an independent study group. This was essentially a self-taught physics class that turned out to be a disaster due to lack of discipline on the part of the students. According to Newt, "It was a total fiasco."

Newt also served as Jim's campaign-manager for senior class president. At that time most people observing them would have predicted that Tilton would be the politician. Newt made speeches for Tilton and directed his campaign. He was one of the most popular students at Baker and won easily. This was Newt's debut as a campaign manager and he thoroughly enjoyed it.[13]

Though Newt had decided early on that he was going to marry his math teacher, Jackie Battley, he had to be careful. Teachers dating students was frowned upon and could get them both into trouble. They went places as part of a group with Tilton and other teachers like Nancy Armstrong. They were remarkably successful in keeping their relationship a secret until Newt accidentally drove Jackie's car and ran it into a tank trap on the Fort Benning reservation and had to call her father to get them out.

Because of Jackie's father's disapproval, and that of his parents, they courted quietly and Newt was careful not to talk about the relationship.

---

[11] Ibid.

[12] Ibid.; Newt Gingrich, interview, 1993.

[13] Newt Gingrich, interview, 1993; ibid., 13 January 1992. Ball and Yielding, interview, 1993.

Even though Newt took her to the Junior-Senior dance neither Ball nor Yielding had any idea they were dating. His parents, however, understood the seriousness of the situation and recommended that Newt go to Emory University in Atlanta after graduation. Though Newt did enter Emory, the ploy to separate them did not work. With some help from her aunt, Jackie got a job teaching in Atlanta at Avondale High and they were married his freshman year in college. Newt was nineteen at the time.[14]

Tilton served as best man at the small, inexpensive church wedding. Bob totally opposed the union and refused to attend. Out of respect for her husband, Kit also did not attend. Only after the birth of Newt's first child, Cathy, were Newt and his parents reconciled.[15]

Newt did well at Emory and worked at outside jobs to help support his family and helped with the chores. He stayed busy with his studies and his family but maintained contact with Tilton who traveled to Atlanta often, and they visited him at the University of North Carolina at Chapel Hill. Newt kept up his contacts with the Republican Party and was always involved in politics at Emory. He convinced Tilton to buy a mimeograph machine so they could print leaflets to distribute. Jim and Newt were together in most everything and they shared whatever they had.

While at Emory, Newt continued his plan to get advanced degrees. He got advanced placement in history and "blew the top off the history part of the SAT." He worked at the Atlanta Public Library and for the Atlanta Finance Company as a collection man. With this income, some help from parents, and a National Defense Education Act fellowship and a Georgia State Scholarship he was able to get through Emory.[16] One of his professors, Dr. Douglas Unfug, remembers Newt as a student and a friend and occasionally visited him in his home. "Newt was a very interesting student. I remember having dinner with him at his apartment and later Professor Joe Matthew's and I converted him to history instead of political science." Newt's political activities on and off

---

[14] Tilton, interview, 1992; Ball and Yielding, interview, 1993; Robert and Kathleen Gingrich, interview by author, tape recording, 22 March 1992, Gingrich Papers, State University of West Georgia Archives, Carrollton.

[15] Tilton, interview, 1992.

[16] Ibid.; Newt Gingrich, resume in the personnel file, State University of West Georgia, Carrollton.

campus also stuck out in the professor's mind: "He was *real* active in local Republican politics."[17]

While a student at Emory, Newt continued his contacts with state and local Republicans. While attending a 1963 GOP meeting in Augusta, Georgia to hear Senator John Tower, he met Jack Prince. Prince was a Republican from Georgia's Ninth Congressional District, a mountainous district running from just above Atlanta to the Tennessee border. He was a bright, attractive businessman in his late thirties and a good speaker. He was vice-president for marketing for the J. W. Jewell Poultry Company and a GOP district official who headed the Nixon & Goldwater campaigns in the Gainesville, Georgia, area.

Newt asked Prince for a ride back to Atlanta. He told Prince's driver that "I'm confident that the legislature will reapportion the congressional districts so that DeKalb County will be in the ninth district and this will give us a chance to win there." He got Prince to consider running for Congress from the ninth and to commission Tilton to do a survey to see what chance he would have to win. The survey backed up Newt's view of the situation and showed that it was remotely possible to win even without DeKalb. At least the campaign would help build a two-party state.[18]

As a result of the survey Prince hired Newt. "Newt managed the whole campaign and he hired the staff." Newt brought Tilton and Shiela O'Brien on board to act respectively as fieldman and office manager. They set up headquarters in Gainesville, and ran one of the most professional operations ever seen in that area. There were lots of small contributors and some money from the local poultry interests but most of the money had already been secured by their incumbent opponent, Representative Phil Landrum, a six-term Democrat. The entire campaign cost about $100,000.

No Republican had ever carried the ninth district but that did not discourage Newt and Prince. Newt "was well organized and energetic and the wheels in his mind were turning all the time," said Prince. "Newt had an extraordinary gift for strategy and for evaluating people

---

[17] Douglas Unfug, interview by author, 30 November 1994. Gingrich Papers, State University of West Georgia Archives, Carrollton.

[18] Tilton, interview, 1992; Jack Prince, interview by author, tape recording, 28 November 1994. Gingrich Papers, State University of West Georgia Archives, Carrollton.

such as the local leadership in given counties and the likelihood of their support." He would pick counties in which long time established GOP leaders worked closer with the Democrats than with Republicans and set about getting some volunteers for those areas.[19]

According to Gordon Sawyer, a Republican advertising executive in Gainseville who loaned space for their first office, "[Newt] had an exceptional memory for things historical that he could use for perspective—he was the strategist for the whole thing." In his campaigning and dealing with the workers, it was not an academic thing he was doing...he understood absolutely and instinctively what politics was all about." Newt and Jack traveled together around the district. "Newt was one of the most focused people I've ever met. We talked essentially about the campaign...no small talk. He was one of the most intelligent and natively gifted political animals I'd ever run across."[20]

"Newt was younger than Jack but could see things in politics and taught Jack how to be a candidate. As he taught Jack, the words *coming out of his mouth*, his instructions and directions, were those of an experienced, confident, very sensitive person." Jack agreed that he learned a lot from Newt. He composed talks for the candidate and gave him key points to include in his speeches and sometimes spoke for the campaign. At a Jaycee meeting one night Newt encountered two hostile critics. "He handled their combative commentary so well that I was inordinately impressed with him. He was very fast on his feet," said Prince.

The campaign was strictly grass-roots. "Newt took a map of the county, marked every one of the major roads going from Gainesville to the Hall County line and said to me, 'I want you as the sun goes up to be at this point at the edge of the county, on this road on this date and you start working your way toward the city and you stop at every house that has a light and you go in and ask them to vote for you.' I did that and I think it helped," Prince recalled.[21]

---

[19] Ibid.; Jack Prince, Interview by author, 28 November 1994, Gingrich Papers, State University of West Georgia, Carrollton.

[20] Ibid.; Prince, interview, 1994; Gainesville *Daily Times*, 20 November 1994, p. 2A

[21] Prince, interview, 1994

The campaign did not get much help from the state GOP and had to qualify by petition because no Republican had run from the ninth district in decades. Post office Republicans and those working with the Democrats were little or no help. Money was short. After Landrum defeated future governor Zell Miller in the Democratic Primary he went on to beat Prince almost two to one in the general election.

Prince accepted the loss as an effort to help party building and said, "Newt took it stoically and professionally." "We did all we knew how to do. We don't have to feel badly about anything. We made the effort," said Gingrich. Prince noted, "we suffered a defeat, not a rout. That is nothing to be ashamed of."[22]

The themes and issues used by Prince were ones Newt would use himself in his races for Congress: Pocketbook issues, the need to be a "watchdog of the American tax dollar," to "openly represent all the people of this district," "a conservative who will remain conservative," the need for a two-party state, "ability in action for you," and the ethics question Landrum was questioned about hitching a ride in an Air Force airplane back to Georgia.[23]

While Prince learned a lot from Newt he also helped teach his manager. "Newt dressed a little sloppy at the time and I stood him in front of the mirror in my living room and taught him how to tie a tie properly." Newt learned more than tie tying; the campaign experience brought something to Gingrich. "I learned a lot and I grew a lot," he later noted.

Newt graduated from Emory University with a bachelor's degree in history in 1965. He had already made a decision to go on for advanced degrees and entered Georgia State University in 1966 before being accepted by Tulane University to study history. He moved his family to New Orleans and began his studies. His professors were impressed. Dr. Joe Baylen, head of the history department at Georgia State University, sent an unsolicited letter of recommendation to West Georgia College when Newt applied for a teaching position there. He was described by his Tulane professors as "thoughtful and provocative," "top man in the class," "a tremendous worker, enthusiastic, analytical," "a man of tremendous drive, zeal and energy." His major professor, Dr. Pierre Laurent, noted, "I have found him a most outstanding student, mature

---

[22] Prince, interview, 1994 and Newt Gingrich, interview, 13 January 1993.

[23] Gainesville, Georgia, *Daily Times,* 28 October 1964m 11-2-64.

and thought-provoking beyond even the superior student...articulate, well-read, and as a teacher, inspiring." He was a graduate instructor at Newcomb College where he taught US history survey courses. He passed his doctoral orals with distinction, only one of five to do so in twenty years.[24]

Newt's life in New Orleans did not begin and end on campus. He joined the Baptist church there, had a second daughter, Jackie Sue, taught Sunday school, got involved in protests defending freedom of the press at Tulane, tried marijuana, partied, stayed involved in Republican politics and made new friends with whom he spent endless hours talking and debating.

One new friend was Alton Estes who was a fellow history graduate student. Alton's love of life was infectious. He seemed to have the view that "life is doing enough history to not lose his fellowship...and then go drink." Newt enjoyed Alton tremendously. Bob Gingrich had introduced Newt to alcohol but it was Alton who taught him how to drink. Another new friend was David Kramer who had recently moved to New Orleans from the Watts area of Los Angeles. These were two very different young men. According to Kit Wisdom, a GOP associate of Newt's, "David was the most rebellious graduate student, or undergraduate student, I've ever met." He was angry at the establishment, the war, politics, and hated Richard Nixon. He and Newt, odd friends at first glance, had something to offer each other. "They were co-conspirators in life." Dave enjoyed Newt's "charming and mannerly style of delivery during a fray" and gave to Newt "a vicarious and hard-nosed perspective of his view of life." According to Wisdom, "They came from very different backgrounds which is why they could be friends. However, it wasn't ever going to be a friendship which could out-last graduate school. Their worlds were just too different to survive life away from the Tulane campus." Another friend was Charles "Chip" Kahn, a high school student who got involved in politics with Newt and would later become his campaign manager during his first two races for Congress. Kahn looked up to Newt and was excited to be involved in national politics. He would frequently ride his bike to the Gingrich apartment to "hang out," talk and share meals.

---

[24] Newt Gingrich personnel file.

Kit Wisdom was a Republican activist in New Orleans, who worked on GOP politics with Newt. The daughter of an Eisenhower-appointed federal judge, Kit considered herself moderate to liberal and worked at one time or another for or with John Tower, Nelson Rockefeller, Charles Percy, John Lindsey and Jacob Javits. It was during the 1968 GOP primary that she met Newt. Newt had volunteered to help Rockefeller following King's assassination. "I felt a moral obligation to support the candidate who was intensely for integration." Kit viewed Newt as very pragmatic and "a very savvy guy who was a good team member and had incredible raw energy." "He was businesslike and could do what had to be done." He was someone "who thrived on confrontation," but had little commitment to Rockefeller personally.[25]

One of the events Kit and Gingrich worked on was to get a large crowd out to meet Rockefeller when he flew into New Orleans. They hired some busses stocked with beer and made signs. The Eureka Brass Band played and people appeared out of nowhere. The crowd was large and the event successful enough that Kit, Newt and David were flown to New York by the Rockefeller campaign to see if they should send a field-man to Louisiana and possibly allocate more money there for national publicity and the upcoming state convention. Though they worked hard to get delegates for Rockefeller, with his defeat Newt switched to support Nixon, the party's nominee. This decision bothered Kit a lot and led her to feel that "he was willing to make changes to suit his personal agenda."[26]

During 1968 Newt received his masters degree, passed his doctoral exams and the next year moved to Brussels, Belgium with his family, including his mother-in-law, to do research for his doctoral dissertation on Belgian colonial education administration in the Congo. While in Europe they traveled widely and, seeking new experiences for the girls, they enrolled the children in Belgian schools as they had in head-start programs in New Orleans.

As Newt's research neared completion, he began seeking teaching positions back in the United States. In late 1969, Newt applied for positions as a history professor at the University of Georgia, Georgia State University, Georgia Southern College, and West Georgia College. Though some of his Tulane professors urged him to consider schools

---

[25]Ibid.
[26]Gingrich personnel file.

outside the South, Newt wanted to repay his Georgia State scholarship by teaching in the state while moving closer to his wife's home as well as eventually establish a base for a run at Congress. Because his wife had relatives in Carrollton, Georgia, Newt was encouraged to receive a response from West Georgia College and sent a formal application with a three page letter explaining why he wanted to come to the 6000-student liberal arts college.

In the letter he wrote, "I am in history because I enjoy it and I feel a deep need to learn more about man and his world." After listing his academic record and accomplishments he confessed, "I am probably not a very good professional because I feel too deeply to stand off and deal with my material coldly." He went on to say, "I am deeply concerned about the state of American higher education. I agree with Jacques Barzun's warnings of Mandarinism. On the other hand I agree with Jencks and Riesman that American higher education has probably been a good influence. I am more a critical progressive seeking reform rather than a new leftist advocating radical change."

At this stage of his career Newt understood reform to mean trying different approaches to see what would work. He had not turned to the idea of revolutionary change in education but still had hope that reform was possible in spite of the bureaucratic domination of those wanting to preserve the status quo. His doctoral dissertation had, after all, shown that Belgian bureaucrats had been among the most competent people involved in colonial education. This belief changed a decade later due to his own experiences and the examples of thinkers like Alvin Toffler, Bill Bennett and a host of others seeking serious new directions in both public and higher education.

Dr. Ben Kennedy, chairman of the History Department, was impressed with Newt's academic credentials and intrigued by his approach. He offered Newt an assistant professorship in March 1970 that would begin 1 September 1970. After Newt accepted the position at West Georgia College, the Gingriches quickly settled into the routine of a junior professor and newcomer to town. They joined the First Baptist Church, where Newt became a deacon, and became active in church and community affairs. Newt would later join the Kiwanis and Moose Clubs. He quickly adapted to academic life and fit in easily with his colleagues. His first office-mate, Floyd Hoskins, who had also just arrived at West Georgia, found him to be "a totally enlightening person, a truly challenging professor. Students would come by the office after class to continue their discussions. He made them think." Newt continued his habit of learning from older people by closely questioning Hoskins about his experiences in World War II in order to add the personal dimension to his teaching. Hoskins, a Silver Star recipient and naval captain, had also served with the CIA in Germany during the first stages of the Cold War.[27]

Hoskins was opposed to the Viet Nam War, seeing it as one primarily of nationalistic goals rather than a communist effort toward world domination. Being a decorated veteran and intensely patriotic, he refused to protest while US servicemen were in the field. He and Newt frequently discussed the war and the younger man came to sympathize with Hoskins' point of view. These discussions were frequently carried on during all night pig roasts at Newt's house. Society, politics, history, religion and war were regular topics at the roasts and the parties held by Newt and his history colleagues. One of the participants at Newt's parties was another office-mate, Jim Gay, who arrived at WGC in 1971.

Gay remembers Gingrich as "energetic and busy" and interested in environmental matters. "He was a popular teacher. The flow of students through the office was obvious." Newt was not "dominated by politics" at that time but was "very open." The faculty was quite diverse and got along fairly well. Newt was "absorbing a lot of ideas and developing some at the same time. I did not see him as narrow in any way." Gay saw Newt as "very political" but in an academic sense. "He seemed ambitious early on but more in the academic arena."[28]

Three events testify to that academic ambition but more from an experiential viewpoint than a power one. In 1971 Newt submitted his name for the position of President of the college. He had read much on higher education reform and thought he might have something to offer from a new, youthful perspective. He was not seriously considered for the position. Later in 1972, the chairman of the history department, Dr. Kennedy, decided to step down. Newt put his name in for that position

---

[27] Floyd Hoskins, interview by author, tape recording, 12 November 1994, Gingrich Papers, State University of West Georgia Archives, Carrollton.

[28] Jim Jim Gay, interview by author, 23 November 1994, tape recording, Gingrich Papers, State University of West Georgia Archives, Carrollton., interview by author, 23 November 1994. tape recording, Gingrich Papers, State University of West Georgia Archives, Carrollton.

so that he could experiment with his ideas about educational reform; also, the position paid more than the $11,600 he was making at the time.

Though it did not occur to Newt, some of his colleagues viewed this decision as disloyalty to another colleague who had served as interim department head and had placed his own name in contention. Others considered Newt's decision brash or arrogant. "I thought it was interesting, brash, premature," remembered Gay. "He was filled with all sorts of ideas. I liked him but thought he would be a disaster as a chairman."[29] Still, Newt had some support and made it to the final four candidates. The job went to a Vanderbilt University professor named Steve Hanser who would become a friend of Newt's, a political supporter and a close and valued advisor to Gingrich.

In February 1971 Newt prepared a paper entitled *Some Projections on West Georgia College's Next Thirty Years.* This paper caused some of Newt's colleagues to respond negatively but one, Dr. Jim O'Malley who said, "Newt was not afraid. Newt didn't stand on titles or formalities. If he thought he had something to say he wasn't beyond saying it. Some saw him as an upstart, 'How dare this young man from Tulane think he had anything to say to Ward Pafford about running the college.' Some professors, though they agreed with him politically, felt he should wait his turn."[30]

The new president, Dr. Ward Pafford, was impressed with the paper. In a note to Newt he observed, "I have read this statement with concern and, I hope, appreciative interest. It represents the kind of thinking I like to see taking place among our teaching faculty at any level and in any subject-matter field. Many things come to my desk from various organizations, agencies, or individuals outside West Georgia College. Most of this material is impersonal, exceedingly repetitive, and stereotyped. It needs to be balanced off by some hard thinking and profound immediate concern within our own ranks. I hope you will make an early occasion to arrange for an appointment so

---

[29] Ibid.

[30] Jim O'Malley, interview by author, tape recording, 13 December 1994, Gingrich Papers, State University of West Georgia Archives, Carrollton.

that we can discuss at least the salient points of your statement along with their implications."[31]

Pafford was about to restructure the college. He saw Gingrich as bright and innovative and asked him to help think through the human issues of change at WGC. Newt consulted with Dr. Mike Arons, a disciple of humanistic psychology, who sent him an older graduate student, Daryl Conner. Conner was not sure he wanted to commit himself as a graduate assistant but went by as a courtesy to Newt. He meant to stay five minutes and stayed five hours after which he went home with Newt and accepted the assistantship.

Gingrich and Conner spent a year working on the project with Pafford and other college administrators. When asked what reactions and cooperation they got during this project, Conner remembers there was some resistance to change but that overall most faculty and administrators participated because they had Pafford's blessing. President Pafford's memory is that there was no real resistance but some skepticism among administrators about approaching it from the "humanistic" direction.[32]

The great majority of the students Conner knew were intrigued by Newt and were taken by his capacity to make them think, though some viewed him as being extreme. The faculty was about evenly split into three groups. One viewed Newt as "intriguing as a person or understood and agreed with what he was doing. Another saw him as a blip on the screen or as mildly irritating or irrelevant and another was threatened by him."

Newt's personal and professional actions during this period give an early look at the complexity of the man. On the one hand he was working with Pafford to bring about major structural change as smoothly as possible and explaining to campus administrators how it could be done. On the other hand Conner remembers Newt as being less smooth as he approached faculty and department meetings. "He was not very subtle, or didn't care about college politics and was direct. This threatened some faculty."[33] Jim O'Malley thinks Gingrich knew exactly what reactions he would get when he ran for college president

---

[31] Ward Pafford memo, 19 November 1971. Gingrich Personnel File, Gingrich Papers, State University of West Georgia Archives, Carrollton.

[32] Ibid.; Pafford, interview, 1994.

[33] Conner, interview, 1994.

and department head. "This wasn't his first rodeo." "Some faculty like Dr. Sumner Long, a friend of Newt's and Geology Department chairman, advised him to 'tone down' his approach at faculty meetings and Newt said he would say it another way but he would say it." "In the meetings with Pafford and vice-president John Martin Newt was respectful but very direct. Both men, at times, were uncomfortable with that directness."[34] Nevertheless, Gingrich and Conner continued their project to the general satisfaction of both Pafford and Martin.

Gingrich and Conner were sufficiently interested in how to get people to be responsive to change and how to guide the change agents in the best possible way in achieving their goals that they formed an organization to study and explain how institutions transform themselves. The Institute for Directed Change and Renewal focused on educational change with limited success. They had only one client and spent more time preparing than producing and advising.

In 1972 Newt's interest in environmental affairs came to the forefront of his activities. Newt proposed a two-year pilot program on environmental studies with himself and the Science Division chairman, Dr. Charles Masters, as coordinators. This program was interdisciplinary and had broad appeal for students and support from administrators. Gingrich himself had earned the approval of administrators in his two years at West Georgia. Dr. Don Wells, chairman of the Political Science Department, recommended him for Director, Special Academic Programs (Honors). "Dr. Gingrich's greatest asset is his ability to work outside 'normal' hierarchical channels to effect change and implement programs....I think you will find few individuals who surpass Newt in an understanding of how extra hierarchical processes function and in effectiveness in working in those processes." In 1973 Newt was recommended for appointment as official coordinator of the Environmental Studies program by Dr. Doyle Mathis, Associate Dean of Academic Affairs and by John Martin who referred to him as "an invaluable member of the staff." Dr. Eugene Huck, Social Science Division chairman, had recommended him to teach special advanced high school courses for bright students at Newnan High School in addition to his duties at the college.[35]

---

[34] O'Malley, interview, 1994; Pafford, interview, 1994.

[35] Gingrich Personnel File, Gingrich Papers, State University of West Georgia, Carrollton.

In 1974 Newt moved to the geography department and was welcomed by chairman John Upchurch who thought he was the "most charismatic teacher on campus" and sure to bring bright students with him. Jim O'Malley remembers him as being not much older than the students and some of the brighter ones were always hanging around him as they bounced ideas off each other. "He thought of himself as a populist even then." The program was science based with social scientists teaching it and supported by science teachers. "Newt covered it from his own historical perspective. He noted that other civilizations had made these kinds of mistakes and this is what happened. If we continue to make these kinds of mistakes this is going to happen to us."[36]

Two of Newt's students, Arthur Fessenden and Frank Gregorsky, were impressed enough with him that they worked for him when he entered politics. Fessenden, a geography major who took Newt's Year 2000 course, said, "Newt was a fantastic teacher and had the respect of all the students; they felt comfortable around him." He presented a relaxed atmosphere and always gave oral exams to probe the extent of the student's knowledge. Some of the class sessions were held in his home around coffee and donuts. "He would challenge you with facts. He would come in and ask, 'What happened today?' If you didn't know what was going on in the world you wouldn't know enough to change it."[37] Gregorsky found him to be "serious and earnest." He was simultaneously "friendly but distant."[38] Dr. Mac Martin, a Carrollton surgeon who was GOP county chairman, had two daughters who took Newt's courses and thought he was "a wonderful teacher who challenged you."[39]

Newt's years at West Georgia College were a testing ground for his ideas and for himself. He proved to be an exceptional teacher and found a fertile ground for the development of his own political, social and intellectual growth. His dean, Dr. Richard Dangle, who quickly became

---

[36] O'Malley, interview, 1994.

[37] Arthur Fessenden, interview by author, tape recording, 30 November 1994. Gingrich Papers, State University of West Georgia Archives, Carrollton.

[38] Frank Gregorsky, interview by author, tape recording, 2 December 1994. Gingrich Papers, State University of West Georgia Archives, Carrollton.

[39] Mac and Carol Martin, interview by author, tape recording,14 December 1994. Gingrich Papers, State University of West Georgia Archives, Carrollton.

a friend and advisor, found him to be a rational, reasonable and bright teacher who absorbed and generated ideas, a teacher who did not force his ideas on his students but who encouraged them to form their own ideas and philosophies.[40]

Some of Newt's ideas shared with Dangle had to do with his views of the role of a representative and the obligation of an educated citizenry to interact with and support their representative, be it on a state or national level. Newt also shared these ideas with a number of other professors and students who thought he was on the right track and became political supporters. Though Newt would cast a wide net for political support all across the sixth congressional district, the college served as the launching pad for his political ambitions and many of his colleagues and students served as the foot soldiers in his first three campaigns.

[40] Richard Dangle, interview by author, tape recording, 16 December 1994. Gingrich Papers, State University of West Georgia, Carrollton.

3

BUILDING A BASE

Typical academic politics held no real interest for Newt because he was not planning to be a part of that world. The traditional route to tenure and promotion, research and publishing scholarly articles and books, was not the path he chose. Newt was more interested in teaching and learning and in finding more effective ways to transmit knowledge. Whereas some professors considered time spent with students a waste and yearned for more research and writing time, Newt often discussed with his other colleagues the need to encourage and reward teaching in a school like West Georgia College, which was not a major research institution. He was also more interested in party politics. When asked by the *West Georgian* in 1977 why he did not apply for tenure he said, "It would be presumptuous for me to apply for tenure after taking two leaves of absence to run for Congress. I made the decision two or three years ago that I'd rather run for Congress than publish the papers or academic books necessary to get promoted."[1]

Many of Newt's students were also interested in politics because of their interest in government policy or in the environment. Some were interested in politics because Newt thought it was important. For whatever reason they encouraged him in his political activities and many worked actively in his campaigns. Some students were able to use their class assignments to help Newt with his campaigns and provide information for campaign issues. This was especially true of environmental issues. Frank Gregorsky tailored a research paper assignment to study the impact of the Kennedy tax cuts in order that

---

[1] West Georgian, 14 October 1977.

Newt might use it in his support of the Kemp-Roth bill.[2]

Newt also depended on the research skills of Dr. Chester Gibson's debaters. West Georgia had a championship debate program which included some very bright students who were eager to help and learn from Gingrich. Gibson would critique Newt's speaking style and the student debaters would provide supportive research for the campaigns.[3]

Having met social critic Alvin Toffler at a conference, Newt was familiar with "future shock" as well as the general concept of futurism. He had taught a course on the future while at Tulane and was already incorporating many of the futurist ideas into his environmental studies and history courses. While teaching a team-taught course on "The Modern World" in the early seventies he would frequently begin a discussion with statements such as "Brazil will be the dominant country in the Western Hemisphere in the next century." Whether an accurate prediction or not, the assertion stirred comment and discussion and caused Newt and the students to explore why and how this might happen based on the history of the country and the current and possible future direction it was taking.

Newt was asked by Toffler to be on a panel for a congressional conference in Washington. The panel was mostly Democrats and a Republican was needed for balance. "Then I remembered a young Republican futurist in Georgia who said that he was running for office, so we invited him to balance it." Newt had been impressed with Toffler and his ideas at their earlier meeting. He began to include Toffler's third wave concept in his lectures and class discussions. The meeting with Toffler began a relationship that has continued for over two decades.[4]

Toffler influenced Newt and his application of futurism to politics. He and Jim Tilton had projected Nixon's "southern strategy" in 1960 following the Kennedy victory. He saw that a conservative wave was coming. What he developed in the next decade was the sense of how to ride, and help direct, the wave that was so much a part of him, and of

---

2 Frank Gregorsky, interview by author, tape recording, 2 December 1994. Gingrich Papers, State University of West Georgia Archives, Carrollton.

3 Chester Gibson, interview by author, tape recording, 12 December 1994, Gingrich Papers, State University of West Georgia Archives, Carrollton.

4 *The Atlanta Constitution*, 20 December 1994.

the country.[5]

The 1971 reapportionment of Georgia's congressional districts had redrawn the sixth district, which included Carroll County where Newt lived. It now contained twelve counties and part of Fulton County that contained southwest Atlanta and the Atlanta airport. This new district was now more urban and showed a history of strong conservative voting. The Nixon-Agnew ticket had done well there in the 1972 election and after making a careful study of the election returns Newt thought the time was right for a serious Republican candidate.

A Republican victory in the sixth would be a long shot. No Republican had ever won in that district. The incumbent, John J. Flynt, was a former district attorney and state representative who had gone to Congress in 1954 in a special election and had been reelected ever since. He had a reputation as a conservative "good old boy" politician who stayed in close with the people back home and tended to constituents' problems. Flynt also had the support of the business community, the legal profession and the courthouse politicians as well as African-Americans and "yellow dog" Democrats. Seniority was appreciated in Georgia and Flynt had plenty of it. He also had money.

Newt realized, however, that reputation and reality are not always the same. The voting patterns suggested to Newt that the voters in the sixth district would vote for a Republican, at least for president. They would certainly support a conservative. Watergate was breaking and Congress was not doing well in public opinion polls. In addition, a city commissioner from Flynt's home town, Skeeter Norsworthy, had come to Newt with a story about Congressman Flynt taking money from Ford Motor Company to park cars on some land he owned and about ethical problems related to a dam being planned in his area. All of this indicated to Newt that there might be a chink in the Democrat's armor.[6]

Newt had maintained his contacts with the Republican Party in Georgia while in college. He was a regular attendee at party conferences, conventions and meetings while in school and since returning to Georgia in 1970. He had worked to help Howard "Bo" Callaway in his race for governor in 1966 and had managed Jack

[5]Jim Tilton, interview by author, tape recording, 26 March 1992, Gingrich Papers, State University of West Georgia Archives.

[6]Newt Gingrich, interviewed by the author, tape recording, 13 January 1993, Gingrich Papers, State University of Georgia Archives, Carrollton.

Prince's campaign for Congress in 1964. He had been active in Callaway's bid for GOP National Committeeman. He had supported Nixon's candidacy in 1968 and was sixth district chairman for the President's reelection campaign in 1972. He maintained contact with party leaders, including future US Senators Mattingly and Paul Coverdell, and was active in party affairs where his ideas and advice were actively sought.

Being young, bright and energetic naturally caused many Republicans to approach Newt about running for office. Most wanted him to run for state representative or state senator. A colleague in the history department at West Georgia College talked politics with him during this period from 1971 to 1973. He tried to talk him into getting involved on a state or county level as a Democrat because he thought Newt would have a better chance of winning if he ran as a Democrat. In the fall of 1972, however, the two met in the Nixon reelection office on the top floor of the Times Georgian building where he had his political office. Newt made it clear that he was interested in Congress and not a state position. Indeed, he was not sure he could win against a local Democrat for state office.

Newt felt he could legitimately define Flynt as an out of touch Congressman who had ethical problems and was more interested in serving his own interest than in representing the "bread and butter" needs of his constituents. Since few people actually know their Congressman and most voters can describe little or nothing about his stands on issues except what they heard at election time, there is no personal connection like that that existed in local elections. This lack of familiarity with the Congressman can allow an opponent the opportunity to define the incumbent in the minds of the voters. In local races the voters are apt to personally know the candidate or his relatives and thus already have an established an identity for the incumbent.

The most daunting question was whether Newt, a thirty-year-old college professor who had been in the sixth district only a little over three years, could find the support to make a serious run at Jack Flynt. Though a number of WGC professors had opposed Flynt in 1972 as a representative of the "old politics" Newt sought his first support from the Republican Party and not the college. Flynt had done few favors for the GOP and Newt thought they would provide the core support he needed to get off the ground. Bo Callaway had been elected to Congress in 1964 and ran a close race for governor in 1966. Ben Blackburn and Fletcher Thompson were elected to Congress from the Atlanta area in 1966 and Thompson was running for the US Senate against Sam Nunn in 1972. These three Republicans had shown that the party could get behind candidates and win. Nixon carried Georgia in 1972 and Newt's contacts made during the reelection campaign would prove invaluable now. Indeed, some of those who had worked on Thompson's staff now brought their campaign and congressional experience to aid Newt in the south Atlanta area.

Newt had approached the party regulars at district and county meetings. At first he did not mention he was running, but just introduced himself around, handed out a simple card with his name, address and phone number on it and generally tried to be helpful. He asked a lot of questions and kept a list of key people who might be helpful in the future.[7] Party leaders knew Newt but many of the rank and file in the newly reconstituted sixth district, which included Carrollton, knew little, if anything, about him. In 1971, 1972 and 1973 he attended every Republican function he could and assumed or was assigned some official role.[8] He even thought about writing a war novel to help educate people about the dangers of a third world war.

Newt genuinely wanted to help the state party. He thought it needed to broaden its base and appeal if it were ever to make electoral in-roads. Bill Shipp, a political reporter for The *Atlanta Constitution* remembers Newt briefing the press after a 1971 visit to Atlanta by Vice-President Spiro Agnew. After a closed door meeting with party officials and contributors at the Marriott Hotel, Newt talked to reporters about what Agnew had said and to their astonishment predicted that Senator George McGovern would be the Democrats' presidential nominee in the 1972 election.[9]

Gingrich was convinced that the nomination of first Hubert Humphrey in 1968 and George McGovern in 1972 sent a signal to Southern conservatives that the national Democratic Party was moving

---

[7] Jan Whaley, interview by author, 28 December 1994, , Gingrich collection, State University of West Georgia Archives, Carrollton.

[8] Barbara Scruggs, interview by the author, 27 December 1994, Gingrich Papers, State University of West Georgia Archives, Carrollton.

[9] Bill Shipp, interview by author, tape recording, 8 December 1987, Gingrich Papers.

to the left. The 1964 Johnson-Goldwater race had opened the door for conservatives in Georgia where Goldwater carried every congressional district but one. The 1968 and 1972 campaigns saw many heretofore Democrats splitting their votes and turning to the GOP on the national level. The refrain of "I didn't leave the party, it left me!" was heard more and more often. Affirmative action, set-asides and quotas favoring minorities coupled with the left's anti-war protest, led many conservatives both in and out of the labor movement to vote Republican. Nixon was able to tap their resentment in 1968 as thousands broke with their leadership to support the Republicans. No longer could the Democrats take labor's vote for granted.

Newt did a serious analysis of the recent elections in Georgia and came away convinced that Republicans could be elected to Congress. Blackburn and Thompson had already represented the Atlanta area in Congress and Callaway the west Georgia area. In the early part of 1973 Dr. Steve Hanser, chairman of the history department at West Georgia College, had a conversation with Newt concerning the need to move now for a successful bid for Congress. Newt would turn thirty that summer and felt he had time to pursue his political goals. "I'm still young," Hanser remembers him saying. Hanser, on the other hand, pointed out that life could be unexpectedly short, Hanser's father having died in his fifties, and that thirty was not that young. This advice seemed to focus Newt on the need to expedite the course he had set for himself over a decade earlier.[10]

Newt and his wife, Jackie, talked a good deal about what it would take to run for Congress. The decision to run would not be easy on the family. Newt could stay in the academic world, research and write articles, teach and get tenure, and lead a relatively secure and enjoyable life. If he wanted that life he would have gone to a university instead of coming to West Georgia College. Contacts had been made by his Tulane professors and that option had existed. If he decided on the political rather than the academic option he would be, in effect, deciding against seeking tenure and the security of the professorate. There would not be time for both.

Jackie strongly opposed Newt's running at that time. She felt it was too early and their debts were too great. She pointed out that teaching

---

[10] Steve Hanser interview, 6-8-95 UWG archives, Gingrich collection, State University of West Georgia Archives, Carrollton.

full time and taking care of the girls would leave her little time for campaigning. In spite of the reservations they held, the family decided to support Newt's run for Congress if he thought that was what he had to do.[11]

Early that spring Newt began to line up a team to consider the options and prepare for a campaign. Dr. Mac Martin, a surgeon, and his wife, Carol, were early supporters and would hold coffees in their home to let Newt discuss the race with other conservatives, both Democrat and Republican. A local businessman, Chester Roush, and a group of civic leaders met and encouraged Newt to run and quietly sought bipartisan support for the effort. The Martins remember him as "very earnest and keyed-up." They had worked with him in the Carroll County Republican Party and though he was the first person who had offered to run for Congress as a Republican in that district, they were concerned that he might not make it as a Republican. They were impressed enough with Newt that they asked him to consider running as a Democrat. "He was very idealistic," said Carol, and told them, "I am a Republican and will run as a Republican."[12]

Carol Martin worked with Newt at a state GOP state convention where, in the heat of the moment, "someone accused him of some impropriety and he really was bothered. He hadn't done anything wrong and insisted on defending himself." Though some candidates may have ignored the remark, Newt made sure the situation was resolved. He had not run from the attack or tried to excuse his way out of it. He faced it squarely and settled it.[13] He would follow this pattern the rest of his career.

Newt began talking to Republican Party leaders and contacts about running for Congress. He also started seeking support from some of his West Georgia College colleagues. In an early morning discussion Newt thought for hours about his chances of victory. Spreading out the maps and going over the data, Newt pulled no punches. "I want to run for

[11] Jackie Gingrich, interview by Frank Gregorsky, tape recording, 29 April 1979, Gingrich collection,

[12] Mac and Carol Martin interview, 14 December 1994, Gingrich collection, State University of West Georgia Archives, Carrollton.

[13] Ibid.

Congress and I want to show you why I think I might be able to win."[14] Newt outlined the results of the recent redistricting and went over the recent election results from the counties included in the new sixth congressional district. The results were fairly clear. All the counties voted conservative, almost all had voted at least once for a Republican President, and the counties in the metro area around Atlanta were clearly moving toward the political right. A few had even voted for Republican candidates for governor. It was just possible that the right candidate with the right kind of campaign might be able to upset Jack Flynt. But was Newt that candidate?

Newt now turned to Daryl Conner. "Newt was my best friend and I was ready to help him with whatever he wanted to do," said Conner. Though he was basically non-political, Conner would be helpful in offering Newt organizational advice, helping him decide how to structure his campaign and serving as someone with whom Newt could bounce ideas around and help work through problems with no self-interest involved.[15]

Jim Tilton was establishing a law practice at this time but offered personal and some limited financial support. He hocked his life insurance to get money for Newt and came in occasionally to serve as a sounding board and to offer advice. "Newt was a visionary and concerned about the future of our country and what we would leave our grandchildren. I did what I could to help out." Tilton noted that he did not always agree with Newt and with the management of the campaign, particularly in terms of the campaign's professionalism and the amount of local control in the campaign.[16]

Newt also turned to the Republican Party regulars to help him get started. Jan Whaley, a Newnan housewife and party activist who had worked in the Goldwater campaign in 1964 and in numerous national and state efforts since then, remembers Newt coming to her during a sixth district Republican meeting in 1973 and asking her to serve as his campaign chair. She had met him a few times before but was not particularly close to him or his family. She had watched his work as

---

[14]Mel Steely, interview by Frank Gregorsky, tape recording, 15 November 1980, Gingrich Papers, State University of West Georgia Archives, Carrollton.

[15] Daryl Conner, interview by author, 3 October 1994, Gingrich Papers, State University of West Georgia Archives, Carrollton.

[16] Tilton, interview, 1992.

chairman of the 1972 state Republican platform committee and thought he had done a creditable job and had seen him at a number of party meetings. She thought it odd that he would select her for that critical position.[17]

Gingrich, however, had done his homework. Between 1970 and 1973 he had gone to every party meeting he could and had watched and made notes on a variety of people. He knew who the workers were and which were respected and listened to by the others. He knew who could raise money and who could get volunteers. He knew who had real experience and who had enthusiasm. Whaley had good contacts in the party, having worked on a variety of campaigns throughout most of a decade. She was a respected Republican from his district in a county, Coweta, that was turning Republican. She was credited with being a good organizer and a tough, no-nonsense manager. He felt she would be loyal and hard-working. Whaley, as his chairman, would give him a quick start in organizing and staffing his campaign. Newt was delighted when she accepted his challenge.[18]

With little money at the start it was necessary to get Newt around the district as much as possible to raise his visibility and get his name known to the voters. The various chambers of commerce were contacted in the district to get the names and addresses of the various civic club leaders and then write them, in the interest of "expanding the community service function" of the college and offer to provide speakers on a variety of topics.

The two speakers recommended to the civic clubs were "two of the more popular civic club speakers" in the west Georgia area, Floyd Hoskins and Newt Gingrich, both members of the history department. Hoskins would talk on China and Asian-American relations and Newt had four topics to maximize the chances of his getting invitations to speak. The topics he could discuss were, "The Year 2000," "The Future of Education in Georgia," "The GOP in Georgia Today," and "The Energy Crisis and What Can Be Done About It."[19] Both men received numerous invitations and publicized the school as well as their ideas. In addition to getting the opportunity to speak before small groups of civic

---

[17] Jan Whaley, interview by author, 12 December 1994.

[18] Ibid.

[19] Mel Steely Papers, (1974 campaign folder), Gingrich Collection, State University of West Georgia Archives, Carrollton.

leaders they almost always received local newspaper coverage and made contacts that would prove helpful in the future.

Newt also reached into his past for campaign support. He had kept in touch with a young student, Charles "Chip" Kahn, who had worked with him in 1968 in the Rockefeller campaign in Louisiana. Kahn was finishing up his undergraduate work at Johns Hopkins University and admired Newt since his New Orleans days. Newt recognized Kahn as very bright and loyal and presented him with the opportunity to be part of not only a political campaign for Congress, but part of a "crusade" to help change the Republican Party and the country as well. Kahn would ultimately become the 1974 campaign manager.[20]

Newt now had the core of a campaign in place and began putting together an organization. Conner helped think through the grass-roots organization that would be needed and the sort of appeal that would be needed to swell the ranks of volunteers. Ways to get Newt more visibility were devised and Newt worked with advisors to put together ideas on what would be needed to win, what short-term goals Newt would need to achieve during the next six months, and making key contacts that would be helpful in the campaign. Newt, working with Whaley, concentrated on developing his base within the Republican Party. He also became the chairman of "Operation Breakthrough," a project of the Georgia GOP designed to expand the party and break through the Democratic hold on the voters.

Newt had begun the process of putting together a campaign. The leadership of the Georgia GOP was supportive of Newt's effort. He had a campaign chairman and a core group of his friends and colleagues who wanted to help defeat Jack Flynt. He was beginning the process of expanding that base through high visibility and the efforts of his team to recruit other supporters and contributors who wanted change. Then he began to have doubts about timing and whether he was ready to make the commitment necessary to carry on a major campaign against an entrenched incumbent.

As the summer of 1973 was drawing to a close he decided to visit his parents who were stationed in the Canal Zone. Jackie still had doubts about the effort and a few days might give him the time he needed to

---

[20]Charles Kahn, interview by author, tape recording, 10 February 1995, Gingrich Papers, State University of West Georgia Archives, Carrollton.

think it through and make up his mind.[21] He disclosed his doubts to a trusted friend and asked him to put together a paper on what would be needed to win the campaign and to give him his thoughts on efforts to recruit other supporters and some of the contacts that Newt had made during the summer.

Newt received a later memo dated 20 August suggesting that he see a missionary while in the Canal Zone to buttress his talks to church groups and to make some decisions one way or the other. Fundraising was a major problem worrying Gingrich. Newt *hated* raising money. Asking other people to give him money for the campaign was especially difficult for him. As the memo urged him, "You have to be positive about running or no one is going to give you a dime."[22]

Likewise, Newt thought 1974 might not be a good year for Republicans. Vice President Spiro Agnew was having problems and was only months away from resigning in disgrace. The first steps of the Watergate journey were becoming noticeable and off year elections were usually unkind to the party in the White House. Nevertheless, Flynt appeared to be in trouble, Newt had great appeal and it appeared that the press might be friendly. The district had showed its willingness to vote Republican and many Democrats could be expected to switch parties in the congressional race.

An advisor argued that the scandal may harm overall voter turnout, but may not necessarily produce a negative reaction against the Republican party as a whole. Further, the advisor suggested that Tom Glanton, a young developer who was running for the state legislature as a Democrat was behind Newt and could talk to some of his colleagues for Newt. Tom suggested some key officials who did not like Flynt and thought they might be helpful.[23]

Kahn had been asked to put together a think-piece "to lay things out for you [Newt] in black and white." Kahn had been at a Sunday meeting at Newt's home along with a small group of supporters including Conner and his wife Ann, when Newt discussed his ambivalence about running just before leaving for the Canal Zone. He

---

[21] Gingrich, interview, 1979.

[22] Steely to Gingrich, Carrollton, 20 August 1973. Mel Steely papers (1974 campaign folder) State University of West Georgia Archives, Carrollton.

[23] Ibid.

and Conner were also concerned about Newt's attitude.[24]

Kahn put together a nine point document outlining why various groups such as GOP polls, finance people, close friends and campaign workers would support Newt and how they would be affected if he continued his indecisiveness. He noted that at that stage of the campaign personal loyalty was in low supply and indecisiveness could have a very negative impact on most of those currently interested in the campaign. He wrote in his 21 August memo to Newt that Gingrich needed to be a "suitor" and needed "to develop a base of your own" before he could really have a solid group of supporters who would be dependable enough to stay with him for the long haul. "Although you may have established yourself as the key intellectual force behind the Georgia Republican Party, as a candidate you are still an unproven quantity—in essence you are still only your potential." Writing as "campaign manager," that appointment not yet finalized, the loyal and idealistic Kahn was hard-hitting and blunt in his assessment.[25]

Upon returning to Georgia, Newt seemed ready to get on with the campaign. The race would be good for him even if it was not for the GOP at large. He stood a chance to win it all and even if he were defeated a good race would get him the name recognition he would need for a second race. He did not discuss his ambivalence again.

His key leaders agreed that Newt needed to concentrate on three priorities for the rest of the year. Organization, finance and visibility were all critical to getting the campaign off the ground. Newt needed to identify and recruit thirteen county chairmen and to flesh out his staff for his main office. He needed to spend the next four months contacting those who could give or raise money to be in a solid position by January 1974. The Carrollton area and Atlanta were the target areas because those were the places where people either knew Newt and would invest in him or because they had money and would support Republicans and conservatives from their immediate area. He needed to maintain or increase his current level of exposure through public appearances district-wide insofar as his teaching schedule would allow him time to travel.

Newt decided to establish regularly scheduled meetings every other

---

[24] Kahn to Gingrich, 21 August 1973. Steely papers (1974 campaign folder) State University of West Georgia Archives, Carrollton.

[25] Ibid.

Sunday evening for his "executive committee." The first was held 30 September 1973. Newt told his committee that being open and honest had to be the hallmarks of the campaign. "People have been sweet-talked too to often," he said. He thought that people had to actually see and participate in the whole campaign in order to believe it was honest. He and Conner talked about them "co-sharing" the campaign as if it were their own and thought this "co-sharing" and "co-owning" should extend as much as possible to all "our" volunteers and contributors. Though they were aware this level of idealism would engender considerable confusion they thought it might work in building the first less-than professional low-cost campaign. [26]

Reflecting his own practicality and his acceptance of the Franklin Roosevelt method of management, he went on to describe the campaign as "actually an experiment." "We must not be afraid to try new ideas, discard those which fail and try again, until we discover what works in practice." Believing in this approach, Newt would use it again and again in future campaigns, in running his congressional office, and in working to gain a GOP majority in the House of Representatives.

Newt Gingrich loves lists. There are multiple steps, points or reasons in every enterprise in which he engages. He listed his "six basic rules for the campaign":

1. Honesty in everything about the campaign
2. Co-sharing in power, information, etc.
3. We go slow now in order to go rapidly later
4. Keep everything simple, stick to fundamentals
5. Keep trying, openly admit mistakes, learn from each other
6. Have some fun along the way

In his commitment to openness and learning he suggested that minutes be taken of each executive committee meeting and reproduced and made available to libraries, schools, and all other interested parties. He wanted to apply the "sunshine law" to the campaign. This suggestion struck almost all the committee members as naïve but was indicative of his belief that when people understand what he is doing they will be supportive of the effort. It was decided that minutes would

---

[26] Executive Committee meeting minutes, 30 September 1973 Steely papers (1974 campaign folder) State University of West Georgia Archives, Carrollton.

be kept but that publication would be no earlier than the spring. Jefferson's idea of "trust the people" was seldom held more firmly by an American political figure than by Newt Gingrich.[27]

Following a discussion of the breakdown of the voters in the sixth district and of possible opposition in the primary, the meeting ended with Newt expressing his desire to pattern the campaign on Sam Nunn's 1972 US Senate campaign. Nunn had used the slogan, "Get Tough in Washington." He had handily defeated David Gambrell, an incumbent appointed by Governor Jimmy Carter to replace Senator Richard Russell following his death in 1971.[28]

Assignments were made concerning the gathering of a large volunteer group in Carroll County, the start of formal scheduling, getting a list of the media, and developing mailing lists. The need for a campaign car was also noted. Newt had been using his own car and those of volunteers. Jackie needed the family car to take care of the family needs and volunteers could not always be counted on to be available when needed. Ivan and Betty Taylor, GOP supporters from Griffin, Georgia, helped solve the transportation problem by purchasing a used $500 Rambler station wagon.

The fall of 1973 was an extremely busy time for Newt. He began his work as coordinator of environmental studies along with his teaching and also was appointed chairman of the West Georgia College Planning Council by President Ward Pafford. These responsibilities took a good deal of his time as did being a deacon in his church, an active member of the Kiwanis Club and the Georgia Conservancy. In addition, he now needed to make as many speeches as possible around the district to gain greater visibility for his campaign. It was at this point that he came to grips with the need to be better organized in the way he used his time. He adopted a set of schedule organizers that broke his time into fifteen-minute intervals. He set aside specific days for family and for political activity. He recorded all his class and student advisement obligations, committee meetings, and so on, and then filled in the rest of the time with speaking engagements whenever possible.

It quickly became apparent that depending on volunteers to drive him was uncertain at best. He was frequently exhausted after a full day of teaching, meeting and speaking and driving himself was impractical.

---

27 Ibid.
28 Whaley, interview, 1994.

A regular, reliable driver was needed. Bob Claxton, Mel Steely, Kip Carter, and Richard Dangle all served as drivers at one time or another, as did other volunteers who were associated with the college. Jeff Reid, a bright student who wanted to be a golf professional, signed on as the first driver and "fieldman" in October. Later another student, Steve Ford, would serve as driver.

Newt scheduled his classes early in the day or in the evening so that he might have blocks of time to campaign. After he finished classes and office hours one of his drivers would meet him at the college and they would travel to Atlanta for a party meeting or to a speaking engagement somewhere in the district. The acting chair of the Kiwanis Public and Business Affairs Committee arranged for Newt to be assigned to his committee to work with local education, business and industry leaders and get to know members of the Chamber of Commerce who might be helpful. The Whaleys got him engagements in Coweta County, the Taylors and Betty Sowell in Spalding, Cary and Dot Hall in Henry County and a former member of Congressman Fletcher Thompson' staff, Claudine Williams, and volunteers like Dot Crews helped in the south Atlanta area. It was a grass-roots operation.

Newt crisscrossed the sixth district again and again in the waning weeks of 1973, speaking, planning and meeting with his campaign committee. Whaley raised money to buy him a suit and passed on to Newt some of her husband's shirts and his watch. She was astounded at Newt's lack of interest in clothes and material possessions. "He basically had nothing. He was young and poor," she noted. His clothes, his house, his car and his furniture reflected his disinterest in having material possessions.[29]

In January Newt sent a letter and poll to his GOP mailing list. The overall purpose was two-fold, to prospect for money and to get an early reading on grass roots opinion. The letter did not mention Newt's candidacy but instead focused on the need to "plan an aggressive, hard hitting, 1974 campaign at every level of government." He went on to urge a "return to the grass roots to discover the real issues that are bothering people. We must build a grass roots campaign that by-passes the liberal media's desire to dominate and direct public opinion." The letter was signed by Gingrich as chairman of the 1972 Georgia Republican Platform Committee.

---

29 Ibid.

The poll letter was only one part of a growing campaign. Newt had held seven executive committee meetings in seven counties and meetings with volunteer workers in the seven major counties before Christmas. A basic press operation was ready by November 1973 with biographical packs, lists of stations and phone numbers and key news people. A Newt newsletter was planned and the poll letter was the first step in that direction. Voter registration drives were planned. Coffee chairmen, pledge card coordinators, canvass chairmen, office managers and leaflet chairmen were recruited by early in 1974.

Newt's first campaign was a genuine grass roots effort. Money was always a problem. Most of it was raised by pledge cards, event ticket sales and solicitations. Newt traveled to New Orleans and Columbus, Georgia to seek support from former friends and active Republicans who might contribute. He turned to Key Republican contributors from the Atlanta area and was invited to meet with the "Loose Group." This was a group of conservative, mostly Republican, businessmen who pooled their contributions to help conservative candidates of both parties.

Some funds made their way to the campaign but it was always short of cash. More than once small groups of supporters, mostly from the Carroll County area, co-signed notes with banks to raise needed cash. These were small notes for a few thousand dollars each. Some of the co-signers were Democrats, like Tom Glanton, who suffered a good deal of abuse from their party colleagues for supporting Newt.

To cut costs, the campaign produced its own signs. Billboards cost too much so smaller signs were needed for name recognition. Wood for the signs and posts was donated when possible and a couple of silk screens were purchased. An old abandoned warehouse was offered to do the silk screening. There was no electricity so gas lanterns were used as volunteers labored late into the night painting and silk screening signs to have them ready for pick up the next day. Volunteers with pickup trucks would carry them back to their home counties and see that the signs actually got put up in key locations. Students and teachers at the college and Carrollton residents were the backbone of the sign project.[30]

The college also supplied help to Newt in other ways. Dr. Gibson and his debaters had worked with Newt and Conner in their consulting efforts and continued to help Newt as he prepared for speaking

---

[30] Ibid.; Sign project documents.

engagements and later for campaign debates. The students would research problems Newt selected as main campaign issues. They would then meet with him, go over the material and, with Dr. Gibson, actually walk through debates with him on each of the issues.[31]

Colleagues like Jim O'Malley served on phone banks to do polling and get out the vote. Many of Newt's fellow historians at WGC put up signs in their yards and many co-signed notes with Newt. The Dean of Arts and Sciences, Richard Dangle, became a close and trusted advisor and worked with Newt to help raise money. The administration worked with him to get him leaves-of-absence in order for him to campaign. President Pafford occasionally helped the Gingrichs with grocery money during the periods of unpaid leave. Others held coffees, passed out leaflets in shopping centers, town squares and at stoplights. They also helped staff his Carrollton office and would drive when his regular drivers needed a break. All in all, the campus provided a solid core of support for Newt during his first campaign.

Newt's wife, Jackie, and his daughters, Cathy and Jackie Sue, were also deeply involved in the campaign. Jackie, now committed, was an active participant in the discussions and was insistent that Newt's time had to be used wisely and to best advantage. She and the girls were almost always at each local bumper sticker blitz and frequently handed out campaign literature at county fairs, shopping centers and high school football games.

Newt continued to consult with party regulars such as Mack Mattingly, Bob Shaw, Dick Lane, Paul Coverdell, Virlyn Smith, Dorothy Felton, Johnny Isakson and Bob Bell. They were very helpful in opening the door to possible contributors and as issue advisors. Many were elected officials and Newt was, at this stage of his career and later, concerned about looking at the upcoming election as a team effort. He wanted to be elected but he also wanted the GOP to do well. While he did not follow this plan himself he did think that politics was like a baseball farm team program. Local GOP officials would supply candidates for state office and state GOP officials would supply gubernatorial and national candidates.

His desire to push a team effort had to be carefully handled because he personally needed large numbers of people who normally voted Democratic to vote for him. If he were overly partisan he might lose

---

[31] Gibson, interview, 1994.

support among those voters. While always identifying himself as a Republican he did not stress the point when campaigning in the sixth district. He did stand with other Republican candidates on all levels but personally campaigned as a reformer, an outsider and a change-maker—not as a Republican first and foremost.[32]

Newt's campaign literature usually mentioned the word Republican only once—on the back page. The cover urged "Elect Newt Gingrich... Isn't it time you had a Congressman?" He adopted the theme that the politicians have had their chance, now it is time you had yours. This positioned him as an outsider not to be blamed for what was currently going on in Washington. When pressed he would note that it was the Democrats who had run Congress for over twenty years and they had to bear the burden of Washington's failures.

By January 1974 Newt was openly being considered a candidate by the press. The Newnan *Times Herald* noted his candidacy and his use of contemporary problems to illustrate the failure of those in power and as a platform for his own ideas. Speaking to a Newnan Kiwanis Club he was bipartisan in his assessment of the national leadership in the handling of the energy crisis. "The energy crisis is a result of stupidity on the part of our government which did not act in time to circumvent a serious problem." He blamed congressional overspending for inflation and noted, "Taxypayers are acting as suckers today tolerating inflation, an inactive government and a group of politicians who tell them when to sell their gas, who to sell it to, how much to pay for it, and how much they may sell."[33]

Speaking at a county GOP meeting later in January he described himself as a "common sense conservative," when he talked about national defense. "The real choice we face is not between the hawks and the doves, but between the eagles and the ostriches." A few months later, he expressed his feeling that while we need a strong military trained and ready for quick and sustained response, we should not be blind to the extensive waste in the defense budget. He had read and understood Eisenhower's farewell speech warning of the military-industrial complex and the dangers it presented to America's future by bloating the budget and thus increasing the deficit. Newt was as

---

[32] Campaign literature, Steely papers (1974 campaign folder) State University of West Georgia Archives, Carrollton.

[33] *Newnan Times Herald*, 10 January 1974.

committed to common sense spending as he was to a strong military.[34]

There was considerable debate among Republicans about Watergate in early 1974. Resignation was eight months away and many felt that President Nixon was being unfairly attacked by the "liberal" press for doing what all presidents had done. Newt was not sure just how guilty Nixon was, nor of what he was guilty, if anything. Still, he thought there was something substantial here and in March told his audience, "The nation can stand nothing less than the truth. The House Judiciary Committee is now a grand jury. The President has to come clean. He must supply what the Committee says it needs."[35] Even though he had served as Nixon's reelection chairman for the sixth district in 1972, Newt did not want to make a decision about the President's guilt or innocence until he had all the facts.

The next month he brought a sobering message to the Republican Party as well. "The Republican Party is in danger of dying. It often resembles the old Whig Party with its lack of clear-cut leadership and strong vision of a better America." He said most Americans view the GOP as "the party of hard times, of the country club, and of big business." He went on to look ahead to 1976. "Let me warn flatly that we are kidding ourselves. If the party which people think of as the party of hard times still has a recession on its hands in 1976, or has raging inflation, then [anticipating Nixon's removal from the scene] President Ford will have a hard time beating any middle of the road Democrat."[36]

Also important to Newt were issues of social justice, issues dating from his own grade school days. He felt strongly that minorities had to be included in the political process in a meaningful way and sought to do that in his campaign. He understood that it would be an uphill fight but thought it was absolutely necessary, not to win, but to run an honest campaign open to all voters.

Newt had been in contact with the Scott family who owned and published *The Atlanta Daily World*, an African-American newspaper aligned with the Republican Party. The Scotts were friendly to Newt and helped open doors in the African-American community. In February he spoke at the Locust Grove Baptist Church during Negro

---

34 Clayton *News Daily*, 25 April 1974.
35 *The Atlanta Journal*, 3-27-74, G.V.R. Smith editorial.
36 *Atlanta Constitution*, 10-5-75, David Nordan column.

History Week and praised Martin Luther King, Jr. and his goals. Later that month he was the featured speaker at the Lincoln-Douglas Banquet for Black Leaders in Atlanta. He praised Lincoln and Douglas as men who "did so much in healing and reconciliation and in enabling a people to live together as human beings."[37] He would continue to speak at African-American churches throughout the district for the duration of the campaign.

Congressman Flynt's record on civil rights was less than inspiring. The Gingrich campaign put out a flyer entitled, "Congressman Jack Flynt and Civil Rights." This document stated "If Rep. Jack Flynt has been anything in his 20 years in Washington he has been a consistent opponent of civil rights legislation. He has spoken out in Congress more times on this subject than any other." While in the Georgia legislature he had pledged his strength, blood and life to resist integration. He had voted against Civil Rights Acts, the US Commission on Civil Rights, the Voting Rights Acts, the Economic Opportunity Acts, the Equal Employment Opportunity Commission and the Food Stamps Program."

A second flyer noted, "There is a story circulating in the Sixth Congressional District of Georgia that Rep. Jack Flynt died in office some years ago and was never replaced. This is probably because very few voters in that part of the state have ever seen their congressman. Actually, the rumor is not true. Jack Flynt is very much alive and continuing his notoriously consistent record of voting against the best interest of black Americans....Some men change with the times. But not Jack Flynt. He never missed a chance to vote against the future of black young people."[38] Though Newt did not believe in smear tactics, he insisted that an elected official should stand on his record and be accountable for his votes.

Though it became clear early on that Rep. Flynt's approach to the African-American community in his district was to ignore them and depend on their loyalty to the Democratic Party, Newt now sought to erect a campaign tent that was large enough to include African-Americans as one of the special interest groups to be approached by the campaign. He contacted and sought the advice and support of local African-American leaders in communities throughout the district. He believed that they, like any interest group, had special concerns but he

---

[37] *Atlanta Daily World*, 2-26-74 and Henry Weekly Advertiser, 2-7-74.
[38] Campaign literature. Steely papers (1974 campaign folder).

also believed that they had the same basic problems, hopes and frustrations as other Americans and should be approached on that basis.

Other special interest groups were also the focus of the campaign. Airport workers were important. The Atlanta airport was the biggest generator of jobs in the district. Government workers such as policemen, firemen and city and county employees were important because many of them were as concerned as Newt about making the system work, getting rid of red tape, dead wood, and useless or excessively restrictive regulations, and fighting fraud and corruption. They served as an important source of information for the campaign.

Young people, newcomers to the district who were not locked into the local Democratic Party, and Republicans were other groups approached by the campaign. Newt personally visited high schools throughout the district talking with school newspapers and other students about the future and about his work in Coweta County with advanced students. Teachers were critical to the campaign. Jackie was a public school teacher as were many of the wives of Newt's supporters. These women and teachers across the district thought Flynt was not a friend of education. Newt, on the other hand, was young, married to a teacher and personally taught college and advanced high school students and had experienced many of their concerns firsthand.

In February 1974 he outlined two futures for public education in an article in the *West Georgia Educational Development Program Newsletter*. The first future would be one where the "anti-education, cost cutting forces" join with other special interest groups to divert budget support, fire teachers as enrollment declines, and replace teachers with technology. "This approach will almost certainly lead to a weaker education system and it will be very attractive to some people." The second future would be where teachers, students and parents work together to cut class sizes, give sabbaticals, provide for more planning and in-service training and use technology to "supplement and enrich teacher-student activities."[39]

Though Newt acknowledged that the second future would be more expensive than the first, he genuinely believed in public education and felt that the problems it faced could be worked out through a reform of the system. He thought it needed to be more democratic and open to

---

[39] West Georgia Educational Development Program Newsletter, Jan.-Feb. 1974, p. 2. Also see the Carroll County Georgian, 3-21-74.

outside input and to the student learning process as well. At this stage he saw teachers' organizations such as the Georgia Association of Educators and the National Education Association as allies. They returned the feeling with formal endorsements.

In August, invitations to teachers were sent asking them to come to a meeting to organize "Educators for Gingrich." The special interest advisory committee would be a favored device used by Newt through the early 1980s. The educators committee met and named an executive committee. They scheduled regular meetings and passed out assignments concerning recruiting Newt supporters among the faculty members of sixth district schools. The committee would advise Newt on educational issues and serve to recruit other teachers to pass out literature, hold teas, serve on phone banks, and so on.[40]

The educators committee was made up of college, public and private school personnel. Often secretaries and staff would participate and work actively in the campaign. There was a sense of a "crusade" about Newt's campaign. The educators were, in their opinion, working to get "one of our own" in Congress and were determined to remove someone they felt was not attuned to their needs.

Other special interest groups were also involved against Flynt...though not especially for Newt. Flynt had virtually no environmental concern. He favored federal spending for rural areas and neglected urban areas, opposing such developments as rapid transit, and expanded medical and legal services. He was anti-labor, opposing the Peace Corps, aid to Israel and against foreign aid generally. He was strongly supportive of veterans and retired people as well as large farmers. Many liberals who normally voted Democratic supported Newt. Some thought he was a liberal and others supported him because they thought he had to be more liberal than Flynt.[41]

Newt did not go out of his way to correct those who thought he was a liberal. He consistently described himself as a "common sense conservative." Because he was chairman of the local chapter of the Georgia Conservancy and was pro-education as well as strongly for social justice, many thought of him as liberal. These assumptions would

---

[40] Campaign literature. UWG archives, Steely papers (1974 campaign folder) State University of West Georgia Archives, Carrollton.

[41] Bob Claxton, interview by, author, tape recording, 2 February 1995, SUWG Archives, Carrollton.

later lead to confusion when he stressed economic conservatism, small government and a strong military.

The truth was that Newt was neither exclusively liberal nor conservative. He believed that government should protect freedom and not constrict it. He did not believe in big government as the answer to all problems. When governmental intrusion was necessary it should be to help solve problems rather than to become another problem.

What was troubling to Newt in 1974 worried a lot of his fellow citizens. Government, in what was a well-meaning attempt to solve social problems and bring social justice, had itself become the problem. As he had stated when he opened his campaign, "indifference and incompetency" was what our leaders were giving us. Congressmen "neither listen to the people nor let the voters know what they are doing." He thought that trust and openness were important and compared the open approach of his campaign to the closed doors of government committees in Washington. His promise to be a congressman who would help solve problems for the average citizen and get government "off our backs," brought him a good deal of support.[42]

One of the groups that liked his pledge to listen and to be their spokesman in Washington was the small business community. Young professionals and small businessmen all around the district gave him support. As he began his tour of the district in April and May he determined to travel every road and pig-path and shake hands in every store he passed.

The beginning of that tour came with the formal announcement of Newt's candidacy the night of 8 April 1974. A small but excited group of Newt's supporters waded through mud that rainy evening to gather in his Carrollton headquarters on Watson Street. A local dentist, Dr. Alvin Crews, had rented the campaign an empty warehouse with an office attached to serve as headquarters. Volunteers provided punch and homemade cookies, but only the local Carrollton newspaper chose to cover the event. The reporter, Allen Gunther, generously reported seventy-five attendees.

Newt said he was running because, "I am fearful for this country as it enters a changing world with leaders who do not understand the nature of those changes." He promised a campaign of honesty and

---

[42] *Carroll County Georgian,* 9 April 1974.

openness and declared himself a "common sense conservative" and declared "I am undertaking what promises to be a long, uphill fight because I can no longer sit idly by while my future and the future of this country is endangered by political hacks who don't understand what is happening to the people they supposedly represent."[43]

The next day Newt traveled to Atlanta with a group of his supporters to declare for Congress at the state capitol so that he might draw more press coverage. He had taken the precaution of checking to be sure that press would already be there to cover other events. He made essentially the same speech and did draw better press attendance. He did not, however, get the coverage he had hoped for because Atlanta Brave Hank Aaron hit his record breaking home run that day, relegating Newt's announcement to "other news."

Newt then started a handshaking tour around the principal cities in the district. He had taken an unpaid leave of absence to devote full time to the campaign. His days started early with a breakfast with a civic group or with supporters and were a whirlwind of activity lasting late into the evening. He would typically park at one end of a main street and go door to door up one side of the street and back down the other. He smiled, talked, left campaign literature and asked for support and names of other people to see.

On one of these tours, in East Point, Georgia, he visited the office of an optometrist, Dr. Crook. Crook was so taken with Newt's personality and message that he began to accompany him as he went through the business district. Crook was the prototype supporter any candidate would relish. He was young and energetic. A successful professional, he knew the chamber of commerce and the business community. He was a scoutmaster and a Civitan. He and his wife were active in the church and the community and were ready to become part of a cause they believed would help change the country for the better.

"I thought Newt was honest and had integrity. He was very bright and helped shape my beliefs," said Crook. He introduced Newt around South Fulton County and accompanied him to ask for money. "Newt had a lot of difficulty asking for money. I'd go with him and close the deal by asking for a specific amount to pay for a specific item such as $200 for yard signs or $100 for radio ads."[44]

---

43 Ibid.
44 Gary Crook, interview by, 12-28-94.

Crook later became co-chairman of the campaign and served in that or some other meaningful capacity in the next four campaigns. Another optometrist, Dr. Wayne Brown from Carrollton, had provided similar help to Newt in that part of the district and served as Newt's second campaign treasurer. Cary Hall, from Henry County, like Crook, Brown, Whaley, Taylor and many others, served as an advisor and provided a place for Newt to spend the night and get fed. Hall, an irascible retired naval officer and regional official in the Nixon administration, was almost like a surrogate father to Newt. Ever critical and difficult to please, he always demanded the best from Newt. Newt respected and admired Hall and always listened to what he had to say. The day Newt was sworn in as speaker two of the original team were in the gallery and Hall was one of them, filled with emotion and proudly watching the culmination of what he had help start two decades earlier.

Newt consistently drove home his views on seven major areas of concern. High prices, tax reform and health care were the key pocketbook issues. Education, the problems of "our older citizens," and the environment spoke to key constituents and the lack of proper representation remained the keystone for attacking all the above. Many of these would remain central to all Newt's future campaigns as well.

Newt described the health care situation as one of "crisis." He insisted that it demanded a new approach that would "deliver better treatment, not more red tape. I believe this can be done without socializing medicine." In general terms he said we should encourage health care organizations, increase preventive medicine and reform the delivery system, all of which should result in better care at a lower cost.[45]

"America needs a return to moral values, to individual and fiscal responsibility," he said. "These are the proven ways which built this nation and keep it great. We must bring these values back—not because they are old, but because they are true." He went on to say, "The only *special interest* a congressman should have is the people he represents.[46]

Throughout April and May Newt crisscrossed the district, recruited volunteers and sought every possible opportunity to get free press to get his name known. The campaign organization grew in size and

---

[45] Mel Steely Papers, (1974 campaign folder).
[46] Ibid.

structure but contributions were still at a premium. Carroll County continued to provide the core of the campaign with volunteers. One of the themes of the campaign developed around the idea that even the staff, manager, field workers, secretary, and so on were working for almost nothing because they were dedicated to the cause.

A former student of Newt's, Michelle Shallum, ran the local headquarters, a former professor, L. H. Carter, served as the treasurer, other professors were in charge of signs, canvassing and telephoning. Mitt Conerly and Steely served on the advisory committee and local Republicans like Carol Martin and Aubrey Duffey helped with election procedures and organization. Following qualifying in June a main office was opened near the Atlanta airport in Fulton County. Attorney and GOP official John Stuckey helped get space over a restaurant/bar at a modest cost and Atlanta area Republicans helped staff the office.

At the qualifying Newt called for electoral reform for spending limits. He proposed a $90,000 limit for the primary and another $90,000 for the general election. He also called for full disclosure of income for candidates. He said that he thought it was time for action instead of talk.

At first Newt thought it would be good to qualify by petition rather than to pay the qualifying fee and worked successfully to get enough people to sign the petition. A lot of his supporters, however, objected to qualifying by petition. They thought the candidates should bear the cost of the election and if someone could not get people to give him money to run then maybe he should reconsider. Since the petition already had enough signers Newt decided to qualify both ways.

Newt's lifestyle helped sell his message. It was clear to anyone who saw how he dressed and visited his home that he was not a materialist. He had returned to Georgia, in part, because teaching in the state would help pay off his debt. His home was a small house on Howell Road which was modestly, though adequately furnished. His green plastic covered sofa and reclining chair that automatically reclined when anyone sat in it became the stuff of legends. When new furniture was required Jackie had to insist on buying it. Money just was not something he thought about except as it paid bills and helped him achieve his goals.[47]

He was making headway, he felt, by mid-summer. David Broder had noted in the *Washington Post* that "Gingrich and a handful of others

---

[47] Conner, interview, 1994.

insure the Republican Party's future regardless of what happens this fall."[48] Likewise many of those who were close to him in this campaign also thought that Newt was "special." There was a dedication and a certainty about him that conveyed the assurance that he would play a major role in the future of the country and the volunteers thought they too were a part of this rather historic activity.

In the thank you notes sent out to contributors Newt noted that they were now "shareholders" in the campaign. Some more money came in but it was always a balancing act to pay all the bills at the end of the month. In a copy of "Notes From Newt," the campaign newsletter, Newt noted that volunteers are the key to victory, "but money is the key to survival until the election." He set $6,000/month as the base figure needed and said that since he would not accept over $1,000 from any one person or $3,000 from any group then it would be necessary to find hundreds ready to support the campaign with small contributions. His pleas were answered.

More press support came in. On 7 August 1974 he received his first newspaper endorsement from the *Atlanta Suburban Reporter* reflecting the paper's dissatisfaction with the level of representation provided by Flynt since South Fulton was reapportioned into the sixth district. Reg Murphy, editor of the *Atlanta Constitution*, became the first major commentator to say that Newt had a good opportunity to defeat Congressman Flynt.[49]

As the 13 August primary approached, more and more volunteer cards came in and county and town organizations were constantly strengthened with new blood. While there was a lack of coordination and most county organizations were given little guidance there was a shared enthusiasm that was infectious. Many in the campaign put in long hours phoning, canvassing, working on sign projects, and staffing the local offices.

A week before the primary Newt attacked Flynt for once again placing special interests ahead of the public. Flynt had supported the 1971 Sugar Act Extension Bill and Newt charged that the incumbent Congressman was favoring the sugar growers "at the expense of housewives" and consumers. Sugar sacks eventually became a symbol during Newt's first campaign ad where he stood and denounced Flynt

---

[48] *Atlanta Journal*, 1 July 1974.
[49] Ibid.

beside a table piled high with five pound bags of sugar.

While Newt was denouncing the sugar interest supporting Flynt the GOP was taking a body blow with the resignation under pressure by Richard Nixon on 8 August 1974, less than a week before the primary. While Newt accused the Democrats of being ineffective and corrupt, the Republicans hardly offered a better alternative. Vice President Spiro Agnew had resigned less than a year earlier (10 October 1973) facing charges of bribery and ten months later the president also resigned leaving most of America with the impression that he really was a crook. Still, Newt had been openly critical of Nixon and demanded that he "come clean" early on. He did manage to insulate himself personally from the fall-out but did not benefit from an increased party vote by those fed up with corruption.

Newt was certain of a primary victory because no one was running against him. He and other supporters gathered on primary night to watch the returns and talk about the "campaign really starting." Toward the end of the month "evenings with Newt" were held to raise money in various parts of the district. One held at North Lakeshore Park in Carrollton was typical. Held on 14 September, on a Saturday afternoon it offered the regular political fare, chicken and fish. About 100 attended paying $10.00 each for the privilege of visiting with Newt, listening to a short speech and watching each other's children play. Newt's message was standard: "[Y]ou are important in helping me carry the message to Washington. Your money and your time volunteered to the campaign make it possible for me to get on the road with the tools necessary to do the job."[50]

People called in with sign locations and their production was coordinated, distributed, and erected through local contacts. Whaley and Marge Krauth coordinated pledges and finance, Lee Howell handled press and Dot Crews took care of special projects. County organizational meetings were held in those counties not already organized. Newt opened with remarks and a question and answer session followed by Kahn's outline of the campaign and a colleague's comments on campaign needs and organization. Discussion groups were encouraged and individual meetings with Newt were held by local leaders.

On 8 September 1974 President Gerald Ford issued a pardon to

---

[50] *Carroll County Georgian*, 9-17-74.

Richard Nixon confirming the belief for many that there were two systems of justice in America. Once again the cynicism of the voter was rekindled. The view that "they are all alike" made the rounds and made it harder for Newt to push the idea that he was not like those in Washington. It seemed to many supporters that every time the campaign got on track something would happen to send it off track.

Newt's ability to stay focused was remarkable as was his ability to reframe a situation to make it a positive instead of a negative. He understood what Ford was doing but thought it was wrong nonetheless. He represented the view that more than ever we needed someone in Washington to represent us. His slogan that "the politicians have had their chance and now it is time the people had theirs" seemed to fit the moment.

Newt reported to his district organizational meeting on 15 September that the bitterness had eased somewhat but had the election been held a few days earlier there would have been an almost definite defeat. "We have to work harder now," he said. Plans were set for him to visit a factory shift each morning, then a large office building and finally a kindergarten or elementary school at pick-up time. Weekends he would visit shopping centers shaking hands and do bumper sticker blitzes. Jackie would attend coffees and whatever else she could work into her schedule. Advertising took on a new priority and it was decided that radio and newspapers would not be enough.

Educators, cattlemen, unions, conservationists and senior citizens were targeted and Newt took every possible opportunity to visit radio stations and newspapers as he passed through their communities. He continued to be a whirlwind of activity making it critical to have Dot Crews, who had become a scheduler as well as special projects person, keep tabs on what was happening and select the priority events for his personal appearance. Interestingly, a young law professor from the University of Arkansas named Bill Clinton was similarly engaged in his first quest for congressional office.[51]

Claxton reported that Newt's was the first effective challenge Flynt had in his ten terms in Congress. The League of Conservation Voters endorsed Newt because of his leadership in the Georgia Conservancy and his opposition to the Sprewell Bluff Dam project...a project that Governor Jimmy Carter also opposed. The Georgia Association of

---

[51] David Maraniss, First in His Class. (NY: Simon and Schuster) 1995.

Educators also gave him their endorsement and editorial cartoons began to appear that opposed Flynt.[52]

Flynt did not take the challenge lightly, though he was slow in recognizing Newt as a serious threat. He increased his campaigning and spent more time in the newer parts of his district. He branded Gingrich as a "liberal college professor" and refused all offers of joint appearances or debates, claiming that his Washington duties prevented such appearances.

Newt had accused Flynt, Chairman of the House Ethics Committee, of unethical conduct when he took $12,500 from Ford Motor Company and then supported efforts to ease automobile emissions standards. Flynt denied there was any connection. He also had sold a narrow strip of street-front property to avoid paying a $4,000 assessment by the city of Griffin and Newt made an issue of it. Flynt again denied any impropriety though later he paid the assessment and admitted, "It was the most stupid thing I've done in my life."[53]

In spite of the ethical concerns, Flynt's poor voting record on civil rights, education and the environment, and the public's disenchantment with Washington politicians the incumbent Congressman had numerous advantages. He had twenty years of contacts in the district and vastly greater name recognition. He had the courthouse officials working for him and a number of people owed him favors. In addition, Flynt was clearly seen as a conservative in a conservative district. Finally, this was an off-year election where the party out of power usually picks up congressional seats.

A late poll showed the race fairly close with Newt within the margin of error and gave hope that he might pull it out. The campaign had again begun to move and Newt was starting to get positive receptions as he continued his hand shaking tour. Radio and newspaper ads were increased at a relatively small cost and some television was purchased, mainly on cable and during mid-afternoon shows directed at women because the poll had shown Newt had some strength in that area.

Kahn had put everything he had into this campaign. In September, while handing out campaign literature at a local football game, he had watched the players and decided you had to give it your all if you wanted to win. He met Newt after the game and asked him, "If I put in

---

52 Claxton, interview, 2 February 1995.
53 *Atlanta Journal.*

money will you raise the rest for television?" They both felt that might be the key to winning and so Newt agreed to raise the necessary money. Kahn then borrowed $5,000 using his trust fund to secure the note. They made the sugar ad and another one with Newt facing the camera stressing the new versus the old. Flynt did not use any television ads. Newt and Kahn thought they had to be real to the voters. The television ads did make an impact and resulted in some earned media as the press covered the ads but in the end the polls showed it had a very negligible impact and the election still looked close.[54]

On Sunday evening, 3 November, two days before the election, Newt gathered his team together for one last strategy meeting at his Hapeville headquarters. He opened the meeting by going around the room and thanking each person there mentioning something they had done to help the campaign. He noted that they had one more day to get those last votes needed to win.

Reports came in. Over 14,000 calls had been made to those on the voter's list (220,000 voters). There had been 600 volunteers in the campaign across the district and twelve full time volunteers in what was a massive grassroots effort. As usual, money was needed, $17,000 to be current. To that point there had been over 1,000 contributors, most of whom gave less than $100 each. It was estimated that Newt had traveled over 40,000 miles and it was anybody's guess as to the number of hours volunteers had put into the campaign.

During the last strategy meeting people seemed reluctant to leave. Preparations for Monday went on and on. Plans for the election night celebration were gone over and over again. There was a sense among those present that they had been part of something special and if Newt won or lost it would never be quite the same again. Newt, Jackie, Kahn, Steely, Conners, Conerly, Whaley, Carter, and the rest of the team had mixed feelings about what would happen on Tuesday. Most, including Newt, thought victory was possible but felt deep inside that though he would make a good showing they would have to wait until 1976 for the win they wanted so badly.

Early the next morning Newt was in Bremen at the Arrow shirt factory working shift changes with a team of volunteers. He then traveled to Clayton County stopping off in Douglasville, which had

---

[54] Chip Kahn interview, 2-10-95.

proven to be a stronghold of support, on the way. The Douglas County team were passing out leaflets and felt sure that they would carry their county easily. He then went to busy intersections in the metro area and worked at traffic lights asking drivers for their support. He visited the shopping centers in the area, then back to Carrollton to work the late shift change at Southwire, and home to get a few hours sleep before election day.

Newt woke up to a rainy election day and shook hands at an early shift change in Carrollton before he and Jackie went to vote. Hopes were high all day as he moved from group to group around the district. No one talked about losing as they listened to WSB radio reporting on how the voter turnout was going. The rain slowed voters down somewhat but this was a year when Georgia elected a governor to replace Jimmy Carter and that race, along with other state constitutional officers, helped turn out a decent vote of about forty-three percent of the registered voters. There was considerable debate about whether that would help or hurt Newt's chances.

Newt's election night party was held at Crowley's Bar and Restaurant close to the Atlanta airport and in the same building as his Hapeville headquarters. Starting early in the evening reports were coming in that irregularities were going on in the voting in some of the rural counties. This was especially true in Lamar, Coweta and Heard, the smallest county. In Heard the Democrats seemed to take every Republican vote very personally and did what they could through intimidation at the polls to stop it.

Kahn and Tommy Engram, the security advisor, worked with a small staff at headquarters to gather voting results from around the district from supporters who had agreed to call in with the totals. Most of Newt's supporters were gathered at Crowley's with the candidate going back and forth from the restaurant to headquarters and back. The vote was close all evening but sometime around 9:00 P.M. Kahn came down to the restaurant and told Newt that though he was carrying some key counties such as Clayton, South Fulton, Douglas, and Carroll, he was not carrying them sufficiently to overcome Flynt's considerable advantage in the more rural counties. "It just ain't going to happen."[55]

At this point Newt and his key advisors huddled to decide how seriously to take the charges of irregularities. When the final totals came

---

[55] Ibid.

in Newt had lost by 2,774 votes and had 48.5 percent of the vote. Flynt got 49,082 (51.5 percent) and Newt 46,308 votes. The small counties had gone big for Flynt and the irregularities had come from those counties. It was unlikely that a recount would change the outcome but nevertheless it seemed important to Newt that a challenge be made to set a baseline for the future. He decided to make a challenge in the three counties.

Newt was right about the outcome of the recount. A few numbers were changed but Flynt still won the election and there was little evidence of massive vote fraud. Still the closeness of the race was considered by many to be a great achievement. Newt and his advisors were pleased and somewhat surprised that it was so close. Everyone associated with the campaign thought this was the first step toward a second campaign in 1976 and thought that one would probably bring victory for Newt.[56]

Newt was disappointed. He was especially disappointed because the election had been so close. One would, however, have thought he had won when he spoke to his supporters at Crowley's. Conner remembers him saying, "This is where we go from here." Conner continued, "Campaigning was a task that he'd experienced and endured and would continue until he got elected. It was never a question in his mind of whether he was going to get to Washington. If ever there was a person I've met who perceived their destiny, it was Newt."[57]

The race for 1976 began immediately.

---

[56] Kahn, interview, 1995.
[57] Conner, interview, 1994.

4

SECOND TRY

Jim Gay was not disappointed about the 1974 election loss. "I really thought he'd probably lose and I think he did too. He was laying the groundwork for the next time. The result was not anything that was negative to most people who supported him. They thought it was a good base and a good start and very respectable for a Republican."[1]

Newt seemed to share Gay's view of the loss and began immediately to plan for the 1976 race, though developments in his personal life took precedence. The 1974 campaign had placed a tremendous strain on his marriage. Newt had a brief affair with a staff member and his wife had found out about it. He and Jackie had experienced problems since before they left for Belgium. They had agreed though to make sure their personal problems never touched their daughters. Strange as it seems, the family was strong but the marriage was rocky. "Newt was struggling with his marriage, not his family," remembers his friend Daryl Conner. "What I remember is that they were a very close family. They had a pleasant, positive, affirming, warm family unit." [2]

The experiences of the campaign and the growing apart over the previous decade led Newt to seriously consider divorce in early December 1974. He talked about it at length with Jan Whaley, Cary Hall and Ivan and Betty Taylor. Working through it with these friends led Newt to commit to making the marriage work in spite of the differences between him and Jackie. "The whole time I knew him his

---

[1] Jim Gay interview, 23 November 1994.
[2] Daryl Conner interview, 3 October 1994.

attitude was 'how do I make this work?'" said Conner. "He turned every stone to make the marriage work. Both he and Jackie seemed to feel 'how do we get over our differences and get this to work?'"[3]

By January 1975 Newt and Jackie put thought of divorce aside and worked to restore the marriage. He returned to planning for the next campaign and to his work at college. The inner circle that had worked with him in the 1974 effort stayed close and involved. Chip Kahn had returned to New Orleans to work for the mayor. He had grown to think of Carrollton as a second home and traveled back and forth during 1975. The municipal job was just to make money and gain experience while planning Newt's strategy for the 1976 campaign. The entire inner circle felt the same way. The 1974 campaign had been a long shot and a test run, now it was time to get serious about the next campaign. Even Jackie, who thought the odds longer and hopeless due to Jimmy Carter's decision to enter the race for president, felt better about this race than she did the first one though she noted that the "spirit of adventure" was gone and it was like another job.[4]

For Gary Crook and his wife, Katherine, there was still plenty of romance left in a Gingrich campaign. Shortly after the election, in December 1974, they drove to Carrollton to visit with Newt and Jackie. They talked about the previous campaign and discussed the prospects of a second run for Congress. Gary Crook gave Newt a $250 check to help pay off the campaign debt which was less than $20,000 at that point and returned home pleased that Newt had agreed to another race.

Crook, for his part, had agreed to continue to help recruit volunteers and raise money for the 1976 campaign. His two main problems were convincing people that Newt was not a liberal who was running as a conservative and overcoming resistance to Jackie who "didn't seem to fit the mold of a congressional wife." He reminded supporters objecting to Jackie that it was Newt they were electing and he was certainly no liberal.[5]

Newt's concerns over the environment and social justice no doubt contributed to the confusion about his conservative political nature. On 14 January 1975 he appeared on an ACLU panel for Bob Claxton

---

[3] Ibid. Also Jan Whaley interview, 12-28-94.

[4] Jackie Gingrich interview, 29 April 1979.

[5] Gary Crook interview, 28 December 1994.

discussing "Civil Liberties in an Uncivil Environment." Two weeks later he attended and spoke at a state meeting of the Georgia Conservancy held at Callaway Gardens. State Senator Paul Coverdell and Lieutenant Governor Zell Miller were afternoon speakers at the meeting. Newt, as head of the Carroll County chapter of the Conservancy, was proving it possible to be an environmentalist as well as a conservative but, again, those not attending could have misunderstood because some equated the Conservancy with liberals. He followed this the next week with a proposal for the Georgia Extension Service extending its activities to cover suburbia instead of only the rural areas of the state. While this is accepted practice today it raised eyebrows in 1975.[6]

Newt returned to the West Georgia College campus and officially headed the environmental studies program moving from the history department to the geography department. Newt continued to attract students to his classes and some came on board to help with the campaign. Arthur Fessenden and David Butler were part of Newt's student following. They came to his house from time to time to continue discussions after class and often stayed for dinner. During the summer of 1975 they noticed that his house needed painting and they volunteered to paint it if he would supply the paint. They knew Newt did not have the money to pay a painter nor the time to do it himself. Fessenden also later served as Newt's driver and spent the next four years working with Newt in the campaign or with his congressional office.[7]

Roger Miles, a local druggist and supporter, agreed to work as treasurer. Bob Claxton agreed to store the 1974 campaign materials and hold them for the 1976 effort. Conerly and his crew at Real Estate West agreed to provide logistic support and help raise money. Chester Gibson and his debaters continued researching the issues for Newt. Whaley, Taylor, Hall and a host of other key leaders in the 1974 campaign continued setting up speaking engagements for Newt and helping raise money in their counties almost as if the campaign had never stopped.

---

[6] Bob Claxton papers and interview, 2 February 1995.

[7] Arthur Fessenden interview, 30 November 1994. UWG Archive, Gingrich Papers.

Newt was concerned about more than local support and his own election. He knew he had to encourage the building of the state Republican Party. As luck would have it a friend and supporter was elected party chairman in the spring of 1975 and shared Newt's view that the GOP in Georgia had to expand its horizons if it was to do more than elect a Republican here and there. The party had reached a low point with no federal elected officials, no statewide constitutional officers and only a smattering of state senators and representatives.

Mack Mattingly, from St. Simons Island, Georgia was elected state GOP chairman at this crucial point in the party's history. Mattingly, a transplant from Indiana and an Air Force Korean War veteran, was a marketing manager for IBM and at that time was opening up his own office supply business on St. Simons. He had served as Barry Goldwater's district chairman in 1964 and had run for Congress, unsuccessfully, in 1966. He had been active in state GOP politics since 1962 and would go on in 1980 to be the first Republican elected to the United States Senate from Georgia since 1871.

Gingrich and Mattingly worked hand in glove with other Republicans like Senator Paul Coverdell, the new Georgia Senate minority leader and Representative Mike Egan, the House minority leader. For so long the party held little hope of electing candidates and focused instead on internal politics within the party. If the party was to grow, if good, creditable candidates were to be recruited, then the party had to change.

Newt was after more than simply getting himself elected to Congress. Georgia had three Republican congressmen elected in the 1960s and 1970s and by 1975 all were gone. Newt was working for a Republican majority in a truly two-party state. After that was done he could work for a majority in Congress as well.

One of the problems facing the development of a unified Republican party in Georgia was the challenge Ronald Reagan, the California governor, was starting to make against President Gerald Ford. Georgia Republicans, like those nation-wide, were split between the conservative Reagan and the more moderate and traditional Ford. Many Georgia Republicans had come to the party during the Goldwater period in the 1960s and had advanced in county and district offices. They were ready to move the party toward conservatism. The traditional Republicans supported President Ford.

Newt's first task was to make sure that sixth district Republicans stayed united behind him. That would not be easy because both sides wanted his support and would likely be disaffected if he supported one or the other. While publicly standing with Ford, he nevertheless praised Reagan and even insisted that Jan Whaley "take over Reagan's primary campaign in the district as well as serving as Newt's campaign co-chair with Gary Crook."[8]

Newt had, in fact, been pulled to Reagan in 1965 when he debated Bobby Kennedy and said, "Do any of you honestly believe that if Stalin had a monopoly on the A-Bomb that we'd be free?" Reagan's stand on defense really impressed Newt and he was a Reagan supporter from that point on. Though he supported Reagan, Newt did not feel comfortable openly opposing Ford as president. At the same time he did not want to oppose Reagan, not only because it might destroy the unity in the sixth district, but also because Reagan might be what was needed to change the direction of the national party. Having Whaley run the Reagan campaign in the sixth, with strong ties to the state Reagan people and explaining that Newt was not opposed to Governor Reagan, worked well enough to hold the district Republicans together and keep them focused on electing local GOP candidates as well as fighting over the presidential primary. Civility and tolerance were preached regularly to the faithful. Reagan's eleventh commandment that, "Thou shall not speak ill of another Republican" was often quoted.[9] The party leadership shared Newt's interest in unity—no matter who was nominated for president—and worked to that end. Newt's efforts within the sixth district were successful and received the support of both camps in his effort to replace Representative Flynt.

In its attempt to do just that the 1974 campaign's main internal failure was that of organization. Newt had provided the intellectual construct for the campaign with the themes of ethics, service from the representative and changing a Congress that was out of touch with the American people. However, there was no serious plan carried out to coordinate the message in each county and community and few understood the need for television to legitimatize a congressional candidate. The 1974 campaign was a true grass roots effort, people to people, hand to mouth from week to week. As such the campaign

---

[8] Jan Whaley interview 28 December 1994.
[9] Newt Gingrich interview, 13 January 1993.

created great volunteer involvement and excitement among those who worked in the campaign, but did not carry to the mass of voters the reasons why they should vote for Newt instead of Flynt. In analyzing the 1974 effort Newt and his advisors felt, in spite of Watergate and Nixon's pardon, that the campaign could have been won if run properly.[10]

The 1976 campaign was better organized with more professionals getting involved. Buddy Bishop continued to be involved but Russ Evans and Wilma Goldstein brought their expertise and experience to the campaign. Like Bishop, they were experienced in district and state-wide campaigns and had solid ties to national GOP organizations. The Republican National Congressional Committee was now more interested in Newt because of the closeness of the 1974 campaign. In addition, Representative Flynt was now the chairman of the Ethics Committee in the House and that focused renewed light on Newt's charges from 1974 and the press became, in a sense, an ally.

"In 1976 we had a plan and played it out. The cleavage issues were the same except now we had Koreagate and Flynt was the chairman of the Ethics Committee. 1976 was a real campaign on both sides."[11] This time no outside factor could be foreseen to blindside the campaign as had the Nixon pardon late in the 1974 campaign. Jimmy Carter had announced his intention to run for the presidency and Newt and his team could figure that into the equation early on. It was clear that Newt would have to run well ahead of President Ford if he expected to win because it was anticipated that Carter would carry Georgia if he got the nomination.

Regular weekend strategy meetings were begun in 1975 and Kahn and the other consultants were in regular attendance along with what had begun to be called the "Carrollton Mafia" as well as other key leaders from the 1974 campaign team. As the leaves began to turn in Georgia, Newt warmed to one of his favorite themes: warning against big government assuming more and more power. Newt quickly targeted a current proposal for Atlanta to annex and consolidate with Fulton County. He called the attempt an "arrogant and outrageous act of government" and compared it to the Townsend Acts prior to the American Revolution. "Bigness itself had become an enemy of free

---

[10] Jan Whaley interview, 28 December 1994.

[11] Chip Kahn interview, 12 April 1995 and 19 February 1995.

societies." Annexation without a referendum would be the "worst possible way for Georgians to celebrate the 200th anniversary of the signing of the Declaration of Independence." He pointed out to a Kiwanis Club gathering in Union City that "small governments that are close to hand allow people to relate directly with their government and to talk with their leadership."[12]

Newt had been concerned about the trend of governmental growth since he came to West Georgia College and had frequently discussed his concerns with colleagues. He was no more pleased with Nixon's expansion of government than he had been with that of the Great Society. He was not opposed to federal control and involvement when needed but felt that too many people thought that wisdom resided only on the federal level. He thought that large bureaucracies made worse rather than better decisions and taught people to expect others to make their decisions for them.

Speaking to the Griffin chapter of the American Association of University Women on 2 October 1975 he said, "George Washington and Thomas Jefferson rebelled against a government too big and too distant to listen to the people." He went on to note that "freedom is ours only for one generation at a time." The way for citizens to keep it was to go out and fight for it at the ballot box or lose it.[13]

On 4 October he carried the anti-big government message to his own party. Speaking to the Georgia Federation of Republican Women he observed, "The Republican Party is in danger of dying." He warned that President Ford would have a hard time beating "any middle-of-the-road Democrat" if either recession or "raging inflation" were present in November 1976. At that point he noted that the only major difference between the two parties was that "Republican presidents favor big business while Democratic presidents favor big labor."[14]

Newt went on to tell the GOP Women that he blamed the Democrats in Congress for the economic situation but said the Republicans had failed to produce leaders "with the courage, the intelligence, and the charisma to lead us out of the wilderness of misgovernment." After seven years of a Republican presidency, he noted, "Medicaid has jumped from $3.7 billion to $12.6 billion. Welfare has gone up from $2.5

---

12 1976 Campaign Scrapbook, Newt Gingrich Papers, UWG Archives.
13 Ibid.
14 *Atlanta Journal*, 5October 1975.

billion to $8.5 billion, food prices rose $105 per family with farmers getting only $1.00 of that and that we were in the worst recession and suffering the worse inflation since World War II." In addition, "The party of conservatism and local government has now presided over the greatest amount of court intervention and busing in American history."[15]

Newt was for what he called "limited, effective government" but not a wasteful and bureaucratically bloated one. In his mind it was illogical to send money to Washington, establishing a new layer of bureaucrats to decide how to spend it on people and problems they had never seen and of which they knew little. This theme has stayed with him throughout his career.

Newt received a positive response from the Republican Women and a few weeks later from the DeKalb Young Republicans when he took the message of party reform to them. John Crown, a political columnist for the *Atlanta Journal*, noted on 14 November 1975, that "He is young and refreshingly idealistic while being reassuringly realistic." Newt told the Dekalb organization they should follow four points of reform. First, they should not be so exclusive. Second, they should shift their focus from the internal matters of their group to the real world of political activity, such as working to elect serious GOP candidates. Third, they should encourage the state party to establish a "Commission on Georgia" to hold hearings around the state to talk about issues. Finally, they should encourage the 1976 national platform committee to be a model of openness and make good use of the mass media. The message he gave to the Young Republicans was the same message he gave to the rest of the party.[16]

Newt became something of a darling of the press. They liked his talk of reform and openness and the *Atlanta Constitution* followed the *Journal* in praise. "Cheers for Newt Gingrich," they wrote. They noted that Newt Gingrich and John Savage were the top GOP candidates in 1974 and stated that, "If the Republican Party does have a future, it is with candidates like Gingrich and Savage" and recommended that "Georgia Republicans would do well to listen carefully to Gingrich." Jim Wood, editor of the *Clayton County Daily Recorder*, and a future opponent of Newt's, described him as "an attractive alternative to

---

[15] Ibid.

[16] John Crown editorial, *Atlanta Journal*, 14 November 1975.

Congressman Flynt."[17] In describing Newt and his campaign, David Nordan, a political writer for the *Atlanta Journal*, said Newt was a "middle of the road, young and candid" candidate who was considered the Georgia Republicans' "best hope for recapturing some of its lost dignity in the next round of elections."[18]

Gingrich had run well in 1974 against a formidable and entrenched opponent. His message was received well by the press and the public and many expected him to run successfully in 1976. As his popularity picked up with the public and press some of his early supporters from the college began to show irritation. "I must admit I was quietly irritated," said Jim Gay. His former office-mate did not understand why Newt had moved to Geography and thought he was spending less time with students and more on campaigning. "In 1976 I did not openly support him and I did not vote for him."[19]

Other faculty colleagues like Hanser, Gibson, Dangle, Claxton, and O'Malley continued their support. Newt sent a letter to his backers thanking them for their support and promising his continued hard work in the future. In his letter to O'Malley he said, "I remain committed to fight for these ideas. As often as possible I will be making speeches and writing articles for a stronger, more effective America."[20]

One of the ideas for which he was committed to fight was getting the government off the backs of America's small businessmen and women. Irvin Kristol had written an op-ed piece for the *Wall Street Journal* 13 November 1975, that crystallized much of Newt's thinking in that area. "The New Forgotten Man" stated "A whole new class of forgotten men has emerged—chivied, harassed, and bankrupted by a political process that takes them for granted. I refer to the small businessman." Newt thought regulation and taxation were unfairly slowing down the nation's enterprise, killing jobs and hampering the traditional American spirit of entrepreneurship.

In order to effectively enlist the Georgia GOP in his crusade to unify and move the party forward Newt put together a six-page package as a road map to GOP victory in the near future. The five topics covered were "Georgia Republicans Need to Look Ahead," "The Role of

[17] 1976 Campaign Scrapbook, Newt Gingrich Papers, UWG Archives.
[18] *Atlanta Journal*, 5 October 1975.
[19] Jim Gay interview, 23 November 1994.
[20] Steely papers, 1976 Campaign folder. UWG Archives.

Precinct Organization and Other Activities in Party Building,"
"Training in the Georgia GOP," "Communications for the Georgia
GOP," and "Some General Rules for Communication."[21]

Newt advocated looking ahead to 1982 and to preparing a list of
candidates for that election with winning the governorship and a
majority in the legislature as the goal. He argued that an emphasis on
long-term growth would aid recruitment. If precinct organization is
used properly, "best seen as the harvester rather than the plow," and
with proper training for a complex endeavor then electoral victories
could be expected. "Politics is the most complex business in a free
society short of warfare," he said. The training program should develop
a synergism between general ideas and skills and the specific problems
and opportunities of the local leaders. This should develop into a
combination training/planning program."

While training and planning were critical to success they would be
meaningless without communicating the objectives and goals to the
public. "Communications are the lifeblood of a political party," he
noted. This included internal communications such as newsletters and
bulletins, direct mailings to key groups and a heavy reliance on the
mass media. "Despite our traditional distrust of the media, we have to
recognize that they are the key to building a statewide program."[22]

The state party leadership and elected officials accepted most of the
document and worked to implement it. One of the key steps related to
the media was for Chairman Mattingly, Senator Coverdell and
Representative Egan and John Savage, as well as Newt, to look for press
opportunities and make news. The same held for each of the other
twenty-three Republican members of the Georgia General Assembly.
While their efforts did not result in a blizzard of news stories they were
diligent in their search for ink and air time and gradually began to get
their message to the public.

Receiving encouragement from the new head of the National
Republican Congressional Committee, Congressman Guy Vander Jagt,
Newt extended his ideas to the national level with a paper entitled,
"National Republicans Ought to Plan for a National Majority: A
Proposal from Carrollton, Georgia by Newt Gingrich." He began by

---

[21] Ibid.
[22] Ibid.

stating, "The 1976 presidential election should be one of the great realigning elections comparable to 1896 or 1932."

An opening summary of the paper noted "1976 offers Republicans an opportunity to once again become the majority party if they will simply take public opinion polls seriously and realize that the American people are disgusted with politics." He advocated "A thoroughly revised Republican strategy" that he thought "could lead to a sweep in the House and revitalization in local parties as well as a Presidential victory." He cautioned, "This proposal requires that Republican leaders plan a coherent strategy including issues, structure, and campaign tactics. Focusing on isolated campaigns and tactics will simply waste money and energy without yielding significant gains." In concluding his summary he promised, "The proposed strategy will both rebuild local parties and minimize the threat of a Wallace third-party next year."[23] The national strategy explained in the document would not be heeded in 1976 but would be partially implemented in 1980 with some positive results and would be followed closely in 1994 resulting in the kind of realigning election proposed for 1976.

The heart of the recommendation was for a competitive and decisive campaign. Newt noted, "Put simply, realigning elections are divisive, not appeasing. They emphasize the differences between two view-points. They are competitive, not cooperative, and seek to oppose the other party at every opportunity. They are moralistic rather than pragmatic and tend to become crusades for their vision of America." Gingrich continued, "They have a philosophical base but are not fanatically ideological. Their philosophy includes an umbrella broad enough to cover an amazing range of local idiosyncrasies but they are willing to anger traditional supporters (as FDR lost many northern conservatives in 1936). Finally, realigning coalitions attract large quantities of new, often younger activists who sweep out established politicians who have lost touch with their constituencies."[24]

The young activists Newt brought into his own campaign came from both parties and he did not stress the divisive approach in his own race. He still needed Democrats to put him over the top and did not have the strength of a mature state Republican Party to help him. Indeed, had he

---

[23] Ibid.
[24] Ibid.

advocated realignment publicly many would have viewed him as a dreamer at best.

Likewise, he did not follow his own advice to the state party concerning communications. By 4 January 1976, a seventeen-group direct mail list had been created which targeted both votes and money. The list did not include GOP party lists as these would be sought from Mattingly. At the same time the GOP members of the General Assembly were in legislative session and used that as an opportunity to comment on numerous bills and policies and develop press relationships. Letters and "Newt Notes," the old "Notes from Newt," continued to go to the faithful 1974 volunteers, encouraging, informing and getting them ready for the 1976 effort.[25]

Unpleasant though it was, Newt was active in raising money wherever he could and in February had the House Minority Leader, Representative John Rhodes from Arizona, fly in to speak at a fund-raiser in College Park. Newt had noted earlier that "We must stop making the American taxpayer *Uncle Sugar* to the world." He now said that "The US can not be the policeman of the world. When we tried that in Vietnam they beat us up." He continued, "We must fight to win or stay out" of foreign intervention. He favored a balanced national budget and a foreign policy that would maximize our strengths. About 450 people attended the event and it was successful at generating publicity and raising money.

In March columnist Jack Anderson said in his column that Representative Flynt, as chairman of the Ethics Committee, had taken Representative Robert Sikes, facing charges of influence peddling, aside privately and told him not to worry about an ethics investigation. This again connected Flynt to the ethics question and questioned his own personal ethics. Newt made the most of it. In addition, Flynt was put on the "Dirty Dozen" list by Environmental Action, Inc. and listed as a "Consumer Zero" by the Consumer Federation of America.[26]

Shortly after the end of winter quarter, Newt took a leave of absence from the college and on 22 March 1976 he announced that he was a candidate for Congress. He began his day in South Fulton speaking to supporters and the press and then visited Griffin, Newnan and Douglasville doing the same. He ended his day in Carrollton with an

---

[25] Ibid.

[26] Jack Anderson, *The West Georgian*, 3 December 1976, p. 4.

old-fashioned announcement rally on the town-square speaking from a flatbed truck.

Speaking to an enthusiastic crowd he said he was running again because, "the American middle class is under siege. Inflation, red tape, concentrated economic power in both labor and business, the decay of social discipline, the decline of a belief in hard work, the concentration of bureaucratic power in Washington, all have worked to weaken and undermine the working, tax-paying, middle class of this country." Newt went on to propose "a political counterattack on behalf of the working tax-payers that are the backbone of this society. A solid common sense conservative program which outlines clearly the direction we must go if the American middle class is to survive." The program he proposed included a welfare policy that stated, "No able-bodied adult should be paid federal funds." He said, "There is plenty of work for everyone to do; we have just been uncreative in how to get it done. I had much rather see a person paid to work in public service jobs than paid to do nothing."[27]

On education, he said, "American education policies have been frustrated for the past decade with attempts to teach too much too easily and without parental involvement. Furthermore," he said, "schools have been used as a vehicle for social experimentation. The federal government is more concerned with where my children go to school than what they actually learn." Concerning the budget and governmental waste he noted, "America stands at a cross-roads between the free, individualistic country we are, and the bureaucratic society we are becoming." "The fiscal policy of the US government," Newt said, "is a nightmare of irresponsibility. The federal government wastes money and resources. We cannot continue to pile up deficits which our children will have to pay." He promised, "I will propose a constitutional amendment to require a balanced federal budget except in times of war or national emergency. I will work to cut waste in the Pentagon, the Department of HEW and especially congress itself."[28]

Newt noted that there were problems with social security and worried that it would not be adequate in the future. He supported and encouraged private pension plans and warned that "American pensions and retirement policies are heading towards crisis." On crime he said,

---

[27] Newt Gingrich Papers, 1976 campaign scrapbook. UWG Archives.
[28] Ibid.

"We must realize that the best way to keep guns from being used in violent crime is to lock up the criminals who use them. I favor a mandatory ten-year sentence for anyone using a firearm in a felony."

Newt criticized Flynt for being more concerned about unauthorized leaks to the *Village Voice* by the Intelligence Committee than Koreagate or the Sikes investigation. He made sure that ethics would remain a major issue in the campaign in every way he could. The ethics question remained at the forefront when columnist Jack Anderson accused Flynt himself of leaking military information. Flynt protested noting that the leak had been "authorized by officials" and was "merely a backgrounder for the press." Newt marveled at Flynt's gall and continued doing his best to bring the ethical conflict to the attention of the public.

Mitt Conerly stepped up his fundraising efforts among the real estate people and John Stuckey agreed to approach attorneys and party regulars. He also agreed to help find an office in the airport area. Planning started for the 3 May sixth district meeting to be held at Woodward Academy in South Fulton County. Marge Krauth helped schedule a support group for Newt at the convention while Stuckey agreed to take care of the hospitality suite and help with the organization needed at the meeting.

While banners and signs were made for the 3 May meeting and other organizational aspects of the campaign were being carried out, Newt kept up his schedule of speaking and working to get news coverage. On 24 April he spoke to the Coweta County GOP convention. He continued his message of party reform noting Republicans "have to get their own house in order before they can begin working to solve the problems confronting American society today."[29]

Newt outlined four steps that should be taken by the GOP if they hoped to avert "the death of the party." First, they had to talk "honestly and without fear about the history of our times and the issues which dominate" and give the Democrats credit for the problems they had brought after twenty years in power in the Congress. The second point in his "renewal plan" for the GOP was to "recognize we are involved in politics and not merely in a debating society." "We must learn to talk the language of the average American."

---

[29] Ibid.

Continuing his focus on the average American, he stated his third step. The Republicans must "design programs for the middle class." If his party were to win it would have to be "by unifying these people." "We can only convince working, taxpaying Americans to believe in our philosophy if we learn to talk about their problems, to listen to their hopes and fears, to understand their vision of America." Newt concluded that section by pointing out that "Republicans preach too much and listen too little; that is why we have such a small flock."

Gingrich's final point was that the Republicans "must practice evangelism and pursue every possible voter." He had set the example for this when he decided to stay in the Republican Party, instead of running as a Democrat. He believed that we needed a two-party system and that the core beliefs of the GOP were closer to his own. Three traditionally Democratic groups, women, minorities and organized labor, should be targeted. "Whatever we believe, whoever we recruit to carry our banner, all is for nothing unless we adopt an evangelical spirit."[30]

It was about this time that Richard Rudman replaced Lee Howell to handle the press for Newt and to act as campaign photographer. Rudman, another former student of Newt's, relieved some of the tension between the staff and the press. The press, though generally favorable to Newt, was persistent and could be as critical to Flynt. Rudman worked well with Chip Kahn in the everyday tasks of getting out press releases and putting together speech outlines for Newt.

Vice President Nelson Rockefeller endorsed Newt in a fundraising appearance in Atlanta netting $12,500 for Newt's campaign. Senators Bill Brock, Bob Dole, and Barry Goldwater and former Treasury Secretary John Connaly would also come to Newt's aid. Each visit brought much needed press coverage as well as contributions.

While receiving help from the national party, Newt supported local GOP candidates. He and his staff, principally Bob Claxton, met with Quincey Collins, the GOP candidate for the seventh district congressional seat. They gave Collins advice and shared with him Claxton's research in the race against Larry MacDonald, the Democrat from Marietta known for his alliance with the John Birch Society. Newt also worked with a multitude of statehouse candidates.

---

[30] Ibid.

The Democrats were not complacent about the threat Newt posed to their party. Representative Tom Glanton, a Democrat who supported Newt, endured strong pressure from other Democrats and in Douglas County the Democrats sought to expel two local Chamber of Commerce officials for their support of Newt. Flynt also took this campaign more seriously than the he did in 1974 and spent more time on the stump, especially in areas that had gone for Newt the first time around. He also increased his radio and newspaper ad campaign though he still did not use television.

Interestingly, Flynt's Democratic opponents began to sound like Newt in their attacks on the incumbent. One opponent, state Representative Frank Bailey, even consulted with Newt's staff to obtain information that might be useful against Flynt. One candidate accused him of spending too much time in Washington while another accused him of spending too much campaigning and not tending to the issues of his constituents. Another opponent contacted the Ethics Committee asking for an investigation of its chairman. Newt's almost-successful effort in 1974 had excited opportunistic Democrats who saw a chance to beat Flynt. The democrats, hoping that with no record of their own to attack, thought they could defeat Gingrich because they would represent the change Newt preached and deny him the cross-over Democratic vote that was essential to his victory. Their assessment of Flynt's weakness was misplaced and he went on to win the August primary without a run-off garnering 56 percent of the vote. [31]

Even with help from the national party Newt's campaign was still slow in raising money. In a 21 May memo to the Policy Committee Kahn listed priorities in three parts; survival expenses, campaign materials and radio advertising. He noted, "It is obvious that at this time we are far from meeting the minimal survival needs of the campaign." Still, the money did come in through small contributions, loans and through fundraising events such as the visits from nationally elected GOP officials. Minimal salaries, rental fees and pressing bills were paid and brochures and bumper stickers were bought.[32]

Newt continued to depend on large numbers of volunteers who would work with him as he toured the district making speeches and carrying on literature and bumper sticker blitzes. Each county would

---

[31] Ibid.

[32] Newt Gingrich Papers, 1976 Campaign folder. UWG Archives.

have a core of volunteers who would be waiting at shopping centers or malls to meet him and help hand out campaign material.

Early in the campaign a special filing project was set up to raise the money needed to file for candidacy on 7 June. The cost of the filing was $1,330 and the project sought to get 133 individual contributors to give $10.00 each and then appear with Newt at the state capitol for a news conference and media event. The money was raised and Newt appeared with his supporters at the capitol. "This filing fee could easily have been sought in a back room from one or two wealthy individuals, but it was not...our filing is both a practical and a symbolic example of what responsible self-government means. I will return that tradition of responsibility to Washington." Having "co-filers" supply the fee did get news coverage and continued the grass-roots operation that was the hallmark of both the 1974 and 1976 campaigns.[33]

As part of the grassroots operation Newt set up a CB radio operation talking to citizen band radio addicts about the campaign and having his supporters do the same. As it turned out this was not one of the more productive ideas during the campaign. Most CB users were traveling through the district and those living there wanted to talk about something else in addition to politics.

More important were the traditional campaign techniques including the "campaign event." One such was when Newt and his photographer went to Washington in June for Newt to be photographed outside the Ethics Committee door "knocking on the door asking Flynt to open it up to public scrutiny." In August he appeared with Flynt at an NAACP meeting where he challenged the incumbent to tell African Americans what he had done for them and to explain to the public why he had been in Congress twenty years and had no serious bills passed. Each of these events got considerable media coverage.[34]

Newt continued attacking Flynt for failure to accomplish anything in Washington except to bring home a little pork. He repeated the 1972 Ford "car storage" incident and the sale of his strip of land to his administrative assistant to avoid paying a city assessment. In addition, he blamed Flynt for stalling lobbying reform and for covering up corruption by failing to investigate Sikes and Hayes. In spite of all the attacks on him Flynt won the Democratic primary on 11 August without

---

[33] Ibid., 1976 Campaign Scrapbook.
[34] Ibid.

a run-off. Newt had no opponent and was declared the Republican nominee. Two weeks later on 28 August, Newt held his formal kick-off at the recreation center in Carrollton with an old style political rally and a speech.

Newt thanked his supporters for their help in 1974 and 1976 and then attacked Flynt: "At voter forum after voter forum" Flynt did not show up. "Ironically, the man who wasn't there was the one candidate being paid by the taxpayer and the only candidate who for 22 years has been paid by the taxpayer." He noted that the taxpayers showed up but Flynt did not appear. "I say to you tonight the number one issue in this campaign is whether or not John Flynt is willing to stand up and answer questions from the people who have paid his salary and paid for his trips and paid for his staff."

Baldy, in an editorial cartoon in the *Atlanta Constitution*, supported Newt's charges with a drawing of Newt speaking at a rally holding up a speech reading "Flynt barring the door to the Ethics Committee as Newt tries to get in" and another of Flynt telling Newt he is young and smearing in part of campaigning.[35] Within days after these charges were made Flynt was hospitalized for chest pains which were diagnosed as an anginal disorder. This condition effectively kept the incumbent off the campaign trail well into October and muted the failure to debate the charge.

Every Sunday night Fessenden would add up all Newt had done the previous week and lay out the week ahead in a report to the seven key leaders in the campaign and then relay their reactions back to Newt late Sunday evening. Newt also held regular meetings with his key volunteer leaders from each county. These could turn into rather raucous affairs with each expressing their own ideas about what needed to be done. Newt encouraged everyone to speak and would allow differences of opinion to surface and work themselves out while he weighed both sides and made the final decision.

Newt stayed close to the state party leadership during the campaign. He worked especially close with chairman Mack Mattingly who felt committed enough to Newt and his effort to personally help pay some of the campaign debt. Both men knew it was important to make a strong showing on 5 November if they were to do serious recruiting in

---

[35] *Atlanta Constitution*, 9 September 1976, p. A4 and 31 October 1976, p. A21.

1978. Newt carried his message every way he could. He bought more television ads than in the 1974 campaign and circulated and mailed considerably more literature. He also stepped up his radio and news-paper advertising using the slogan, "The politicians had their chance. Now you can have yours."

Newt's newspaper ads used the campaign slogan and each ad noted, "The real issue is whether or not you're going to let the bureaucrats run your life." He noted that "Every year the Congress passes more and more legislation that discriminates against the middle class....We're paying for the welfare mess. And the unfair tax system keeps eating away at our hard earned dollars." "We need a congressman that's as angry about the current mess as you are," said the ad.[36]

Newt went on to promise representation close to the people by having offices around the district and through a mobile office that would go from town to town. "When Newt Gingrich goes to Congress, he'll put an office in your hometown. On a regular basis, throughout the year, Newt Gingrich's mobile congressional office will visit your town. You'll be able to sit down with your Congressman and tell him what's on your mind. And Newt will listen. Just like he always does."

A series of flyers were handed out directed toward specific groups of voters. Each carried a picture of the young Newt on the go, jacket off and tie loosened, ready for action. They all started with the phrase, "Isn't it time...." "Isn't it time Georgia's parents, students and teachers were represented in Congress?" "Isn't it time Congress did something about high prices?" These flyers and others like them followed the lead question with the inevitable list of steps that needed to be taken. They contained hard information that described the bureaucratic mess in Washington. It ended with a request that they send "$1.00 or more to cover the cost of this leaflet."[37]

Newt told the voters in speech after speech that the government was destroying our neighborhoods and making deals that cost us money at the grocery store. He advocated cutting the federal budget and reforming the tax system. He wanted to cut red tape "so business, schools, doctors, and all of us can get back to work." He said, "We

---

[36] Newt Gingrich Papers, 1976 Campaign Scrapbook. UWG Archives.
[37] Ibid.

should never have had an energy crisis," and we should "invest more in research for new energy and productivity."[38]

His efforts paid off with a series of endorsements such as the one from the NEA/GAE, "We believe Newt Gingrich is closely attuned to the needs of students and educators throughout the district." It also paid off in the volunteer efforts of many teachers who manned telephones for Newt and helped pass out bumper stickers and leaflets in shopping centers and on town squares and helped turn out the vote on election day.

Through September Newt had outspent Flynt $85,000 to $75,000 and was turning out a few television ads that were considerably more sophisticated than the sugar ad from 1974. They were a series of negative ads followed by late campaign positive ads and seemed to be working according to the polls. Newt was certainly within striking distance as the campaign came to a close.

Election day dawned and the voter turnout was higher than usual. The Democratic Party ran ads asking for strong support for Carter by voting a straight ticket. The turnout was viewed as support for Governor Carter and the Gingrich camp worried that voters who might be for Newt might also want to give all the support they could to the first Georgian in recent memory who had been nominated for the presidency.

Newt continued campaigning around the district ending up in South Fulton and Clayton Counties. He handed out leaflets at intersections and asked for votes. Fessenden drove Jackie and the girls over for the election night rally and the car broke down as it turned onto Virginia Avenue about ten miles from the hotel where the party was to be held.

Most of the crowd gathered that night still held high hopes for a victory and the returns were close most of the evening. Everyone knew it would be an uphill fight but, as good partisans, did not see how the voters could send Flynt back to Washington after all that had come out during the campaign. While hopeful, Newt was back to reality by the time returns started coming in and it was evident he was not winning enough in the counties he was carrying. The probable loss registered in his mind but he did not let it discourage him. He was already thinking about a third campaign. Fessenden remembers Newt being a little

---

[38] Ibid.

down but not letting it show: "He realized it'd be tough but he was never scared of losing. If you do lose you just go on from there." Newt had confidence that he was destined to be in Congress and viewed this defeat as one more step along the way.[39]

When the final votes were tallied Jack Flynt had narrowly defeated Newt again. He received 77,532 votes or 51.7 percent of the vote to Newt's 72,400 or 48.3 percent. President Ford's pardon of Nixon, the heavy support for Carter and the black vote for Carter and the Democratic ticket pushed Flynt back into office. The *Atlanta Constitution*, which had endorsed Newt, noted, "Blacks Gave Flynt Victory" and commented it was "ironic because he [Flynt] had opposed voting rights legislation throughout his career."[40] Flynt's strategy of laying low and riding Carter's coattails had worked. Coattails or not, Flynt was going back to Washington and Newt was planning for a third campaign.

---

[39] Arthur Fessenden interview, 30 November 1994
[40] The *Atlanta Constitution*, 6 November 1976.

5

YES, NEWT!!!

Following the Christmas holidays in 1976 Newt once again settled into the routine of teaching and campaigning. While making sure that he completed all his obligations to West Georgia College and his students, he continued his campaign for the sixth district's congressional seat. "The period from the start of the 1976 campaign until Newt won in 1978 was almost non-stop campaigning," remembers Arthur Fessenden who stayed on as Newt's driver. While campaigning abated somewhat during 1977, Newt was still campaigning at a regular pace. "He thought the third one would either make or break him and never considered not running again."[1]

As coordinator of environmental studies Newt was now housed in the geography department. Newt quickly returned to the demands of academic life. "He never let his teaching slide and always carried out every committee assignment I gave him. He was very involved in campaigning but gave his students 100 percent," remembers his department chairman Dr. John Upchurch. "As a teacher he is probably the finest classroom instructor I've ever seen. He stirred student interest and caused them to think...he was an outstanding instructor."[2]

The president at West Georgia College, Dr. Maurice Townsend, had politics somewhat more liberal than Newt's but had confidence in him as an individual and a teacher. When questioned about why he

---

[1] Arthur Fessenden interview, 30 November 1994.

[2] John Upchurch interview, 1 April 1995. Newt Gingrich Papers, UWG Archives.

frequently voted for Gingrich when his philosophy was more liberal, he responded, "He's done a lot for West Georgia College and he's had pygmies running against him." Townsend thought enough of Newt that he recommended his reappointment for 1977-1978 as an assistant professor of geography and coordinator of environmental studies, a decision supported by Dean Richard Dangle.[3]

Townsend enjoyed politics and frequently spent time going over the latest political gossip with Newt and a mutual friend. In February 1977, he was also helpful to Newt in a political sense when he appointed him as a board member of Community Action for Improvement, Incorporated, an organization in which Newt would represent the interests of the college while making useful political contacts. Two months later, as required by college policies, Townsend sent Newt notice that 1977-1978 would be his last year at West Georgia College unless he received tenure.[4]

Newt did not intend to request tenure because he had already made the decision to seek a seat in Congress. Likewise, given his lack of research and publications over the past years, it is unlikely he would have been granted tenure. Those close to Newt were concerned about what he would do if he did not win the 1978 election. Newt's response was almost philosophical. "I'm not sure but there are a lot of options. I might teach somewhere else or go into some sort of consulting." He went on to point out that what was important was to win in 1978 so he would not have to face those decisions.

Meanwhile, Newt continued politicking, making speeches as well as contacts. He and the new state GOP chairman, Rodney Cook from Atlanta, got along well and continued the cooperation established with Mattingly. While maintaining his contacts in Washington, he stayed with his old teacher, Nando Amabile, who provided him with a car and a bed. "Newt was worried that there would be a feeling that he'd had his two shots so he came seeking support and mending fences where necessary." "He'd get up at six and come in at two in the morning and then start all over again."[5]

---

[3] Newt Gingrich Personnel Folder, UWG Archives.

[4] Ibid.

[5] Nando Amabile interview, 6-16-84.

One of those Newt met with while in Washington was Representative Guy Vander Jagt, chairman of the National Republican Campaign Committee, who had provided him with support in 1976. The NRCC chief was not at all sure Newt would run again in 1978 and wished to insure that race. "Newt, we dramatically increased the help we gave you over 1974 and you won't believe what we'll do for you in 1978 if you'll run again." New assured him that he would run again and that he would need all the help he could get with Jimmy Carter in the White House. Carter was at the crest of his popularity at this time and it was feared that he would help other Georgians in the next election.[6]

After losing two extremely close grassroots-based campaigns Newt was giving thought to make the third one more professional with better control and more central direction. With a promise of more support from the NRCC, professional consultants could be brought in on a regular basis. He intended to take advantage of everything the Washington-based specialists could offer him.

Newt understood, however, that all the professionals in the world could not win it for him. He would be the candidate and the campaign would be built around him and he had to do his part or it would not work. He was the form around which the campaign would be molded. Who he was and what he had to offer had to be the core of the effort. The professionals might offer him the winning edge but the issues and goals he had run on in 1974 and 1976 were still valid and he was still the driving force behind his candidacy.

He took every opportunity to speak before civic groups to keep his name alive and active. Each news story covering his speeches mentioned his previous races and his possible candidacy in 1976. He tried to focus on local issues as they tied into the broader picture of bureaucratic intrusion in the lives of his listeners. When he spoke to the Douglasville Lions Club in March he talked about how the interstate highway coming through their county would change their lives as it related to growth patterns. Government could be helpful when controlled and directed. It could help with planning for the expected population and industrial growth that would come with the highway,

---

6 Guy Vander Jagt interview, 8 November 1994.

but only if the people who lived there took control and did the planning.[7]

Also during this period early in 1977, Newt first committed to his idea for writing a novel to paper. One of the ways Newt relaxed was to play the historians' game of "what if." What if there was a Soviet conventional attack on Western Europe? How would it come and how would the NATO forces defend against it? Could it be stopped? Would it lead to a third world war? He had begun to think this scenario would make a good novel and decided to write it. He would need to go to Europe and see the area that would be covered in such an attack and talk to the NATO people involved in defense.

To acquire the funds needed for research, he decided to offer the book as an investment opportunity and shortly after the first of the year he put together a three page document outlining the proposed project, its purpose, investment procedures, timeline and budget. He optimistically thought he could have a first draft together by 1 September 1977 at a cost of $17,000. There would be two general partners, Newt and the Dorchester Corporation. Chester Roush was the president of the corporation and a businessman with a shrewd eye for a profit. He agreed to manage the limited partnership open to contributors of $1,000 each.[8]

In addition to traveling to Western Europe, Newt planned trips to Fort Knox, Fort Benning, Fort Bragg and the Air Force College in Montgomery, Alabama to understand what could be expected of the equipment and the men facing the onslaught. He also wanted to walk over and make notes about the area where the fighting would take place.

Some of his political supporters were critical of his taking a summer to research and write a book when there were no votes in such a venture. Better, they said, that he should stay home and spend his time working the district in preparation for next year's congressional race. He listened to their suggestions and went to Europe anyway. The book would be interesting and fun and if it worked it would help with name recognition and get some media attention.

---

[7] *Douglasville Sentinel*, March 1978.

[8] Chester Roush interview, 12-14-94 and Newt Gingrich Papers, Dorchester Corp. folder, UWG Archives.

Newt left for Europe on 4 June. For the next month and a half he crisscrossed Germany and Holland researching and interviewing. The American Army allowed him to fly with the attack and scout helicopters and it really educated him insofar as their ability and strategy. Following the flight he met with the entire company of thirty pilots for a two-hour discussion of tactics and problems. He got similar treatment from the Air Force at Ramstein regarding the new F-15s. The Bundeswehr gave him an excellent tour of their First Corps area and the armored school at Munster. They showed him new weapons and talked strategy.[9]

The trip was an exhilarating experience for Newt and he arrived back in New York on 14 July, stopped off for a day or two in Harrisburg to see his family and returned to Georgia on 17 July. Soon thereafter, he set to work on writing the first draft of the novel. Most of his days were spent writing to meet the September deadline. Still, he did make time for the occasional speech or political meeting. The first draft was finished in September and circulated to some friends whose opinion Newt respected.

Amabile, after reading Newt's effort, recalls that it was "the most garbagy piece of a novel" he had read. "The characters were wooden but the plot had some promise," he said. Professor Bill Doxey, who taught creative writing at WGC, had a similar opinion and thought it needed a lot of work if it were to be published. Later when Newt was accused of taking money that summer and never writing a book, Doxey noted for the record that "Newt wrote a book; it wasn't much of a book, but it was a book." Their criticism and that of other readers caused Newt to do some rewriting over the next year but not enough to send it to a publisher.[10]

In addition to the criticism of the book, Newt also was faced with the resumption of classes in September and the need to get back into the campaign cycle and prepare for the 1978 election. Two writers tried to work with him to improve the book but due to the pressure of teaching, faculty committee assignments, student counseling and campaigning, he was not able to find large blocks of time to work with them.

---

[9] Newt Gingrich Papers, Dorchester folder.

[10] Nando Amabile interview, 8 November 1984. The manuscript is in the UWG archives under Nomonhan Book.

While Newt was out of the country the campaign began recruiting former volunteers and campaign workers and announced: "It's July, 1977, thirteen months away from the August primaries, and we are gearing up." It listed six categories needing help and gave the names and phone numbers to contact if one wished to volunteer. Some new talent recruited from the 1976 campaign came on board including Dan Rainwater, Pete Rintye, Jimmy Bone and Lynn Bradley. The response was heartening. Though politically inexperienced, these new recruits would play important roles in the campaign. [11]

In addition to writing his novel, Newt found another cause in which to get involved upon his return to the States. Jimmy Carter had decided to sign a treaty with the Panamanians giving back the Panama Canal. Many Americans were outraged at this idea and their protest was led by Ronald Reagan, former governor of California and presidential candidate. Newt's father had served in the Canal Zone as his last duty station and Newt had visited him there. Newt felt strongly about the Canal and signed on as chairman for the Georgians Against the Proposed Panama Canal Treaty. He was supported by GOP state chairman Rodney Cook and Sam Tate, the Reagan for President chairman for Georgia. Their goal was to get 50,000 Georgia signatures on a petition to send to President Carter and to try to influence Georgia's senators, Herman Talmadge and Sam Nunn, to oppose the treaty.

Newt supported a strong and aggressive foreign policy based on the real interest of the United States. To be effective he thought that policy had to have public support. He pointed to the war in Vietnam as an example of what can happen when public support is lacking. "The only way to build a solid foreign policy in a free society is to bring the public in early and candidly so that they can join their leaders in a process of mutual education. The way to destroy public faith in a free society is to tell the people last, to blackmail them into agreement, and to manipulate them into acceptance." It was the wrong treaty offered in the wrong manner and was little more than an effort to once again "bail out a dictator and our own economic establishment at our expense. I say no," he said. Most of those present agreed with him.[12]

---

11 Newt Gingrich Papers, UWG Archives. 1978 Campaign Scrapbook.

12 *The Atlanta Constitution*, 28 September 1977.

While the canal issue took some of his time, Newt still kept his focus on the campaign. On 29 October he held his kickoff dinner at College Park. The crowd was large and it was a financial success. Newt was the main speaker and told those present, "You are the key supporters who have made my campaign possible. You have been faithful in defeat and you have encouraged me to run again despite the frustration of 1974 and 1976." He said he was certain of victory and would depend on them and their neighbors. "We will convince them that with their help we can fight to solve America's problems and build America's future."[13]

Newt's December newsletter noted the success of the kickoff dinner, talked about his hope to block ratification of the canal treaty, asked for help in fundraising and to distribute tabloids, and discussed the need to build a strong base in black communities around the district, "not just to win the election in 1978, but to learn how to represent all the people in the District after we win." The newsletter described the work Newt had started in August when he met with potential black supporters to listen to their concerns, the walking tour he had taken canvassing in the black areas of Ben Hill and the various contacts he had made with black business and political leaders. "Mutual trust and frank dialogue do not` just happen. It takes a lot of hard work from all involved. The process has only just begun."[14]

Also in December Newt got his first primary challenger. He was the only Republican running in 1974 and 1976 but Flynt now looked like he could be beaten and opponents from both parties were getting in line for the opportunity. Party chairman Cook made a speech wherein he said Newt would oppose Flynt again. This statement brought a response from a toy salesman from College Park, Mike Ester, who announced that he too would challenge Flynt and would be running in the Republican primary against Newt in August.

A fellow Carroll County Republican, Dave Barrow, also made a decision to run for Congress in 1978. Barrow was mayor of Bowdon, a small clothing industry-based town west of Carrollton. He had been involved with the Republican Party since the early 1960s and had served on the city council and as mayor. He was a close friend of

---

13 Ibid, 30 October 1977. See also 1978 Campaign Scrapbook.
14 Ibid.

Representative Flynt, who had helped his community on more than one occasion. Barrow had pledged to Flynt that he would not run against him. In late 1977 it became apparent to Barrow that Flynt might not run again.

When Flynt announced in February that he would not seek another term Barrow was quick to announce his intention to run for the seat. Many Republicans were surprised that Barrow would run against Newt. He had, however, never been a strong supporter of Gingrich due to his friendship with Flynt and because he felt he needed to remain neutral as mayor and work with both sides. "Jack Flynt was an old personal friend going back many years. It was awkward. Jack was good to me and to Bowdon. I basically did not trust Newt. I felt like at that time Newt was singing a more conservative song than he really felt."[15]

Neither Barrow nor Ester seemed to have any real issues or direction other than a desire to be a congressman. Barrow was running against Gingrich because he suspected he was not conservative enough. Esther simply was running as a far right, patriotic Republican leaning heavily on brochures covered with flags and military pictures.

Newt, on the other hand, was running on the same issues he had in 1974 and 1976 and was insistent on advocating a responsible Congress that listened to and responded to the people back home. In 1977 Representative Trent Lott, chairman of the National Congressional Council (or NCC), appointed Newt as co-chair of the council. The NCC was a coalition of community leaders who provided counsel to Republican leaders to keep them in touch with local issues.

Newt was also in the process of putting together his new campaign staff. Vander Jagt had sent Bob Weed, a GOP consultant, to advise Newt on the campaign. Weed and Newt had met but had not worked together. Another professional to sign on was Carlyle Gregory who had worked with Weed in the College Republicans in Virginia and on the Paul Trible campaign in 1976. He was working in Trible's district office when Weed and Wilma Goldstein recommended him to Gingrich as campaign manager. Frank Gregorsky, who came to West Georgia in March 1978, signed on and worked as a volunteer driver and researcher.

---

[15] Ibid.

Gregorsky had gone by to meet Newt on the advice of his academic advisor who knew he was interested in conservative Republican politics. After a discussion of Gregorsky's interest in politics, it was agreed that he would be a substitute driver. After a while it became clear that Gregorsky was more interested in issue research than in driving and felt that would be a better use of his time. Newt told him to see the newly-hired campaign manager to resolve the details. Newt also suggested that he do a study for his political science course paper on the Kennedy tax cut and compare it with the Kemp-Roth tax proposal. This work was very helpful to Gingrich and the Kemp-Roth bill became a centerpiece of the campaign.[16]

Gregory had just signed on with the campaign, and was assigned to work with Gregorsky, who turned out to be a gifted researcher and writer. On Weed's advice Gregory contacted Newt in a letter dated 1 February 1978 hoping to work for "the kind of new South Republican that our party so badly needs." Later in February the Gingrichs and Gregory met and discussed a possible position and Gregory's background and ideas. The next day Gregory met with a larger group of key leaders in College Park including Kip Carter and Daryl Conner. He wanted the job with Newt. These key leaders were also impressed with Gregory and recommended to Newt that he be hired. He was and joined the campaign in April.[17]

Gary Crook had obtained an office in East Point that was up and running. When Gregory arrived Pete Rintye was working as organizational coordinator tasked with keeping in touch with the GOP county chairmen and getting out the campaign tabloids. Gregory walked into an ongoing operation. He talked to Kahn by phone and got a good deal of background, what had and had not worked in 1974 and 1976, and Kahn's advice on strengths and weaknesses of the key leaders and Newt himself. His main advice was for Gregory to get control of the money and Newt's schedule as quickly as possible.[18]

A week after Gregory met with Newt in February, Jack Flynt announced his decision not to run for reelection. This development changed the campaign in a major way. Flynt's ethics and poor

---

[16] Ibid.

[17] Carlyle Gregory interview, 9 February 1995.

[18] Ibid.

representation were out the window as issues and a new strategy had to be devised without knowing who the Democrats would offer. In comparison to Flynt Newt had been a moderate conservative but he was likely to be to the right of anyone the Democrats would nominate and could run as the conservative in the race. The negative focus would remain on Washington and Congress and he would continue pushing the Kemp-Roth tax plan and a series of tax and bureaucratic reforms that would be used no matter who the Democrats nominated. He would continue to describe himself as a "common sense conservative" as he had since 1974 but this time he would be more conservative than his opponent.

Newt had decided to put out his own tabloid newspaper, the *New Georgia Leader*, to get out his ideas and tell people about the campaign. The first edition came out in April and headlined, "Cut Taxes One-Third Says Newt Gingrich." It pictured Newt walking in front of the Atlanta airport, the largest employer in the district, and talking to a Newnan taxpayer in front of the Coweta County courthouse.[19]

The paper, edited by Chip Kahn's wife, Mary, and Weed, stressed the Kemp-Roth tax cut, a full page on Newt and his family with pictures and a full page letter from Gary and Katherine Crook asking the readers for money and support for Newt. The back was a full page ad asking for the defeat of the proposed Panama Canal Treaties including a petition readers could clip and get filled out. The ad was paid for by the Georgians Against the Proposed Panama Canal Treaties thus helping with the cost of the tabloid. The *Atlanta Journal* writer John Crown reported favorably on the tabloid and quoted liberally from it. He called Newt a "Capable, hard-working, frank citizen who would bring a large measure of moderation and responsibility to the Congress."[20]

After qualifying, Newt was one of nine candidates seeking the sixth district congressional seat, three Republicans and six Democrats. Ester was clearly the far right candidate from the Morton Blackwell school of campaigning. Barrow was the folksy and good-natured mayor of a small town who always had a story to tell and probably was the best liked of the nine. He ran as the only Republican candidate with both business and government experience. Esther chose to wrap himself in

---

[19] Ibid. See also Newt Gingrich Papers, 1978 Campaign scrapbook.

[20] The *Atlanta Journal*.

the flag which seemed odd to many who knew Barrow had served in both World War II and in the Korean conflict and had been awarded the Navy Cross.

The three leading Democrats in the field were Betty Talmadge, former wife of Senator Herman Talmadge, State Senator Virginia Shapard and State Senator Peter Banks. Talmadge was very much like Barrow, folksy and down home. She spent more time talking about Talmadge hams and giving her sausage recipe than serious politicking and became friends with Barrow. Banks was a moderate and respected senator who was probably the best old-fashioned campaigner. Shapard was the wife of a Griffin, Georgia textile mill owner and a slightly left of center senator who sought to give the impression in dress and action, of a serious, no-nonsense candidate who could be as tough as the males in the race.

The most dangerous candidate, from Newt's point of view, would have been State Representative Tom Glanton, a man who was not in the race. Glanton, a supporter of Newt's, gave serious consideration to entering the race after Flynt said he would not run for reelection. He had no problem with Newt but viewed the race as a chance for personal political advancement. He called some of his close friends and supporters together for a lunch in Atlanta and then a meeting at his home in Carrollton to explore the possibility of running. At the meetings it became apparent that Glanton's problem was that many of his supporters were also Newt supporters including industrialist and former mayor Henry Lumpkin, Harrell Fountain and a host of bankers and businessmen including his partner, Chester Roush and Dr. Mac Martin. All were interested in the advancement of both men and did not relish a fight between them that would divide their base.

Newt met quickly with his key Carroll County supporters to discuss how to make sure Glanton did not enter the race. Mitt Conerly, one of Newt's chief finance people and a superb strategist, came up with the idea of holding a lunch for Newt's key financial supporters, who were also in many cases, Glanton's regular supporters. The idea was to get them committed to Newt before Glanton approached them. At this point it was not widely known that Glanton was considering running. Conerly was put in charge of the project and moved quickly to set up the lunch. He invited the prospective contributors by phone due to the necessity for quick action. The lunch was two days later at a private room at Danyel's Restaurant and Mitt refused to let them leave without signed checks or pledges in his pocket. With the check or pledge came a commitment to support Newt.

In the next forty-eight hours Glanton contacted a number of those present at Newt's lunch and was told that while they liked him, they had no idea he was considering running and had already made a commitment to Newt. Glanton, a businessman who lived on the financial edge, always ready to get rich or go broke, had no independent financial base and with his core financial supporters denied him made the decision not to run. Glanton was an excellent campaigner and would have cut into Newt's financial and political support in both Carroll and Coweta counties.

Conerly proved invaluable many times in the campaign. "He was a prince," remembered Gregory. "He was a voice of reason and very level-headed." Mitt took a leave of absence from his job in real estate the last three months of the campaign and devoted all his efforts as a volunteer fund-raiser. He put together breakfasts, lunches and dinners with ten or twenty businessmen using the technique he had tried during the "Glanton" lunch. This approach was successful and raised considerable donations for the campaign. Conerly also developed a slide show to educate the finance committee on how to hold these dinners and get contributions. "Mitt really came through when we needed TV money late in the campaign."[21] The campaign also used a good deal of direct mail to raise money along with special events with name speakers.

Controlling Newt and the "Carrollton Mafia" was just as difficult as getting control of the finances. "Newt often told me that the earlier campaigns were more fun," said Gregory. "'Seventy-eight was slower and more bureaucratic. I saw my job as keeping us on the *track* at forty miles per hour." As a result of Gregory's drive to control the money and the schedule, some of the old supporters felt the campaign had been turned over to Washington consultants who knew nor cared anything about Georgia. They felt all they were used for was as sources of money and as volunteers to hand out materials at shopping centers.

"We did care about Georgia, but they were right about the rest." The Carrollton Mafia did not make the day to day decisions as they had

---

[21] Carlyle Gregory interview, 9 February 1995.

in the past. Instead, decisions were made quickly by professionals who knew what they were doing instead of at strategy meetings. "In the earlier campaigns no one was saying 'no.' Newt and the key leaders would forever come in with interesting ideas about something they wanted to do and off they would go." In the earlier campaigns projects were started and never finished with little regard to priorities already set. With help from Connor, Gregory learned how to tell Newt no. "Newt had so many ideas and many of them were good. He was such a good campaigner...he won votes whenever he got out...it was hard to say 'no' but when we looked at priorities he would work with me, however reluctantly, to stay on track." Linda Kemp regulated campaign accounting and kept spending on track, and Tommy Engram derived a production system for direct mail. These staffers, and others like John Grunden (who kept older machinery operating), would stay with Newt for the next decade.[22]

At this point the press was not against Newt, but he was no longer their darling fighting the corrupt Flynt. He was, however, still interesting and good copy. Some reporters, like Colin Sedor at WXIA in Atlanta paid attention to his ideas and his actions and developed a friendly, if wary, relationship with Newt. While many key campaign leaders were leery of the press, Gregory and Warnick adopted Newt's approach of being open and honest with the press. Newt thought Sedor proved you could convince the press that what you were doing was right. "Newt used the press to deliver his message," said Gregorsky, who served as assistant press secretary. Newt, Gregory, Warnick and Gregorsky did not view the press as evil and had a rule to "never lie to the press...it'll cost you one way or another." Newt made lying to the press, or to him or Gregory for that matter, a firing offense and stressed it frequently.[23]

Having opposition in the primary actually helped Newt keep sharp and develop his message. This competition also got press and forced the campaign organization prepared for the general election campaign in the fall. Likewise, the primary was unusual in that it played out without much rancor or hard feelings. "In spite of the fact that eight of us were shooting arrows at Newt because he was the front-runner, we

---

[22] Ibid.

[23] Frank Gregorsky interview, 18 May 1994.

all became remarkably close, often riding to candidate forums together. I think that campaign was the basis of my friendship with Newt today, even though I ran against him."[24]

Newt won the August primary without a run-off, though election night gave Barrow some hope early on. The first returns, small though they were, came in from Jasper County, a relatively rural county on the eastern fringe of the district. They put Barrow in the lead and caused great excitement among his supporters. The excitement did not last long. As further returns came in it became clear early on that Newt would win. "I think Esther conceded just after the polls closed and I did around 10:00 P.M.. I went over to the Holiday Inn to congratulate Newt and met him as he was leaving for a TV station. I then went back and partied into the night. Shapard called and asked for my endorsement but didn't get it," said Mayor Barrow.[25]

Newt had selected the Holiday Inn because it was where Betty Talmadge held her election party and she was certain to draw the most television coverage. He carefully chose the ballroom beside hers for his party and filled it with cheering supporters. He then strategically placed Gregory and Warnick outside between his room and Talmadge's. As reporters left her party Newt's supporters directed them immediately into Newt's ballroom. Only one television station did not cover the parties live and Newt was on his way to that one for an on-air interview when he met Barrow coming with his congratulations. After winning two uncontested primaries and losing two elections it was important to Newt that he be seen as a winner.

In something of a mild upset, Virginia Shapard won the Democratic primary, though her victory party would weaken her coming campaign. Shapard decided to hold her party at her home in Griffin, an hour's drive for Atlanta television crews. The reporters and crews were received in what they considered a "mansion" and transmitted that image by camera angles, one shot from the ceiling through a large chandelier. This image gave the impression of an upper class tea party and set the tone for the campaign: rich mill owner's wife versus poor college professor. Even her cheery bright yellow campaign color was contrasted with Newt's new, serious, patriotic blue.

---

[24] Dave Barrow interview, 28 March 1995.

[25] Ibid.

Newt and his team were worried about how to campaign against a woman in the South. While there was no direct attack on Senator Shapard's gender, Newt did appeal to local gender norms when Shapard raised the issue of her family life. The senator made a point of telling reporters that she would not move her family to Washington but leave the children at home in the care of their father and the maid so their lives would not be disturbed. A male making such a statement probably would have been acceptable to most voters, but a mother leaving her husband and children to go to Washington was something else in 1978. Newt made the most of the situation by stressing that he would be taking his family with him to Washington.

Newt also emphasized family interest in his tabloid, *New Georgia Leader*, in articles and pictures about Jackie and his daughters. The September issue contained an interview with Jackie, who had just won a bout with cancer, talking about the campaign being a family effort. The October issue contained an article entitled, "Newt's Family Is Like Your Family."[26] Newt's desire to identify closely with the voters' family issues was also reflected in his selection of a shopping cart as the campaign symbol.

Jackie also sent personal letters to "fellow teachers" stressing their commitment to education and telling them "I don't want to tell you about these issues. Newt is doing that. I want to tell you about Newt and our Family. And I want to let you know that Newt is a good man who will make you a great Congressman." The campaign also produced "handwritten" letters from Jackie addressed to "Dear Neighbor." In these Jackie began, "I'm writing to you because I think your family may be a lot like mine." Both letters compared the Gingrich family to the average sixth district family, going to church, shopping at the market, and stressing "Newt knows the value of the dollar to a family with growing children." Each letter contained a picture of the family and a request for votes and financial contributions. The "Dear Neighbor" letter contained a postscript: "You probably see Newt's opponent on TV a lot. A bank loan of almost $150,000 paid for those ads. Newt and I could *never* borrow that kind of money." This was followed by an appeal for individual contributions.[27] The "Jackie"

---

26 Newt Gingrich Papers, 1978 Campaign Scrapbook.

27 Ibid.

letters were tremendously successful. People wrote her at home sending pictures of their children and many called the campaign headquarters and the Gingrich home to talk with her about similar problems and to offer support.

The September issue of the tabloid carried the cart symbol headlined with "Increase take-home pay, and stop rising prices." This article attacked rising inflation and advocated the Kemp-Roth tax cut, quoting Professor Arthur Laffer from the University of Southern California as he explained his "curve" and how it would lower taxes and raise more money for the government. A related article noted Senator Sam Nunn's endorsement of the Kemp-Roth tax cut. It also had the results of an opinion survey from the previous tabloid and a picture of Newt "listening to local opinions."[28]

The tabloid also compared the candidates' personal backgrounds, family backgrounds and work experience. Shapard was born in New York and went to school there and at a woman's college in Virginia. She was an Episcopalian and worked for the county welfare department and her husband ran several textile mills. Newt, on the other hand, graduated from a Georgia high school, "where his father was stationed at Fort Benning," and from a Georgia University, Emory, before attending Tulane University. Newt was a Baptist and a history teacher at West Georgia College and his wife was a high school teacher.

In comparing the candidates' stands on the issues Newt also pointed out that Senator Shapard had voted against a tax cut and welfare reform. The campaign manager, Gregory, said, "She was trying to run as a competent person without ideology, a very ethical person. This gave her, due to her TV buys, some momentum toward the end of the campaign and we had to stop that." A television advertising professional was hired and produced two pairs of ads. The first pair were positive and showed Newt discussing issues in front of a group. The second pair of ads, run in October, attacked Shapard on her votes against a tax cut and welfare reform. These latter ads were run at times to target white females and proved to be effective in slowing Shapard's momentum. A fifth and final television ad ran during the final days of

---

[28] Ibid.

the campaign and showed Newt and his family with a full shopping cart while they discussed the problems of inflation.[29]

The campaign also printed a flyer entitled "Newt Gingrich is going to Washington" that listed the six points for which Newt would fight. The first point was small business. Newt promised that he would fight for "a small business Bill of Rights that will eliminate the red tape, over-regulation, and taxes which stifle new ideas, cripple the economy, and lock the poor into poverty." Secondly, he would fight for "an American energy policy designed to encourage new fields of energy utilizing new technology and our American ingenuity in free enterprise." His third fight would be for a home owners' savings plan. The fourth fight would be for "a 30 percent across the board tax cut over the next three years." Newt's fifth fight would be for "a realistic welfare program that encourages people to work for a living while providing livable supplements for those who are not able to provide for themselves." Finally, he would fight for "a strong national defense, second to none, because if we are not alive and free of foreign domination, nothing else counts."[30]

Newt continued to draw fairly good press. "The media still liked him. He was not a crazy right-winger but was fun and interesting. Newt was a professor who really tried to teach. He was always looking for an analogy to make it real to people. He used colorful language, metaphors and similes to jolt people and get their attention."[31] He also used historical events or people to make his point, such as comparing a situation he or others faced to one faced by a historical personage like Winston Churchill or Franklin Roosevelt.

By September, the team in the main headquarters in East Point had been honed to a fine edge, and all the positive press, hours of hard work and hand-shaking began to pay off. Volunteers were showing up regularly at a store-front "volunteer office." In addition to the offices in East Point, five or six local offices were opened around the district and coordinated much better than those in 1974 or 1976. Neighbors for Newt, a new organization inspired by Conerly's preemptive

---

[29] Carlyle Gregory Interview, 2-9-95.

[30] Newt Gingrich Papers, 1978 Campaign Scrapbook.

[31] Carlyle Gregory Interview, 2-9-95.

fundraising lunch against Glanton, distributed materials door to door and recruited volunteers.

In October the campaign's efforts to cultivate bipartisan support for Newt succeeded in convincing Carroll County's Democratic County Commissioner, Horrie Duncan, to produce a series of radio ads for Newt. There was no question of Duncan's conservatism. He had supported Jack Flynt in the two previous campaigns but thought Shapard was much too liberal. He also thought the Democratic Party made many demands on its candidates and gave precious little to help them. He deplored the massive inflation that was growing steadily and thought President Carter offered little hope for the future. "I just felt it was in Carroll County's interest to support Newt," said Duncan, "I didn't care what party he belonged to." Senator Culver Kidd, a colleague of Shapard's in the state Senate, was quietly helpful in the western part of the district and a host of local officials across the district gave Newt a good deal of assistance by letting him know where to go speak, when events would be held and who he should see, and especially by talking to key people in their counties and encouraging them to support Newt.

By the end of October Shapard was appearing bored when appearing publicly with Newt and talking about the same issues again and again. She had begun to attack Kemp-Roth as unworkable and said it would cause 15 percent inflation but seemed to lack conviction. She was calling Newt, sarcastically, "professor" and he took to calling her "student" and took the position that he was trying to educate her. She boasted of her Senate record and Newt attacked it. While the tax cut remained the centerpiece of the Gingrich campaign, the identification with the voters through the shopping cart, emphasis on family, the promise of a mobile office and the possibility of a toll-free number to let constituents call him along with the promise of offices in Griffin, Newnan and in Carroll County all helped in drawing support.

Senator Shapard also made a minor mistake late in the campaign when she had First Lady Rosalynn Carter appear at one of her fundraisers. The event was held on a Friday afternoon and was not well attended, a fact noted by the press. In addition, Mrs. Carter's presence did not lend credibility to Shapard's claim to being a conservative. Though President Carter would again carry Georgia in 1980, he did not, in 1978, have the popularity he had in November 1976 and Shapard did not get the boost she expected from a First Lady's visit.

The Georgia GOP helped Newt as best it could but was still relatively weak. Senator Paul Coverdell and former state GOP chairman Mac Mattingly were especially helpful. The party did provide some mailing lists that were useful in raising money but the state organization was still lacking cohesion and direction. Gingrich, as well as the other candidates, still had to depend on his own resources generated from within his campaign.

Election Day came. It rained. Most of the staff and key leaders had been up late or got up early to put up the last of the Newt signs on the routes to the polls. Newt was shaking hands and asking for votes in Carroll County and then in the south Fulton and Clayton County areas. Gregory got up at 5:00 A.M., an especially early hour for him, and went with some of his friends to put up posters. They had worked until 2:00 A.M. and had less than three hours sleep. Everything told them that they were going to win. Their spirits were high as they returned to the office to prepare for the night's activities.

Gregory had put up a large precinct chart in preparation for counting election returns. Gregorsky, meanwhile, stayed home. "I have an introvert's hobby of taping election returns." It seemed that he was the only supporter missing at the victory party. Gregory and a small group stayed at headquarters to take returns which were called in by supporters in each of the counties so Newt could get them as quickly as possible and know exactly how the count was going.

The early returns were even better than had been expected. Without Carter at the head of the ticket the black vote was lower than in 1976 and the margin that carried Jack Flynt was not there for Shapard in 1978. In addition, the labor vote was split with the UAW quietly supporting Newt. Newt's organizations had worked hard at turning out their vote and were successful. Precinct after precinct came in supporting Newt somewhat better than had been hoped. Gregory called Newt and gave him the news that he would win the election. By 11:30 P.M. Newt was ready to claim victory.

While it was a victory for Newt it was not a great triumph for the Republicans statewide. Governor George Busbee, Lieutenant Governor Zell Miller and Senator Sam Nunn all won reelection by over 80 percent of the vote. The other nine congressional seats remained in Democratic hands as did all other elected state officers. Still, Newt's election was the first step toward changing the Democrat's domination of the state. With shouts of "Mr. Congressman" ringing in his ears Newt had told his supporters, "I want you to force us to be accountable. Stay alive. Call and raise cain. We need you to be an angry customer just like you would in any business."[32]

Soon after the celebration the realization dawned on the new congressman and his family that a number of priorities now presented themselves. Newt and Jackie would need to go to Washington to look for a house. He would need to attend a couple of sessions for new congressmen and meet with Weed and members of the minority staff to see about committee assignments, office space, and so on. He would not only have to get a house in the Washington area but would have to furnish it. He and Jackie had decided to keep the home in Carrollton and that meant they would need new furniture. These objectives all involved expenses and that was money Newt did not have. It had been over six months since Newt had drawn a paycheck from the college and the campaign had nothing left. One of Jack Flynt's friends, Harrell Fountain, who supported Newt in 1978, decided to hold a dinner and sell tickets with the money going to help cover his expenses until he could get his first congressional check. Fountain was put in charge with the stipulation that those invited were to be friends and constituents rather than lobbyists. Ticket prices were low, $25.00 each, the room was full, and everyone enjoyed an evening with the Gingrichs.

---

[32] Ibid

6

THE NEW
REPRESENTATIVE

After his victory, Newt's staff and key leaders were already looking ahead to 1980 when President Carter would again be at the head of the Democratic ticket and were starting to plan strategy for that challenge. Newt was not thinking about 1980 but he was thinking about January 1979. After his speech and a round with well-wishers and the press, he telephoned Bob Weed and offered him the position of administrative assistant. Newt was already thinking about organizing his congressional staff and agenda. He obtained Weed's acceptance and went on to give him a list of items he wanted Bob to start working on as soon as possible. Weeds was challenged first with listing various tasks that Newt would need to accomplish as a newly elected Congressman. Getting an office, furnishing it and staffing it were top priorities.

A problem emerged from this phone call to Weed that was a harbinger of a criticism that would persist throughout Newt's career. Newt had not discussed appointing Weed administrative assistant with his staff or with his key leaders. He had made the decision after carefully considering what he thought he needed to set up an effective office. He picked Weed because of his experience and his brilliance as a strategist. Newt wanted his administrative assistant to be more than an office manager. He wanted someone who could think ahead and do serious planning on a number of fronts, including policy, once they were up and running in Washington. Newt had focused narrowly on what was needed. He did not consider how his decision would impact those around him. He viewed it as problem-solving while others thought of it as insensitive, uncaring and ungrateful behavior.

Carlyle Gregory, the victorious campaign manager, came to the victory party full of good spirits and ready to accept congratulations. After hearing Newt's speech he happily joined the party. Returning from his call to Weed, Newt approached Gregory and excitedly informed him about Weed's acceptance as administrative assistant. "He was delighted with Bob's acceptance. 'Isn't it great?' he asked. All I could do was stammer, 'yes.' It was a punch in the nose," said Gregory. "Newt wasn't thinking about what anybody thought. He just sort of did what he thought he needed to do. He didn't give any thought about how people would take it."[1]

Gregory was not the only person to get bad news. Newt's former campaign manager, Chip Kahn, was also disappointed. He called Newt to congratulate and exult. Kahn viewed Newt like a big brother and felt almost family pride in the night's accomplishment. Kahn wanted to work for Newt. He wanted a good job. He had paid his dues since the sixties in New Orleans and Newt had been a part of his life for a decade. He had worked for free at times and had personally loaned the campaign money. Like Gregory, he was a true believer, totally committed. Newt did not say "no" but told him that Weed was now administrative assistant and that Kahn would need to interview with him.[2]

On election night there was concern about who would be the district administrator and work directly with the constituents. Though Newt's staff in Washington would aid Newt's national role, the Georgia staff was critical to taking care of his constituents and to Newt's reelection. After talking to Weed, Newt offered the job to Kip Carter. Carter accepted and welcomed the task of representing Newt in the Sixth Congressional District and making sure that Newt paid attention to his constituents.

Carter was put in charge of developing the district staff, subject to Weed's and Newt's approval, and Weed was tasked with drawing up hiring guidelines and with the overall responsibility of hiring the staff, especially for the Washington office. Some of the campaign staffers were

---

[1] Carlyle Gregory Interview, 9 February 1995.
[2] Chip Kahn Interview, 10 February 1995.

upset over having to interview for a job, feeling that they had already proven themselves. Newt thought this was a matter of learning to delegate and of separating his personal feelings from making decisions about what was in the best interest of a smooth running and efficient office.

Though he was returning to college to finish his degree and had no stake in the hiring, Gregorsky sat in on some of the staffing sessions with Newt and Weed. "I was struck by the utter professionalism of Newt and Weed as they reviewed positions and goals on staff picks. When somebody was let down or bitter, Weed'd say, 'It's a tough business.'" It was a tough business and Newt even brought in a consultant, Marc Rosenburg, to help Weed perfect the staff structure and at the same time give him someone other than Weed on whom he could depend. He also consulted his old teacher, Nando Amabile, who worked in personnel for the Secret Service, to get an outside opinion.[3]

Some of the staff and volunteers were already talking about sharing an apartment, so sure were they that they would be going to Washington with Newt. When he had them interviewed, competing with each other for a relatively small number of positions, they had to recognize that Newt, while appreciating their contributions to the campaign, was committed to making his office as professional as possible. Job descriptions were devised and applicants were selected based on qualifications. They thought they would automatically get the jobs they wanted based on their loyalty and work in the campaign and expressed considerable disappointment noting that they had certainly "been more loyal to Newt than he had to them."

Even some of those who were given jobs were not happy with the particular position awarded to them and expressed bitterness over pay levels or lines of responsibility. They failed to understand that all jobs were temporary insofar as Newt was concerned. You could move up or down depending on your performance. He was also looking for thinkers and policy wonks to staff the Washington office as well as those who could do the particular job to which they were assigned.

During one of the days visiting the district Newt went to Griffin for a meeting with Jack Flynt. Newt wanted to talk to the Congressman about the practical aspects of running an office and seek any other

---

[3] Ibid.

advice Flynt might have for him. His feeling was that Flynt was a professional and even though they had been opponents. He thought Flynt would seek to be helpful to the man replacing him.

Flynt was cordial and full of practical advice on how to manage a political office. He advised, for example, that Newt start his staff off at minimum or slightly higher salaries so they would be grateful when they got raises. If they were started at the top they would quickly become disaffected when raises were not forthcoming.

After visiting with some of his supporters and city officials they drove back to Carrollton. Newt talked about his meeting with Flynt and was genuinely pleased with the way it had gone. He too tried to be helpful by offering Flynt the use of the office in the transition the Congressman faced as he returned to private life in Griffin. Newt was impressed with how long Flynt had stayed in office. Newt believed he could equal that by being even more responsive than Flynt in constituent services and staying in close touch with the people in the district. The mobile office would help, he thought, as would outreach programs wherein his district staff would visit counties without a congressional office at least once a month to do intake and generally make themselves available to the voters. They discussed setting up special interest "advisory committees" to meet with Newt at least twice a year and share their views on problems and possible solutions related to their particular interest such as aviation, farming, banking, education and health care. Newt also said he wanted to set up a committee to recommend appointments to the military academies rather than doing it by himself as favors for supporters.

During this period as congressman-elect Newt thought a lot about his new job. He took seriously his obligation to the people who had elected him and felt a strong commitment to truly represent them. His 16 December memo, which was not circulated until 1982 as part of a staff newsletter, was entitled, *A Proposed Contract Between Congressman-Elect Newt Gingrich and the Citizens of the Sixth District of Georgia*. The use of the word contract is instructive, as it will be in 1994, as to the seriousness with which he took his obligation.[4] Gregorsky, as newsletter editor, printed the contract in 1982 to give the staff a better understanding of their boss. In describing the contract he noted, "In it

---

[4] Ibid. Frank Gregorsky, "Staff News" 9-13-82.

one grasps the burning idealism and unorthodox mentality of a man who worked twenty years to get where he was, and the sense of another several decades' work just starting."

Newt describes his time off with family and in-laws as helping him "get away from some of the pressures," but quickly turns to his concern about President Carter's recognition of Communist China the previous day and how his relatives have reacted to it. He talked on the phone to his staff at length about it and gave an interview to the Atlanta newspapers. Even while relaxing he could not turn away from business.[5] Newt took the opportunity to "confront the question of my role in politics and to look again at my beliefs and the system's assumption." He wrote, "Ten days in Washington were enough to convince me that there is a grave danger of being socialized into impotence. By my last day in DC, the only realistic information source I had was the Doonesbury cartoon." He went on, "All around me there were attitudes and habits which accurately reflected the Capitol Hill clique but which were totally out of touch with the rest of the world."

Newt also complained that, because the press finds Congress hard to understand and Congressmen expect to be misunderstood or attacked by the media, "there is little effort to communicate Congress's role and responsibilities to the people. As a result the President has almost a total monopoly on setting the national agenda and focusing the national dialogue...by default." He goes on to contrast the hard-working, decent people back home, whom he had recently visited, with the situation he found in Washington. He saw Congress as "smug," "inactive," and "indifferent to corruption." Newt wrote that his constituents' "simple decency and love for this country, their hope for their children's future and their belief in the American dream" moved him and "renewed my commitment to fight with all my being to change the course we are now upon."

In 1979, as Gingrich was just entering Congress, those politically close to Newt, knew that he would serve his first few terms as Congressman from Georgia's Sixth Congressional District learning the ropes and positioning himself within the Republican caucus to have influence over the long haul. Newt was prepared to do that as long as the leadership was moving toward a positive goal that he could support. Consolidating

---

[5] Frank Gregorsky Interview, 5-18-94.

himself politically in the district and becoming familiar with how the House worked were primary goals for Gingrich. Few who knew him doubted that Newt would be in Congress for a long time or that he would make a major impact on the Republican Party, the Congress and the nation.

7

BACK HOME IN GEORGIA

In the fall of 1980 Newt clearly felt the need to do some serious thinking and writing. While his first term was successful on the national level, Newt's level of success in Georgia was somewhat mixed. His staff was going through the process of shakedown and change. On a personal level he was, in his own words, "disintegrating as a person." His marriage was ending. He was concerned about his children Some of his friends were becoming critical of who he had become since going to Washington. He had a reelection campaign to wage and a vision to maintain. 1979-1980 were to be years of stress and survival for Newt Gingrich...and for many of his friends and supporters as well.

In spite of all the care and preparation taken in building a staff Newt faced serious problems within his own organization. Some supporters blamed Newt for these problems, arguing that he would see someone performing well in one area and assume their ability to perform well in other areas. Someone might be excellent when working directly with people but not as good at bureaucratic follow-up. Another individual might possess tremendous ideas and vision, but not possess any teamwork to implement those ideas. Others felt it was not that Newt had misused them as much as they were not up to the job given them.

By the end of the first term six of his key staffers were no longer on the staff, including his two main administrators, Kip Carter and Bob Weed. Carter was a very good people person and a competent administrator. He saw his role as district administrator as representing Newt and almost as a junior congressman in the district when Newt was not present. Carter attended civic club luncheons and official receptions, visited businesses and industries, met with constituents, played golf, and worked with governmental agencies in order to make contacts and resolved problems.

Carter and Newt were friends. They had been close since Newt protested Carter's termination at West Georgia College when they were colleagues in the History Department. They talked on a regular basis even when Newt was in Washington. It was not enough for Carter. He thought Newt was getting too absorbed by national affairs and spending too little time in the district and dealing with district problems. The model of a congressman Carter was expecting was Jack Flynt. Newt was not Jack Flynt.

Newt's difficulties began when constituents came to Washington to see him, or called him and wanted to know why he had not followed up on a given problem. "When I told them I didn't know anything about it they said they'd talked to my man Carter and he said I would take care of it. I told Kip he'd have to start reporting these meetings and let me know what commitments he'd made so we could follow up. He said I could call him each night and get a report, that he was not a bureaucrat." He did not want to be bothered with having to write reports. Newt told him to dictate them to a secretary who would mail them in. When Carter balked at that Newt told him he could have a recorder to tape his reports and he could give the tape to the secretary. He refused that too. In addition to the reporting difficulties Newt was having with Carter, another district staff member, Linda Kemp, the scheduler, had complained to Carter and Newt that Carter was using his congressional office to run a personal family cotton waste business. Newt was not sure how important this issue was but it bothered him on ethical grounds.

The whole matter came to a head in April 1979 in a phone conversation between Newt and Carter. According to Newt, the pair were trying to work out the reporting problem. The conversation became heated and the other staffers in the East Point office could hear Carter's voice rising through the closed door. It finally reached a peak when Carter said, "If you don't like it fire me!" Newt confirms the conversation and responded by telling Carter, "All right. You're fired." Shortly thereafter Carter emerged from his office and told Kemp that she would have to fill-in for him with a scheduled appointment to tour a warehouse.[1]

Weed's difficulty lay in his management style, which served to alienate many of the staff. By the spring of 1980 he was a most unpopular man in the office. Weed volunteered to go to Georgia to manage the troubled reelection campaign and Newt told him that he could return as administrative assistant after it was over. While Weed was in Georgia, being replaced by David Warnick as administrative assistant, Newt became convinced that it was best that Weed not return to his old job. "I was very upset," remembers Weed. He felt betrayed. He sent Newt a memo in September clearly expressing his feelings and accusing Newt of disloyalty. "You resigned to become campaign manager and the campaign is over," Weed remembers Newt saying. In spite of his hurt, Weed maintained contact with Newt and the two worked closely together on a number of GOP projects in the years to come.[2]

Though there were normal staff problems with any new group working closely together, the real depression did not set in until June 1980 when Newt announced that he and Jackie were getting divorced. Newt had discussed his marital problems with Daryl Conner, Mitt Conerly and a few others but most of the staff had no idea that the marriage was in such trouble. Newt's distracted behavior the past spring had been noted by many staffers, but few had suspected marital problems as the cause. Though the staff suffered the typical difficulties of a new group working closely together, these problems were further complicated in June 1980 by the announcement of Newt's divorce.

Earlier in 1980, Newt began working later hours at the office. What many took to be Newt's typical determination was, in fact, Newt's dread of going home to a difficult situation. By late spring, Newt began discreetly informing Steely, Carter, and Fessenden (no longer on staff as

---

[1] Linda Kemp Interview by author, tape recording, 11 February 1995, Gingrich Papers. State University of West Georgia, Carrollton; See also Newt Gingrich, Interview by author, tape recording, 5 May 1988 and Judith Warner & Max Berley, *Newt Gingrich: Speaker to America.* (NY: Signet, 1995) 76-78.

[2] Bob Weed, Interview by the author, 27 March 1992.

the mobile office proved to be too expensive). One by one Newt was telling those close to him what to expect.[3]

Newt had even spent the night with Conerly discussing the marriage. The two stayed up until early morning talking about what Newt described as the "deep pain" he was in over the situation. The two friends talked over the various options, the impact on Newt's daughters and the personal and political consequences he would face as a result of a divorce. Conerly assured him there would be serious political consequences and urged Newt to weigh them against the pain of keeping the marriage together. By the time they went to bed Conerly felt that Newt had made up his mind to seek the divorce because he "just couldn't go on with it [the marriage] anymore."

In the spring of 1980 Connor had similar conversations with Newt at his home in Virginia. Conner was well aware of the marital problems Newt and Jackie were experiencing and had counseled Newt as far back as 1974. During the intervening years they had talked off and on about the struggle to save the marriage. "So many times Newt asked, 'How do I make this work?'" Conner said. "He turned every stone to make the marriage work." Up until 1980, remembers Conner, Newt never considered that it would not work. The question he asked Conner was "how do we make it work?"

While staying with the Gingrichs, Newt and Conner took a long walk around the neighborhood and talked. Conner felt that Newt knew the marriage was over but refused to acknowledge it. He confronted Newt on this and by the end of the long walk Newt agreed that Conner's assessment was probably accurate but was reluctant to give up, possibly because of the impact it would have on his daughters.[4] Similarly, Linda Kemp knew about the problems in the marriage from a conversation she had with Jackie during the 1978 campaign. She knew they had been in counseling for five years and felt "if you can't make it work in five years then go on and get another life. I think mentally they were divorced before the summer of 1980...he had stood it as long as he could."[5]

---

[3] Arthur Fessenden, interview by author, 30 November 1994. Gingrich Papers, University of West Georgia Archives, Carrollton.

[4] Daryl Conner, interview by author, tape recording, 3 October 1994, Gingrich papers, State University of West Georgia Archives, Carrollton.

[5] Kemp, interview, 1995.

Whatever Conerly, Kemp or Conner thought, Newt still had to make the decision. He made it by the first of June and then notified his staffs in meetings in Washington and Georgia. The Washington staff meeting took place on 12 June. To the further surprise of the staff, it was also announced that Weed would be going to Georgia in July to take over the campaign. Newt told Weed, Warnick and Gregorsky that he was "no longer willing to play out a psychodrama" concerning the divorce. Weed was needed to "save the campaign" not only because of the divorce but because the current campaign manager was not working out and the reelection campaign needed to be put on track.[6]

Those supporters worried about voter reaction to the divorce had good reason to be worried. The emotions of a divorce played out in the middle of a political campaign are almost always volatile. The divorce was not all that was on people's minds. Some of Newt's old supporters were becoming disenchanted with their congressman regardless of the divorce. Many supporters had campaigned for Newt in more than one election and considered themselves to be good friends with a special claim to his time and attention. Before the election Newt had spent nights in their homes, attended their parties, shared ideas with them about the Republican Party and the campaign, and generally paid a good deal of attention to them and what they thought. As Newt's role as congressman placed different demands on him, he no longer had that luxury.

Before the election the campaign and the party were the focus of Newt's attention. He truly needed the input of his supporters because they knew a good deal about what was happening in their district and he trusted their instincts. Now that Newt was in Washington new issues and problems became the object of his focus. He now needed advice and counsel from a new group. He also found that his time was being filled up more and more with just being a congressman.

"Newt, you have to tell them you aren't the man you were. You've changed, the job has changed and the time demands have changed...they'll understand," Fessenden told Newt. Newt tried to follow up with scheduled town hall meetings, advisory groups, speeches and appearances throughout the district, but the old support-

---

[6]Frank Gregorsky, interview by author, tape recording, 18 May 1994. Gingrich Papers, State University of West Georgia Archives, Carrollton.

ers wanted personal visits in their homes or offices. They wanted to have lunch with Newt and not have the whole Kiwanis Club attending. They wanted him to hang out in the barbershops and country stores like he had when running for office. When the scheduler would call to arrange such a meeting some were offended that he did not personally call or that it was not a spontaneous happening.[7] "Tell him to forget about working with the national Republican Party and all those party people and spend more time back here at home walking the squares and listening to what people think," advised Richard Dangle.[8] He made a point to stop by favorite local restaurants like the Lazy Donkey and Jerry's Country Kitchen, Buddy's and Melears BBQ as often as he could. He would drop by the Maple Street Mansion where he use to spend afternoons into the evening having a beer with his colleagues at WGC. O'Malley remembers, "Newt would come back for supporter's parties at first. They invited him and he came. When he got busy and couldn't come they took it personal."[9]

Newt had become a congressman to establish a GOP majority in Congress and move the country toward a more conservative vision. Only by doing this, he thought, could he "save the country" and avoid the looming disaster he saw just around the corner. He knew that if one did not satisfy one's constituents one did not get to stay in Washington to make national changes. He told his staff that they were the troops who would buy him time to do the national stuff. This policy worked for the average voter who seldom expected to see his congressman, however, it failed to placate those who had worked with and for Newt when he was running for office. They wanted and expected more from him. They did not want to see staffers, they wanted to see Newt.

Other supporters were disappointed because Newt seemed to them to be more and more conservative. The truth was that he changed little. The emphasis shifted from time to time. He had been moderate or liberal compared to Jack Flynt but rather conservative when compared to Virginia Shapard. He had identified himself in his first campaign as a conservative and in each campaign thereafter. When he started acting like one in Washington it disappointed them. They were also concerned about the partisan approach he was taking.

---

[7] Fessenden, interview, 1994.

[8] Richard Dangle, Interview by the author, 16 December 1994.

[9] Jim O'Malley, Interview the author, 12 December 1994.

The day after the election in 1978 Newt and his family had returned to their home on Howell Road to a community celebration with banners and food in his front yard. Local officials gave congratulations and made speeches and County Commissioner Horrie Duncan presented a proclamation to the applause of a large number of old friends, new friends and supporters. By the summer of 1980 Newt had to be wondering if he had seen another day like that in his hometown.[10]

Newt's reelection effort was losing ground. Before he made the divorce decision he and his principal advisors had predicted a victory of better than sixty percent. While that margin was still the objective, many felt they would be appreciative of a fifty-four percent "holding our own" victory. Without minimizing the dangers, many felt it was possible if Newt worked as hard in 1980 as he had in 1978. Though he might lose some of the old disillusioned supporters, he was gaining new ones all the time.

Conversely, this campaign lacked certain disadvantages present in the previous two races. In 1974 Newt's campaign was burdened with the Nixon pardon. In 1976, Carter was a strong presence on the ticket. In 1978 the Democratic machine was out in force to reelect Governor George Busbee. In 1980, while Carter was running for reelection, all the polls showed that he was vastly unpopular and that Ronald Reagan was likely to win, bringing with him new GOP congressmen and senators. While native son Carter was expected to take Georgia it was not expected that he would have long coat tails. The key would be Newt's opponent. If he or she were a strong, attractive candidate from one of the more populous counties it would be difficult, though not impossible, to pull out a decent victory.

Dolorese Shanks, the new district administrator, worked hard to represent Newt in the most positive light, especially in the south metro area. Her contacts with local officials helped offset opposition to Newt, even though he was not a Democrat. The Georgia staff followed her lead and were building a reputation as a good, responsive group of professionals. Newt's outreach program was helping them, and him, get to know his constituents.[11]

---

[10] *West Georgia News* (Carrollton), 10 November 1978.

[11] Gregorsky, "The First Two Years."

The 1980 campaign sought to keep strong candidates out of the sixth district race. In the early days of 1980, word was spread of a particularly strong campaign to intimidate Newt's possible opponents. The legislature was targeted as the most dangerous port for potential candidates. Virginia Shapard still had a sizable continuing debt that she was struggling to pay, a point that Newt's supporters pointed out to possible candidates.

The campaign also paid considerable attention to Speaker Tom Murphy. As a staunch Democrat, Murphy's support for Newt was out of the question, but his support for Newt's opponent could be devastating to the reelection effort. The campaign hoped to neutralize and placate Murphy as much as possible, particularly with redistricting coming up in 1982.

One particular candidate, Representative Nathan Knight, was a particular threat to Newt because he was close to Speaker Murphy and could raise money if he ran. The strategy singled out Knight and showed him how well Newt served his county. Newt already had an office in Newnan and that also helped Newt's image with Knight. Steely talked with Knight about the problems one would face living in Washington and asked if Knight really wanted to give up his lucrative law practice to take his family there. Knight, for whatever reason, decided not to run.

With Knight out of the race Speaker Murphy indicated that he would not run anyone against Newt. Newt had acted on Murphy's recommendation about staffing, had appointed residents of Murphy's county to advisory committees and to federal positions on committees and boards such as the Agricultural Stabilization and Conservation Committee and paid special attention to constituents in Haralson County. Newt made sure that staffers worked the county on outreach and he made a point of holding town hall meetings there whenever possible.

Newt also made a point of working with Georgia's lieutenant governor, Zell Miller. They had remarkably similar backgrounds in politics. Both were young and aggressive with a practical approach to politics. Both had been college professors teaching history and both held the military in high regard, Miller being a former Marine. Both were men consumed by politics. Miller ran his first race for Lieutenant Governor in 1974 when Newt ran his first congressional race. Miller won. Like Murphy, Miller did not intend to go out of his way to help Newt, but the Newt team did not want Miller's opposition either. Miller was president of the Georgia Senate and could encourage opponents and would appoint the Senate committee dealing with reapportionment. Newt and Miller would develop a respect for each other and work together on issues affecting Georgia over the next decade.

No member of the legislature ran against Newt. Still, there was no question that there would be a Democrat to run against him. Newt's supporters addressed all the possible opponents to get them not to run. Some had debts and did not want to risk losing and incurring more debt. Others did not want to move their families to Washington and some were making too much money to take the pay cut. A few had actually lost elections and were no longer viable as candidates. The Carrollton Mafia again set up a "Democrats for Newt" organization, this time with a former Democratic county chairman, Henry Lumpkin, one of the most respected men in Carroll County, heading the organization. While "Democrats for Newt" was never a major factor in the campaign it did give cover to Democrats who wanted to split their vote.

In the end all the work with legislators to encourage them not to run either paid off or was not necessary. Two outsiders ran for the Democratic nomination to oppose Newt. Jim Huffman and Dock Davis were both new to politics. The assessment was that Huffman could be dangerous as a rank amateur. He had personality, roots and appeal but was almost ignored by Davis in the primary while he concentrated on attacking Gingrich.

Davis, an attorney from Heard County, the smallest and most rural county in the district, had law offices there and in Atlanta. He had never held elective office and did not have Huffman's personality. Still, he possessed some advantages. He had served on the Democratic Executive Committee and had been appointed to a number of party positions. He was a former naval officer who had served in Viet Nam and had run, unsuccessfully, for a seat in the Georgia House.

During the primary campaign in the summer of 1980 Davis, who had served in Jimmy Carter's gubernatorial administration, had targeted Newt for his criticism of the Carter administration. He asserted a Georgian should be helping the president and not working to undercut him. Because of Newt's aggressive attacks on the Democratic Congress Davis accused him of being negative and of offering nothing positive, saying, "He's only there to tear down."[12] This change might have been effective if Carter had been popular. Many other Georgians were also critical of President Carter and the accusation did not strike home with the voters.

That fall Carter returned the favor by appearing with and endorsing Davis. This endorsement was about all the help Davis received. All the Democratic money was directed to help Carter and Senator Herman Talmadge get reelected. Talmadge was opposed in the primary by Lieutenant Governor Miller in an expensive and grueling campaign which the senator won but which exhausted his financial resources. He had an unexpectedly difficult general election campaign to run against former state GOP chairman Mack Mattingly due to ethics problems and the strenuous primary. Talmadge needed all the money he could get and this diminished Davis' hopes for fund raising.[13]

The Davis organization was not without some tactics, however. Through Connie Plunkett, a strong Carter supporter from Carrollton, they even approached Kip Carter to seek his help against Newt. Carter met with them and explained why Davis could not win and refused to join their campaign.

Davis won the primary to the satisfaction of the Gingrich team. "We wanted Davis," remembered Conerly. Davis seemingly had no real background in politics and came from the smallest county, the only one without a single traffic light, and thus would have a small base from which to run. Under ordinary circumstances Newt could have run up over 65 percent of the vote.

Newt had appointed Ben Nobel to be his campaign manager in the spring. Nobel, inexperienced in politics, turned out to have organizational and management problems and these were exacerbated by Newt's decision to seek a divorce. By early June the campaign was deteriorating and the decision was made to send Weed to Georgia to manage the campaign. Newt was no longer expecting a 60 percent margin, he just did not want to lose.

Davis made a strong effort early in the campaign. "Newt Gingrich has changed." He attacked the size of Newt's staff and budget. He accused Newt of hypocrisy. Being divorced himself, Davis did not

---

[12] Dock Davis, interview by author, on videotape, 25 May 1998, GPH, Ingram Library, State University of West Georgia, Carrolton.
  [13]Ibid.

openly campaign on that issue but rather pictured Gingrich as two-faced and allowed his audience to draw their own conclusions. Telling people "He'll vote the way he talks" Davis stressed his ties to the Democratic Party and President Carter. Newt was for the all volunteer army, Davis was against it. Newt helped put together the "Budget of Hope" and Davis opposed it. "I don't think Newt understands the district. He has no rapport with working people, with rural people." Newt was a professor, after all, and he thought everyone knew they live in ivy covered towers and were out of touch with reality.[14]

The real issue for Davis was the fight to stop a hazardous waste dump being located in his home county. Davis had worked his county hard. It was a strong Democratic county where the mayor of the county seat told voters as they entered the polls that they could not vote Republican. Newt had not carried it in 1978. The county embraced Dock and he embraced their issues.

Dock was comfortable at home. The people of Heard County were his people. The plan for the Gingrich campaign changed slightly with this recognition. It was decided to do all they could to encourage Dock to spend his time in Heard County and away from the larger counties. A debate on the dump was now accepted. A campaign debate was scheduled for the county. Newt's people worked the county at first saying how worried they were about losing the county. After the idea had been established, Newt's supporters began talking about how Newt's strength was growing in the county in an effort to get Davis and his people to spend more time there.

Weed had been instructed by Newt to go to Georgia and do what he could to "not lose" the election. He was nervous because of the divorce but still believed it was his to lose. Newt decided to spend most of his time in the larger counties and came home as often as his obligations in Congress would allow. He told Weed, "Nothing fancy, just don't lose it for me."[15] Newt wanted to be called when the polls showed him at less than sixty percent. The call was placed sooner than anyone expected.

Newt's people knew the divorce would hurt his standing but still felt confident about the victory. The negative reaction in Carroll County shocked them. There was also a good deal of negative reaction in the

---

[14] Newt Gingrich Papers, Steely file, 1980 Campaign folder, State University of West Georgia Archives, Carrollton.

[15] Weed, Interview, 1992.

largest county in the district, Clayton, especially in Jonesboro. Supporters were reporting that it was hurting. The media, especially the local Carrollton radio station, WLBB, and the Atlanta newspapers were hostile on the issue.

When he was on the campaign trail he talked about issues that were a continuation of his previous campaigns—jobs, the right to real representation in Washington, ethics, the budget, cutting taxes and a strong military to defend America's interests in a troubled world. He had help from the party in Georgia and nationally. Even the dean of the Georgia delegation in the house, Representative Jack Brinkley from Columbus, a Democrat, spoke for him. Brinkley spoke at one of the meetings Newt held for his major givers in Atlanta. At one of the meetings where Newt returned the favor speaking for Brinkley, the Democrat said in introduction, "Newt Gingrich is the delegation's professor. He's smart, thoughtful and not doctrinaire. He approaches issues on the basis of merit, does his homework and gets along well with people. He is a valuable member of the Georgia delegation and serves with distinction on the Public Works Committee."[16]

Laurie James, Newt's personal secretary, told Gregorsky that Newt was "undergoing personal turmoil" as an explanation for his being more or less "out of touch" with his Washington staff during May and June 1980. This was accurate. With Weed leaving for Georgia and the campaign, the uncertainty created by the divorce, and the gloom spreading from the Georgia staff, the DC staff was becoming discouraged and wondering what next to expect.[17] The staff was confused about Newt and his direction and an intensity of feeling aimed against Weed. While Newt had remained focused on his chief goals he had confused the staff by throwing out ideas and projects only to apparently lose interest in them after a short while. The staff was uncertain when to take his ideas seriously and when they were just passing.

Tension was also apparent back in Georgia. The campaign headquarters was located in the same building as the congressional office in East Point. Shanks set up strict rules for congressional-campaign contact that resulted in a very clean ethical approach, but served to

---

[16]Newt Gingrich Papers, 1980 campaign folder (press accounts), State University of West Georgia Archives, Carrollton.

[17]Gregorsky, "The First Two Years."

breed hostility between the two groups. The separation of the two groups was ruthlessly maintained and Shanks came to be disliked by the campaign people and Weed by the congressional staff. Cooperation between the two groups, especially over things like scheduling Newt's time, became increasingly difficult.[18]

Newt's first 1980 campaign manager, Ben Nobel, had good contacts with money people but they had not paid off. Weed now struggled with fundraising. Warnick told the DC staff that Weed's strategy was one of low risk and not vote maximization. Due to Weed's suspicions of the Carrollton Mafia they were not informed of the new strategy to run a low risk campaign. They were still working toward voter maximization to compensate for votes lost to the divorce issue. It was almost as if two campaigns were being run: one in the western part of the district and another in the rest of the district.

Weed was nervous about a volunteer-based campaign and sought to do almost everything from within his own staff. He would later regret this. "We should've demolished Davis," he said. "We got staff heavy and the volunteer based campaign didn't work as well this time." In his own defense he noted that though Davis was not an especially strong candidate, "Newt was in the middle of a divorce and was not giving a lot of attention to the campaign." When the candidate is the greatest campaign asset and is not available, the campaign suffers in every area.[19]

The divorce was weighing on Newt and the campaign. Ultimately, Newt told his lawyers, "I can't deal with this anymore. I want Jackie and the girls taken care of. Give her whatever she wants." Newt was advised that he was just speaking from guilt and that he would eventually regret the decision. Newt declined any other negotiations: "I know what I'm doing, give her whatever she asks." A few years later Newt was asked if he made the right decision in the settlement. Newt responded that it was "one of the best decisions I've ever made."

The divorce was costly to Newt personally, financially, and politically. He now shifted his concern to his daughters. Some of the rumors in Carrollton were vicious, such as the accusation that he had presented divorce papers to his dying wife in the hospital and

---

[18] Ibid.

[19] Weed, Interview, 1992.

demanded that she sign them. Though untrue, he worried about how all this was affecting the girls. He determined to spend as much time as possible with them and assure them the divorce was in no way their fault. By the time the divorce was final, 31 January 1981, he had adjusted to it and had set a pattern of visiting and talking with both girls.

He was not visiting and talking with voters in the western part of the district, however, and this worried the Mafia. They believed his presence was particularly effective there and thought Newt could turn some of this around by his policy in the western counties. Weed disagreed and held rigidly to his plan of Newt appearing in the more populous counties. Weed did visit some of the western areas, including Carroll County. His personality and insistence on keeping Newt in the eastern part of the district did little to help western supporters. The Carroll County Commissioner, Horrie Duncan, was so incensed by Weed that he told Newt to keep him out of Carroll: "If I see that [expletive] in my county I'll cut his damn head off." Speaking with some fervor, Duncan made his point and Weed never visited Carroll County again.

The campaign ran one rather complex television ad showing various Washington politicians, including Representative Trent Lott, endorsing Newt and saying how important it was to reelect him. Conerly and Catherine Brock thought this played into Davis' hands by stressing Washington instead of Georgia. Local people were calling in volunteering to do "local" ads telling how Newt had helped them with a variety of problems but Weed vetoed using them. That further incensed the Mafia who thought he was out of touch with the constituents.

The polls showed that Newt had a moderate lead in the major population centers and holding even in the rural areas despite the divorce. This information was not shared with the Mafia and they continued to worry. By October Davis pointed to the waste dump issue to show that Newt did not care what happened to the people back home. He also accused Newt of mud-slinging and lying by saying that Davis would shut the Carrollton office. What Davis had said was that he had not made a decision about where he would have offices, a vague statement sufficient to scare many of the Carroll County voters.

Knowing he was below 60 percent in the polls, Newt made appearances throughout Carroll County as well as a few in Haralson and Coweta during October. Ads were run locally in the western counties — paid for by money locally raised — that showed people how to split a ballot. They even made a point of noting, with pictures, that you could vote for Jimmy Carter, Herman Talmadge and Newt. They also had Horrie Duncan do some radio ads on local stations endorsing Newt and put on some of the ads that Weed opposed.[20] Newt's presence helped and the campaign's decline seemed to be reversing toward the end of the month.

At that point Weed began soliciting donors for Mattingly's senatorial campaign against Talmadge. He sent out a letter over Newt's signature asking Newt's contributor list to help Mack Mattingly. Unaware that Newt had instructed Weed to go to Mattingly's aid, the Mafia and many supporters exploded. Newt had made pledges to Talmadge that they intended to stay out of his campaign. He had stayed out of Newt's and aside from endorsing the Democratic ticket, as Newt had endorsed the Republican ticket, he had played no part in the race against Dock Davis. The fear was that the Talmadge people would feel betrayed and quickly turn against Newt providing the margin necessary for Davis to win in the rural counties.

With the expectation of backlash from Talmadge supporters, tensions were particularly high between Weed and the Mafia. Weed was adhering to his plan, and feared the Mafia's meddling. In one instance, Davis' ex-wife contacted Newt's campaign with what was potentially damaging information against Davis. Weed vetoed using information though she agreed to go on television with what she alleged was evidence proving her story. This decision further upset the Carrollton workers and did little to heal the breach between the two sides.

As the campaign moved toward election-day Davis improved and became more confident debating Newt. He also was spending a good deal of time in his home county where he was strongest. He pictured himself as a person with "real world experience" and tried to tie himself to the Democratic Party, "The party of Roosevelt, John Kennedy and Richard Russell." Since Newt felt there was a strong reaction against Carter in Georgia, he was pleased that Davis publicly connected

---

[20]Gingrich Papers, 1980 campaign folder, Mel Steely Collection.

himself with the Democratic Party. Newt believed Carter would carry Georgia, but not by the 1976 margin.

Newt stressed his cooperation with state and local officials and his ability to deliver for Georgia. His ads advised voters to "vote like your future depends on it." He stressed his support for tax cuts and his opposition to tax increases. He was for cutting spending. He opposed the hazardous waste dump and worked to help solve problems at the Atlanta airport. He pictured a great future under Ronald Reagan and announced, "It's time for hope and it's time for leadership."[21]

With all the problems in his own campaign Newt had also gotten involved in the presidential campaign and tried to make the congressional elections national ones with a common theme. At a meeting, one of AT&T's vice presidents, Charlie McWhorter, suggested to Newt an event involving Republican congressional and senatorial candidates, along with Ronald Reagan and George Bush. He suggested they all meet on the steps of the Capitol in Washington to announce a centerpiece for all Republicans to support and unite behind. This centerpiece was the Kemp tax cut proposal, which would quickly become the Reagan/GOP tax cut proposal. Newt was active in the development of the Capitol steps event in the summer of 1980 and was delighted when Vander Jagt reported to him that "Bill Casey [a key Reagan advisor] already thinks Newt is working on the 'Republican team approach' to the fall campaign."[22]

By early fall it was clear that the GOP would do well in senatorial elections and possibly carry the Senate. This knowledge helped Newt make up his mind to help Mattingly in Georgia even at the risk of stirring up "straight ticket" Democratic voters who might have voted for Newt, too. Ladonna Lee, a GOP consultant, told Newt that there was a good chance that at least sixty Republican House candidates had a "fair shot" at winning. If true, the Republicans would not have a majority, but with the help of conservative Democrats, the Republicans would have a chance of controlling the House on a number of critical issues. The challenge now was to build a farm team of good GOP candidates on the state level.

---

[21] Ibid.
[22] Guy Vander Jagt, Interview, 1994.

Though the 1980 GOP event on Capitol steps was the genesis for the 1994 event that showcased the Republican "Contract with America," it had a more immediate development. It also convinced Newt that serious work had to be done to get viable candidates to run as Republicans. This objective became the work of GOPAC when Newt took over as chairman from Governor Pete Dupont in 1986 and focused on House elections. Even before GOPAC Newt had begun traveling the country trying to help elect GOP congressional candidates and was planning, with his policy staffers, how to achieve that goal as soon as possible.

With all Newt's concern for nationalizing the election Newt's race remained to be won in the sixth district. The Mafia was continually concerned about Newt's letter asking help for Mattingly. A state GOP official, Matt Patton, was publicizing an appeal for county commissioners to switch to the Republican Party. This plea, along with Newt's support of Mattingly, caused many Democratic office holders to get nervous and hampered any alliances toward supporting Newt.

Weed continued a low profile, high ad course, in the eastern part of the district. In the west the Mafia was running bumper sticker blitzes and using Newt at every opportunity. His presence raised over $4,000 for local use in radio and newspaper ads that were locally targeted. He also enthused a large number of local volunteers in the last weeks of the campaign and their public presence helped dispel the impression that everyone in the west was against Newt. The $4,000 also provided some "gas" money to drive people to the polls for use in the African-American community and to help turn out the vote for Newt in those areas.[23]

By election-day most everyone with the campaign felt fairly confident that Newt would be reelected though the margin of victory varied widely with each prediction. Some topped sixty percent while others were as low as fifty-one percent. All were in a pretty good mood when they gathered for the victory party in a hotel just south of the Atlanta airport.

After claiming victory in his race Newt met with some of his key people and thanked them for sticking with him through a rough campaign and congratulated them on "their" victory as well as his own.

---

[23] Gingrich Papers, 1980 campaign folder.

He had only lost four counties, traditional Democratic ones. One, Speaker Murphy's home county, was lost by only sixty-three votes. Davis had, as expected, carried Heard County by a wide margin. Newt carried the largest county, Clayton with 60.7 percent. Carroll County was hard hit. Newt carried his home county, but suffered serious losses when compared to the 1978 election (66 % in 1978 versus 51 % in 1980). Newt won the district by fifty-eight percent.

Early in the morning Newt had a staff member drive him up to Mack Mattingly's headquarters to congratulate the new Senator-elect. Mack had been part of the original team, with Paul Coverdell and Bob Irvin, that had worked to revive the Georgia GOP with Newt and now it appeared that they would be working together in Washington to do the same thing for the national Republican Party. The final vote was not yet in and Mack was cautious about claiming victory. Newt assured him it was over and arranged to get together to make plans for future cooperation in Georgia and Washington.[24]

---

[24]Mack Mattingly, Interview by author, on videotape, 16 February 1987.

8

REAGAN AND
REAPPORTIONMENT

The year 1981 held huge promise. Newt had been reelected and was joined by Georgia's new junior Senator, Matt Mattingly. They were to be led in their fight for a conservative revolution by President Ronald Reagan and a new team in the White House. Having a Republican Senator from Georgia helped Newt in many ways. While Mattingly could hardly be called a clone of Gingrich, the two did share the same goals, a close friendship, and a genuine desire to help Georgia and their country. The Republican take-over in the Senate meant the appointment of conservative judges and bureaucrats who shared their goals and objectives.

New Republican blood had also been added in the House. Vin Weber from Minnesota, who was to become one of Newt's closest allies and friends: Bill McCollum from Florida, Steve Gunderson from Wisconsin, Dan Coats from Indiana, Duncan Hunter from California, Bill Emerson from Missouri, Chris Smith from New Jersey and a number of others were all new and ripe for recruiting to the ranks of the developing conservative revolution that was growing in the House. Newt remained fixed on his three main goals: working for conservative control of the budget and lower taxes, building a Republican majority in the House, and serving the needs of the people of the sixth district of Georgia.

Newt had met Marianne Ginther on a campaign trip to Ohio and now she was working in Washington for the Secret Service. She began to play a major role in his personal life and they were married in

August. She would be key to encouraging him in his work and in curbing some of his more exuberant tendencies. She certainly was part of the promise of 1981.

Newt was delighted with Ronald Reagan, who personified so many of the things in which Newt believed. Reagan was clearly the heir to Barry Goldwater as leader of the conservative cause. His affable manner and ease of communicating with the American people would go a long way toward paving the way for the Reagan Revolution. This revolution was Gingrich's as well and the Reagan appeal would make it easier to get popular support for the Kemp-Roth proposals and for recruiting promising candidates needed to provide the GOP majority in the House. The Republican Party had to connect with the conservative movement as it never had before. The military was in dire need of reform. The budget had to be brought under control and minority citizens had to be brought into the political mainstream.

Newt knew each item on the conservative agenda was important and insisted on being involved in each in a major way. Separate structures and support teams had to be built for each issue and, oftentimes interconnected. In addition, to build the internal structure, popular support had to be galvanized to encourage and support that structure. Technology and the mass media seemed the answer to this latter problem. Newt became a supporter of widespread computer usage. He stepped up his press exposure. He began to open lines to the rising talk show explosion that would shortly produce a series of conservative shows, Rush Limbaugh's being the most notable, that would reach out to Americans and allow them to carry on a conversation as to the country's direction. Newt and his conservative colleagues helped lead that discussion through the regular media and especially through the use of C-SPAN in statements from the floor and in "special orders" following the end of business each day. It would be difficult to overestimate the impact these efforts had as hundreds of thousands tuned in to C-SPAN around the country and millions listened to the talk shows.

Most of these themes Newt had embraced from the beginning. He had opposed racism in all its forms. He sent his children to a heavily black Head Start program in New Orleans while in graduate school to make sure they had the experience of interacting with children of other races. He had been inspired by Martin Luther King's rhetoric and grieved at his death. He had worked for Nelson Rockefeller because of "Rocky's" commitment to integration. He stressed black involvement in his political campaigns and kept his promise to hire a number of black staffers equal to the percentage of the black population in his district.

As a congressman, Newt strongly supported the Martin Luther King holiday even when a majority of his district opposed it. He backed the open housing legislation of the 1980s and was one of the few Republicans to take a strong stand favoring a ban on US investments in South Africa because of their racist policies. In a 1984 letter to the South African ambassador to the US, he and thirty-five other GOP House members supported the curtailing of "new American investments" in South Africa and the organization of "international diplomatic and economic sanctions." "Let us reiterate our strong view that an end to apartheid is instrumental to the maintenance and growth of the relationship between South Africa and the United States," they said. They wanted to work for stronger ties between the two countries, "but the reality of apartheid and the violence used to keep it in place make it likely that our relations will deteriorate. Those obstacles to a constructive alliance must be ended."[1]

He was just as emphatic in his insistence on involving blacks in his campaigns and in seeking the black vote. He knew the majority of blacks were wedded to the Democratic Party but thought the effort had to be made. When aides pointed out the futility of expending great amounts of time, energy and money on the black vote, using their vote for Jack Flynt as a case in point, Newt responded, "We've got to bring this country together. The alternative is terrible. We've got to keep trying." Newt used the same logic about his support of the King holiday both with aides and at town hall meetings back home when questioned about his vote.

The small number of blacks coming by his offices troubled Newt and some of his Georgia staffers. Less than 10 percent of Newt's casework related to blacks. Catherine Brock, Jan Savage and Virginia Lamutt, all concerned with outreach, noted similar figures in their fourth year reviews.[2] Though some speculated that blacks did not want

---

[1] Newt Gingrich Papers, 1984 correspondence. *The Atlanta Journal,* 8 August 1985, "Gingrich Constituents at odds over South Africa," p. A1.

[2] Frank Gregorsky,., *The Second Two Years,* Newt Gingrich Papers, State University of West Georgia Archives, Carrollton.

to talk to Republican legislators, state Democratic legislators reported the same lack of contact with blacks. Given that blacks had the same problems as other citizens, the conclusion drawn by Newt and the staff was that most blacks in the district were not aware that such help was available. Newt would have to reach out to them.

Mark Florio, a Washington staff member, noted in 1982, "I think I've been around Newt long enough to know that his outreach to blacks is sincere; it's very real, and it seems we never build on it until it's too late." Newt did not think it was too late to start building. From 1983 on a minority outreach project was a regular part of district staffers tasking. Faye Williams, a black former teacher, had been put in charge of the military academy appointments selection process because of her competent ability to relate to school counselors. Likewise, Newt felt strongly that it was symbolically important to have a black associated with excellence.

More than symbolism was needed. A 3 August 1983 memo to Mary Brown listed Newt's goals in the newly established black outreach program. The three main objectives were to help establish more black businessmen in the sixth district, to establish a base of black contacts in each county, and finally to establish black awareness of services offered by the congressional office and raise the number of black constituents served directly in casework.[3] The goals were to be achieved through four subsections of the overall black outreach program: a black entrepreneurs program, a series of meetings with black leaders, visits by Newt to black churches and reunions, and national or congressional legislation.

The first entrepreneurs' meeting was held in Carrollton 1 September 1983 with a local bank as sponsor. Over forty minority businessmen attended, black and Hispanic, from five counties. Each offered suggestions as to how Newt could be helpful. One suggestion was for Newt to bring in someone from the Small Business Administration to meet with them. A meeting with the deputy district director for the SBA was arranged for 1 December 1983 in Carrollton.[4]

---

[3] Mel Steely papers, "Black Outreach" folder, Steely staff memo, 3 August 1983, Newt Gingrich Papers.

[4] Ibid. Mel Steely, staff memo, 3 September 1983, Black Outreach folder, Gingrich Papers.

Black leaders were to be organized by county so Newt could be sure to visit them as he visited their counties and staff could work with them on a regular basis. Newt developed a good working relationship with Atlanta's three black mayors, Maynard Jackson, Andrew Young, and Bill Campbell. Contacts were opened with Fulton County officials like Marvin Arrington and Ira Jackson. Newt attended meetings and parties in black homes where businessmen gathered and worked to develop a continuing relationship with them.

Invitations were sought to black churches and family reunions and Newt's schedule included them on a regular basis. J. W. Lemon, a black leader from Griffin, met with Newt during office hours there and suggested that Newt present a set of framed Black Heritage postage stamps to the churches where he would speak. Lemon thought this reminder of blacks in history would serve to inspire black young people. Newt liked the idea, paid for it from his campaign funds, and made it a regular part of his black outreach program. Sometimes Newt would give a short inspirational talk and tell the congregation about his local office and the services it provided and sometimes he just attended the service and be available to talk to church members.[5]

Whether it was attending black churches, holding dinner meetings with black entrepreneurs, or meeting with leaders in the local black community, Newt consistently worked to build a bridge to the minority community. Later these efforts were expanded to the Asian, Indian and Hispanic communities as their numbers grew in the sixth district. Strong contacts were established in the Indian community through the help of leaders like Krishna Srinivasa, a local computer software businessman and leader in the Indian-American Political Forum. Newt, or someone from his staff attended and spoke at their conventions with some regularity. Staff appearances at annual Chinese and German celebrations were also fairly regular.

The efforts of Newt and his staff were marginally successful in getting more constituent casework and more so in opening contacts in the minority communities. The outreach did not, as some aides had hoped, yield greatly at the polls where Newt often received less than 20-25 percent of the black vote. Newt was undaunted. He thought the

---

[5]Black Stamp Project folder, Dallas New Era, 3 December 1987, Gingrich Papers.

number of black Republicans would grow as they came to realize the value of voting in both parties and understood their personal interests were the same as his. Newt's priorities were that contacts be opened, inroads established into the minority communities and that all minority constituents understand that he was there to be helpful and supportive.

Moving the state party on the inclusion issue was not easy. At one Georgia GOP state convention in the early 1980s the resolution committee had to overcome substantial debate before creating a resolution welcoming and encouraging the inclusion of young people and minority groups. Inclusions did grow in the party however. The party nominated a black for lieutenant governor in 1978 and another was elected county school superintendent in Douglas County in 1988, a largely Republican county in the Atlanta suburbs and in Newt's district

Other problems faced the Georgia GOP and Newt. The Reagan forces had worked hard to elect their candidate. With Reagan in office, they expected control over patronage and the right to appoint their own people. During the campaign they had been less than supportive of other GOP candidates. Newt was not allowed to put a window sign in their headquarters in Carrollton, nor was any other Republican candidate. The Reagan chairman for Georgia, Ted Stivers, would normally have been, with the state GOP chairman, the deciding factor in patronage matters. In 1980, however, Georgia elected a Republican US Senator, Mattingly, and he controlled the patronage and had his own ideas about how patronage should be run. The 1981 state GOP convention was a raucous affair with Stivers' allies actively competing with the Mattingly/Gingrich forces for control of the state party with a Stivers stalwart leading the opening prayer and praying for God's help in stopping the Mattingly/Gingrich coalition from taking control.

While supporting Ronald Reagan, Newt backed Mattingly and sought some accommodation for the Reagan people in Georgia. Mattingly allowed Newt to control patronage for northwest Georgia and Steely was placed on Mattingly's patronage committee and J. Eugene Beckham, Newt's personal attorney, on Mattingly's judicial appointments committee to represent Newt's interests. The most notable and contested of Newt's appointments was that of Lynn Duncan, Commissioner Horrie Duncan's son, as US Marshal for north Georgia. While other qualified candidates such as a former sheriff and a state trooper, were available, Newt owed Horrie Duncan for his support in 1978 and

1980 and Newt paid his debt. Duncan turned out to be one of Newt's most outstanding appointments and was honored by the Marshals Service more than once for his outstanding work

Many Georgia Republicans believed that their elected officials in Washington should not interfere with state party politics and resented being "told how to vote." Still during most of the 1980s the Mattingly, Gingrich and Coverdell coalition dominated the state Republican Party. Emphasis was placed on candidate recruitment and training. Reagan, Dole, Bush, Kemp and Pat Robinson alliances were made and Coverdell was eventually elected in 1992 and re-elected in 1998, to the US Senate to replace Democrat Wyche Fowler who had upset Mattingly in 1986.

National and local politics blended in a number of areas. Reapportionment, as mentioned previously, was a major concern for the GOP, and for Newt. The national air traffic controllers strike of 1981 was also of considerable concern, particularly in Newt's area. Postal employees and air traffic controllers had talked of going on strike in 1980 and the controllers, having their demands rejected, decided to strike. The Reagan administration's position was that this action would be illegal and the president would fire the controllers if they struck. Many of the controllers lived in Newt's district and sought his support. He advised them not to strike and to return to the bargaining table. "This is not Jimmy Carter you're dealing with," he told them, "President Reagan intends to fire you if you strike. Go back to bargaining and I'll do all I can to help but I can't support an illegal strike." The controllers viewed Newt's stance as an unacceptable lack of support.[6]

The controllers' bitterness came out through attacks on Newt and Reagan in the press and especially at town hall meetings Newt held around the district. At one such meeting in Fayetteville, Georgia, south of the Atlanta airport, tensions rose to the point that Newt had to go into the crowd to break up heated arguments. At this meeting a young uniformed Boy Scout stood up and asked Newt why people who were making $70,000 a year were striking. He said his mother had worked hard just to buy him his uniform and to support him on less and could not understand why people who made that much were striking. The controllers did strike and President Reagan did fire them. Popular

---

[6] Air Traffic Controllers folders, 1981-1982, Gingrich Papers.

opinion sided with the president and did not do much damage to Newt politically because many in the sixth district saw Newt as standing up to the unions. Still, the whole situation bothered Newt considerably. The postal employees, seeing people lined up to apply for their jobs, decided not to strike.

Up until this strike Newt's relations with the unions were cordial. They had supported him against Shapard and were relatively neutral during the 1980 reelection bid though their vote swayed somewhat toward Davis. They saw President Reagan's actions as strike breaking and union breaking and thought Newt could have stood with them in their hour of need. While this disagreement did not completely destroy his relationship with the unions it did strain it considerably. The Eastern Air Lines strike a few years later would cause a rupture in that relationship.

Ironically, his strong support of the president's decision helped him in reapportionment by giving him an image of strength. The 1982 session of the Georgia General Assembly was the reapportionment session based on the 1980 census figures. In 1980 work was already underway to make sure the key figures in the process would not harm Newt's reelection by redistricting him into a more Democratic district. Newt had been attentive to their legislative and constituent needs and had developed personal friendships with a number of the key legislators, especially those from his district.

Newt met with Representative Joe Mack Wilson, chairman of House Reapportionment, in the fall of 1981. Newt did not ask for favors but rather sought to learn from Representative Wilson how the process would develop. Wilson, a "yellow dog" Democrat, described the ebb and flow of the process, how many maps would be submitted reflecting the various interests of those concerned and how the winnowing process would come down to the final weeks and days. After Newt asked a series of technical questions, Wilson finally pronounced the words Newt had come to hear, "Newt, we're not going to try and hurt you but we're not going out of our way to help you either."

Two members of the Senate Reapportionment Committee were from Newt's district, Senator Perry Hudson and Senator Terrell Starr. As with House members, Newt worked closely with them as well as with Lieutenant Governor Zell Miller and a handful of other key senators such as Senators Culver Kidd, Render Hill, Nathan Dean and Wayne

Garner. Newt had one thing going for him. To cut up his district very much they would have to do serious damage to the surrounding districts occupied by favored Democrats. The Democratic Congressmen did not want their districts tampered with any more than was necessary. If counties were taken from them to give to Newt they would have to take someone else's counties to make up for what they had lost. Many maps were drawn, as Wilson predicted.

Wilson's assurances aside, the process was not easy. The final map for congressional redistricting took away four of Newt's counties on the southern and eastern fringe of the district. Polk and Paulding counties were added at the northern end of the district. Though all the counties added and subtracted were considered Democratic, the new counties were considered ultimately beneficial to Newt. Paulding County was adjacent to perhaps the most Republican county in Georgia, Cobb, and the population explosion was moving out of Atlanta in Paulding's direction potentially increasing that county's conservative vote. A close supporter of Newt's had been raised in Polk County and had contacts that might prove valuable to Newt.

Court challenges carried the process into the summer and as August 1982 approached it was unclear whether or not primaries would be allowed and whether the general election could be held on time in November. In the end, after a special session of the legislature, the map was finalized and approved. Newt had his two new counties, and though he still had Heard County, the constituents of that Democratic county decided they liked having two nearby congressional offices, one in Carroll County and one in Coweta County, and fought, through Senator Hill, to stay in the sixth district. Newt was satisfied and threw a small dinner party for key legislators and their wives to thank them for being especially helpful in ensuring that his district was acceptable.

In Georgia as in Washington Newt continued to stress the need for a balanced budget and for tax cuts. Newt found himself in agreement with the president's core economic concerns: cutting taxes along lines advised by the supply-side economists, increasing defense spending, and balancing the budget. He agreed with the need to speed up economic growth and provide more jobs. Federal tax rates needed to be reduced and the income tax brackets needed to be indexed. Reducing government and cutting bureaucracy had become a holy mantra for most Republicans as had eliminating waste in government. Newt was at first less sure about giving the President line-item veto power because it would reduce the power of the House and upset, to a degree, the balance of powers so necessary to the functioning of the republic. After a few years, Newt's experience inside Congress led him to support presidential line-item veto.

Newt's team was in place. He had added to it by sending out materials to GOP candidates stressing the need for a national agenda and pushing the Capitol Steps event. Fifty-three freshmen had been elected and more than a dozen had emphasized to Newt how much his materials had helped them. Many of these now joined the Hope and Opportunity budget group. The team had learned much from the 1979-1980 budget fights. "I'll bet you that's the model for how to run a project in the House thirty years from now," Newt told his staff.[7]

Added to the new members and the Budget of Hope team were also conservative Democrats such as Representatives Phil Gramm, Richard Ray and Ed Jenkins. Most of the Democrats came from the south and were dubbed the "boll weevils." They supported the president and conservative legislation almost as much as did the GOP and at least one, Gramm, actually switched parties. These members were finding the Democratic Party less and less hospitable as they felt a multiplicity of liberal and radical interest groups had undue influence in the party.[8]

Though this coalition of these conservative members assisted in a dramatic string of victories for President Reagan and the GOP in 1981 such as the Economic Recovery Tax Act in July, the AWACS bill in October and the farm and foreign aid bills in December, Reagan's success seemed to stall. Reagan's initiatives were moving slowly if at all and most House Republicans repudiated the Administration's budget proposal with the 1982 tax increases. Newt, though a great admirer of President Reagan, was not about to go back on the most consistent plank in all his campaign platforms: the need for a tax cut. At one point Newt was sufficiently upset that he accused the Senate Finance Committee chairman, Bob Dole, of being "the tax collector of the

---

[7] Gregorsky, *Second Two Years*, Gingrich Papers.

[8] Richard Ray, Interview by author, on videotape, 6 July 1989, GPH, Ingram Library, State University of West Georgia, Carrollton. Also see Jenkins, interview by author, on videotape, 21 May 1991 and 28 July 1998, GPH, Ingram Library, State University of West Georgia Archives, Carrollton.

welfare state," a comment that would be repeated by the press as evidence that Newt should not be taken seriously.

Newt had no interest in feuding with his President but his first loyalty was to the people of his district and to the principles he had espoused for years. Newt could respect a stand with which he disagreed if it was on principle and for what one considered the best interest of the country. Referring to criticism of Representative Ron Dellums, Newt said that Dellums was patriotic in his own way and was "sincerely trying to work for a better America as he understands it. While I disagree with him, I still respect him." He thought he owed it to his party and his President to disagree, as he would later with President Bush, when he thought he was right and to confront them with that disagreement in the hope that they would be open to change.

While planning the year's agenda with his staff in January 1982, Newt proposed to introduce thirty-four bills embodying what would become the Conservative Opportunity Society's (COS) legislative agenda. The staff collectively recoiled at the prospect and said he was in danger of "overreaching." He responded, "Over-reaching is the most admirable and the most American of the many American excesses...."[9]

While many Republicans now took their cues from the White House regarding legislation, Newt had his own agenda and supported the president when both agendas could be reconciled. He supported Reagan on most issues but thought the Administration was not properly selling the President's program as it should be sold. While Newt did not mind compromise, he did mind capitulation. He saw the GOP as deferring too much and too often to an arrogant Democratic Party leadership in 1982.

In 1982 he found neither the Democratic leadership nor the White House willing to engage him in serious legislative debate. While this situation was irksome at times it did free him to accomplish goals he felt were essential. Likewise, his staff, led by Gregorsky, dissuaded him from pursuing his thirty-four bill proposal, a decision he later rather wistfully regretted. Building the Republican majority, strengthening the national defense, reforming the military, pushing for a tax cut along the lines of the Kemp-Roth proposal, and developing the Conservative Opportunity Society topped Newt's agenda. He saw the COS as an

---

[9] Gregorsky, *Second Two Years*, Gingrich Papers.

organization that would advocate and work for conservative ideas and programs offering opportunity rather than dependency.

Building the GOP majority and the COS were inextricably linked. Properly done the COS development would draw not only conservative Republicans but also conservative Democrats and independents to his cause. "We must define ourselves in such a way that most Americans identify with us." Early in 1982 Newt had Catherine Brock type for him what would become a standard handout at his appearances. In the handout, Newt delineates his understanding of the differences between the COS and the "liberal welfare state." He compared, in stark comparison, the two different ways of viewing government and life.

COS "Government"// LWS

Honest money without inflation // A return to double-digit inflation
Jobs through economic growth // Jobs through temporary make work
Decentralized and flexible govt. institutions // Centralized & rigid govt. institutions
Local official needs to understand local community // Local official must follow federal rules and bureaucratic red tape
Citizen with problem talks to official closest for results // Citizen with problem has to go to the highest ranking official possible.
Stable tax levels & some tax cuts // Higher taxes on almost everything
Speeding up the arrival of the jobs & technologies // Propping up the failing businesses of the future and structures of the past.
Protecting the innocent by stopping criminals especially drug dealers // Criminals & drug dealers are not a real threat to our freedom — police are.

"Life"

People are responsible for what they do whether it's bad or good. // Society is ultimately responsible for everything that happens.
Traditional family values // Radical lifestyles
Equality of opportunity // Equality of result
Man creates resources // Resources limit man
Competition expands choice // Competition wastes resources
Savings and investing // Borrowing and overspending

Foreign nations are dangerous & the US is good // Foreign nations are
    benign, it is the US that is the problem.
We are the children of God, so voluntary prayer in school is natural. //
    God does not exist, or He is irrelevant, or He should be kept out of
    public life.

Newt included a COS reading list of four books: *The Third Wave* by
Alvin Toffler; *Megatrends* by John Naisbitt; *The Effective Executive* by
Peter Drucker; and *In Search of Excellence* by T.J. Peters and R.H.
Waterman.

When speaking at West Georgia College at a symposium on energy,
Newt distributed this handout. Some of Newt's former colleagues, while
praising his speech and agreeing with most of it, resented the COS
handout because it was much too simplistic. "The world is just not that
clear-cut," insisted Dr. Don Wagner, a friend and supporter. Wagner
and others argued that there were gray areas and the handout defined
the differences too sharply. Newt acknowledged their arguments but
responded that the handout was accurate and details about overlaps and
gray areas would defeat the purpose of the exercise. He thought his
point was made based on the responses he got showing that people
remembered the two alternatives even if they disagreed with his
simplistic presentation. If people look at the two choices they will, he
thought, choose the COS over the LWS. He continued using the
handout.

The structural organization needed to begin implementing the COS
doctrine was multifaceted. The structure needed in the GOP leadership,
the White House and the Senate consisted of four groups. The first
group, the GOP Whip Planning Committee was headed by Trent Lott
(who Newt called the "Godfather of the COS") and included Jack Kemp,
Guy Vander Jagt, Dick Cheney, Jim Martin and Phil Crane with Bob
Michel as ex officio. The committee provided strategic approval, project
oversight, tactical support and to coordinate with official GOP
leadership in the House, Senate and White House. Under Newt's
prodding the GOP Whip's office was expanding its duties far beyond
the traditional task of vote counting.

The second group was the GOP Wednesday Team that met at 9:00
A.M. every Wednesday. This group included Vin Weber, Bob Walker,
Dan Coats, George Brown, Henry Hyde, Ed Bethune, Mickey Edwards,

Judd Gregg and Dan Lungren. Their job was to figure out what strategy the team should use concerning timing and presentation of actions taken within the House itself. They controlled project coordination and were central to the development of the COS movement. Whether it was developing ideas or leading floor fights, recruiting or delivering "special orders" on C-SPAN these members provided the energy, ideas and leadership to make COS work.

The third group, the Outside Strategy Group, met each Wednesday for lunch and had a fluid membership depending on need and who was in town at a given moment. It was drawn from economic and social conservatives, conservative lobbyists, conservative intellectuals, GOP campaign strategists, general news media, and pollsters. It was primarily an advisory group that could also be helpful in spreading the word about COS efforts.

A fourth group, the Senior Advisory Group, was devised to meet once a month for a working breakfast and also had a fluid membership of GOP stalwarts such as Don Rumsfeld and Bill Brock. Their assignment was to give general advice and, more specifically, to help think about and plan for the long term creation of a national conservative GOP majority.

Newt met and worked with each of these groups and served as de facto chairman of three of them. To aid in crystallizing the thinking of the members, and more importantly, of many supporters, he and his wife Marianne put together a document entitled "Building the Conservative Opportunity Society: The Challenge in 1982 for America." The document noted that too many people were focusing on the wrong questions and on problems instead of opportunities.[10] "Let me reverse these current negative feelings. Frankly, I'm optimistic. The country continues to move in our direction. Americans continue to share our broad general vision of the future. Republicans as a party may lose elections. We may mismanage the economy enough that people reject our partisan label in some districts and some elections. But the public will almost certainly not embrace liberalism. Democrats will increasingly win to the degree that they accept the conservative opportunity society."

---

[10] 1982 campaign folder, Gingrich Papers.

He noted the forces favoring a conservative opportunity society were a somewhat fragile majority and were made up of three groups: economic conservatives, national defense conservatives, and social conservatives. He discussed how the liberals might try to drive wedges to break up the coalition. It is the job of the conservative leaders to "design issues, build alliances and pose questions in such a way that we bring together our three groups of conservatives."[11]

While Newt had his own reservations about the administration he still appreciated what it, and the President, offered for the conservative agenda. "Ronald Reagan is the great articulator of this basic value shift. The President is our best ally. If our values are correct, publicly advocating them will attract supporters. He challenged the readers, "Let us go out to the nation, to the people, to the political leaders of the next generation, and begin that building job. We have the resources, the energy, and the personnel to shape a nation if we have the courage to do so." He ended, "Let us join together in 1982 to build the bridge to a healthy conservative opportunity society. This is the challenge to our generation of Americans."[12]

In addition to engineering the building of the COS, Newt continued his recruitment of new members to the COS and worked hard to help elect Republicans to Congress. He also decided to put his ideas before the public by writing a book about his view of the future. Newt and Marianne created a first draft of *Window of Opportunity* toward the end of 1983. After receiving comments and suggestions from many of his colleagues, Newt rushed the manuscript to printer. By February it was ready, in time for the 1984 GOP national convention in Dallas, Texas.

The book is subtitled, "A Blueprint for the Future" and begins with these words, "There exists for the United States today a window of opportunity through which we can look, and—with luck and hard work—reach to create a bright and optimistic future for our children and grandchildren." [13] *Window of Opportunity* contained all the now famous Newt ideas contained in COS doctrine. When later criticized by his opponents for the book deal and for the way it was written as well,

---

[11] Ibid.

[12] Ibid.

[13] Newt Gingrich, *Window of Opportunity: A Blueprint for the Future.* (NY: Tor Publishing, 1984) p. 1.

Newt responded, "My book was a real book with real content and sold in real book stores."

Newt did more than write books and articles. During early summer 1982 he met with executives from his home district representing Southwire, Inc. (the largest wire distributor in the free world) who were concerned about high interest rates and continuing deficits that were costing them millions and causing layoffs. The 1982 budget deal the president had cut, Newt thought, would trade higher taxes for cuts in interest rates and an expansion of credit. Though the president's budget was supported by many Republicans and Southwire's owners, Newt had always opposed tax increases and supported tax cuts. He thought it would harm the Republicans in the November elections because "it made us no different than the Democrats." Two of his main goals, tax cuts and electing more Republicans to the House, were challenged by Reagan's actions. Newt talked to key leaders back home in the sixth district, met with his COS allies and checked the polls. Newt decided to oppose Reagan's budget.

"[Newt] quickly became the most prominent elected Republican to use the national media to defeat the President on a key vote," remembered Gregorsky.[14] Newt was everywhere on television in July and the first week in August. Taking the floor to speak against the bill he told his colleagues: "What you will decide in the next hour is simple: Who really matters to you? Do you listen to the strange, unexplainable alliances of powerful political opponents, who together form a political establishment in Washington? Or do you listen to the long, anguished voice of the American people, which in every referendum, every poll, every vote, for four years has begged us to cut taxes, not to raise them?" He continued, "You, the Members of the People's House, are the country's last stronghold against mistaken policy. I urge you, I beg you, to vote against this bill."[15]

By the end of the year Newt was offering new solutions to the budget problem and the deficit. Newt argued that the key to the budget dilemma was fairness, not national defense. He proposed a government-spending freeze on everything except new retirees becoming eligible for social security. Any federal spending growth in the future

---

[14] Gregorsky, *Second Two Years*, Gingrich Papers.

[15] *The Congressional Record*, vol. 128 August 1982, 19799-19802.

would have to come from new revenues. No special cases, defense or otherwise, would be considered. The President liked the idea and was indeed able to get partial freezes on hiring but the House rejected the idea of a general freeze.

Newt believed that the American people would accept some sacrifice as long as they believed that it was being asked of everyone. If one group seemed to be favored the freeze would not work. The country had pulled together during the Great Depression and World War II when the American people felt "we are all in this together." Franklin Roosevelt had pulled the people together in those great efforts and Newt thought Ronald Reagan could do it as well.

The tax conflict brought a clash with a former Budget of Hope ally, David Stockman. Stockman, now Director of the Office of Management and Budget, supported the tax increase. The debate between the two became heated and sometimes public. Stockman had agreed to come to Georgia for a Newt fund-raiser and honored that commitment. The tension and anger between the two during that event was almost palpable as Newt and Stockman talked in hushed whispers in the hallway outside the ballroom where Stockman was to speak.

While 1982 was a contentious year because of budget issues, it was also a confusing election year because of the suit challenging congressional district lines. Racial politics were alleged with the chairman of the House Reapportionment Committee, Representative Wilson, being accused of using racial epithets. Candidates were not sure when or if primaries would be held or the date of the general election. The primaries were finally held at the end of August with newspaper publisher and state legislator Jim Wood becoming the Democrat's nominee and Newt being unchallenged.

Newt's own campaign began strongly. He and his team had decided they needed to have a continuous campaign rather than trying to restart every two years. They used the name Friends of Newt Gingrich as their organizational umbrella and had added various groups in election years as needed. One example was Neighbors for Newt, an election year group that held coffees and blitzed subdivisions with literature and stickers for Newt. Also, under the direction of John and Pat Grunden a system was developed around a yearly fundraising dinner called the "Forward America Dinner" with a major conservative as guest speaker.

Wood was from Clayton County, the most populous county in the district and was a state representative. In addition, the governorship and all state offices were on the ballot and the Democrats worked to maximize their turnout. In keeping with this goal, Wood ran an especially negative campaign and seemed to be working to divest himself of much of the support he would normally expect. His treasurer in Coweta County went to the press and resigned from the Wood campaign because of its negativism. Newt's former aide, Kip Carter was now traveling around the district and working actively for Wood. Wood held "tomato sandwich rallies" and handed out "Wood Working Kits" and leaned heavily on the straight party vote. Representative Jim Jones, House Budget Committee chairman, and Senator John Glenn came in to speak for him and he associated with every state and local Democratic event possible.[16]

The Democrats were finally alert to the potential disaster of a rising GOP in Georgia and were running as a team on the idea that "if we don't stop them now every Democrat will be challenged down to the city council level." The Republican candidate for governor, Senator Bob Bell, a popular and well-qualified candidate, also ran on a straight party ticket. As a result the election was polarized as never before. This ruled out the Democrats for Gingrich and some of the bipartisan support he had received in past elections.

Wood sent a letter to all Democratic candidates and office holders stating, "The Republicans have a long range plan to capture every courthouse position and every elected office in the Sixth District. Don't be fooled by any overtures or accommodations which have been made — your job is on the Republican's list. Therefore it is in the best interest of all local Democratic officials to work toward the election of a Democratic Congressman."[17]

Wood attacked Newt at every turn. Speaking to the Douglasville Kiwanis in August, he said, "Newt is the chameleon of the Congress. He changes his stand on issues when it would be politically to his advantage." And "Newt is not a conservative, he's a radical." Wood accused Newt of letting "hundreds of special interests buy into his campaign," while he was accepting endorsements and money from

---

[16] 1982 Campaign Folder,Gingrich Papers.
[17] Ibid.

labor groups and the NEA/GAE [National Education Association/ Georgia Association of Educators. Negative stories about Newt were being spread around the district and were especially harmful in the new counties, Polk and Paulding, where the voters knew little about Newt and generally voted for Democrats on the local and state level. "We have a congressman who wants to make taxes easier for big business and the ultra rich. But not for us." Finally, Wood accused Newt of wanting to destroy Social Security and hurt senior citizens. Wood's negative campaigning continued until election day.[18]

Newt answered Wood in a series of four debates, though Wood wanted twelve. Newt stressed experience as the major difference between the candidates. He received endorsements from teachers in the Carrollton school system as opposed to the NEA/GAE. He used radio and newspaper ads that had him in conversation with "down-home folks" who told him what a good job he was doing. He stressed in his newspaper ads, "Newt Gingrich Is A Leader in fighting for things that concern your pocketbook." He hired consultants and, following their advice, handed out a series of flyers targeted at special interest groups stressing his concern for small businessmen, teachers, veterans, textile workers, tax payers, federal retirees and senior citizens. Using his usual large number of volunteers, Newt blanketed the district with these flyers. Some flyers were tailored to counties where debates were to be held, stating, for instance, "Douglas County [or whichever other county was relevant] Needs to Ask Jim Wood Three Questions." The flyer would then list three questions, damaging to Wood, that would serve to make him especially angry and ill-tempered as he tried to answer them at the debates.

In a letter to black constituents Newt reminded them he had voted for the Voting Rights Act and Wood said he would have voted against it. Newt had helped Morehouse Medical College get almost $6,000,000 in grants and had worked with Senator Sam Nunn, Georgia's senior senator, to develop minority business outreach programs with the Defense Department and with Lockheed. He also had served as the GOP spokesman in passing a bill to place a statue of Martin Luther

---

[18] Ibid.

King, Jr. in the Capitol and promised to do all he could to help them with their social security, veterans, disability and Medicare problems.[19]

Newt touted his record of "bringing home the bacon." He was asked how he could be for cutting "pork" spending and then be responsible for so much coming to Georgia such as highway, rapid transit (MARTA) and airport money. His answer used the metaphor of the level playing field. So long as everyone is playing by the same rules, then competition for federal funds is fair. He wanted to change the law so everyone was playing by the better set of rules. "You ought to fight for a cheap, overall budget, and then, within that overall budget, you ought to fight for as much as you can get for constituents." said Newt. As 2 November approached, Guy Scull, Newt's campaign manager felt confident of victory. Newt knew he would win but wanted to get over 60 percent in order to ward off possible future opponents.[20]

At the Gingrich victory party at the Ramada Renaissance Hotel at the Atlanta airport he stayed in his room getting results from around the country in hopes that the GOP was doing better than Jim Baker had predicted. The numbers were not good for the Republican party. Some observers used the word "disastrous." Whereas the GOP had gained thirty-three seats in 1980 they lost twenty-six in 1982. Newt had not expected such a poor showing for the conservatives.

When he claimed victory that evening he was doing so with a 55.3 percent majority, not the 60 percent he had wanted. Though he did not show it to the crowd, he was disappointed. His own vote was down from 58 percent in 1980 and he lost four counties (the two new counties, Polk and Paulding, and two of the same Democratic counties he lost in 1980, Heard and Haralson.)

Even with his percentage of the vote down and the national losses there were reasons for optimism. He had run 17.4 points ahead of Bell, the GOP candidate for governor, in the sixth district, done well when other Republicans were losing around the country and he had raised his numbers in his home county, Carroll, from 51 percent to 53.5 percent. All in all, he viewed his second term as positive. The voters agreed by sending him back to continue his work.

---

[19] Ibid.

[20] Guy Scull, interview by author, tape recording, 5 April 1995, Gingrich Papers.

9

DREAMING HEROIC DREAMS

In a meeting shortly after Thanksgiving 1982 Newt met with Gregorsky, Laurie James, and Steely to talk about his "essential job for the next two years." He began by saying that 1982 had been sobering. He said he would try to "avoid fights and avoid trying to directly influence the behavior of the Republican Party and the White House." While all present knew this goal was an unattainable goal given his nature and previous behavior, Newt's statement did reflect his feeling at the time. "I really can't influence the White House—nor can anyone, even the President."

Newt had taken some criticisms from the "old Bulls" of the party for the 1982 losses. Unwilling to dwell on those defeats, he viewed them as a learning experience and directed his time and effort toward his larger goals. "The Republican Party is sufficiently in disrepair that its central problem is one of right doctrine and right cadres, and it doesn't do any good to preach right doctrine to people who have no capacity for learning it."[1]

Newt said he'd try to model "right doctrine and right behavior," less opposition and more cooperation, within the party framework, at least for the developing COS core group. He saw no purpose in directly opposing President Reagan or other party leaders. He thought it would be much better to enlarge his own forces and conquer by indirection. Newt focused on formally organizing the COS and on working to elect more GOP congressmen.

---

[1] Frank Gregorsky, *The Second Two years*, Gingrich Papers.

Following the 1982 campaign Newt and Marianne had moved to Clayton County close to the Atlanta airport. After their marriage in 1981 they lived for a while in a small farmhouse in Carroll County until a broken shower pipe forced them to find other accommodations. They lived in a Carrollton apartment for a year and then decided to move to Clayton County to be closer to the airport and Newt's main district office.

After winning reelection by 55% in 1982 Newt worked to establish the COS and develop himself as a speaker to help elect other GOP candidates. He supported the M. L. King holiday, advocated a larger space program, voted for the Alaska Land Act, called for Interior Secretary James Watts's resignation, and polished his use of C-Span to reach a National audience. His third term was working out successfully. Nineteen eighty-four was an election year almost without an opponent. The Democrats nominated Representative Gerald Johnson, a five-term state legislator from Carroll County, and a friend of Newt's. Both candidates knew the outcome from the start and hardly a crossword was uttered by either against the other. Newt did not even bother to hire a full-time campaign manager but used his district administrator, Liz Camp, to supervise it after she finished work each day and on her lunch hour. A full-time organization was established for Friends of Newt Gingrich (FONG) with all the necessary accoutrements such as fund raising, barbecues, yard sign projects, bumper sticker blitzes, debates, and so on.[2]

Camp and the FONG organization ran the campaign with Newt paying little attention and showing up in the district only when it was necessary. He carried out his normal congressional duties but was not overly concerned about his reelection. He even left the country, for a debate with the Vice President of Nicaragua at the Oxford Union in England during the campaign. Most of the time he was traveling around the country helping GOP candidates. While some of the FONG people were irritated at his absence from the campaign, Newt spent that time building toward his goal of a GOP majority in Congress and improving his relationships with the newly elected members who would later remember Newt during votes for GOP leadership positions.

---

[2] 1984 Campaign folders, Gingrich Papers.

Johnson was nominated because he was the only serious candidate to offer. Speaker Tom Murphy did his best to recruit someone against Gingrich but with no success. Gingrich carried the election by his highest percentage ever, 66.53 percent, carrying every county in the district. Asked why he had run, Johnson, a real estate broker, said, "I needed to do something to make a living. I was spending so much time legislating that I wasn't selling real estate. I needed to go into one or the other full time and it seemed like a good idea at the time." He had hoped the Democrats would nominate a strong presidential candidate to bolster his own campaign. They nominated Walter Mondale and President Reagan ran a "Morning in America" campaign that handily defeated Mondale and helped carry a host of other Democrats with him, including Johnson.

During his fourth term Newt worked at changing his aggressive image. He worked for a balanced budget with Senator Mack Mattingly and became involved with military reform. He expanded his national speaking schedule as he focused on building a GOP majority in the Congress and in state houses all across the country. Two years later the Democrats ran Crandle Bray, a bureaucrat from Clayton County, the most populous in the district. Bray had both experience and good party ties. He was popular in his home county and people liked him. Newt took him more seriously than Johnson and the press pronounced him a worthy candidate to take on Gingrich.

The first debate with Bray virtually decided the election. In the debate, each candidate made an opening statement and then asked his opponent a question. Newt went first. He noted that Bray described himself as a "conservative Democrat" and wondered if he would mind telling the audience who he had voted for president in 1984. Bray sputtered momentarily, but no words came out. Newt said he was proud to have voted for Ronald Reagan. Under prodding, Bray finally admitted he'd voted for Mondale.

Newt renewed his travels for GOP candidates, helping them raise money and offering advice at every opportunity. Issue papers, workshops, and similar activities were coordinated through the party. Newt knew he could raise his election numbers by spending more time in the district but decided, because he knew he would win, to work with the Republican candidates to help build a GOP majority in the House.

Bray was a more capable candidate than Johnson and improved as the campaign went on. Newt's absence from the district and the Democrats' effort at straight party voting with Governor Joe Frank Harris at the head of the ticket lowered Newt's victory margin to 54.27 percent.

Marianne's health complicated the campaign as well. She injured a spinal disc and was in considerable pain much of the time. While talking to visitors she would frequently lie on the floor with her legs over an upside down chair trying to get some relief. Her absence from the campaign trail caused all manner of rumors to be spread by the opposition's supporters of Newt's opponent and that disturbed her. Physical therapy improved her condition and she was back on her feet by Christmas but it was a rough time for the Gingrichs.

The greatest blow of the 1986 campaign for the Republicans was the loss of the GOP majority in the US Senate. One of those who lost was Newt's close friend Mack Mattingly. Sen. Mattingly ran a lack-luster campaign and stayed in Washington voting and tending to business while his opponent, Congressman Wyche Fowler, campaigned all over Georgia asking people if they had seen Mattingly. Fowler also had the full support of the conservative Democratic establishment, including Speaker Tom Murphy.

While the Mattingly loss cut Newt deeply, the 1986 election held some promise for the Republican Party. Georgia's fourth congressional district elected a second Republican, Pat Swindall, to join Newt in the House. Others Newt had campaigned for also won around the country and the ranks of Republican House members were slowly changing to include more activist members.

Ever since coming to Congress Newt had been concerned about Social Security. He had introduced bills regularly, with no success, to make Congressmen pay into Social Security and he had refused to take the Congressional pension until they did. He did finally enroll in the pension plan and Congress did join Social Security as well as their own retirement program. Newt was concerned with the state of Social Security but each time he raised the subject his opponents would accuse him of attacking the elderly. Still, all the serious reports he was hearing concerning Social Security and all the in-house talk among House members, told him that something had to be done or the system would fail.

Newt was concerned about preserving and protecting the benefits for the elderly. He was also concerned about what the exploding cost of medical care was doing to younger Americans. Many young adults thought the system was failing and would not be around for them. In the fall of 1980 at a town hall meeting in Riverdale, Georiga at the fire station a former West Georgia student, Kurt Jocoy, asked him, "Why should I have to pay into Social Security? Where are the benefits for me? I'd do better by investing it." Newt told him that is just the way it is and Jocoy, somewhat upset at such a dismissive answer, told Newt "You are full of shit! You are just an opportunist." Though the exchange was unpleasant it did draw Newt's attention to the seriousness of Jocoy's questions.[3]

Toward the end of the 1986 campaign Newt told a small group of key advisers that he was working on a proposal to help salvage the Social Security system. The staff was aghast, thinking Newt was about to introduce this proposal in the waning days of the campaign. Instead, he intended to introduce it at a Congressional Club dinner election night and release it to the press the next day. It was entitled, "A Stable, Permanent Social Security System: An Opportunity Society Answer to James Roosevelt."

Newt discussed the problems with the Federal Insurance Contributions Act pointing out that the system could not sustain the financial burden very much longer. He noted that change had happened in all our lives and Americans dealt with change. Grandparents were worried about their financial future and therefore "we should create a financially sound retirement system so senior citizens won't have to worry." He proposed abolishing the FICA Social Security tax and replacing it with mandatory individual retirement accounts (IRAs) as well as establishing an anti-poverty retirement fund financed by a value added tax instead of the FICA. Social Security and Medicare trust funds would be taken off budget so they could not be used to balance the rest of the budget. "A new off budget trust fund would be created to raise all senior citizens above the poverty level."[4]

Newt said he would abolish restrictions on seniors working beyond the age of sixty-five and also abolish taxes on Social Security benefits.

---

[3] Mel Steely, notes on Jocoy conversation, 1995, MSC, Gingrich Papers.

[4] 1986 Campaign folder, *A Stable Permanent Social Security System*, Gingrich Papers.

He openly admitted his was not the only possible solution and invited others to join him in proposing solutions. He wanted to start a debate. He was starting a Chamber of Commerce state-wide tour talking about upcoming legislation and used the tour to spread his ideas around the state. He felt the time had come when senior citizens and others were ready to talk about change and would be supportive in finding a solution to the problem. He was wrong.

The press and his opponents came to realize that Newt had waited until after the election to propose his ideas. He was accused of duplicity and of wanting to "do away with Social Security." In a sense both were accurate charges. He had waited until after the election to avoid giving his enemies a cudgel to use against him and with the hope that people could focus on what he was saying instead of automatically turning the issue into partisan activity. While he did not want to destroy Social Security he felt it must be changed to provide for future needs.

His colleagues regarded his proposals with astonishment and an old friend and ally, Jack Kemp, questioned his sanity at having brought up the issue at all. The AARP wanted to keep the system as it was with more money being added as needed. The Democrats intended to use any discussion of Social Security as a wedge issue against any Republican who raised it. The future Speaker learned the lesson well. In 1995 when budget changes were being discussed Newt made sure that Social Security was taken off the table for discussion. He was not ready to start that fight until the other changes were already made.

While realizing the risks inherent in discussing Social Security he was upset about what he considered a callous disregard displayed by the Democrats and the organizations that were supposed to have the interest of the elderly at heart. "You'd think they don't understand what is going to happen. This is a train wreck coming and they are not willing to do anything to stop it," he told his staff.

He also opened himself to criticism with his emphasis on the space program. From the outset Newt was a great advocate of space exploration and the practical uses it might provide. After the 1980 election he had encouraged Bob Weed to set up an organization to support the space program and had utilized a space devotee, Jim Muncy, to create position papers and working documents on space issues.[5] In the early days Muncy spent so much time around Newt's office that some thought he was on the staff. A major section of Newt's book, *Window of Opportunity*, was devoted to space.[6] He had talked so much about space and technology, including computers, that he received a staff memo in February 1982 warning that his constituents were concerned that he was not putting his voters' issues in perspective. His staff urged that issues like crime, defense, inflation and jobs needed to be put before space exploration. Newt's opponents and the press had fun tweaking him about "space citizenship" and space wars.[7] In April Newt was front and center speaking about Space Week 1982. He would not be deterred from pushing the space agenda he thought was so important though he did increase his attention to the other issues as well.

Newt has been fascinated with space and the promise it holds. Not only did he encourage Weed to establish a space organization, but he also founded the House Space Caucus and worked to make sure funds for NASA were not cut any more than necessary. After a visit to a NASA facility he instructed his staff to adopt NASA procedures and check lists to become more efficient. He was fascinated by space movies such as *2001 Space Odyssey*, the *Star Wars* trilogy, and recently the heroic, NASA-centered *Apollo 13* drama. He supported President Reagan's SDI defense system and compiled a "Space Bill of Rights." In an article published in 1984 in *Future 21: Directions For America in the 21st Century*, he advocated investment in space as a natural byproduct of the opportunity society.[8] He met with his space staffers in January 1983 to plan strategy to work for a space station and popularize space concepts. He spoke to the NASA Advisory Council in February and worked with Dr. John Keyworth, President Reagan's science advisor, to help advance the SDI program. He appeared on national television whenever there was an opportunity to advocate space causes. The Atlanta media started referring to Newt as "Newt Skywalker" and stated that his interest seemed to be more in outer space than down

---

[5] Jim Muncy, Interview by author, tape recording, 3 December 1994, Gingrich Papers.

[6] Newt Gingrich, *Window of Opportunity,* Chaps. 11, 12.

[7] Space Folder, MSC, Gingrich Papers. See also Warner & Berley, *Newt Gingrich*, p. 106.

[8] Space Folder, MSC, Gingrich Papers.

here on earth. While not giving up his space interests, Newt was aware that these comments were not helpful to his overall agenda. He began to focus again on issues of more immediate interest to people in the sixth district. One such issue was national defense.

By the late 1970s the modern US Army was at its nadir. A lost war in Vietnam, low public esteem and the exodus of the professional non-commissioned officers' corps were serious problems. Also rising illiteracy, drugs and race problems plagued the military. The administration offered little hope that the situation would improve in the near future. For Newt, all these factors painted a dismal picture of US national defense.

The lessons of Verdun were still close to Newt and he strongly believed in the need for an informed, prepared military. He agreed with John Philpot Curran's sentiment, "Eternal vigilance is the price of liberty." In the late 1970s Newt believed America was not prepared. Our NATO forces had been stripped to fight a war in Vietnam and had not been restored to combat strength. National resolve was indecisive and the shameful treatment inflicted on returning Vietnam veterans caused many to leave the military and potential recruits to decide not to join.

Newt was likewise dissatisfied with American foreign policy. Though America had forced out dictators in Nicaragua and Iran, each was replaced with a decidedly anti-American government. Our allies in NATO complained of indecision and lack of leadership and some European leaders such as Chancellor Helmut Schmidt were distinctly hostile to President Carter over such issues as the neutron bomb deployment and pressure from Carter to expand Germany's economy more than he felt was prudent. The Soviets had moved into Afghanistan forcing Carter to issue his "Carter Doctrine" proclaiming the Persian Gulf in our area of national interest.

After he was elected Newt became dedicated to doing all he could to resuscitate the American military. Between 1979-1980 Newt made contacts in the Pentagon to learn some of the key players. The most important military relationship Newt developed was that with General E. C. "Shy" Meyer, the Army Chief of Staff. Meyer was as concerned as Newt about what was happening to the Army. He was a first class soldier who was determined to reverse all the negative trend lines and restore the US Army to a position of excellence. Meyer introduced

Gingrich to General Donn Starry, the commander of the Army's Training and Doctrine (TRADOC) Command. Starry too, felt the Army was becoming one of managers and careerists instead of soldiers. The Army had to reequip itself and properly train its personnel with appropriate doctrine.[9]

Two clusters of military reformers were developing outside the formal military structure in the early 1980s. The Military Reform Caucus was made up of Senators and Congressmen, including Newt, Dick Cheney and Gary Hart. These officials described themselves as "cheap hawks" and were concerned with the state of the military and a common determination to recreate a totally dominant military force. A second cluster, the Military Reform Group, was made up of neither legislators nor military people. They were largely young men, some veterans, some congressional staff or those attached to quasi-military organizations in Washington. They supported the idea of maneuver warfare, a concept adopted by the US Marine Corps, rather than the old concept of attrition warfare. They were also against super technology and very complicated weapons. To them the Bradley vehicle, the M1 tank and the F-14 fighter were all a waste of money.[10]

Newt did not belong to the Military Reform Group but interacted with them, as did Hanser as Newt's agent. In 1981 Hanser took an unpaid leave of absence from his teaching duties and came, at Newt's request, to Washington to work with Newt and the military in something of a crash program to redesign Army doctrine. He and Newt visited all the Army schools and most of those of the other services.[11] Newt, indeed, began to lecture somewhat frequently at most of these schools. He also became the speaker, on a regular basis, at the Capstone Dinner for newly appointed general officers of all the services, a practice he continued as Speaker.

The Army had begun to make changes in doctrine in 1976 with the development of the "Active Defense" manual (100-5). Change was needed and the Army knew it. General Creighton Abrams, the Army Chief of Staff, told Starry, who was on his way to be a corps commander in Europe, to "Go out and get the Army off its ass!" Starry says at that time the troops felt "they were just speed bumps for the Soviets on their

---

[9] Gen. E.G. Meyer Interview, 20 September 1995.

[10] Ibid.

[11] Hanser Interview, 8 June 1995.

way to the Rhine." About the same time Abrams was putting together a new arrangement of the old Continental Command. It would now be in two parts. Command would be housed at Fort McPherson (FORSCOM) and training and doctrine (TRADOC) at Fort Monroe. General Bill Depui was the first commander at TRADOC. Depui was an ROTC officer who served with the 90th Division in Europe during World War II. While there he witnessed fatal accidents involving soldiers. As a result, he wanted to limit the occurrence of such unnecessary and costly accidents. He soon took over TRADOC at its inception in 1973 and pioneered in the doctrine and internal reform areas. By the time Starry took over at TRADOC in 1977 the Army was changing.[12]

Starry noted quickly that congressional criticism of "Active Defense" was a problem. There was some justification for that criticism. The 1976 version of the 100-5 manual had stressed countering the enemy's first echelon attack but did not do much to address the follow-up echelons. Starry decided to have a bright brigadier general, Don Morelli, take care of that problem. Morelli was tasked with the problem of going to see the critics and in effect co-opting them. One by one he took to his task. He was personable and diplomatic in addition to being bright and was able to persuade his critics to sign on to help bring about the needed change.

Starry read a speech Newt had given on the House floor in extension of remarks of 24 September 1980. The speech was entitled "Blunt Talk About War, the Military and National Survival" and discussed problems facing the military. Starry was impressed and sent Morelli around to see Gingrich. Starry was open to legislative leaders who wanted to make a substantive contribution and Morelli delivered that message. Some like Sam Nunn and Newt Gingrich responded constructively. Others were critical with little or nothing to add and were considered irritants by the military but important nevertheless because they could at least put the issues out where people could talk about them.

"You've got to talk with this guy. He's got some good ideas," Morelli told Starry after visiting with Newt. Starry found Gingrich to be very interested in how to change large organizations. Newt had been

---

[12] Gen. Donn Starry Interview, 12 December 1995.

through some of this during the changes President Pafford made at West Georgia College. Newt had worked with Mattingly and Coverdell to change the Georgia GOP. While he was working with the Army to bring about change in that organization he was at the same time trying to spur changes in the Republican Party in the House.

The Conservative Opportunity Society (COS) was the vehicle for that change. Newt reorganized the minority whip office by broadening its traditional role and later, as Speaker, changed the role of the Speaker, the House, and in a sense, the role of government itself. He aspired to redirect the course of American history away from the liberal welfare state model. He had been a reformer all his adult life...not for the sake of change alone but to bring about change for the better. Newt wanted to, in the words of the Black Panthers, bring back "Power to the People" and away from Washington.

Generals Abrams and Depui had seen what Abrams called "the horrible price we pay for non-readiness...a price of lives lost in battle." The Army was on its way to change when the Reform Caucus came along. Once they understood what was happening some, like Nunn and Gingrich, became ready participants in that change. By 1980–1981 General Meyer was telling Starry, "Go ahead. Newt's very supportive of what we are doing; we've got Newt on our side." He was indeed on their side. Starry remembers, "His support was essential. He was a very useful fellow. He and Sam Nunn kept Congress off our backs so we could do our work...they helped defuse dissent."[13]

According to Hanser, Newt had several roles: [H]e interacted with not only the commanders but with individuals, for example, the principle writer of the new 100-5 worked with Newt who edited and corrected the first drafts of the manual. He wrote and participated in conferences and workshops such as the 1982 Callaway Workshop on Modeling and Simulation of Land Combat where he gave a speech on 'The Need for Historical and Political Inputs to the Modeling and Simulation of Warfare.'"[14] He also spoke at the 1984 Callaway Workshop sponsored by Georgia Tech. In 1983 he, Hanser, Walter Jones and David Warnick put together a 150 page paper entitled, "On Survival: A Comprehensive Critique of Our National Defense System." As late as spring 1992 Newt was being interviewed for *ASWlog*, the

---

13 Ibid.
14 Hanser Interview, 8 August 1995.

antisubmarine warfare magazine, where he talked about technology and the future of the Navy as he argued for a "coherent national strategy" at the end of the Cold War.

In addition to writing and speaking about the military, Newt also served as an advisor, educator and inspirer as he regularly lectured at the various military schools. Hanser has noted that one of the most valuable things Newt does is to teach the proper interaction between the senior military officers and the civilian political leaders. By now almost all the senior military leaders have heard or worked with Newt.

General Ed Burba, now retired, is a Purple Heart veteran of Vietnam and has worked with Newt for over a decade. He and Starry continued their advisory association after retirement and according to Newt have been "very helpful." Burba was a colonel working for General Meyer in the Pentagon in the early 1980s when he first had contact with Newt. He then served as assistant commandant and commandant at the Infantry School at Fort Benning before eventually becoming FORSCOM commander in Atlanta at Fort McPherson in the early 1990s.[15]

Burba's most vivid memory of Newt was of Gingrich's second visit to speak to the annual Infantry Conference at Fort Benning in 1987. A dinner was held at the commandant's home following the day's activities. The Army and its current situation was the general topic of discussion. After the dinner Newt and the officers adjourned to the living room where Burba had set up a terrain board for use in discussing new weapon deployment on the battlefield using various tactical vignettes. Special emphasis was put on the use of the new Bradley fighting vehicle and its importance on the battlefield. Burba had planned for the discussion to last two hours but they were there until after 2:00 A.M.

One of the participants was Colonel Bill Hartzog, later TRADOC commander. Hartzog commanded the 197th Infantry Brigade and had exercises planned for the next morning. Newt said he wanted to watch these actions personally because they were concerned with urban warfare. After two hours' sleep, Newt rose at 4:00 A.M. to watch Hartzog's troops go through their paces implementing some of the policies Newt had discussed the previous evening. Burba was impres-

---

[15] Gen. Ed Burba, 5 July 1995.

sed with Newt's willingness to sacrifice for the sake of improving the military..[16]

"Newt fired everybody up," Burba remembers. "Everybody just immediately had ideas based on his ideas. He used that as a point of departure for a lot of very stimulating discussions that occurred. He used the Socratic method to bring out what he wanted to know. He was an honest broker and didn't have his own agenda but was seriously looking for answers. He was willing to do his homework and he knew his subjects."

In November 1987 Newt went out to Fort Ord to talk with Burba about light infantry and then down to the National Training Center (NTC) at Fort Irwin, California. Newt was accompanied by Bo Callaway, former Secretary of the Army, West Point graduate and Korean War veteran. Steve Hanser also attended and had begun regularly accompanying Newt and going as his emissary to the Naval War College and other military schools as well.

Callaway and Hanser stayed in VIP quarters at the training center but Newt insisted on going into the field with the troops. Burba had been impressed with Newt's "grasp of tactics and doctrine as well as his instincts for warfare fighting...cogent and interesting." He was honing these at the NTC, in the field, unshaven, unwashed and exhausted most of the time. The last twenty-four hours Newt switched sides and joined the opposition forces and participated in a night attack on the "American" forces wherein the "American" position was infiltrated and the operations officer was captured by the opponent forces. Newt greatly enjoyed the exercise. So did Hanser, who participated in the final tank attack in one of the new M1 tanks. The two then sat in on the postmortem, i.e., debriefing, of the battle.

Newt depended a good deal on Hanser to be his eyes and ears concerning military issues. A military historian by training, Hanser was described by Burba as "Newt's right-hand-man. He is a man of substance. He was there because he believed in Newt Gingrich, what Gingrich stood for and what he was seeking to do and felt like he could help him...and he did."

Burba was impressed with Newt's concern for the National Guard and Reserve units. That concern went back to the early 1980s when the

---

16 Ibid.

Guard came up with a report called "Vista 1999." Newt and his aide Mike Burns worked diligently to have the Defense Department study the report because he thought it would improve the Guard. The Army responded and when an amendment covering its cost was added to the FY 1983 budget on 29 July 1982, it passed the House with Newt's support and encouragement. He was worried about Guard readiness and went with Burba to visit the Guard in the field, the Mojave Desert, for two days to look at every aspect of combined arms operations. After returning he phoned the General with the message, "We've got to do better by the National Guard." He sent the same message in a letter to both Burba and to the Army Chief of Staff, General Carl Vuono. The Army listened and though they were already moving in that direction with a new summer program they modified it according to his insights.[17]

The Army depended on Newt for help in other areas. He had helped Burba with an issue of Reserve Command and Control that was involved in pending legislation. By this time Newt was the Minority Whip and responded to the general's request by inviting him up to Washington to hear him out. They scheduled a breakfast meeting for the following morning. Later that afternoon Newt made his stand on the budget rejecting the tax increase approved by President Bush. Newt was immediately under fire but impressed Burba by still finding time for him and then making sure the Army received what it needed. He was also helpful in making sure the Bradley fighting vehicle received congressional approval in spite of strong opposition. He had watched the weapon work at Fort Benning and thought it was needed.

When Newt came back from visiting the troops during the Gulf War he stopped by Fort McPherson to discuss with Burba what he had seen there. About two thirds of the troops sent to the Persian Gulf were under Burba's command and Burba had asked Newt to please pay special attention to two or three issues while there. Newt "reported in" and walked through a whole series of issues with Burba and his senior staff. He had done this before 1988 when he spoke to a large group of general officers in Atlanta.

Respecting their experience, Newt called on military leaders as well as civilian experts whenever he thought their advice would be helpful.

---

17 Ibid.

Newt and Starry met with Senator Barry Goldwater, Steve Hanser and Goldwater's aide, discussing how to change a large organization while maintaining the organization's order and operations. Starry recommended note taking in a special book and Newt was quick to take the advice and follow up. Starry also stressed delegating, as he had done with Morelli.[18]

Newt was taking what he had learned about organization and applying it to his House efforts at change. One of the political experts he consulted concerning organization and motivation was Richard Nixon. By 1983 Newt understood that his staff could not handle all the necessary tasks. Newt and Marianne flew to New York during the Christmas break and met with former President Richard Nixon to seek his advice. Newt admired Nixon's grasp of strategy and tactics and sought his advice on how to win the GOP majority in the House.[19]

Over dinner they discussed a wide range of issues and the Gingrichs found Nixon a delightful host. As it turned out he, like Newt, was concerned about the attitude of the Republican leadership concerning change. Nixon too thought they had accepted the idea of being in a permanent minority status. "Change would not come easy," he warned. According to Newt, Nixon thought to achieve a change in attitude Newt and his group would have to become more active and force the issue. In an interview with the *Washington Post* he said Nixon commented that the House GOP had to become "more interesting, more energetic, and more idea-oriented." He was advising the right man because Newt was already thinking in that direction. Like Nixon, Newt "thinks in terms of decades, he forces the implementation of grand strategies, and he has an overarching, if often inexplicable, perspective based on long studies of government and the human condition," noted Gregorsky. Newt's approach had long-term benefits but confused and frustrated his staff at the time because he did not communicate to them what he was doing.[20]

Newt was concerned with staff reaction and the fact that much of what he wanted was not being accomplished. He asked Steely to interview the staff and give him a report on the problem. Steely interviewed ten of the key staffers and reported in a 10 April 1983

---

[18] Starry Interview, 12 July 1995.

[19] Gingrich Interview, 11 August 1984.

[20] Ibid.

memo to Newt, "...staffers feel intellectually and professionally confused by you and your most recent behavior. They don't know where you are heading and have the feeling that you don't either. Or, at best, you know and simply don't know how to communicate your vision to them. The feeling seems to be that you need unlimited money, unlimited staff and general support to pursue unlimited goals."[21]

Of course, the goals were limited, but of grand design. Acquiring a Republican majority, changing the course of American history and "saving the west" were not on the agendas of most congressional staffers. Better organization and control, delegation and the use of step-by-step projects was needed. Communicating intent in a clear manner was important. Staff, other activist Members, and GOP Party leaders, as well as the public, had to understand what was expected. Newt and Marianne had put together a couple of papers earlier outlining the problem, the "Key Steps" document and "Building the Conservative Opportunity Society." They carried the message that "We...are in fact building a new America around a new statement, a statement that *traditional American values work and when combined with advanced technology will allow us to build a conservative opportunity society"* (Gingrich's emphasis). [22]

Newt was carrying the COS message to the Party and the public before his talk with Nixon. He had been using the phrase "opportunity society" for a couple of years as he compared it to the "liberal welfare state." He identified his group by carefully defining his opponents in such a way that few wanted to belong to their group. "Everyone who does not consider themselves part of their group should be ours." While he was carrying the message, and having some success receiving party and press attention, his success was more mixed within the House itself. The losses of the 1982 election, the meeting with Nixon, and the realization that his staff would not be able to carry the load for him all came together at about the same time. The formal organization of the COS would be the answer.

The activists around Newt had worked together using guerrilla tactics to gain a victory here and there. By 1983 Newt had developed a close relationship with a handful of colleagues, especially Bob Walker

---

[21] Mel Steely, staff memo 10 April 1983, MSC, Gingrich Papers.

[22] Gregorsky Interview, 2 December 1994. See also Gingrich Papers, 1984 Campaign Folder.

and Vin Weber. Walker's love of action on the House floor opened the door to the great success they had using "special orders." Walker, even before knowing Newt, had been awarding the "tarnished peanut award" to some Carter official who had been especially incompetent that month. He thought, "The minority party was at its best on the House floor because it was there that they were at their greatest strength." There was little or no chance to accomplish anything in committees so the floor was the alternative.[23]

Walker traces the COS to the late 1979 "Project Majority Task Force" which "had high hopes but drifted off into nowhere." It gave the activist something to do and served the COS leadership's purpose but it had no mechanism for acting on ideas. Newt had been somewhat successful working with the Republican National Congressional Committee because of Representative Vander Jagt but no major changes were made.

Gingrich was certainly key to the development of the COS. As Walker expressed it, "He was the one who decided if we were going to be successful we needed to weld together an organization with a dynamic." Walker continued, "He recruited activists one by one. He got about twelve of us meeting in his Longworth office working in a coordinated fashion. The driving force that welded this [COS] together was the Reagan Revolution. Seeing the results of the 1980 election was the motivation that encouraged us to come together, to try to promote that agenda more actively." Their agenda and that of President Reagan coincided in many ways and while they no longer had Carter to attack they had Reagan to support.

The Reagan administration did split the Party in a way. Those who wanted to govern found themselves resenting those activists, like Newt and Walker, who could not give up bomb throwing. "It became harder to make activism a part of overall policy. We developed ideas and sought out allies."[24] One ally in the leadership was Representative Trent Lott who Newt described as the "godfather" of COS. Lott was especially helpful by hosting a weekly luncheon for the group to meet and plan strategy. He served as a bridge between the Old Bull leaders and the upstart activists. His main service was to interpret their

---

23 Walker Interview, 17 July 1989.
24 Ibid.

activities and plans to the leadership and keep the latter off the activists' backs.

Lott was also helpful, as was Dick Cheney, in helping the COS work within the party. "We had to become better at what we did, at explaining ideas and making alliances," remembers Walker. Jack Kemp served as the symbolic leader of the movement but was never very actively involved in the day to day activities or running COS. "The whole Kemp aura helped us. His kind of political style of wanting to be positive and wanting outreach to new groups was the essence of what we were trying to achieve." Bringing in new allies was important. Newt, speaking to Georgia Republicans in May 1984, told them he was not worried about Jesse Jackson registering new minority voters. "The ones who want to get ahead and have their children live better are with us. We need to bring in everyone who is not one of them."[25]

Bob Michel, the Minority Leader, was willing to communicate with Newt and the COS and to accept some new concepts. He had frequent conversations with Lott and Newt as well as other members of the leadership. "Michel always listened," said Walker. Newt always spoke with great admiration, sometimes mixed with frustration, about the leader. "He puts up with a lot from me," Newt said. There was no feeling that Michel needed to be replaced, according to Walker, but rather a feeling that when they were at cross-purposes they had a responsibility to "move him along."[26]

By spring 1983 it was time to move the COS organization along. Newt simply approached those congressmen whose records suggested activist allies and invited them to a meeting. According to Walker, "The process was evolutionary and ultimately produced a fairly cohesive group with four up-front men (Newt, Weber, Walker, and Connie Mack) who took the lead on issues with solid backing from the other ten or twelve.

Newt was beginning to understand the difficulty of managing organizations, as reflected by his meeting with Starry and Senator Goldwater where they discussed management and delegation. Newt approached individual members he thought would be receptive. He then sent an invitation via a "Dear Republican Colleague" mailing to the rest of the House GOP.

---

[25] Gingrich Papers, 1984 Campaign Folder.
[26] Walker Interview, 17 July 1989.

The 8 June "Dear Colleague" was essentially a document exhorting them and inviting them to a meeting to discuss "possible management and communications reform."[27] Newt caught much criticism for this publication because it did not acknowledge work already being done by the leadership who, with their allies, saw it as presumptive. A week later a more humble letter went out, on the same theme, stressing cooperation with the leadership. Newt noted that "the idealized model of a more powerful system is not a reflection of personalities....What is lacking is the systemic approach to multiply the effectiveness of individuals and to draw all Republican Members into the effort." "Virtually the entire leadership," he said, "has been aggressively involved in developing new systems and new approaches." He ended the letter with an effort at keeping the bridge to the leadership. "My talk to the Conference and the follow-up Dear Colleague letter were meant to outline the framework for a Republican effort to build a majority. Since these ideas had been developed in coordination with the leadership, they should be seen in that context."

At this point he neither wanted to change the leadership nor saw himself taking a leadership position in the near future. He later told Dick Williams, "I was the senior planner. I didn't have any thoughts about being in the leadership. I thought it would be five or six years before that would happen and, when it did, Cheney or Lott would be the Republican leader and I'd be the senior planner."[28] The "four up-front men" signaled their intentions on the first day of the 1983 session. Walker spent an hour and a half to request one hour during special orders each day of the session for each of the four members. Unanimous consent was refused and they did not receive their hours that day. But the message was sent.[29]

Throughout 1983 the four activists, and others, did a series of special orders and made their point week after week. It was clear that they were pushing the principles of the Reagan Revolution. Newt thought they would have accomplished more if the White House staff would have cooperated with them, especially regarding economics. Newt did not just want "Reagan to be Reagan," he wanted the staff to also "be Reagan." To Newt this was clearly a struggle of the COS versus the

---

27 Gingrich Papers, COS Folder.

28 Williams, *Newt*, pp. 98-101.

29 Walker Interview, 17 July 1989.

Liberal Welfare State and he wanted the entire team to operate from the same playbook.

Walker told Judith Warner and Max Berley, for their *Newt Gingrich: Speaker to America*, "We felt that you needed conservative solutions and by that time we meant that you needed to base more and more decisions-making in the hands of individuals and you needed to move decision-making toward localities." They wanted to reduce tax burdens, government debt and government spending in order to provide opportunity. The COS team thought "the concept of society" should be community and neighborhood-based rather than "in the sense of a liberal welfare state where the national government had a command-and-control kind of role to play."[30]

The team argued for the conservative cause on economics, government regulation and foreign policy. They organized and recruited. They reached out to and encouraged GOP moderates, knowing GOP activists of any stripe helped their cause on the floor. Following up on the inclusive theme, the team began planning during the summer for a conference that would draw together Republican Members to talk about the future. "The Baltimore Conference [of House Republicans] in October 1983 was the first attempt to say we'd looked at a planning strategy," remembers Walker. "We thought there were certain issues that the Republican Party focused on we could move toward majority status. We needed to get all the Members of the Party together to talk about these things. We needed to give them data to interact."[31]

Connie Mack, a banking executive from Florida and grandson of the legendary baseball manager, was given the project. They went up to the Hunt Valley Inn (not actually in Baltimore) and ran a conference for and by the House GOP. They brought in Daryl Conner to set the parameters "and ended up with a lot more people, in the Party at least, who understood where we were coming from." Activists were recruited for the COS, and non-COS members responded by becoming more active on the floor. "We pulled it off. The leadership realized they had a real group to contend with."

Though the Baltimore Conference did not accomplish all that the COS leadership wanted and as they hoped, they did attract the attention of the leadership of both parties. By 1984 the GOP leadership

---

[30] Warner & Berley, p. 93

[31] Walker Interview, 17 July 1989.

had taken over the concept and the next conference was held in downtown Baltimore with Michel's sanction. There was a debt left over but Newt assumed it personally. "I don't want us to worry about the money. I'll take care of it. Let's move on."[32]

Though the COS focused mostly on the economy and the budget it was foreign policy that brought them, and Newt, their first great television success. President Reagan had sent troops into Grenada on 25 October in one of the first steps in the new Reagan Doctrine. This not only made clear his resolve to fight Communism in the Caribbean but by extension in Central America as well. Newt was delighted. For the first time the US had taken back territory claimed by the Communists and sent a message to the Soviets that none of their colonies were inviolate. Newt saw this as a major step to winning the Cold War. For the next couple of years Newt held teach-ins on the anniversary of the liberation of Grenada to celebrate the action and to explain why it was necessary. He was shocked that some in Congress were critical of the effort and were actively opposing American activities in Central America to stop the spread of Communism. His impression was that many of these legislators had consistently opposed US actions against Communism.

This impression led Newt to ask Gregorsky to do some research on the subject and come up with information that would show whether or not there was consistent congressional opposition against US action. Gregorsky, a superb researcher, did indeed come up with quotes from a number of Democrats who currently opposed the policy in Nicaragua and Central America. Newt took the Marxist/Leninist leader of Nicaragua, Daniel Ortega, at his word when he said he intended to spread Communism throughout Central America and Mexico by the end of the century.

Newt was further incensed when in early May 1984 a group of House Democrats, including the Majority Leader and future Speaker, Jim Wright, wrote a letter to Ortega beginning "Dear Commandante" offering to negotiate peace. Shortly after receiving the letter Ortega flew to the Soviet Union to pick up some Soviet aid. Newt took Gregorsky's document to the floor and accused the letter writers of "being blind to Communism" and of taking a view that America was always wrong

---

32 Ibid.

when dealing with communist governments, a message that Ambassador Jeanne Kirkpatrick would deliver later that year at the GOP convention in Dallas, Texas. The "always blame America first" crowd had to wake up. Learn from the experience and open your eyes, pleaded Newt. Speaker Tip O'Neill and the Democrats were furious. They did not see the anti-Communist Contras as freedom fighters, as did Newt and Reagan, but rather as thugs. Taking this view they had done what they could to cut off any support for them. In their minds, Newt's attack was very, very personal.[33]

On Monday, 14 May 1984, Speaker O'Neill went to the floor and attacked Newt, while he was not there, accusing him of attacking Democrats while they were not in the House Chamber. Newt and the COS group were accused of not letting the House Democrats have time to make short statements during "Special Orders" but rather consuming the time themselves for long speeches. They also were accused of attacking Democrats by holding them to unfair standards—that is Newt had quoted their own words back to them. They were accused of not notifying Democrats that Newt intended to refer to them by name in his "Special Orders" speech and had thus denied them an opportunity to defend or explain themselves.[34]

Newt was in Atlanta while the Speaker was making his charges and had not been notified that O'Neill would attack him personally on the floor. Newt liked O'Neill personally. "Tip is a wonderful Irishman, who would probably do great on that TV show about the Boston bar (Cheers). He's not a wonderful Speaker." Most previous Speakers, while partisan, were also institutional Speakers...even Sam Rayburn. Newt did not see O'Neill as an institutional Speaker. "He is really not Speaker. He is majority leader for the radical wing of the Democratic Party, and as a consequence he weakens the whole House," the future Speaker told a GOP gathering in Atlanta a few days after their confrontation.[35]

No one on the Republican side expected O'Neill to respond as he did. They thought he was to much savvy and professional for that to happen. The Speaker was tired of seeing COS Members on C-SPAN during "Special Orders." There was something false about speaking to

---

[33] *Congressional Record*, 10 May 1984.

[34] Ibid., 14 May 1984.

[35] Gingrich Papers, Georgia GOP Convention Speech, GA GOP Folder.

an empty chamber he thought. He and the Democratic leadership still did not realize the growing viewership of Brian Lamb's cable channel. Lamb, one of the great innovators of the modern media, was satisfying a growing need for people to watch their representatives in action without the media in the way, interpreting what was done and said. Some have estimated viewership at that time to be around 250,000. These viewers were people who were not watching reruns and were knowledgeable about and interested in their federal government.

Walker understood the power of C-SPAN much earlier when he started receiving mail from all around the country after people saw him arguing the conservative cause. He had advocated the use of C-SPAN and was appreciative of the fact that it did irritate the Democrats. "We'd been getting on their nerves. They tried to debate us and we sent them away whimpering," he gloated. Frequently, at the end of a short day which ended around 6:00 P.M., he would go to the other up-front men or to other COS activists and point out that 6:00 P.M. in Washington was 3:00 P.M. on the West Coast. "Let's do a couple of hours of special orders," he would say, and off they would go with little or no preparation. "Tip was using the rule against us to keep us from speaking during the regular session and this was our way of getting our message out...getting it heard."[36]

The day after the speaker's attack, Newt and the team, including Lott, prepared for action. Newt went to the well and noted, "The Speaker yesterday, as recorded in today's *Congressional Record*, made a series of statements which require an answer." Tip gave him an hour and commented, "The Chair wants to listen with keen interest to the Gentleman from Georgia."

Newt began by letting another Member, Ike Skelton, a Democrat, introduce his pastor from back home in Missouri. He then noted that the Republicans always tried to be accommodating during their special orders times. He said he felt the speaker had been misinformed or uninformed when he made his statement on Monday. As an introduction Newt noted that he had entered two-thirds of the Gregorsky study into the *Congressional Record* and would enter the rest later. He described the study (actually, a GOP Study Committee Report): "It is a serious historical study. It is an effort over a certain

---

[36] Walker Interview, 17 July 1989.

period of time to say certain things were said and certain things happened. It questioned the wisdom and the approach toward foreign policy of some people in this body." It was entitled, "What's the Matter with Democratic Foreign Policy?"

Newt said they had sent a letter to each of the Members whose names would be mentioned the next day in the special orders and invited them to be present. It said, "The basic theme of the study is that today's national Democrats have a pessimistic, defeatist and skeptical view toward America's role in the world. This world view could fairly be called radical because it violates every US citizen since Truman's time and ignores basic lessons about how the world works." It was signed by Newt, Walker and Weber.

Newt noted that he and Representative Stephen Solarz had debated the "Dear Commandante" letter earlier and hoped to have a similar debate over the Gregorsky document. He said he had seen, in the Speaker's Lobby, on 4 May, a propaganda document for the Communists but did not say who had put it there, though he knew. Representative Jim Wright immediately jumped up to defend the "Dear Commandante" letter and claimed it was not propaganda and how dare Newt impugn their patriotism. Newt responded that he was not talking about that letter but one listing victims of the Contras but found it interesting that Wright would think his letter might be considered communist propaganda.

"At that moment I looked up and there was Tip, who is a genuinely imposing figure. He is, physically, a very big man; Jim Wright, who is the best orator in the Democratic Party in the House; Dave Obey, who is very, very bright; Tom Downey, who may be brighter; and Ron Dellums, who is very articulate; and they were all five queuing up to fight me," said Newt. "Samuel Johnson once said that nothing so focuses a man's mind as the notion that he will be hung in the morning....And I realized it was about to get exciting."[37]

Newt stated quickly that he had been specific in his original statement, to which O'Neill objected, in that he did not question the good will, good faith or patriotism of his colleagues. He said he questioned their judgment. Again, he stated, "Let me make my position very, very clear. What we are seeing comes all too close to

---

[37] *Congressional Record*, 15 May 1984.

resembling a McCarthyism of the left. We believe it is legitimate in the system of this House to raise two sets of questions. The first was whether the "Dear Commandante" letter violated the Logan Act by communicating with a foreign dictator with whom the US was in conflict. He said, "By signing the letter the gentleman, meaning well, made a serious mistake with serious long term consequences. That's worth debating." The second issue was the Gregorsky paper.[38]

"When you look at statements made by gentlemen in this body, statements about South Vietnam, about Laos, about Cambodia, Angola, Afghanistan, Ethiopia, Grenada, Nicaragua, and now about El Salvador and you see a consistent, what some of us would regard as inaccurate judgment, I say to you, as strongly as I can, it is *not* a question of their patriotism, good intentions, or decency; it is a question of their judgement, their historical record, what they said and what happened in reality. It is perfectly American to be wrong." He went on to say he made no charge of unamericanism and he resented their saying he had. "I resent it bitterly. Is it wrong to ask what has happened in thirty intervening years (1954–1984), for historians to raise questions of history, to go back and do the research and lay it out?"

At this point the speaker entered the fray. He mentioned the word "apologizing" and Newt said he was explaining and not apologizing. O'Neill thought it was wrong for Newt to dredge up statements made twenty or thirty years ago and use them against a member. He compared it to a "have you stopped beating your wife" type of question. O'Neill was frustrated and had difficulty staying within the rules of the House at this point. He was a big man with a red nose but he was not Santa Claus. He did, however, give Newt a gift. "My personal opinion in this," he said, pointing his finger at Gingrich, "You deliberately stood in that well before an emptied House and challenged these people and you challenged their Americanism and it is the lowest thing I've ever seen in my thirty-two years in Congress."

O'Neill, in his pique, had attacked a Member personally on the floor. This attack was against the House's rules. Walker and Lott were on their feet before Newt could respond. "Mr. Speaker, I move that the Speaker's words be taken down," said Lott. After what seemed like an eternity, actually five and one-half minutes, the chair ruled, reluctantly,

---

[38] Ibid.

against O'Neill and his words were "taken down." In the background Jim Wright could be heard asking "What's wrong with that?" He nor the Speaker understood that O'Neill had gone too far. "I was expressing my opinion very mildly because I think much worse," he said.[39] It was the first time a Speaker had been rebuked in over a century and the next night all three television network news shows carried the exchange.

Newt was thrilled as were his supporters back home. Stanley Parkman, publisher of the local Carrollton paper, the *Times Georgian*, called to lend Newt support. The television coverage was a great triumph. "The number one fact about the news media is they love fights. You have to give them confrontations. When you give them confrontations, you get attention, when you get attention, you can educate," Newt said. "I am now a famous person."[40] He was famous, in a way. But that fame was indeed built on confrontation and an aggressive manner that made many uncomfortable. The Republican leader, Michel, was uncomfortable. Even Lott moved quickly "to proceed on a higher plane" and asked that the speaker be allowed to continue within the rules, noting that their point had been made and it was best to move on to the issues at hand.

O'Neill was concerned about Republican partisanship but continued to use the rule against the COS group and the GOP generally. He also continued his attacks on the president stating, according to the UPI, "The evil is in the White House at the present time—and that evil is a man who has no care and no concern for the working class—he's cold. He's mean. He's got ice water for blood." Even Michel was upset at this and rose on the floor to chastise the Speaker for his words as well as those of Majority Leader Wright who, on the floor, called Reagan "intellectually dishonest."

A few days later as O'Neill watched Walker waving his arms in a special orders speech, O'Neill struck back in an attempt to make Walker look ridiculous. He ordered the C-SPAN cameras—that provided gavel to gavel coverage of the Senate and House—to pan the room showing that the chamber was empty and Walker was speaking only to the cameras. O'Neill still did not understand. Walker was speaking to the thousands on the other end of the camera. Lott was

---

[39] Ibid.

[40] Warner & Berley, *Newt Gingrich*, pp. 101-102.

upset and reacted angrily but Walker and Newt were more sanguine. Walker suggested to the speaker that panning the chamber was a good thing and maybe he should order that it be done during regular hours and not just during special orders.

O'Neill took to calling Newt, Walker and Weber the "three stooges." They brought pictures of the comedy greats and hung them in their offices. "They [the Democrats] created a firestorm of support out in the country...they made national figures of us," Walker explained.[41]

Newt moved quickly to take advantage of his new status. He made sure that his book, *Window of Opportunity*, would come out in time to offer it at the upcoming GOP convention to be held in Dallas. The renomination of the Reagan-Bush ticket was a foregone conclusion and the only real excitement was over the platform. Newt and the COS moved to make sure their fingerprints were all over it. It was important that their ideas and issues be embraced by the party at the convention. As a member of the platform committee's executive committee Newt was ideally placed to make his influence felt. His new book gave him intellectual credentials as possibly the principal spokesman for the rising COS movement.

Georgians, especially those delegates and alternates from Newt's district, were exuberant in Dallas. Wearing patriotic or partisan hats and an assortment of buttons and badges that would boggle the mind, they reveled in Newt's popularity and the certainty that President Reagan would be renominated and reelected. Frederick Allen, the brilliant young writer for the *Atlanta Constitution*, was there as were Dick Williams and Tom Houck from WGST radio to do live broadcast back home on their daily, politically centered radio show. Newt made regular calls to radio shows back home and most of the Atlanta television stations had coverage live and on tape. In this circus Newt was one of the main acts. Everywhere he went he was besieged by reporters and admirers. He was even awarded a private interview with Walter Cronkite. "I can't believe how well it is going," Newt remarked after an especially long day.

The platform reflected a COS agenda and had been hard fought from the beginning. It was, in some ways, a preview of the 1992 Houston GOP platform. It was strong on opportunity brought on by free

---

[41] Walker Interview, 17 July 1989.

enterprise and was against communism, raising taxes and was for limiting abortions. Some of the key ideas in *Window of Opportunity*, such as support for space, technology and traditional values, were also reflected in the platform document.

To maximize the distribution of his message Newt brought Eddie Mahe, a respected GOP political consultant, with him to Dallas. They set up a separate room of operations. Eddie brought in people to answer phones and help Newt's overworked scheduler keep track and respond to all the demands and requests coming in that week. Newt enjoyed the media and used it to make his points. Mahe had difficulty keeping him from venturing out on his own to do interviews without first coordinating it with the scheduler. This impulsiveness sometimes resulted in Mahe making excuses for Newt not being available when Mahe had promised. Newt tried hard to do it Mahe's way and that too resulted in problems such as the time a fellow Republican House Member asked him to speak to his local reporter and Newt told him he would have to check with his "publicity agent." That member walked away as something less than an admirer.[42]

As successful as the convention was for Newt personally, it still depressed him. The COS had dominated the platform. Almost all the speakers, Newt not among them, preached the conservative message from the podium. Jack Kemp, an ally and potential presidential candidate for 1988, was well received. The media had been interested not only in Newt but also in other COS members. The team had followed Nixon's advice and had become more active in the House and had been a serious, if not dominating, presence at the convention. Newt should have been content but the teacher in him would not accept contentment.

Always looking to be more professional, he had watched the speakers, the press coverage and the way the convention was run. Many delegates and alternates were not happy with the platform and with its management. Newt was not satisfied with the convention management either. He told Dick Williams, "There's a Nixonian level of control over this convention that's just plain silly."[43] Many saw the convention, with its certain outcome stripping it of any suspense, as entertainment more than anything else. Gingrich, on the other hand,

---

[42] Eddie Mahe Interview, 9 August 1995.
[43] Williams, *Newt*, p. 106.

believed the convention was serious business and the people in charge had failed to use it to its full potential.

The COS message was out. The question now was "who's listening?" and "will they pay attention and follow our agenda?" The particular target for Newt was the White House, though he also felt it was essential to reach out to the Party and to the American people, who, he was convinced, were basically conservative and ready to hear and heed the message if it were properly presented. Talking to Dick Williams he expressed his frustration, and, in a way, his hopes. "We're setting the framework on which all presidential candidates in the GOP will run in 1988. When Reagan and his staff think through the State of the Union address and their agenda for a second term, they better be thinking about what we believe, or they'll face a revolution in their own party."

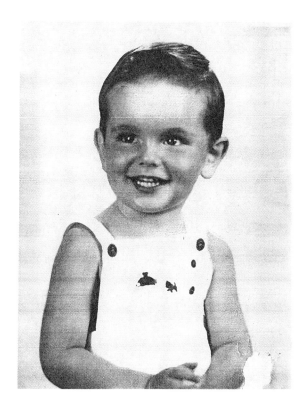

Baby picture of Newt.

Newt as a baby with his mother.

Newt and his mother Kit.

Newt with mother & sisters on way to Ft. Riley 1954

Newt and parents at Verdun (1957).

Newt with friends Calvin Roush and
Jim Tilton 1961.

Baker HS football picture with Newt (82) & Tilton (70) 1962.

Newt as a West Georgia College professor.

Newt runs key leaders meeting at campaign headquarters 1974.

Newt in 1974 campaign.

Newt speaks to Carrollton Optimist 1974 (Dick Folk and Steve Hanser in picture).

Newt speaking to Coweta GOP in 1974.

Newt campaigning (1976).

Newt votes election day 1976.

Cartoon "Lay Low Congressman" Baldy 1976.

Newt, Jackie, and Steely on way to filing in Atlanta 1978.

Guy Scull and Cathy Gingrich campaigning (1978).

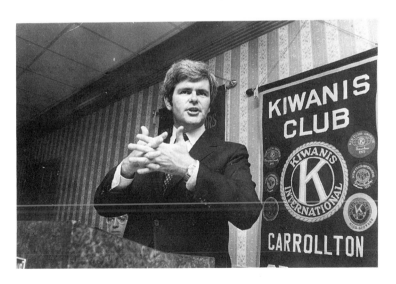

Newt speaks to his home Kiwanis club.

Cartoon "Yes Newt" by David Boyd Nov. 1978.

Newt, Senator Wayne Garner & Steely
(Jesse Sampley photo).

Newt and Bob Weed.

Newt float in July 4th parade Carrollton (1980).

Newt & Marianne on horses at Polk County rodeo (1984).

Newt and County Commissioner Horrie Duncan (1984).

Newt in crowd at BBQ in Carrollton
(Steely & his parents in background
1984).

Paul Walker, Newt's mentor, (1985).

Newt and Sen. Mack Mattingly with BBQ volunteers 1986.

Newt speaks to GA Senate 1986 (Lt. Gov. Zell Miller center behind Newt).

Newt talks with state Sen. Terrell Starr (1986).

Newt meets with WGC AAUP delegation 1984 (Wagner left and Steely).

Newt prepares to speak to Georgia Senate 1986 Lt. Gov. Zell
Miller at podium.

Newt talks highways with Highway Commissioner Tom
Moreland 1986.

Newt talks politics with state Senator Wayne Garner 1986.

Newt with Ken Smith (Smith ran against Murphy 1988).

Newt and West Georgia College colleague
Professor Floyd Hoskins.

Newt with Carrollton staff on inauguration eve (1989).

Newt with Lech Walesa 1989.

Newt & Marianne at book news conference (3-20-89).

Newt & Randy Evans (r) talk to Bill Nigut of WSB-TV.

Newt with Earning by Learning kids 1993.

Hanser, Newt, Steely (1993).

Newt and Bo Callaway at Family Opportunity TV show (1990).

Newt and former press Secretary Lee Howell (1990).

Newt & Mel with Earning by Learning kids, Tom Davidson on 2nd row, second from right (1990).

Newt in 1995 with his high school teacher Katrina Yielding
& Jim Tilton's mother.

Newt & Marianne speak to GOP supporters on inauguration
eve (1995).

Tony Blankley with Mr. & Mrs Eleanor Cliff, election
night 1994.

Catherine Brock (L) and Mary Brown 1994, Newt's
District Adminstration and Administrative Assistant.

Newt and Terry Maples (Director Zoo Atlanta) 1994.

Brian Lamb (C-SPAN), Newt, and Terry Maples (1994).

Joe Gaylord (R) & 1994 campaign manager John Duncan.

Hanser and Newt (1996).

Newt looks at space alien tee shirt (1996).

Cartoon "Trust me" by Macnelly Chi. Tribune Sept. 97, macnelly.com.

TOP TARGET

Cartoon "Top Target" by David Boyd.

TIME

MAN OF THE YEAR

NEWT
GINGRICH

Time Cover "Man of the Year" (12-25-95).

Newt on speaker's balcony
(11-11-98).

Newt's London bus in 1998 campaign.

10

AMBITION AND ARROGANCE

The success of the 1984 convention, at which the COS had their ideas accepted, and the overwhelming response of the American people to Reagan's campaign was encouraging. Reagan, however, had not carried large numbers of GOP congressmen with him. Serious work had to be done from within the House.

Newt had reservations about achieving his personal goal of becoming Speaker, though he never doubted he had achieved his broader goal of gaining a Republican majority in the House. Newt once reflected, "I probably won't get to be Speaker because the tactics I have to use to get a majority will probably prevent it." The truth was that many members were uncomfortable with Newt's aggressive approach and much preferred the more easy-going style of Trent Lott or Dick Cheney, the more likely future speakers. Some also thought he was somewhat too ambitious.

He was ambitious. Up until the 1960s having ambition was considered a positive trait and working to achieve it was honorable. In the last thirty years the ideas of personal achievement and personal ambition have lost favor with many people. Humility and self-efface-ment are considered more becoming. Newt staffer Reid Spearman noted in a paper he did in 1983 that those working for Newt should not have personal ambition. "Personal ambition is trivial," he said. In a note in the margin, Jim Tilton, Newt's closest friend and advisor, wrote, reflecting Newt's thinking, "Personal ambition is trustworthy because it

is a commitment."[1] Commitment and dedication were essential to success, Newt thought, and commendable as long as they did not replace
the goal and in doing so become goals themselves. Personal achievement and success were important insofar as they achieved the overall
goal or furthered the quest.

Newt's view of ambition as a positive force was not shared by
everyone, at least not as it applied to him. His opponents had
challenged his honesty and his ambition on many occasions. In
November 1984 he was the subject of a very effective "hatchet job" by
David Osborne in an article for *Mother Jones*,[2] a left-wing magazine that
seemed to specialize in expose articles. Newt was described as an
unprincipled hypocrite who would use anything and anyone to gain
power and further his ambition. Though the magazine prides itself as
being a "muckraking" journal outside the establishment and notes that
they do not pay much attention to checking facts (the August 1980 issue
boast "If you cannot change the story to fit the facts, change the facts to
fit the story.") the article still gained instant acceptance among Newt's
critics. His Democratic opponents made sure copies were made and sent
all over Capitol Hill. From this point on the charges made in Osborne's
article would reappear again and again in future articles. When
personal criticism was sought the "usual suspects" who had trashed
Newt in *Mother Jones* would be resurrected to repeat the same old stories
for those readers who might not have heard them.

Newt was drawing a great deal of attention. His clash with Speaker
O'Neill, his book, the success at the convention and his leadership in
helping forge post-Reagan conservatism were causing people to take
notice. The columnist David Broder had written favorably of his efforts
and George Will called him a "populist of the Right," intelligent and
impatient, who "exemplifies the Republican Party's current role as the
"party of ideas."[3] Fred Barnes listed him as one of the intellectual
leaders of the conservative movement in a *Washingtonian*[4] article and
his old school's magazine, *Tulanian*[5], referred to him as a "political
swashbuckler with a Ph.D." The daily press was regularly using terms

---

[1] Steely Papers, Spearman Report.

[2] *Mother Jones*, November 1984.

[3] *Newsweek*, 3 December 1984.

[4] *Washingtonian*, November 1984.

[5] *Tulanian*, Fall 1985.

like "maverick," "young Turk," and "revolutionary," when they wrote of Newt and the COS group. For every *Mother Jones* or *Hustler*[6] article, the latter having awarded Newt the "Asshole of the Month" award, there were two or three who took a somewhat more balanced approach. The 1986 edition of the *Almanac of American Politics*[7] listed him as one of the most influential members of the House and many in the media seemed to really be trying to figure out "who is this guy?"

On the one hand Newt thought he had reached a new plateau of political power and the bomb throwing that had marked his early rise in the party might be better left to others. He would assume the mantle of thinker and planner and work on what he considered to be his major goal...electing a Republican majority in the House. On the other hand Democratic arrogance in the use of power was very tempting to a bomb thrower. Ethics would provide the venue for the biggest bomb yet.

The 1984 election had been close in Indiana's eight district. It appeared that James McIntyre, the GOP challenger, had barely won. There was a protest from the incumbent, Frank McCloskey, and the matter would be decided in the House. On a straight party-line vote McCloskey was selected and seated while the election was still being contested.

Newt's involvement in the McIntyre affair is instructive to understanding Newt's attitude toward publicity during this period. "I ran it. Lott had said to me that the test for me was how many other people I could get on TV and how little I personally was dominating the process. They [the House GOP] had a series of leadership meetings that were just pitiful and I came to realize for the first time that we do not have a leadership, we have a group," he said. "The group gets together and deceives themselves because they use the term 'leadership' when really they just sit around and talk with no decision being made."[8]

The Monday conference meeting lasted two and one-half-hours with Kemp doing a good job of explaining they had a crisis over the McIntyre election. After considerable discussion it was decided the leadership would report back to the Wednesday conference meeting. They then held a leadership meeting that Newt attended where Kemp told NFL stories and insisted on a plan for how the GOP representatives

---

[6] *Hustler*, December 1985.

[7] *The Almanac of American Politics*, Georgia, Newt Gingrich.

[8] Newt Gingrich Interview, May 1985.

should respond. Newt approached him and said, "Jack, you know that story you tell about MacArthur where he says his father had warned him against counsels of war because they are always counsels of caution? I never fully understood that until I watched you today act as an agent of caution. Because everybody listening to you toned down their recommendations." "How can you say that about me?" Jack asked. "You were," Newt said. Then Rep. Bill Thomas really jumped him about the same thing. "For a man who thinks of himself as MacArthur at Inchon, that was tough to take," said Newt about his friend.

Newt and Duncan Hunter went into action. All night special orders were arranged and, staying up until 3:00 A.M. Newt and the staff drew up a battle plan for the leadership meeting the next morning, but were disappointed with the response they received. "They didn't read much of it. They didn't understand much of it. They just wanted to talk." Another meeting was set for that evening. This meeting was the third leadership meeting and still no plan. The evening meeting went for a hour and a half and once again produced no plan."[9]

The next morning there was still no plan. Newt refused to brainstorm with Jack in front of the group. Connie Mack was openly contemptuous, Steve Gunderson said, "You know, you guys have no idea how to run anything," and Denny Smith asked, "Jack, I don't understand why you don't have a plan." Kemp offered to resign if they wanted new leadership but no one took him up on that. Later on the floor, Newt went over to Jack, put his hand on his shoulder and said, "Jack, I know this is a tough week, and I love ya anyway." "I needed that," Kemp responded.

Kemp appointed Lynn Martin to chair a committee to come up with a plan for the McIntyre fight. Newt was asked to be on the committee but refused. He offered Lynn a copy of his plan, which she accepted. Bill Thomas, a member of the group, asked Newt to attend the afternoon committee meeting. "You have to be there," he said. "No, I don't." "We need your plan." "You have it." "We need you," said Thomas. Newt agreed to meet with Thomas and members of the committee for lunch before the committee meeting. Almost all the committee attended, including Lynn Martin, and Newt walked through his plan for them. They left and went on to put a variation of Newt's

---

[9] Ibid.

original plan into action. "So, I set up the whole thing. I structured all of it. The whole party walked out [of the House chamber in protest]. Michel and Lott were right there at the front. Bill Thomas was the hero and I never spoke during the major fight."[10] The walkout was stunning. The event made news and pointed out the corruption charge levied against the Democrats. It gave Newt a chance to see the ineffectiveness of the leadership organization and a chance to stretch his own wings behind the scenes as an organizer.

As a result of his efforts during the McIntyre walkout Newt felt that he had earned the right to be the recognized leader on the Central American debate project. Lott and Michel were not so sure. Newt had shown considerable strength during McIntyre. Real action was taken by the entire conference when they walked out in unison in response to the Democratic vote seating McClosky. Would it be wise to let him head the Central American debate? Where would he take it? Was the conference ready to follow him? What should they do? The problem Lott faced with Newt was that, "I'm not just a real powerful ally. I may be the future of the Republican Party in the House. He ain't sure he wants to let that happen and that's a very legitimate reaction I can respect," said Newt.

When talking about the situation with his wife, Marianne, Newt found that she had a feel for why Lott might be hesitant to let him handle the Central American debate. "You can't go from being as dominant as you were on McIntyre, where you reshaped the entire party and pivot three weeks later and do it on Nicaragua. It would just lead to absolute chaos, they psychologically can't tolerate it." Of course she was right. A second effort on his part so close to McIntyre would seemed like he was indirectly challenging the leadership in the minds of many of his colleagues.[11]

Newt was not willing to give up on Central America. He felt very strongly about this issue and intended to have his say. The pro-Contras at the State Department had a collection of weapons that had come through Cuba and had been sent through Nicaragua to El Salvador where they were taken from the communists and sent to the US. They passed them on to Newt when no one at State seemed interested in doing anything with them. To the hard line anti-Communists they were proof that the Soviets were supplying the various revolts in Central

---

10 Ibid.
11 Ibid.

America. Newt would make sure people understood why they were important. Newt took these weapons to the floor and held them up and described them. "I just laid it out item by item," he said. He explained not only where they had originated and but also where they were taken. "Remember this, the next time you want to know why we think the guerrillas in El Salvador are tied to Nicaragua, Cuba and the Soviet Union."

The following day Newt did what he called "an ostrich speech" using the "Grenada Documents" collection just recently published from the Cuban and Russian documents captured during the Grenada liberation. Representative Bill Richardson responded and accused Newt of demagogy. Bob Walker jumped up and asked that Richardson's words be "taken down." This request gave a few moments to allow Newt to think. "No, no, the gentleman's words can stand." Newt then accused him of being blind. He pointed out that he had shown the weapons that tied the communist to El Salvador and the documents taken in Grenada. He then went through the a list of consequences, people dying in Cambodia, South Vietnamese people put in reeducation camps, people dying in Nicaragua, all because "people like you are blind. As long as you are determined to be blind, I'm determined to talk about the facts..." Newt went on to point out that one of the documents described how American liberals and leftists were manipulated and "you fall for it every time," he accused.

Cheney now joined Newt and Walker in urging the Republicans to vote "no" on final passage of an aid bill that did not do enough to help the "freedom fighters" in Central America who were fighting communism. Almost all the Republicans joined with most of the left-wing Democrats to give Speaker O'Neill a crushing defeat. Secretary of State George Schulz called Michel and said they really had hoped something would pass so they could take it to conference and have it changed there. This gave Newt and Cheney an opportunity to lay out the base for a hard line position. Like Lott, Cheney had some reservations about Newt's tactics but after watching him operate for two years, Cheney was moving slowly toward the hard line position. At one point during the Central American debate, after giving an anti-Marxist/Leninist speech, he turned to Newt and commented, "Gosh, I sound more and more like you."[12]

Cheney was moving to the right and away from being a consummate insider, Newt was moving step by step toward a leadership role in the party, and a second term Republican from Ohio, John Kasich, who would become one of the heroes of the 1995 Republican Revolution, carried a monetary policy resolution through the policy committee which referred to monetary policy as a problem for the first time. "Lott and I trained Kasich and he carried the entire fight himself; it was a major step toward our vision of the party," Newt related.

Newt worked hard during the 1986 elections to maximize the number of new GOP House members and the preservation of incumbents. He received help in this effort from an unexpected source, former Delaware Governor Pierre DuPont. DuPont had met Newt in 1981 when they traveled together to represent the US at the independence ceremonies for Antigua. He was impressed with Newt's interest in and grasp of issues, including what was happening in Delaware and how DuPont viewed the Republican Party. Newt impressed the governor as bright, knowledgeable and energetic as did Newt's new bride, Marianne, who later served on DuPont's 1988 campaign advisory committee for the presidency while Newt supported Jack Kemp in the primaries.

Dupont and twelve other Republican governors came together in 1978 determined to organize and help build a "farm system," like baseball, for Congress. They wanted to encourage and support Republicans running for state offices or major municipal positions in order to build up a corps of experienced elected officials from whom congressional candidates would emerge. GOPAC was formed with DuPont as chairman and was active under his leadership during each election between 1978 and 1986.

DuPont decided in 1986 to make a run for the presidency in 1988. It would not be possible for him to continue serving as GOPAC chairman and he and the board determined that they would look for an elected official to replace him. This person had to possess "lots of energy and some vision of what the party should be doing and where it should be

---

12 Ibid.

going." Newt was their first choice for the job.[13] DuPont came over from Delaware and arranged to have an early breakfast with Newt where he asked him to take over GOPAC. Newt was surprised. They talked about what was involved and the governor explained why they thought Newt was the person for the job. Newt wanted a little while to think it over. A couple of hours later, after talking with key advisors, he called DuPont and agreed to take it.

Some might be surprised that he did not accept immediately, given the opportunity GOPAC offered for carrying on his work of seeking a GOP majority in the House. The fact was, though, that Gingrich was on the verge of overextending himself and some of his advisors thought GOPAC would absorb too much of his time with disastrous results for the other areas of his involvement. His normal weekly schedule included six eighteen-hour days and frequently business intruded into his Sundays. Few others in Washington worked longer hours or juggled more different political and policy responsibilities.

What Newt sensed fairly quickly was that GOPAC would make his plan to recruit and train GOP candidates easier. It gave him a vehicle to carry out his program that was not possible through the NRCC or the RNC. With this new tool came more staff and more funding that could be directed toward the effort. He thought that tighter scheduling would provide the time.

Newt was not so much interested in raising money to donate to Republican candidates as he was in training them. Fundraising was important and he would go to their districts to speak at their fund-raisers, but he wanted to train them to a national agenda. "Money is important," he told DuPont, "but let's educate them on issues."[14]

Through the use of position papers, telephone briefings, audio and video tapes and personal appearances Newt was able to share his ideas, and those of other conservatives such as Ronald Reagan, Margaret Thatcher, William Bennett, Jack Kemp, Jeanne Kirkpatrick and innovators like Edwards Deming and Alvin and Heidi Toffler. National conservative themes, tested through experience and polling research, were developed so they would play equally well in Maine or Mississippi, Atlanta or Ann Arbor. The idea was to have Republican candidates all across the country talking about the same issues in much

---

13 Pete Dupont Interview, 15 May 1995

14 Ibid.

the same way and to develop a resonance that would help voters understand what the Republicans were about. This process was in large measure responsible for the GOP success of 1994.

To help him run the organization day to day Newt turned to an old ally, Howard "Bo" Callaway, former Congressman, Secretary of the Army and campaign manager for Gerald Ford's 1976 presidential campaign. Callaway had been elected to Congress in 1964 from the congressional district to which Newt belonged while in high school. He had been very successful in private business but still maintained an enduring interest in politics and public affairs.

Following DuPont's unsuccessful presidential campaign in 1988 Newt also inherited that campaign's research director, Dr. Jeff Eisenach, who would become a friend and ally to Newt and almost a third son to Steve Hanser. Eisenach, a bright Ph.D. in economics, would be active in numerous policy and organizational efforts over the next few years and briefly, after Callaway's exit to return to business in Colorado, would head up GOPAC's organizational effort.

Newt was moving rapidly in his rise as a major force in the House. He had established himself as a leader within the GOP conference. His book and the combination of careful research and a gift for speaking gave him the intellectual credentials necessary to be accepted as one of the key idea men in the party. The COS team, along with moderate GOP activist allies, provided the core of the troops needed to spread the conservative message. The candidates being assisted by GOPAC, in coordination with the NRCC, fleshed out the army.

A new obstacle now appeared. Thomas Phillip O'Neill, Jr. was no longer Speaker of the House. Tip O'Neill had come to symbolize for many conservatives a Congress that was "big, fat and out of control." He had replaced John Kennedy in the House in 1953 and had been Speaker since 1977. He was the perfect liberal symbol for the Republicans to run against, just as Newt, when he became Speaker a decade later, would become the symbol the Democrats loved to invoke at election time. O'Neill was replaced by Representative James C. Wright, Jr., from Texas, the former Majority Leader in the House.

"When Tip left we thought our arch rival was gone and felt we could work with new leadership never understanding Jim would be more partisan and really was a far more closed shop operator than Tip had been...at least with Tip you knew where he was coming from," remembered Bob Walker. "He didn't deal under the table. We had a strained but open relationship." Speaker Wright was considerably different.[15] "Jim Wright operated in back rooms. His effort was to come after us by shutting down our opportunities to effect legislation," said Walker. "That was largely a response to three, four, five years of tactics on the House floor where we'd driven them to a place where they had to use the muscle of the majority in order to preserve their position when they could no longer do it in up-front votes."

It did not take Newt and the COS members long to understand that Wright presented a threat different from that of O'Neill. The speaker's heavy-handed tactics against the Republicans, as well as against conservative Democrats, helped rally the entire GOP Conference against him. By the summer of 1987 Newt was telling those close to him that Wright had to go if they were to be successful in their efforts to obtain a GOP majority in the foreseeable future. It was time for the "vision, strategy, projects and tactics" approach he had been advocating for the last couple of years.

Bob Walker remembers how the arrogance of power exhibited by the Democrats helped unify the GOP. "Wright really became a catalyst for bringing the whole Republican Party over to our [COS] side. O'Neill had enough of a working relationship with our side that the Old Bulls would resent our tactics. Wright made them so mad they accepted what we'd been saying about the majority." Newt and his group presented a genuine option to accepting the humiliating treatment at the hands of the majority. "Tip had friends on our side and Jim Wright didn't. It galvanized the GOP around activist tactics," said Walker.[16]

By the fall of 1987 ten House ethics cases, all Democrats, were before the Ethics Committee. These included Mario Biaggi, a twenty-year incumbent indicted for influence peddling; Harold Ford, a subcommittee chairman indicted for conspiracy to commit bank, mail and tax fraud; and Fernand J. St. Germaine, chairman of the Banking, Financing and Urban Affairs Committee, for using his position for personal financial gain.

"In the context of the House, [violation of] the ethics issue is by definition almost always a function of power, and the people who have power in the House are Democrats," said Newt. "I'm not saying that all

---

15 Walker Interview, 17 July 1989.
16 Ibid.

Democrats are bad; I'm saying that to be part of a machine that's been in power for thirty-four years has its consequences." [17] Newt and others felt those consequences were corruption and unbridled arrogance.

As Newt and the COS group looked around they saw abuse of power as common currency within the Democratic Party in the House. No one had accused O'Neill of corruption nor were there serious charges of abuse of power. He had friends on both sides of the aisle. Off the floor he even managed to get along with Gingrich. Newt had been helpful to Representative Eddie Boland, a close friend of O'Neill's, and Newt and Marianne had sent flowers and a note to O'Neill's wife, Millie, when she was in the hospital. While never close, the two men were cordial and respectful of each other. Jim Wright did not have those sorts of relationships outside a small circle and not across the aisle. Still, he had party support and the power of the Office of the Speaker.

Newt admired Wright as "a technician of power," relates John Barry in his definitive work on the affair, *The Ambition and the Power*. He certainly had respect for the Texan's ability to hinder Reagan's agenda through veto overrides and to curb the House GOP through a skillful use of parliamentary tactics and a willingness to be completely ruthless in their application. Everyone understood that the speaker would be equally ruthless in defending himself against charges of abuse of power or corruption. Picking up the spear to go after the king was not a task lightly taken.

Walker described how the COS group agreed something needed to be done about Wright but no one at that time, including Newt, seemed to be ready to pick up the spear. Newt had outside legal counsel and colleagues who had served as prosecutors go over the evidence. Van Brocklin and others had gathered to see if there was enough to form a case against the speaker and ask the Ethics Committee for an investigation. The answer was no. Newt and Van Brocklin dug deeper and were helped by reporters who had been alerted to the possibilities of a scandal. More information began to come in that supported Newt's case. [18]

"Newt finally said, I'm going to do it. I'm going to see these charges get filed and if no one is behind me then so be it," remembers Walker. Most members of Gingrich's staff were worried when Newt announced

---

[17] *Insight* Magazine, 14 September 1987, p. 24.
[18] Ibid.

on 15 December 1987, that he intended to file an ethics complaint against Wright. Laurie James recalled the tenseness of that holiday period. Noting that he seemed to be alone in his effort, she asked him why he was doing it given the possible consequences. "He seemed a little surprised," she remembered. Being a former Lutheran and a good historian, he told her the story of Martin Luther's confrontation with the Church at Worms in 1521 and dramatically quoted the great Reformation leader, "Here I stand. I can do no other. God help me."[19]

He was right to ask God for help because it seemed that no one else was going to come to his support in this matter. Not even COS members stood with him publicly on this issue. Most members, on both sides of the aisle, stood back to see what would happen. Despite this lack of support and remembering his religion, Newt felt that one should not depend totally on the Almighty to do all the work. God helps those who help themselves and Newt was willing to carry his load in the effort.

Early on Newt had begun to work with the press inside and outside the beltway. He understood the interplay of ideas and how issues are formulated. He developed contacts with Bob Novak, Gloria Borger, George Will, David Broder, Tony Snow, Meg Greenfield, and others and would call them and make sure they knew his side of the issues. He worked the press tirelessly. Van Brocklin swapped information with them and Sheila Ward, his press secretary, did yeoman work in presenting the message.[20]

In March 1988 Wright amended his 1980-1986 financial disclosures to provide more information about an investment company, Mallightco, that he had formed with George Mallick, a Fort Worth developer. Newt sought support from Common Cause but received no response. That Spring all the major papers and news magazines had done stories on Wright's problems as well as a number of regional papers. Newt was seeking resonance.

On 10 May 1988 John Fund of the *Wall Street Journal* wrote an editorial entitled, "Where's the Investigation?" On 18 May Fred Wertheimer, of Common Cause, wrote Ethics chairman Julian Dixon asking for an investigation, conducted by an outside counsel, of Speaker Wright. Six days later Wright also invited an investigation and pledged

---

19 Laurie James Interview, 5 May 1988.

20 Gingrich Papers, van Borcklin File, Jim Wright Folder.

full cooperation. Newt, now backed by seventy-three House Republicans including the leadership, minus Michel, filed a formal complaint with the Ethics Committee.

Newt had orchestrated a media campaign designed to build support for an investigation of the speaker. He now needed to keep up the pressure to make sure a special prosecutor was appointed and that this was treated more seriously than the case of Representative St. Germain, where it was found he had violated ethics rules but no action was recommended. [21]

On 26 July shortly after the Democratic National Convention in Atlanta, the Ethics Committee announced the appointment of Chicago attorney Richard J. Phaelan, a Democrat, as special prosecutor. In September Bob Michel and Dick Cheney asked the Ethics and Intelligence Committees to investigate the possibility that Wright had disclosed classified information about CIA activities. Allegations about improper book deals and improper investments in oil wells and Florida real estate developed slowly, complicating Wright's problems as did his personal diplomacy in trying to bring about some peaceful resolution to the Central American situation. During the 1988 campaign Vice President George Bush and Bob Michel supported the investigation and made Wright a campaign issue as did Ed Rollins, the new NRCC leader, and numerous other GOP candidates including Gingrich. At one event attended by Wright and Bush, the speaker spoke to Bush and took him to task for his criticism. Bush listened, pointed out that Wright had sat by while House Democrats attacked Bush and that he owed Wright nothing.

In April 1989 Democratic Whip Tony Coelho was accused of illegal profiting from junk bond purchases. The next month one of Wright's top assistants, John Mack, was revealed in a story in the *Washington Post* to have brutally beaten a woman with a hammer and left her for dead. He had gone to jail for this crime but Wright had helped him win parole by offering him a job. While Wright saw this act as giving someone a second chance many in the House, especially the women, were horrified. It seemed that everywhere one turned scandals were

---

[21] See John Barry, *The Ambition and the Power* for the best treatment of this incident.

popping up. In September *Insight* magazine did a story on "The House of Questionable Repute."[22]

Newt and the Republican leadership did what they could to feed this perception. To them it was not just a question of Wright's misuse of power but rather of the whole Democratic leadership over the past decades used to being the majority and becoming comfortable with the arrogance of power. Maybe now it would be possible to convince the American people that the only way to clean up the mess was to have a major turnover.

Newt had told Lois Romano, in a *Washington Post* article in 1985, "We are engaged in reshaping a whole nation through the news media." He thought then, after the 1984 convention, that he was playing a major role in that effort. He told her, "I'm unavoidable...I represent real power." Reshaping the House would be a first step toward reshaping the nation. In the same article conservative guru Paul Weyrick, told Romano, "He [Newt] is without question one of the most important conservative leaders in the country because he has taught conservatives how to make their vision of America part of operative debate." This was never truer than during the 1988-1989 period.[23]

The breaking scandals in Washington and the 1988 campaign were the background for the national debate. The trigger for exploding national involvement was the proposed pay raise for 1989 of a 51 percent increase for congressmen. The Commission on Executive, Legislative, and Judicial salaries recommended such an increase to take effect automatically on 8 February 1989 unless both houses of congress voted against it. GOP leaders in both houses denounced it but President Reagan approved it on 9 January. Most members wanted the raise but also wanted to avoid a vote on it because they would have to vote against it publicly. They expected Speaker Wright to provide cover by not calling for a vote. This tactic allowed them to say publicly how they wanted a vote to stop it and tell Wright privately not to call it up.

This situation coincided with the rising influence of talk radio that had been growing since the early 1980s. The king of talk radio, Rush Limbaugh, was just coming into his own as a voice for frustrated conservatives "all across the fruited plain" and was echoed by dozens of regional talk hosts throughout the country. This was seen as a wedge

---

[22] *Insight* Magazine, 14 September 1987.

[23] Warner & Berley, *Newt Gingrich*, p. 110.

issue driving the Democrats away from their core middle and lower-middle class constituency who would not understand a congressional pay raise to $135,000 per Member. Congressional offices were quickly swamped with mail and messages from outraged citizens, spurred on by the talk shows, demanding a vote against the proposed raise.

While the GOP leadership quietly cooperated with Wright to support the raise the RNC, now headed by Lee Atwater, condemned it and the "national Democrats" in his national mailings. In truth, the GOP did not have to do much to build support for opposition to the raises. That issue had struck at the core of voter frustration and had sparked a resonance throughout the country. An ABC-*Washington Post* poll showed that 85 percent of the people opposed it and they were making their voices heard. Some observers trace the rise of Ross Perot and his movement to this issue. People found that their voices could be heard and now felt empowered to express their concerns. With the knowledge, spread by radio, that thousands across the country felt as they did, many began to feel that they "belonged" to a "movement" to change government so that it would be more responsive to the people and their needs and desires.

Gingrich thought the raise was needed and deserved, and when Wright, embattled and bitter at being the target of public outrage, finally called for a vote, Newt voted for the raise after a pledge made by the Democrats that they would not use it against him in the 1990 election or support Democrats who made an issue of his vote. While this agreement provoked outrage from some of his staff and the public it turned out to be rather critical in the failure of his next opponent to defeat him.

In February 1989 Phelan finished his very aggressive investigation and presented his report to the Ethics Committee. It charged Speaker Wright with 117 violations of House rules. The Committee reduced the number of violations to 69. Wright, on 31 May spoke to the House. He noted that he had spent more than half his life there and considered it home. He then offered to give up the speakership in the hope that it would end "this season of bad will that has grown up among us." His formal resignation came on 6 June 1989. Majority Leader Tom Foley, from Washington state, replaced him as Speaker and Bill Gray replaced Coelho, who also had resigned, as Whip. Gray was the first African-American in a major leadership position from either party. Newt, the

RNC and the *Wall Street Journal* continued the attack on corruption. The *Journal* insisted that Wright was not the only problem but rather it was the "imperial Democratic Congress" and the almost certain reelection of incumbents. Newt agreed; after all that had been his argument all along. [24]

Gingrich had slowly become an advocate of term limits for Congress. After forty years of Democratic rule it seemed the only way to effect a turnover that would provide a congress closer to the people. It would also forestall the tendency toward an imperial attitude. Newt would receive criticism from his opponents for supporting term limits and not applying them to himself retroactively. His position was that to do that would only leave the field to those who opposed the idea and would lock in cement that which he was trying to prevent...the continuation of a liberal Democratic Congress firmly committed to the continuance of a liberal welfare state that he thought was destroying America. If all Members were under the same rules he would be glad to have the limits applied to him because that would limit all congressional terms and give the voters a chance to elect a GOP majority.

Term limits was not the only issue of the 1988 election and Newt was concerned with more than his own reelection. He continued talking about the problems of the liberal welfare state and took a special interest in the crime problem and the drug war. He was concerned that drugs were destroying thousands of young Americans and corrupting large segments of society in the process. In a 29 February 1988 memo to White House Chief of Staff Howard Baker he proposed a "communications task force to develop the theme of cocaine, communism and chaos as threats to our southern neighbors. He also proposed "a planning task force to develop the concept of non-violent coercion using high technology vulnerabilities in modern society." He thought this should be under General Colin Powell's direction and that the military had to handle it and make a fast operation to avoid the drug lords corrupting the military. He wanted to be involved in the planning if possible. He also included a private letter to President Reagan warning of the possibility that Panama's General Manuel Noriega might turn to the communists for support if we continued our pressure on him. He suggested that we inform the Soviets and the Cubans privately of the

---

[24] Barry, *The Ambition and the Power*, part VII.

consequences of such intervention and that we establish contingency plans "for decisive intervention should any communist advisors show up in Panama."[25]

At home back in the sixth district of Georgia, Newt was facing the former co-chairman of the 1986 Crandall Bray campaign, David Worley. Worley had just turned thirty when he resigned as an associate in the Atlanta law firm of Arnall, Golden and Gregory and decided to run against Gingrich. He was fascinated by Newt and his success and at the same time opposed to his policies and disliked him personally.

One man who knew Worley well was Randy Evans, a young partner in the same law firm, who had served as county and district GOP chairman and was political director for Friends of Newt Gingrich. Evans was bright and quick and invaluable to Gingrich as a strategist. Working to carry out Newt's goal of enlisting more Republican candidates he held workshops across the district and the state to make sure the candidates had the best possible chance of winning. He also aided in the strategy that designed a campaign which permitted Newt to spend minimal time campaigning at home, and allowed him to travel to help other candidates around the country.[26]

Because Evans was keeping an eye on GOP recruitment in Newt's district and holding workshops, Newt was able to crisscross America in search of more GOP House members. He helped raise money for Republican candidates, made available GOPAC tapes which aided in developing a national message and made contributions of $1,000 to each of them from FONG's coffers. He was also very involved in the thematic and strategic elements of the Bush/Quayle campaign.

Newt supported Jack Kemp in the beginning of the 1988 campaign, but after the primaries began to move toward Bush. Bob Teeter, Lee Atwater and Paul Coverdell, all on the Bush team and all close to Newt, paved the way for his move to Bush/Quayle. By late summer he was seen spending his morning walks to the Washington Monument and back conversing with Deborah Steelman, a domestic policy advisor for Vice President Bush.

Newt pushed for a national theme that would be echoed by the congressional candidates and themes even state house candidates could use. He was involved in the Bush/Quayle decisions concerning the

[25] Newt Gingrich biography folder, MSC, Gingrich Papers.
[26] Randy Evans Interview, 26 September 1989.

Willie Horton ad, crime as a major issue and the flag and pledge to the flag themes. The flag issue became important when the House Democratic leadership opposed having the House recite the pledge. Michael Dukakis, as governor of Massachusetts, had vetoed a bill requiring students to recite the pledge. This action by the House appeared to support the Dukakis veto and brand the Democratic Party as the unpatriotic party. The vote was to refuse the pledge and was carried by a straight party-line vote.[27]

One local candidate who brought Dukakis to the local level was Kenneth Smith of Bremen, Georgia. Smith, a former city councilman, was recruited by Randy Evans to run against Speaker Tom Murphy. Shortly after the Democratic convention in Atlanta, Smith attempted to associate Dukakis with Murphy. The liberal Dukakis, in true ACLU fashion, had done and said so many things the average conservative Georgian did not understand, nor could explain, that it was difficult to defend him. Banning BB guns, opposing the pledge to the flag, opposing the military and restricting the training of his National Guard units and freeing murderers through parole were all potent issues to use against anyone supporting the governor from the Bay State.

Speaker Murphy, the most Democratic of the yellow dog Democrats, who never in his life voted for a Republican, declared his support for the Democratic ticket. Evans was implementing the idea, pushed nationally by Newt, of running candidates for every office on the ballot. He encouraged Smith to go around the speaker's district detailing Dukakis' position on a host of issues and asking the voters to ask Murphy if he supported those positions and if not how he could support Ducks.[28] Murphy maintains that he had personal differences on the issues with Dukakis and that Smith's efforts had little or no impact on him[29]. Whatever the motivation, Murphy, a member of the state campaign committee for Dukakis, announced publicly in September that he could no longer support the nominee.

Murphy was basically a conservative when it came to the economy, defense and patriotic issues, and the law. He had a soft spot, however, for the old, the sick and for children. Many southern legislators were in his mold. His decision came at a time when the Dukakis campaign was

---

27 *Congressional Record*, 10 September 1988

28 Randy Evans Interview, 26 September 1989.

29 Tom Murphy Interview, 14 October 1997.

just gearing up in the south. His decision to back off was seen as a serious, if not mortal, wound to Dukakis in the primary and to his hope of carrying any southern state. Newt was delighted and the GOP cast Evans and Smith in a heroic mold as other candidates across the country were encouraged to follow their example.

Gingrich's own campaign was targeted by the Democratic Congressional Campaign Committee whose chairman, Representative Beryl Anthony, accused Newt of "trying to destroy the Democratic Party" and having that as "his sole mission in life." Worley was sent $10,000 by the DCCC and given technical support through what was called "coordinated expenditures." Anthony would later file ethics charges alleging ethical problems with Newt's book deal for *Window of Opportunity*.

Worley accused Newt of everything from mail fraud to wanting to do away with Social Security. He accused him of supporting Frank Lorenzo in his fight against Eastern Airlines and of taking PAC money from interests outside the state. He said Newt was a hypocrite for calling for budget cuts when his own staff budget was one of the highest in Washington.[30]

Newt responded by talking about his accomplishments. Local ads touted how much he had helped local people and stressed his value in Washington to bring about changes the people wanted. He challenged Worley to a series of debates and began accepting invitations to debate. Worley accepted the challenge but seemed unable to be free when debates were scheduled by the various groups sponsoring them. In the end only one short debate was held on WSB-Televison Station and that turned into a shouting match, mainly over Social Security with Worley making charges and Newt calling him a liar.

Newt used ads tailored to each county requesting the local people, when they saw Worley, to be part of the "Worley Watch" and ask him why he would not come to their county and debate Newt. He cast Worley as a tool of Jim Wright and asked who Worley would vote for Speaker "on his very first vote as a congressman." He also asked, "Does Worley share Michael Dukakis's values?" He handled the pay raise question by giving his raise for 1987 to set up a scholarship for students at Clayton State College. Newt outspent his opponent two to one with

---

[30] Gingrich Papers, 1988 Campaign File.

35.8 percent of his money coming from PACs whereas Worley's PAC contributions accounted for over 63.8 percent of his war chest.

Newt spent enough time campaigning in Georgia to make sure he would have no trouble winning the election. His polls were reassuring and having Dukakis at the head of the Democratic ticket was certain to be a plus for him. GOP candidates for state house races had their pictures taken with him and used them in their ads. Things were going his way. Election night held no surprises for Newt and his supporters and he won with almost 60 percent of the vote.[31]

In 1988 Newt used the national convention as an opportunity to influence the party and the press. He made sure that GOPAC had a major presence at the convention and spread buttons with "Honest Self Government" printed across the top and "98.4 percent" with a red slash across it and "Ask GOPAC" across the bottom. The 98.4 percent indicated the reelection rate of incumbent congressmen and supported the need for term limits.

Bush was sure to receive the GOP nomination by the time the convention met in New Orleans but there was still doubt about who he would pick for Vice President. Newt neither expected nor desired the job and was not involved in the selection. He was concerned about publicizing the COS message and helping develop a national theme for the campaign. The flag and patriotic theme of the 1984 "Morning in America" campaign had worked well and there was no reason to believe it would not work again. The Teeter polls agreed with this assumption and the liberal campaign run by Dukakis almost begged for a rerun of 1984.

Bush's selection of Senator Dan Quayle for the second spot was something of a surprise to Newt but not an unpleasant one. At that point Quayle was seen as a competent and popular two term Senator from Indiana who shared many of the ideas Newt had been advocating all along. The press had yet to begin its effort to trivialize Quayle and picture him as a lightweight. This development would come quickly enough as would the attacks on Bush's manhood and his "resume career."

What was still the most important goal for Newt was having a Republican majority elected in the House. In addition to the 98.4

---

31 Ibid.

percent buttons there appeared buttons with a broom and "clean sweep" on them. As in Dallas in 1984, Newt worked more than eighteen hours a day while at the convention. He gave interviews, he pushed delegates to give greater support to their GOP candidates and spread the conservative message at every turn. Newt was attacking Democratic arrogance and corruption in the House. The Democrats, and some of his GOP colleagues, saw this as an attack on the House itself. In fact, Newt loved the House and saw it as the legitimate voice of the people. He thought it had been taken over by liberal Democrats to carry out their own agenda in opposition to the will of the people, a view shared by numerous conservative Democrats, some of whom, like Representative Ed Jenkins of Georgia, would in the next few years retire in frustration.[32]

In working almost around the clock Newt stretched his time and temper to the limits. During the last days of the convention at a reception Delta Airlines was holding for the delegates, Brown and Brock were awaiting Newt's arrival with Newt's mother and Marianne. Newt was rushing as usual and arrived late and many people had come and gone. He was upset and did not want to hear explanations. He shouted at his mother, harshly and unjustifiably criticized Brown, and did not calm down until Marianne took him aside. It was clear that her reputation as the one person who can control him was well earned. Her influence on him was strong—he listened to her and respected what she said. She approaches him on both a rational and emotional level to convince Newt to examine his behavior at a given moment. The next day Newt sent flowers to Brown and apologized for his behavior.[33]

The most common public emotion exhibited by Newt is anger, or possibly frustration. Those who've worked with him, especially in the early days, saw him quick to anger when he was faced with incomplete or incompetent work by those he depended on. As the years went by his control of his temper improved. By the New Orleans convention in 1988 a public display of Newt's anger was relatively rare because "it is counterproductive," he said. The incident at the Delta reception was an exception but one that worried the staff.

If the staff worried about him being overworked and pushing too hard in 1988 they would have been panic stricken if they could have

---

[32] Catherine Brock Interview, 20 June 1995.
[33] Ibid.

foretold Newt's first quarter of 1989. The Jim Wright situation was coming to a close and Newt himself was coming under attack by the speaker's friends and supporters. Newt thought when the charges against Wright were made and the press and Ethics Committee took them seriously he would be vindicated in making them. At first he did not receive much in the way of personal attacks because people wanted to see if any of the charges would be taken seriously. Newt felt pretty good because of the lack of personal assault. The story is told of his standing in the Capitol waiting for an elevator and telling his staff member, "It really hasn't been too bad. I think it'll be okay." With that he entered the elevator and as the doors shut noticed Representative Jack Brooks, a loyal supporter and close friend of Wright's from Texas, was already there. The staff member noticed the horrified look on Newt's face as the doors shut and heard Brook exclaim, "You son of a bitch!" The introduction to personal animosity had arrived. The Democrats had studied his tactics and were now about to use them to attack and demonize Newt.

The attacks began slowly. In May 1988 Representative Anthony had raised questions about Newt's 1977 book deal and of the 1984 *Window of Opportunity* arrangement as well. Attacks on a national scale, such as ethics charges, could then be used by Newt's local opponents. Worley had used the "unwritten book" as a prop during the 1988 campaign. Not much came from the charge at first. Newt was, however, about to step up to a new level of leadership and with that rise the Democratic attacks became more frequent and much more intense.

President Bush had nominated former Senator John Tower to be Secretary of Defense but in a particularly vicious personal attack the Democratic Senate refused to confirm him partially on grounds that he was guilty of alcohol abuse and womanizing. Even Senator Edward Kennedy joined in against him. With the speaker under attack and the Democrats retaliating against Senator Tower there was a bad atmosphere hanging over the Capitol.

On 10 March Newt heard the announcement that President Bush was nominating Dick Cheney, the House Minority Whip, for Secretary of Defense. There was general agreement that Cheney would be confirmed, vacating his seat as Minority Whip. Newt was back in Georgia on his way to his Griffin office when he was informed of

Cheney's nomination and as soon as he got to the office began to check in with colleagues.

Immediately, Newt's supporters urged him to pursue Cheney's role as Whip. "I recognized that Newt had basically assumed the leadership. He was doing leadership duties and not being given credit for being a leader of the party—this was an unexpected opening at the level Newt should be playing."[34]

"We had calls going all over the nation. I personally made fifty or sixty calls that weekend. Newt called nearly everybody in the conference," reported Walker. "By Sunday afternoon I was calling people who were telling me, oh yeah, I've already had three or four calls about Newt Gingrich....Even people who said they couldn't support Newt were impressed by the fact that the whole organizational thing seemed to come together." The staff had come together in Georgia and in Washington to locate Republican congressmen and those who might influence them to vote for Newt. They then placed the calls for Newt while he talked almost non-stop through Sunday afternoon.

Vin Weber, Steve Gunderson and the COS core started working. Weber's chief of staff, Dan Meyer, provided invaluable assistance in locating congressmen and organizing the staff. "This represented five years of work," said Walker. "They'd started with the absolute loyalists network we'd developed through the COS network, then Jon Kyl, Dan Burton, then to outside allies. I called Don Ritter in Pennsylvania and said, Don, Newt's running for whip, I hope you can support him, and his immediate reaction was, you're doggone right, that's everything we've ever dreamed about so what can I do to help?"[35]

Walker and Newt instructed supporters to call their committees and whoever they could call. "It wasn't organized quickly, rather the result of five years of organization," said Walker. By Sunday night when Newt flew back to Washington he had fifty-five firm commitments. Newt's press secretary, Sheila Ward, worked overtime.

Along with the COS regulars Newt sought to build a core base that included the 92 Group, the Moderate Republicans. He personally called Steve Gunderson, Nancy Johnson and Olympia Snow who agreed to support him. Johnson and Gunderson recommended him to their colleagues as one who had vision, strength and charisma to build a

---

[34] Walker Interview, 17 July 1989.
[35] Ibid.

majority party in the House. Snow agreed to second his nomination as a clear signal that he had the support of the moderate Republicans.[36]

In an 18 March column Jack Germond and Jules Witcover noted Newt "has hit a sensitive nerve with his insistence that his party must follow a policy of aggressive partisanship if the members of the minority are going to be more than so many potted plants."[37] Wright and the Democratic chairmen had helped Newt make his point by their high-handedness and arrogance. The moderates, though they did not always agree with Newt's tactics, were ready to do almost anything to become part of the majority — even make Newt a part of the leadership to send a message. Even though the 92 Group was not as conservative as Newt and the COS, they were activists and wanted an activist leader.

Gingrich stood for confrontation, not accommodation. One GOP member told the *Atlanta Constitution* that Newt "was offering toughness and all out war." Representative Cass Ballenger reported, "He almost did it [built the conservative opposition to the Democrats] all by himself, and that took not only a lot of thinking but a helluva lot of guts. It showed people that he's not only a thinker, he's a doer."[38]

The Democrats continued their attacks. On 20 March, two days before the whip election, the *Washington Post* printed a front page story critical of the arrangement Newt had to promote his 1984 book. He spent a good deal of that day assuring his colleagues that his arrangement was completely legal and did not violate House ethics. Representative Barney Frank and other Democrats noted that electing Gingrich would be good for them because "he produces great unity among the Democrats," much in the same way that Speaker Jim Wright had among Republicans.

In asking for support from other Republican Members Newt armed each of his supporters with a series of ten selling points:[39]

1. It would give an opportunity to ratify the concept of reform and honest self-government.

---

36 Nancy Johnson Interview, 29 September 1995.

37 *Atlanta Constitution*, 18 March 1989.

38 Ibid., 3-19-89.

39 Gingrich Papers, Whip Fight Folder.

2. Newt is a proven product (victories in the House Administration Committee) and has the drive and activism necessary to do the job.

3. Newt is the one person who gives a reasonable hope to elect a GOP Speaker before 2000. Newt will stay in the House.

4. Newt wants the chance to make Bob Michel Speaker.

5. Newt will be *Michel's* whip. He is not pushing for his own leadership.

6. Newt works with the moderates and has a good record on environmental and minority issues.

7. Newt supports women and has a strong record within the House and GOP Conference on that issue.

8. Newt is moving quickly to end this and win without a divisive fight for whip.

9. Newt can work with Democrats. He has in the Georgia delegation and with Coelho on the House Administration Committee.

10. Newt will use the whip position to make it a team effort to include each member of the Conference...super activism. He will reach out to all factions of the party.

Being so partisan some worried that he could not work well with the other party as a Whip must do. He thought experience showed that he could do it. He had worked well with Democrats inside the Georgia delegation and on the Public Works and House administration Committees. Representative Roy Rowland, from Georgia, noted that he had "worked extremely well" with Georgia Democrats and on Public Works. He had worked with Representative Tony Coelho on House Administration in gaining an increase in Republican staff members thus showing that he was capable of negotiation as well as bombast. He made the point that he could be bipartisan. "I am very capable of being bipartisan if it's a fair deal," but added that he would not go along if the Democrats were taking advantage of him or the Republicans.[40]

Newt and his team worked tirelessly preparing for the GOP Conference Whip vote which would take place on 22 March 1989. His opponent, Representative Ed Madigan, was close to Michel and the old bulls. He ran a straightforward campaign but started three days after Newt had begun his search for votes. He offered security and a continuation of the conciliatory approach. Madigan would never surprise one but, many felt, he would also never lead them to a GOP majority in the House. Michel had said he could work with Newt but that Madigan was a friend and ally from Illinois. He also worked hard for Madigan to the point that an emissary had to be sent by Newt supporters to ask him to back off or risk splitting the Conference. Michel's efforts were substantial to Madigan but in the end it was not enough.

Rep. Bill Frenzel, a sixty-one year old colleague from House Administration, who had been in the House since 1963, agreed to nominate Newt. Representative John Paul Hammerschmidt, a sixty-seven year old member from Arkansas who came to Congress in 1967 agreed to second the nomination along with Representative Olympia Snow, a leader of the 92 Group of moderates. Thus two Old Bulls and a moderate woman were Newt's recommenders, not merely the COS supporters. Dan Meyer, Weber's chief of staff and key vote counter and organizer, remembers when Frenzel was announced as the one who would nominate Newt, "Jaws dropped...the Conference couldn't believe it."[41]

The conference met at the RNC building on 22 March with Representative Jerry Lewis presiding. The ballot was secret. Newt won by two votes. Representative William Dannemeyer, an arch conservative from California summed up what many thought. "I voted for Newt and it was the right thing to do. Madigan was a good man but not the activist that Newt is and we needed an activist to grapple with the institution. When you are in the minority, you don't need somebody

---

[40] Dan Meyer Interview, 11 September 1989.
[41] Ibid.

whose strong suit is conciliation. You need a tireless fighter. And Newt, I think, exhibited that."[42]

After Lewis announced Newt as the winner Newt came forward to a standing ovation. He asked Michel, Vander Jagt, his old mentor, and Madigan to come stand with him. He noted the loss of Lott, Kemp and Cheney and thanked Frenzel, Snow and Hammerschmidt for their efforts along with his supporters, Dan Meyer and Vander Jagt. He thanked Marianne who "frankly tempered me a couple of times when I'd have become 'the old Newt.'" A voice from the back of the room shouted, "Keep her around." Newt thanked Michel for his acceptance and his forbearance: "He has tolerated more from me during the last few years than one could reasonably expect from one human being."

Representative Barney Frank sent Newt a letter, signed by two other Democrats, Martin Sabo and Lawrence Smith, asking for disclosure of book project information. At his first news conference the day he was elected Whip, Newt asked those interested to send written questions to him about the book project. He and Marianne would gather the materials needed to respond, collate it, discuss it with their lawyers and accountants and then hold a press conference. He promised that "everything would be disclosed in an orderly fashion."

On 11 April Bill Alexander of Arkansas filed a ten-point complaint against Gingrich. Two weeks later Newt's former and future opponent, David Worley, wrote the Ethics Committee with more charges.[43] The promised news conference was held the same day that Worley wrote the committee, 25 April. Marianne, a general partner who had served in essence as business manager for the project, put the materials together and started answering each written question point by point. The press refused to let her go through the material and insisted on asking accusatory questions before she could finish her answers. The press conference became "stormy." Marianne, unused to the Washington press corps, was stunned, frustrated and angered. She felt those gathered at the press conference did not want to hear the truth but were there to accuse and try to trap her. She and Newt tried to stick to the rules and go through the conference point by point but after constant interruptions Marianne, trembling with anger, walked out of the conference. She waited outside, shielded by staff and the Capitol

---

[42] Warner & Berley, *Newt Gingrich*, 122.
[43] Warner & Berley, *Newt Gingrich*, 125-126.

Police until Newt finished the conference. The group adjourned to the House dining room to assess their next move.

Newt had told the press that while his arrangement for promoting the book was unusual it was not unethical and operated on the same principle as a Broadway play. "We wrote a real book, working with a real publisher, distributed to real bookstores and sold to real people for a realistic, standard royalty and Jim Wright did none of those things."[44] The press did not want to hear it. It was all so neat, first Newt accused Wright of ethics violations which were exposed by the press, and then he himself fell victim to the same charge. Marianne thought the press had accepted Newt's guilt before the news conference began and did not want to be bothered by facts that might change it.

Comparable complaints had been filed. Both Wright and Newt were accused of ethics violations involving book deals, of using their staff to help with the book, of improperly soliciting money, of improperly helping contributors, of having payments made to their wives for non-work. Newt was even accused of having an illegal property deal like Wright. In 1986 Newt had signed a note with his daughter Kathy when she bought a house from Pat Grunden, a long-time Newt supporter. The amount of the sale, $77,300, was a fair price and Kathy paid off the entire mortgage by herself. It did not occur to him to list that as a liability on his reporting form and that was a mistake. He was outraged that somehow this error in judgement could be considered unethical.

Newt knew he would be attacked but had not expected the depth of the hostility accompanying the attacks. His friend Weber told the *Atlantic* in an interview, "I was shocked that he was shocked. He had charged into the enemy camp and killed the king's pig. And he wondered why the king's soldiers were gathering with their swords drawn." Newt had shown how to take down a speaker, now some of the press and the Democrats wanted to use the same blueprint to take down a Whip.[45]

The charges and complaints continued for almost a year. The Ethics Committee had appointed the same firm that had investigated Wright to serve as outside counsel concerning Newt's investigation, the Phelan firm. After extensive investigation, on 3 March 1990 counsel recommended that Gingrich be cleared. The committee did clear him of

---

[44] Gingrich Papers, Book File Folder.

[45] Warner & Berley, *Newt Gingrich*, 129.

any wrongdoing in the book arrangements and procedures but chastised him for not disclosing his co-signature on his daughter's mortgage and for using official stationary in one instance to promote a senior citizens' cruise.

The investigation, which had a special prosecutor, lasted a year, and cost the taxpayers $1,115,851.20, exonerated Newt whereas the Wright investigation had resulted in sixty-nine violations charged by the Ethics Committee. The personal cost to Newt was well over $80,000 leading some to note if the Democrats could not remove Newt at least they could try to destroy him financially and administer some pain.

Nineteen eighty-eight had been a costly year for Newt both in money and energy and yet he felt good about what had been accomplished. His charges against Speaker Wright had resulted in action being taken against him. He was successful at the GOP convention and had been involved in the national campaign. His work to organize the House GOP to be more aggressive was starting to pay dividends. He was set to become the Minority Whip and be officially part of the party leadership. He made it through the 1988 elections with fifty-nine percent of the vote and felt pretty good about his base as 1989 arrived. His positive assessment of the coming year would prove to be premature.

Eastern Airlines was in trouble. Frank Lorenzo had taken over and was at war with the Eastern workers who struck and were determined to destroy the airline rather than let Lorenzo have it. It had been a minor problem in 1988 but festered into a sizable boil as 1989 progressed. The unions wanted Newt to go to the President and encourage him to declare the strike an emergency and force arbitration. Newt noted those powers to declare an emergency related to a national emergency, not to the problems of one airline and refused to go to Bush—an action that would have been futile in any event. The unions felt betrayed and began "boot Newt" demonstrations whenever he held a meeting. He met with them and organized his staff to help them with their Cobra insurance problems and to help them seek other employment. The meetings were emotional and raucous and accomplished little except to give David Worley, now running against Newt for a second time, a cause. Worley practically lived at the union hall giving the members encouragement and in turn receiving encouragement from them.[46]

Worley also attacked Newt over his vote supporting the congressional pay raise and on support for savings and loans at a time when they were being bailed with $500 billion. "Newt can get the government to give his buddies at the S & L's $500 billion but can't get it to help out his own voters who are facing ruin because of Frank Lorenzo." He brought up the book deal again. He accused Newt of wanting to do away with Social Security and of wanting to put old people on the streets. He attacked GOPAC for illegally supporting Newt's activities. He pictured Newt as the ultimate hypocrite for talking about cutting waste in government and riding around in a "chauffeur driven limousine." Worley hired a stretch limousine and driver to ride around the metro area with Newt signs on the car and had the driver yell out the window, "vote for Newt." This tactic resulted in numerous negative calls to the Newt headquarters.

The limousine charge bothered Newt because there was no limousine, it was the standard Town Car used by all the leadership on both sides of the aisle. There was no chauffeur but rather a police driver who served as bodyguard for the Whip, whoever happened to be in that position. The three Democratic leaders, as well as Bob Michel, had the same kind of car and driver. The charge of hypocrisy and use of perks hit home with the voters at a gut level and became the stuff of talk shows and street gossip.

The Gingrich depicted by Worley was one who did not want to help workers or the elderly but voted himself a big raise and drove around in a limousine at the taxpayers' expense. Worley was having a field day. To make matters worse for Newt his most populous county, Clayton, was gaining black, Democratic constituents, as African-Americans moved out of Atlanta into the suburbs to the south. Significant change had taken place since the 1988 election.

Newt understood that he had problems. He spent more time in the district and brought in Joe Gaylord as campaign consultant and chief advisor. They outspent Worley, who had money problems because he had attacked the pay raise and thus the DCCC could not help him. He bought no television ads whereas Newt was on television and radio at

---

[46] Ibid.

every opportunity. Marianne became involved as a sort of super manager the last two weeks to make sure everyone was focused. She spent time with the volunteers and worked with Sharon Kuntz on finances to make sure that every dollar counted.

A week before the election Randy Evans met with Newt at Pilgreen's restaurant near the FONG headquarters in Morrow, Georgia. They had a copy of the Democratic poll which showed Newt's numbers high but beginning to splinter like a crack in a windshield. "These numbers are starting to nose-dive," Evans told Newt. "It'll be a long night and a close race." Preparations were made for tighter ballot security due to the expected close vote. "I'm convinced that this election will be stolen if we don't prepare for it," Newt told his close supporters. Poll watchers and marshals were alerted, especially in the more rural Democratic counties.[47]

Evans was watching the numbers and felt pretty sure that Newt would pull it out, though just barely. When the first set of reports came in early to the crowd at the Airport Marriott Hotel in Atlanta it seemed that it would be a long evening. None of the returns were pushing Newt comfortably ahead as his supporters had come to expect. Worried looks dominated the room as staffers reassured the faithful. Upstairs in Newt's suite concern was also evident.

The race was very close during most of the evening. As 10:00 P. M. passed Evans was the only one who seemed to be confident and enjoying himself. He had the numbers and was sure that Newt would win by about 1000 votes. Catherine Brock, Mary Brown, Joe Gaylord and Newt were going over the returns. As the numbers came in, Newt's victory looked more promising. Evans said flatly. "All the bad and swing precincts are in Fayette County and they'll go big for Newt. He's going to win by a slim margin." Newt's supporters were clearly delighted and urged Newt to go down and claim victory. He declined, wanting to wait until the returns were actually in and he had the numbers in hand. He and his party went down around 1:00 A.M. and in his most subdued victory speech ever, claimed a close win. The small group still there, less than 300, were delighted but too tired and emotionally drained to do anything but congratulate their candidate

---

[47] Randy Evans Interview, 16 August 1994.

and go home for some rest. Newt had won by 974 votes. A recount was federally mandated.

Ballot security had paid off. As soon as it seemed possible that Newt could win Gaylord called US Marshal Lynn Duncan, who Newt helped get appointed, and made sure that he understood the situation and moved quickly to personally supervise the most dangerous county. They checked in with all the other counties to be sure that Newt's poll watchers secured the ballots. Key observers helped supervise the recount to make sure there were no problems or tampering with the boxes or the ballots. In the end few votes were changed and Newt had clearly, though narrowly, held on to his seat.

11

IN THE LEADERSHIP

The 101st Congress had been a mixed one for Newt. He had begun with great expectations. There was a new Republican president, GOPAC was in full swing, Newt just won a solid re-election victory in 1988, he was the new Minority Whip and his ethics challenge to the Speaker seemed to be about to bear fruit. It had ended with him the subject, though exonerated, of a special prosecutor's investigation, a fight with the airlines union and a vicious election that he almost lost.

One of the major accomplishments of 1989 was the reorganization of the Whip's office. Room 219 in the Capitol, the office of the Minority Whip, became command center for Republican activists. Tending to business first, Newt built a whip staff that knew their business and could count and deliver votes. Dan Meyer, from Weber's staff, and Len Swineheart became the central players around which the rest of a very capable team was put together. Meyer, a gifted organizer and vote counter, became chief of staff for the Whip's office. Like Newt, he was dedicated to the election of a Republican majority as were the House members Newt placed as assistant whips.[1]

Newt had been dedicated to building the GOP majority since he came to Congress. His good friend, Randy Evans, who stayed at Newt's house while an intern in Newt's Washington office, noted that in the summer of 1979 he and Newt would drive home at the end of the day in an old Volkswagen and the GOP majority was the topic most often discussed. A decade later it was still Newt's most important goal. He

---

[1] Dan Meyer Interview, 11 September 1989.

now had GOPAC and the Whip office as tools to use in the building of that long sought after majority.[2]

Newt had been elected Whip on a Wednesday afternoon with the Easter recess starting two days later. He had to move quickly because most of Cheney's staff was preparing to move to the Department of Defense with their boss and Newt had to build his own staff. He talked to Margot Carlyle, an Assistant Secretary of Defense for Congressional Affairs and an experienced "Washington hand." Due to philosophical differences over how the office should be run they both decided—with Weber's guidance—that hiring her to be chief of staff for the Whip office would not be a good idea. When the recess ended Newt had yet to appoint someone to that critical slot.[3]

Linda Nave, a trusted and experienced Newt staff member, was brought in to run the regular day to day functions of the office and Len Swineheart as a vote counter. Lynn had been Weber's administrative assistant at one time, was a long-time hill staff member and currently worked on the House Budget Committee. Newt met with Weber and Meyer and told them, "We need a chief of staff, you guys work it out."

After discussing the problem for a while Weber told Meyer, "Why don't you go over to get it set up. We are behind the eight ball now. We'll look for someone to replace you and you can come back as my AA." Meyer complied and quickly took charge. Gingrich offered him the chief of staff position on a permanent basis but Meyer declined. He was happy with Weber who was a rising star in his own right and was also from the same state, Minnesota. As time passed and no acceptable candidate for the position appeared, Newt pressed Meyer to accept the job. Billy Pitts, Bob Michel's chief of staff, helped the cause by telling Meyer, "I know how you feel. You want to get back to the AA's job so you can work with the office budget, decide on who gets the intern slots," and generally described all the negative aspects of the AA's job in a rather sarcastic attempt to persuade him to make the move. Pressured by Newt, and his wife's desire to stay in Washington rather than return as AA and then move back to Minnesota to run Vin's next campaign, Dan accepted.[4]

---

[2] Randy Evans Interview, 16 August 1994.

[3] Dan Meyer Interview, 11 September 1989.

[4] Ibid.

Conscious of the need to be inclusive, Newt rebuilt the whip organization along two lines. First came the central whip function of vote counting and gathering. This task was entrusted to one of two chief deputy whips, Bob Walker, Newt's old friend and ally. Walker, a master at floor procedures and tactics, would represent the COS or conservative wing of the conference. The other chief deputy whip would be Steve Gunderson representing the moderate/liberal wing of the conference.[5]

Newt intended to use the Whip office to do more than round up and count votes. He thought that strategic planning and intra-party communications were lacking and thought the Gunderson group could be useful in improving that area. Gunderson's group was called the "Strategic Whip Organization" and had two deputy whips working under Gunderson, Jon Kyls and Nancy Johnson—one conservative and one moderate. Reporting to them were five assistant whips in charge of theme development (Rod Chandler), pre-floor legislation (Steve Bartlett), outside allies (Larry Craig), communication (Jack Buechner) and professional development (Dick Armey). A series of assistant whips were appointed to work with each of these groups, some of whom, like Representatives Kasich, Goodling and Archer, would become committee chairmen following the 1994 Republican revolution.[6]

Representative Walker described the whip office reorganization as, "an activist rather than a COS model....A COS model wouldn't work very well in a formal structure because the advantage of COS was that it was always basically informal. We had a chairman but not much beyond chairman. The chairman existed to run meetings, but we never really bound ourselves to any kind of a formalized structure beyond that."[7]

This activist model worked well in many ways. It was inclusive, a major objective of Newt's. Almost every member who wanted to was able to play a role. It allowed Newt to "task" members and help them develop their strengths. This was a role Newt played that was, according to Representative Johnson, one of Newt's strengths. "Newt tolerates differences and doesn't let it get to him. He helps others do this." There were times when the moderates did not agree with Newt

[5] Gingrich Papers, Whip File, "Strategic Whip Organization."

[6] Nancy Johnson Interview, 29 September 1995.

[7] Robert Walker Interview, 17 July 1989.

but felt free to ask his advice on how best to shape the debate to make their points and argue their cause.[8]

The model also, according to Tony Roda, staffer for the Strategic Whip Organization (SWO), allowed all GOP Conference members a chance to have their say. The purpose of the SWO, as Roda saw it, was "to shape debate before it got to the floor and work with outside allies to decide on the key themes or issues, to formulate a GOP message and serve as a channel to get that message out."[9]

Despite the advantages of its structure, the SWO did not accomplish all of its goals. The Strategic Whip Organization never realized its full potential. While it did give input and experienced leadership roles, the overall structure failed to develop for a number of reasons. The most important reason was probably that it duplicated part of the purpose of the Minority Conference chaired by Representative Jerry Lewis. It was also outside the framework of the existing organization and this fact caused it to receive less than full support from the Old Bulls.

Representative Lewis, as conference chairman, was responsible for providing materials and backup for members in their work and this same role was given to the Assistant Deputy Whip for Strategy in Professional Development, Representative Dick Armey. Armey, hard-nosed and relatively uncompromising, clashed almost immediately with Lewis who felt he was treading on the conference roles. Armey's opinion seemed to be that if Lewis and the Conference organization were truly doing their job the he would not have to do it for them. He did not intend to back off just to satisfy Lewis' ego.

Gingrich admired Armey and wanted to use him to train and inspire other members to follow his example. Armey had moved the base closing bill through the legislative process as a minority member and saw it from concept to completion. He could train and teach the others and possibly relieve Newt of some of that burden. Though productive, Armey stepped on many toes of moderate Republicans as well as Democrats. One moderate Republican described him as "rigid" and unwilling to honestly listen to other views.[10]

The moderates had an investment in Newt's success and that of the Whip organization as well. Nancy Johnson had witnessed liberal and

---

[8] Nancy Johnson Interview, 29 September 1995.

[9] Tony Roda Interview, 25 September 1995.

[10] Ibid.

conservative Democrats coming to blows in Connecticut and losing their effectiveness as a party. As a result they could draw no more than 22 percent of the vote because they could not communicate and focus on common goals. She, along with Gunderson, Snow, and Tauke, did not want this to happen to their party.

The 92 Group of moderates put in weekend time and worked to plan an aggressive activism based on common ground. "What do we agree on?" was always the question. Newt, Walker and Weber met with the 92 Group in order to take an idea through the process from its origin to a floor vote. This was outside the regular committee structure and having ideas "bubble up from the bottom" was good in theory. However, it conflicted with the committee structure and ranking members became concerned. Like Representative Lewis, they felt their turf was being trampled.[11]

After the 1990 elections the group became concerned more with themes and strategy. Newt would bring in specialists such as Gail Walensky (health care) and Jim Pinkerton (White House advisor) to talk about positioning rather than tactics. These specialists helped Newt, and the other participants, think through broader conceptual ideas while still in a legislative setting.

Altogether this group and others who were brought in from time to time worked to develop a mind set about what was common in the party. They worked to develop communications among the members and to encourage ideas and different points of view so that the big picture could be seen before action was taken. According to Representative Johnson, "this really influenced the evolution of the party." It also helped Gingrich's evolution as a leader. In his new position he was able to disperse patronage and to show that he could accept losing. He helped other members on a personal level work out their own programs, build loyalty and bond personally with the team that would be the 1995 leadership. He also emerged as a heroic leader of a revitalized party who did not hesitate to unsheathe the sword and wade into the foe in the interest of the common goal, gaining a House majority for the Republicans.[12]

While George Bush, Bob Dole and Bob Michel might have some reservations about Newt's leadership, most of the Republicans in the

---

[11] Dan Meyer Interview, 11 September 1989.

[12] Nancy Johnson Interview, 25 September 1995.

House were solidly behind him and his activist style. They also thought he was the only major GOP leader seeking to extend and build on the Reagan legacy. As Whip he was able to display his leadership skills and reach out to the rank and file of the party across the country. His increased travel schedule crisscrossing America attested to his determination to broaden the base of his support within the party and at the same time use that support to elect more Republican Congressmen.

To achieve the goal of a GOP majority, which he had sought since coming to Congress in 1979, he needed an updated plan. He talked with his close advisors and decided he needed to move away from the daily press of politics where he scheduled his life in fifteen-minute intervals and was constantly plagued by phone calls, each more pressing than the other. His friend and colleague at GOPAC, Bo Callaway, offered him the use of a special cabin complex at his Colorado resort, Crested Butte.

"North Pole Basin" is in a remote area of Crested Butte with no phone or electricity. It is designed as a ski camp lodge where one can visit to rest and reflect. Newt decided he and Marianne would go there for almost three weeks and bring in groups of advisors for a few days each to do some long range planning. The immediate target was the 1990 election but the discussions went further and focused not only on elections but also on how to broaden the appeal of the "reform movement" to the country at large and Republican voters in particular. Newt wanted to educate the voters so they would understand turning out the Democrats was in their best interest.[13]

Three major groups were brought to Crested Butte in August 1989: GOP members, political consultants, and contributors and advisors, including a number of GOPAC members. Steve Hanser, Jeff Eisenach and Dan Meyer served as advisory staffers. They mixed work with relaxation and generally enjoyed the mountain atmosphere, hiking with Representative Kyle and singing folk songs and ballads with Representative Walker and his guitar. They also convinced Representative Dan Burton, a man of strongly held opinions, to move in their direction.[14]

---

13 Steve Hanser Interview, 8 June 1995.
14 Dan Meyer Interview, 11 September 1989.

Times were changing and the Cold War was ending. Republican opposition to the Soviet Union was no longer a winning issue and just opposing something was not good enough to win elections. Since his first campaign, Newt had stressed the need to have an issue to stand for instead of just being against your opponent's program. Though he had every intention of pointing out the problems created by the liberal welfare state, he also wanted to offer the American people, and the voters of the sixth district of Georgia, a vision of the country he thought was possible. He wanted to give them a clear choice of two futures, the liberal welfare state or the conservative opportunity society.

The meeting at Crested Butte had helped focus Newt's thinking on a "plan for the 90s" which was to begin in the 1990 campaign. In an Atlanta strategy session a week before Christmas he talked about his plans for the next election and the early part of the new decade. The idea was to follow his old plan of "nationalizing" the 1990 campaign so each GOP candidate, from mayor to Congress, would discuss and debate the same set of issues and have two or three key themes in common with all other Republicans. Other party leaders were supportive of the "nationalizing" idea. Bill Bennett, Jack Kemp and Vice President Dan Quayle, with their strong emphasis on values, supported the concept from their own point of view and in the interest of their own political objectives.[15]

Newt outlined his strategy to his advisors. "The key to the 90s is going to be to focus our activities so that each activity builds on the one behind it and the one ahead of it. We want to launch a reform movement defining the America that can be and translate that down into specific groups so that whether you are a young person wanting to buy a house, or a homebuilder, or a realtor, you understand what the terms, the possibilities [are], and you understand that there are real action steps that can be taken to increase your chances of [achieving] those possibilities."

Gingrich was clearly talking about a national campaign and not just his own reelection effort in the sixth district. He talked about the need for coordination in the "movement" which would open with a national television event and would be supported by a newsletter, a 900 number and training videos for GOP candidates. The effort would be formed

---

[15] Gingrich, Hanser, Steely Tape, 19 December 1989.

around a triangle he had developed. One side would be "responsibilities of government," the second side would be "winning one race at a time in one district at a time," and the third, "the creation of national themes and a national movement."

As Steely's focus was the sixth district race, he raised the question of how all this was to apply to the Georgia effort. "We want to think through the '90 campaign in the sixth district so it becomes a campaign, in part, in which most of the people of the sixth district understand why their personal lives would be better off because Newt Gingrich is reelected to fight for the changes which they think will make their lives better," Newt said. "So it becomes a circular process in which the specific individual can tell you what they care about in their own life and you can tell them about our vision of the 'America that can be' in terms of what their particular concerns are and then we can tell them what it is we are trying to accomplish through legislation of that kind of action in order to achieve the values, the changes that would improve their personal lives," he explained.

In the district target groups would be identified with model group brochures printed. Newt wanted three national organizational efforts to be reflected in the sixth district. The first would be to explain capital gains tax cuts (the Savings and Retirement Act) as a jobs bill. All those having an interest in capital gains reform would then be networked. The second would be a grass roots effort on the prevention of drugs and violent crime. The third would be an effort to integrate African-Americans who are non-governmental, such as preachers, into a self-help organization which would become a "Thousand Points of Light" operation. It would be centered on ten cities around the country, Atlanta being one, wherein fund-raisers would be held, featuring either the President, Vice President, Secretary Jack Kemp or Secretary Louis Sullivan, to finance the volunteer effort "to replace the cultural poverty and help people outside the structure of the welfare state."[16]

Newt continued, "We reintegrate everything by defining my job as reform movement leader trying to develop the sixth district 'that could be' and explaining everything in a way that related directly to the sixth district. With that then broadcasted through my position as Whip, through the House of Representatives and through the movement so

---

16 Ibid.

that it is all the same language and the same issues—in the sixth district first. This then becomes the organizational framework of the congressional campaign." He wanted to make the sixth district a model for the nation.

Newt thought the reform movement should be off the ground by early March. It should include reform language, ideas, documents, etc. Gingrich said the movement was "to create the America that is possible as a launching pad for the 21st century, to recognize that reform has to occur from the school board all the way up. Our goal," he said, "is to change the market place incentives so you do what makes more sense for you."[17]

A similar effort had been tried in 1988 but had failed to materialize nationwide mostly due to the lack of more Evans. In 1988 Newt's plan was driven by individuals—Newt and Evans. This time better organization would make it more workable. What looked like a solid, workable plan in December 1989 that could be used as a model for the national effort ended up becoming a personal, defensive campaign that was anything but a model. The concept did work better, however, outside the sixth district.

The model for the 1990s was also shaken by the president's actions regarding the budget. The budget fight of 1990–1991 and Newt's opposition to President Bush's decision to raise taxes would cost Newt some support within the party. Support for the tax increase would cost George Bush a second term and in an improbable way would open the door for the great GOP victory in 1994.

Newt had stated on more than one occasion that his first loyalty was to the people of the sixth district of Georgia. He had not shrunk from opposing the Reagan White House when he thought they were wrong but he was not in the leadership at that time. Now, as Whip, he had something of a responsibility to help with the president's policies. He felt, however, that responsibility was limited. He had opposed the Bush veto of a bill allowing Chinese students to stay in the US after their visas expired. He said he failed to understand why Bush would do that. He told the *Washington Post*, "I do not believe you gain anything in the long run by letting the Chinese dictatorship believe that you value their friendship enough that you will tolerate brutality and repression."

---

[17] Ibid.

Newt thought that it should not be tolerated in South Africa or China and remained consistent in his opposition. "You can't send those kids back to the Communists. It's not right."

The same stubbornness carried over to the budget fight. Newt and the House GOP activists were not happy with the willingness of the President to give in to the Democrats. It was not that they were opposed to compromise but compromise required a two-sided relationship. To the liberal Democrats the terms compromise and bipartisan meant that you accepted their position and agreed with them. What concerned Newt was an attitude of giving in to Democratic demands in hopes that a conciliatory attitude would pay off in the future. The GOP activists had little hope of the Democrats being fair or "working with" the GOP. What they saw was the Democrats working out their program and denouncing the Republicans as uncompromising if they refused to support that program. They thought it was all one-sided in favor of the Democrats.

Newt first became concerned in February 1990 when an article in the *Wall Street Journal* noted that a "Budget Summit is Possible Between Bush, Lawmakers." It quoted Dan Rostenkowski, chairman of the Ways and Means Committee, as saying a satisfactory agreement could not be reached until the president's "'no new taxes' pledge is history."[18] The next month Speaker Tom Foley was quoted as favoring "spending reductions" and "new revenues." He said both sides would have to "sign on to the unpopular parts of the package. The administration cannot expect Democrats to stand alone on taxes and Social Security spending caps." Newt feared this "sensible" argument that would register with the president and induce him to give in order to appear "reasonable."[19]

The Democrats, throughout April and May, launched a brilliant campaign to persuade the president to agree to a tax increase and also to be first to propose it. They did not want to be the ones blamed for raising taxes just before the 1990 congressional elections. They did, however, want the new taxes and the best way to obtain them was to make the Republicans share the blame for raising them.

George Bush had made a production of asking the American people to "Read my lips...No New Taxes." Most Republicans thought there was

---

[18] Gingrich Papers, Steely Papers, 1990 Budget Fight Folder.
[19] Ibid., "Quotes from the Budget Summit."

no way he could go back on that pledge. Newt was less certain. To give in would deprive the GOP of one of their most potent weapons in the upcoming campaign. The polls showed that the Democrats were thought of as the "tax and spend" party and their insistence on a tax increase would prove that belief. But to go back on the Bush pledge and ask Republican members to follow his lead would betray the pledges they and he had made to the American people and put all GOP candidates in danger at the polls. At that time a president, and Congressmen, were held responsible for pledges they made to the American people. Newt thought betraying the pledge would be disastrous for the president and the GOP generally. He thought it would be bad policy as well as bad politics and knew he could not support it—even as Whip, to help the president.

Even before the budget fight George Bush was not enamored of Newt Gingrich. He saw Newt as the attack dog of the GOP and that was not his style. He was uncomfortable with Newt's style of confrontation as was Newt with Bush's conciliatory approach. Newt was not the president's choice for Whip and he encouraged Michel not to retire when it appeared Newt might replace him. Newt, however, had become Whip and was now part of the leadership. The White House had no choice but to deal with him.

On 7 May 1990, the *Washington Post* reported "Bush, Hill Leaders Agree to Pursue Deficit Talks, Possibility of Tax Rise Expected to Be a Topic." The next day the *Wall Street Journal* headlined "Bush Would Take Part in Discussions on Deficit Cuts Without Preconditions." A day later Richard Darman, Office of Management and Budget director, was quoted in the *New York Times* as "sounding the alarm on a rising deficit."[20]

A rising deficit was a cause for alarm but Newt was just as concerned about what he saw taking place in the White House. Budget summit meetings had begun in early May and it was obvious to Newt, as to everyone else in Washington, that the Democrats intended to have President Bush break his pledge and be the first to call for new tax increases. It appeared that the mind set in the White House was to be "reasonable." The president and his advisors seemed to think that they could explain to the American people that there was an economic crisis

---

[20] Ibid.

and, in spite of his pledge, the president was dealing boldly with it. The Democrats reassured them that the people would understand.

The president accommodated the Democrats when in a 16 May press conference he met their demand to "show the public how bad the problem was." The next month was spent in talks where the Democrats refused to negotiate until Bush made the first move. The Democrats assured Bush he would be seen as a statesman if he agreed to a tax increase. Newt opposed this decision and warned the GOP negotiators it would be disastrous for Bush and the Republicans.

In late June Bush gave in after Speaker Tom Foley warned him that the Democrats would pull out of the negotiations if he did not make some gesture to help them avoid the political blame for any tax increase that might come out of the talks. The *Wall Street Journal* reported on 27 June, "Bush Reversal on Taxes Spurs Budget Talks." Newt and the COS activists were aghast. Discussions in House 219, the Minority Whip's office, extended late into the night on more than one evening concerning what action they should take. [21] The president had sought some cover by repeating his "no new taxes" pledge and declaring that "tax revenue increases" would be needed to shrink the deficit. No one was fooled. The *Washington Post* noted "Bush Abandons Campaign Pledge, Calls for New Taxes."[22]

On 27 July Newt sent a memo to the GOP budget summit representatives containing his assessment of the current situation. He opened with a quote from Woodrow Wilson, "You should never kill someone who is in the process of committing suicide." He continued, "Maybe that explains the current Democratic budget negotiating strategy. Why do anything if the Republicans are willing to kill themselves?"[23] In an eight point analysis he described the summit events. He thought the Republicans gave in time and again while the Democrats stalled, passed "appropriations bills far higher than any summit can accept," and were rewarded by daily photo opts "elevating them in stature and respectability." They then "do nothing but pass more spending bills. The Democrats will do nothing but pass more spending bills and insist on a debt ceiling that maximizes pressure on Republicans by expiring on 15 October." He concluded with a question: "Is it time for

---

[21] Ibid.

[22] Ibid.

[23] Gingrich Papers, "Quotes from the Budget Summit."

Republicans to stop committing slow suicide and start putting pressure on the Democrats while telling the country the truth about Capitol Hill?"

According to the *New York Times* the Democrats had earlier been concerned that the president "with all his credibility, walks into the press room and says, 'I did my best, but the Democrats just won't talk about anything but taxes.'" That tactic, later used effectively by President Clinton, was also Newt's fondest hope but it was not realized. He struggled to be both faithful to his promise and to his obligation, as Whip, to help push the president's agenda. In a 20 July memo to Republican colleagues he listed a series of six requirements before he could support the budget, including economic growth, a permanent capital gains tax cut, adequate funding for defense, real cuts in entitlement spending and reforms in the budget process.[24]

He concluded, "After examining any summit package to insure that these elements are included, then I believe House Republicans will consider appropriate revenue increases." A storm of protest erupted from the activists. Was Newt now to leave them and support tax increases? Newt moved quickly to clarify his position. He told his staff that he probably would "lay low" and vote against the tax increase but did not want to lead the effort because that would rupture his relations with the White House. This period was difficult for Newt. He genuinely wanted to be helpful to Bush but was torn by what he thought a tax increase would do to the president, the GOP and the country. By August he had decided. He would not only vote against a tax-increasing budget but also would not "lay low" and leave the opposition to this budget to others.

In an *Atlanta Journal and Constitution* column, Dick Williams wrote, "An angry Newt Gingrich decides to go his own way. Uneasy lies the crown of leadership," he said. He described Newt as "restive and almost angry." "Even before President Bush went to work full-time on the Middle East, he had abandoned domestic policy to the Democratic majority on Capitol Hill. Republicans have been left to bob and weave as the president rolled back his no-new-tax pledge and settled into a veto strategy," he wrote. He noted that Newt was taking a risk in

---

24 Ibid.

planning "to change House Republican strategy from 'going along to get along' into a force for conservative change."[25]

Newt sensed the country's readiness for his new reform movement and tested his theory at home on the hustings and opened with a speech at the Heritage Foundation on 22 August. Titled "The Washington Establishment Vs the American People: A Report from the Budget Summit," the speech opened with a quote from Bill Buckley, "The profound crisis of our era is, in essence, the conflict between the social engineers who seek to adjust mankind to conform with scientific utopias and the disciples of truth who defend the organic moral order." He described five key goals challenging conservatives: integrity, safety, jobs, new model government and pro-family tax policy. These goals, contained earlier in a letter to his constituents, would provide a "renewed, revitalized America" if achieved—and he made it clear he intended to work to achieve them.[26]

He described how a liberal Congress had worked to undermine President Bush, raise billions in new spending and destroy our basic values in the name of misguided fairness. He proposed a tax cut package that would challenge the Democrats' willingness "to have Americans unemployed in the name of class-warfare, a package that challenges the Democrats directly to see which is the party of jobs and opportunity, and a package that is pro-savings, pro-investment, pro-housing, pro-poor people, pro-family and pro-jobs."

He noted that the struggle was an ongoing one with a long tradition reaching back to Goldwater, Buckley, Reagan and Irvin Kristol. It was now up to the third generation to carry the ball. It was Washington against America. "This is a city which is proud that it has withstood all the screams of the American people for lower taxes, less government, and a replacement for the welfare state," he noted. "I believe that 1990-1992 will be key elections in the struggle for American's future." Immediate action was required and he asked for nothing less than a citizen's movement to achieve it.

Gingrich ended up confessing, "I am sick and tired of being told that we have to put up with some modicum of decay in the bureaucratic welfare state because it's inappropriate in the city to tell the truth. This is a sick process; the Congress is a sick institution. I care about that five-

---

[25] *Atlanta Constitution*, 16 August 1990.

[26] Gingrich Papers, Steely Papers, 1990 Budget Fight Folder.

year-old girl, and as far as I'm concerned, we're going to fight to change this country, to give those kids when they get back from the Middle East a country that they deserve, that they are earning at the risk of their lives."[27] The little girl who was afraid to look out her window for fear of being shot, the decay in the schools due to an uncaring system and unfeeling unions and the welfare state plantation kept alive while it enslaves the poor to benefit bureaucrats and selfish political leaders were all signs that the country had to change—or die as a civilized nation. The crusade was to be more than a political one. It was to be a moral one as well.

Newt could now go back into the budget fray of the summit as a leader of a crusade and not simply as one opposed to a tax increase. His mind was at ease and he was once again on familiar ground—ground that he had walked since his first campaign. He had to defend the traditional anti-tax position that had been part of the dual core, the other being anti-communism, of the Republican position in every election for the past two decades.

Gingrich continued to attend summit meetings and sat with the others at the table. He did not join in the negotiations. He read novels and wrote notes to colleagues and advisors. He listened and waited. The deal finally worked out would have reduced the deficit by $40 billion the first year and by $500 billion over five years. It would do this by raising taxes on tobacco, gas and alcohol, the sin taxes, and by reducing the spending on Medicare. It did not include a capital gains tax cut which was integral to his set of preconditions.

As the summiteers gathered to present the plan to Bush and go with him to announce it in the Rose Garden, Newt spoke up and said, "I can't support this." He explained he had tried hard to find some way to go along but since it did not include economic growth measures nor a capital gains tax cut but did include tax increases he would have to oppose it. Darman and Chief of Staff John Sununu were furious as were the other participants. As they all walked out to make the announcement Newt left by a side door and returned to the Capitol. He was met by the COS activists who supported his refusal to support the package and they began planning to openly oppose the deal secure in the knowledge that it was the right thing to do.

---

[27] Ibid.

Newt had sent a number of warnings other than his memos of 20 July and 27 July. He opposed tax increases in the late summer and fall in his reelection campaign, he refused to be drawn into negotiations and clearly expressed his concern to the White House lobbyist, Nick Calio, in early September by reminding him that his first order of responsibility was to his principles, the people of Georgia and his supporters within the House membership. He also had a responsibility to the president but not necessarily when it went against the interest of the others. His speech to the Heritage Foundation was a clear signal as was an interview he gave to the *Atlanta Journal & Constitution's* Mike Christensen. Gingrich "has taken a novel approach harking back to the early days of Reaganomics: massive tax cuts," reported Christensen on 23 August. Newt argued for tax cuts to stop a recession he thought the Democrats were bound and determined to bring on and said, "Higher taxes would only aggravate a business downturn."[28]

It is possible that since many of his signals were sent outside the Washington beltway they were not picked up in DC. Still, there were enough signs of his possible opposition that they should have been picked up by Sununu and Darman. Calio was concerned enough to confront Newt in early September and should have communicated this concern to the White House. Maybe he did and they would not accept it. After all, Newt had not stated specifically that he would oppose the deal and he was still attending their meetings and raising no objections there. Messages to Sununu and Darman in the two weeks before the Rose Garden announcement contained no statement of his opposition. Some Democrats picked up on it while the meetings were going on according to the *Washington Post* and Newt maintained that he never promised support.[29] Whatever the truth, Darman, Sununu and Bush, as well as GOP leaders were surprised at his defection and felt betrayal when he went public with his opposition. Some thought that opposition helped Bush lose the 1992 election but Newt would remind them that it was not he who broke his promise. "You are killing us; you are just killing us," the president told Newt at a GOP fund-raiser. Newt replied

---

28 *Atlanta Journal*, 30 August 1990.

29 Gingrich Papers, Steely Papers, 1990 Budget Fight Folder. See also Richard Darman, Who's In Control, Chap. 13.

that he was sorry "that this is happening" but did not back off his opposition.[30]

Newt and the activists led enough members to oppose the agreement that the White House had to make further concessions to receive enough Democratic votes to pass the measure. The Bushes felt betrayed and many of the Old Bulls and some of the GOP moderates agreed with them. Republican supporters in Georgia pressured Newt to back the popular president. They thought Newt's opposition might hurt Bush's reelection chances. Calio and others have since confessed that Gingrich had his nose in the wind and read it correctly. "He thought it was going to be a disaster for the Republicans and you know what, he turned out to be right," the White House lobbyist told the *Washington Post*. Still, Newt was viewed by many as a back-stabber and was ostracized by some.

Newt was indeed reading the mood of the country correctly. The people were tired of politics as usual and wanted to see some changes. They wanted to focus on domestic problems now that the Cold War was ending. While Newt supported Bush and his masterful efforts to build an alliance to stop Iraq's aggression he also understood that the American people were fed up with big spending, unsafe streets, an education system that was a disaster and political and economic systems that seemed to care little about the great American middle class. The president and many other politicians failed to read this shift and paid the consequences in the 1992 and 1994 elections.

Newt gave two speeches that were turned into position papers. They were called "A Strategy for Replacing the Bureaucratic Welfare State with a New Domestic Order," and "Creating a New Domestic Order Replacing the Welfare State with an Opportunity Society." These were reflections of previously held ideas with the goal being "to replace the bureaucratic welfare state with a new domestic order that will increase safety, prosperity, and opportunity."[31]

Newt said, "We want to invent a government system that reinforces positive, healthy rules for Americans (working, saving, investing, learning, etc.). To implement this new approach, we are prepared to develop a national effort to recruit candidates and raise the resources to replace the center-left Democrats [who] now dominate American

---

[30] Ibid.

[31] Gingrich Papers, Steely Papers, Book Chap. 13 Folder.

government below the Presidency (and a few governorships) with a center-right reform Republican Party." The first shot of the Republican Revolution of 1994 was being fired.

He noted that we faced two great challenges in the 1990s. The first was to develop a new world order "in which peaceful citizens and peaceful nations have the security within which to pursue their own destinies." The second was a domestic reflection that would provide "opportunity for every American which enables us to create the economic wealth and individual freedom which is at the heart of our ability to provide global leadership. American strength in the world is based on the strength of Americans at home."

Five "key steps" were needed to replace the bureaucratic welfare state with a new domestic order. First was the need to "develop a language of replacement." Second, was "to develop the values, visions and key rules of a new domestic order." The third was to use "baby steps and pilot projects that bring to life our values and vision...." Fourth was the development of "an informal planning, discussion, and dissemination system." Finally, fifth, the movement "should be reinforced by constant small victories and by psychological massaging."[32]

The need for "baby steps and pilot projects" as well as the "reinforcement" were already developing independently. Polly Williams, a former Democratic activist, was pushing voucher legislation for poor children in Milwaukee and Republican governors were experimenting with new approaches toward changing the welfare system. Newt himself came up with the idea of helping "at risk" children become motivated to read and created the Earning By Learning reading motivational program.

Some professors at West Georgia College were concerned about the low level of reading competency. In a discussion with Newt, Newt suggested that one way to motivate the children, who seemed to resist all other motivation to read, was to pay them. He agreed to provide the money, from his speaking honoraria, to support the project that would depend heavily on volunteers for its operation. Steely agreed to head up the pilot project to be run in Gingrich's congressional district. Funding would be handled by the West Georgia College Foundation

---

[32] Ibid.

through donations made specifically for that purpose and plans were made to set up the program in five counties in the sixth district.

At seven sites in five counties 282 third and fourth graders read 3801 books and earned $7,602 in the six week summer pilot project. The next year a sixth county was added. 347 students read 6688 books and earned $13,075. The feedback from their teachers as school started showed increases in reading levels, self-esteem and general academic performance. A large majority read more and their grades went up. They kept reading even they were no longer paid.

Newt included a description of the program in his speeches and people across the country began writing West Georgia College to ask how they could start up an Earning by Learning (EBL) program in their area. By the end of the second year projects were going in at least a dozen states and the program was growing. In 1994 it was decided that the program was growing too large to be handled by one person at West Georgia College and an EBL Foundation was set up with a toll free phone number to respond to request for information. The foundation was located in Madison, Wisconsin and a board of directors was established.[33]

Earning by Learning was exactly the kind of grass-roots program, heavy with volunteers, run by contributions rather than taxes, that Newt thought could help turn around the country. Governor Tommy Thompson of Wisconsin, Mayor Brent Schundler of Jersey City, Governor Zell Miller of Georgia and a host of other officials joined in seeking new solutions to old problems. In each case local solutions were utilized with little or no federal involvement.

The *Wall Street Journal* headlined on 27 March 1991, "In an About-Face, Gingrich Becomes an Apostle of Grass-Roots Politics, Averting Clashes in GOP." The article, by Jackie Calmes, noted that Newt's 970 vote win had influenced him to consider the wisdom of Speaker Tip O'Neill's comment that "all politics is local." He seemed to be trying to manage his relationship with his rivals within the House while turning away from his approach of nationalizing elections. His actions were more tactical than strategic. Representative Mickey Edwards noted, "Newt had conceded that races are primarily local and should be run locally." He then conceded that "there is perhaps more of a role for

---

[33] Gingrich Papers, Steely Papers, Earning by Learning Files.

national issues, as a backdrop." Newt had made a tactical concession and got the other side to accept the importance of a "national backdrop."[34]

Newt had reason to be concerned about grass-roots politics that first quarter of 1991. Not only was he trying to shore up his district politics after almost losing his seat but he also had to think about the upcoming process of reapportionment following the 1990 census that would take place that summer.

Population growth had given Georgia at least one new seat in Congress. This meant that serious changes would be made in the new map to be drawn by a Democratic legislature. His standing with Democratic leaders was not as close as in 1981 and the close 1990 election had their juices flowing. His old nemesis, Speaker Tom Murphy, let it be known that if Newt could not be beat in an election then he could be redistricted out of Congress—or at least out of Murphy's district.

Following the Gulf War George Bush's polls were running high and he looked unbeatable. With Bush at the head of the ticket, Newt had campaigned to elect more Republicans at all levels and threatened to replace many Democrats. It would be politically unnatural for the Democrats to not take their best shot at him. Still, Governor Zell Miller and Lieutenant Governor Pierre Howard saw value in his being in the GOP leadership with a Republican in the White House. He could be helpful to Georgia. They decided not to become involved in trying to hurt him. Murphy, on the other hand, was determined to do what he could to get rid of Newt.

The special Georgia reapportionment session began the second week of August 1991. It appeared, at least on the surface, that Newt might not be too severely damaged in the early days of the session. The Senate, while bowing to Murphy's desire to move Newt out of his district, sought to find him a district that was at least competitive.[35]

It also appeared that the new districting for an eleventh district would result in the creation of a super-Republican district in the North Atlanta area. After consulting with his key advisors Newt decided he would have to move to the new district in the northern suburbs if he was to be guaranteed survival. The problem was that if Newt let it be

---

34 *Wall Street Journal*, 27 March 1991.
35 Gingrich Papers, Steely Papers, 1991 Reapportionment File.

known that he was considering moving his old district would be dismantled. If he appeared to plan on staying in what was left of the old sixth then the Senate might insist on a district there which was at least competitive for another Republican instead of the relatively safe one they had drawn. He decided to stay in the old district if it appeared he could win there but was considering moving if it seemed otherwise. That decision was sent back to the GOP caucus thus allowing Republicans in the new district to plan on running there since they thought Newt would not compete against them. This later caused Newt problems and guaranteed him a GOP primary opponent. It also convinced Murphy of Newt's intentions to stay in the south Atlanta area.

Evans and Steely worked with Lieutenant Governor Pierre Howard and friendly Senators to make the old sixth as viable as possible for a Republican. Along with Gaylord, they were concerned about how the lines were being drawn for the old sixth. While it might be relatively friendly to a country "good ole boy" Republican it did not look as inviting to Newt personally. Gaylord advised Newt that most of what would happen was out of his control and that "if any part of your base is cut out of your district go for the best district. You are the only Republican Congressman and there are many plans that depend on your staying in office. Stay out of agricultural areas. The new plan emaciated the district and I told Newt to move now!" Newt was advised not to think twice about moving to the North side. Though the decision was made early it was not made public until after the final map was drawn.

The Democrats inadvertently made it easier for Newt to move by at the last moment putting Newt's home precinct in with the fifth district of Representative John Lewis so Newt would have to move or run against the popular civil rights hero in a mostly black district. The old sixth was shattered and parts of it went into four districts. Newt was able to say how sad it was that he had been put in with Representative Lewis and forced to move or run in a predominantly black district represented by a popular black leader. Given the circumstances he said he thought he had little choice but to move and that he would be moving to the new sixth district, thoughtfully so numbered by the Democrats, which was the heavily Republican district in the fast growing north Atlanta suburbs of Cobb, Gwinnett and Cherokee Counties.

The irony was that the Democrats had drawn a map that would elect Newt in the new sixth and an old friend and ally, Sen. Mac Collins, to the new third district, the remnant of the original sixth. In addition, the Justice Department had pressured the Democrats to maximize black representation and they had created three majority black districts allowing two more Republicans to win seats in Congress for a total of four GOP Congressmen from Georgia when Newt had been the only one in the last Congress. Politics in Georgia were changing. The 103rd Congress had four Republicans from Georgia, three black Democrats and four white male Democrats. Nine white Democrats and one Republican, Newt had represented Georgia in the 102nd.

Tom Murphy had reason to be concerned. In spite of all his efforts the doctrine of unintended consequences came into play in spades in the 1992 elections, much to his displeasure. He was pleased that Newt's move north to a more compact and more Republican district quickly earned him a Republican primary opponent, State Representative Herman Clark. He and a number of other Republicans such as Matt Towery, a Gingrich ally, had planned to run for the new seat. When the GOP caucus was informed that Newt planned to run in what was left of the old sixth district, Clark made plans to run in the new sixth district, his home district. He was angry at what he considered a double-cross and decided he would run, regardless of Newt. Because Georgia does not have party registration this meant an open primary that allowed Democrats to cross over and vote against Newt in the Republican primary. Murphy still had some hope of getting rid of Gingrich even if it meant helping another Republican to replace him.

Having one of the most Republican districts in the country should have made the 1992 election simple for Newt. By playing it as he did Newt was able to help elect more Republicans in Georgia than otherwise might have been elected. The problem was that Herman Clark and Towery were not included in those elected. Clark had little money and organization and the state party leadership was against him and supported Newt. Still, Clark hired a bright and aggressive attack consultant who helped him run a fairly effective campaign and forced Newt into his second close-call campaign. Clark did benefit from some

Democratic money and votes. Sorry they had not helped Worley more in 1990 the Democrats tried not to make that mistake a second time.[36]

Clark personally campaigned by standing at busy intersections holding a "Vote for Clark" sign and spent considerable time on the phone calling registered Republicans telling them why they should vote against Newt. Newt was pictured as a crude, negative loud-mouth who was dishonest and did not fit in with the Cobb County crowd. Replaying some of Worley's 1990 charges, Newt was accused of being a national politician who cared only for himself and could not relate to the new district because he was, after all, a carpetbagger coming north only to benefit from Republican votes. The use of a limousine was again touted as a damning example of Newt's being out of touch.

Newt helped provide Clark with some ammunition against himself during the 1991 House bank scandal. Early in 1991 an audit of the House bank showed that some members maintained regular overdrafts, which was legal but politically damning as one more sign of congressional irresponsibility. Once more, many thought, they had special privileges not available to the average American. How could they handle the people's money when they could not take care of their own finances? Newt, still focusing on a GOP majority, saw a chance to elect more Republicans and called on Speaker Tom Foley to provide full disclosure of those with overdrafts. He knew that he and some other Republicans would probably be in that number but felt, on balance, that many more Democrats would be damaged. Besides, even if it hurt him personally it was the right decision. The people were tired of cover-ups and politics as usual.[37] He also thought that for the GOP to obtain a majority, the system would have to appear so corrupt to the American people that they would be willing to turn out the Democrats. The banking scandal certainly helped build that impression.

In thirteen years in Congress Newt had amassed twenty-two overdrafts, all of which had been covered. Most congressmen were willing to follow the speaker's lead and only release the names of the major offenders. Newt led the fight for full disclosure. The struggle got serious when he said the speaker was covering up the scandal and that the Democrats' newly appointed House Sergeant-at Arms, "may have been involved in actions stopping the Capitol police from investigating

---

[36] Ibid., Election 1992 Folder.
[37] Ibid.

cocaine selling in the post office." No evidence was made public by Newt and he was accused of McCarthy-like tactics and suffered catcalls on the House floor. He contended that this was just more evidence of a corrupt House run amuck under almost forty years of Democratic domination—more evidence that it was time for a change.

Speaker Foley did eventually release all names, before the election, and a number of Gingrich's GOP colleagues were damaged as well as the Democrats. Representative Mickey Edwards' loss in his primary was attributed to the bank scandal and other Republicans simply chose not to run rather than face attacks of preaching fiscal responsibility and practicing fiscal irresponsibility. One particularly upsetting example of this was Representative Vin Weber, Newt's close friend and ally.

Herman Clark did not miss the opportunity to embarrass Newt. He cut a sixty-second radio spot that was called by Judith Warner and Max Berley in their biography of Gingrich, a "most devastating piece of agit-prop." Sung to the tune of "Ole MacDonald Had A Farm," it went:

Congressman Newt Gingrich bounced 22 checks
  For more than twenty-six grand.
With a bounced check here and pay raise there.
Here a check. There a check. Everywhere a bounced check.[38]

Gingrich had recognized the danger Clark presented in the spring and sought the assistance of one of those who had considered running for the seat himself, Towery, in helping him make the transition to Cobb County and the new sixth district. Though Cobb County dominated the district North Fulton County was also critical. Here he depended on the support of Senator Sallie Newbill, the Senate minority whip. It was Newbill who delivered the votes necessary to put Newt over the top in the primary and would become his chief operative in the 1994 campaign.

While Newt knew there would be problems he did not expect them to be so serious. He spent time in the district, got the endorsement of the local papers and did what he could to help other GOP candidates and the Bush/Quayle campaign. By late June he realized the serious-ness of the problem and fought back at the end of the campaign

---

[38] Ibid.

sending out over 100,000 pieces of direct mail and spending around $100,000 on television ads. He also totally ended his travels for other Republican candidates and focused his attention on the sixth district.

Jackie Conn, who had been running the campaign to this point, was now joined by Barry Hutchinson, who would soon become Newt's invaluable staff aide. Joe Gaylord, a former NRCC executive director and now consultant, took personal charge of the campaign.[39] Gaylord had first met Newt in 1981. A close relationship between them was forged during the 1983-1984 election while Gaylord was at NRCC which spent $84 million on candidates. During that period, relates Gaylord, "We learned a lot from each other. One of the reasons we've gotten along so well over the years is that we've learned from each other." Newt was the idea man while Gaylord would operationalize the best of those ideas and help focus on what was most critical at a given moment.[40]

Gaylord knew the move to a new district would be difficult. Though Newt was well known in the Atlanta area he was not intimately known on the north-side. He would have to run as an incumbent with 600,000 constituents he had never represented. "He had all the baggage of incumbency without any of the benefits," said Gaylord. There were no favors done, no case work to draw on, no newsletters or mass mailings, no town hall meetings that would form a basis to work from. Except for party activists the people on the north-side knew Newt only through the media and if Newt wanted positive coverage from the *Atlanta Journal-Constitution* he would have to buy an ad, which he actually did in the 1994 race. Television coverage was only slightly less biased.

Gaylord said Towery was very helpful initially because he helped present Newt to the neighborhoods and subdivisions around which so much of suburban life revolved. Campaigning in the new sixth was very different from the old, more rural sixth district. "We started from scratch and built an organization with the help of Sallie Newbill in five different counties in a territory where they [the counties] were not closely aligned with one another. There was no sense of community in Cobb County itself. Identification came with communities like Dunwoody, neighborhoods, not Marietta as a city. Towery was very

---

[39] Ibid.

[40] Joe Gaylord Interview, 21 April 1995.

helpful with that but the key was Sallie Newbill who produced the margin of victory in North Fulton which made up for the losses in Cobb," said Gaylord.

Gaylord was clearly proud of his work in the 1992 primary. "Herman played the David-Goliath role pretty well. You can't overlook the fact of the Democrats in the primary. Fourteen thousand more voted in our primary than in the presidential primary. The DCCC spent coordinated expenditures in the primary for Clark. The League of Conservation Voters and Public Citizens lobby opened headquarters in the same building in Five Points [North Fulton County]. It's easy to say 'didn't Newt do bad?' but look at it this way, look what Newt withstood. He faced 600,000 new voters, an anti-incumbent year, the DC check scandal, the entire wrath of the national Democratic party, a pretty feisty opponent and a carpetbagger image and he still pulled it out," reflected Gaylord. "I don't know many people who could've done that." Gingrich won the primary by 980 votes.[41]

Newt's Democratic opponent, a trial lawyer named Tony Center, offered little new. He reran the Clark charges and added the Gingrich divorce, which had figured in the 1980, 1982, 1988 and 1990 campaigns, dredged up the old *Mother Jones* charges once again hoping maybe they would work better in the new district than they had in the old one. Center also, in an ugly television ad, accused Newt of delivering divorce papers to his wife the day after she had a cancer operation. He accused him of leaving "his wife and children penniless" while he benefited from Washington perks.[42]

Newt's youngest daughter, Jackie, responded with anger. She lived with her husband in North Atlanta and was very familiar with the attacks on her father. She considered them to be bogus and unfair. Jackie talked with her father who at first thought she should stay out of it and was upset that the attacks reflected on his children. She wanted to become involved and went to the campaign and said she wanted to do an ad for her father countering Center's charges. In the ad, which ran toward the end of the campaign, Jackie, looking directly into the camera, said "My dad has always stood behind and supported me and my sister in everything we have done. We care about our father and he cares about us." Newt had always encouraged his daughters to be

---

41 Ibid.

42 Gingrich Papers, Election 1992 Folder.

independent thinkers. When they differed they debated the issue with him. Cathy, who lived in North Carolina with her husband, had joined the National Republican Coalition for Choice and opposed the GOP's anti-abortion position. Even with differences, Cathy, like her sister, stood by her father and resented the attacks that she considered unfair.

Center's attacks on Newt for "leaving his wife and children penniless" were nothing new. At one time or another in his political career members of Newt's family were included in attempts to attack or embarrass him. Both of his wives, his daughters, his half-sister and his mother and father have at one time or another been used in personal stories aimed at hurting him.

This time Newt found the Democratic attacks so painful and frustrating that he said he considered dropping out of the race. "If survival in public life means this level of degradation, I don't want to be part of it," he told his supporters and the *New York Times*. Democrats were gleeful that he was feeling pain and pointed out that he "could dish it out but couldn't take it." They mentioned the Studds and Crane cases, Jim Wright's ethics charges, when a Newt staffer repeated a rumor that Speaker Foley might be gay, and Representative Barney Frank's ethics charges. At one time or another all the above had been stung by Newt's attacks[43].

Gingrich thought this was unfair because the charges he had leveled he considered to be true and factual. The exception was the Foley case where he reprimanded the staff member for even bringing up the question. The attacks on him, on the other hand, he thought were untrue or exaggerated. He pointed out that Center, as a lawyer, had won a child support case for a woman and then asked the court to give him the money he had won for her and her child to pay for the legal fees he charged her. "Not much of a moral example," said Newt. He admitted that he was not perfect but said he had learned from the experiences and compared his position and experience with the lack of either on Center's part. He also spent almost $2 million to win reelection, the fifth highest amount spent by any House member in 1992. He won the general election somewhat more handily than the primary and had, he hoped, gotten past his last close race.

---

[43] Ibid.

George Bush was not so lucky. Newt had worked with Dick Darman and Roger Porter to help structure the 1991 State of the Union Address. He made it clear in a 7 January memo to them that he and the conservative activists desired a State of the Union that had a supply side component, capital gains, that called for a replacement for the welfare state instead of a managed welfare state, and looked toward real activities on the cabinet level to back it up. Because of the confusion over what he meant or did not mean during the 1990 budget summit he wanted to be clear. "I want to avoid any confusion about my intentions. I will praise and support a growth and replacement State of the Union. I will criticize and oppose a non-growth, manage the welfare state speech."

Ross Perot was stirring the American people with his George Wallace-like message of a pox on both their houses. Newt thought the feelings Perot stirred were real and dangerous to the two party system. They were certainly dangerous for Bush. The president did not seem to understand this. He knew Perot as they were fellow Texans, and did not take him overly seriously.

President Bush seemed to be seeking a middle of the road in an almost bipartisan way early in 1992. On 17 March Newt sent a letter to the president responding to a speech Bush had made to state legislators. He complained about Bush's targeting "the Congress" and said the speech was "inaccurate and misleading. You suggest later, people are tired of the business-as-usual from Washington. I am too. Your speech yesterday was non-partisan blandness. Nothing we can do as your allies can save us this fall if you are determined to remain vague and inaccurate. You must be clear. You must define the case simply, clearly, and repetitively so the American people can understand this historic choice."[44]

Failing to see any response to clarify the Bush position Newt shared his frustration in a personal letter to Nick Calio, the president's lobbyist. He complained of how Bush preferred to work with bureaucrats and Democrats rather than his own party leaders. "The president seems to oppose change when the party platform called for it. He gives in to and strengthens the Democrats in return for little or no gain." Newt told Nick he tried to talk to Bush, who listened politely and did nothing.

---

[44] Ibid., Bush Documents Folder.

Newt wrote, "I am close to despair about the self-destructive patterns and habits of this Administration. Right now we are not winning reelection. The Democrats are losing. If we continue to drift with self-imposed debilitation we could lose in November. Even if we win, the current pattern will lead to no mandate, no energy and no commitment. The result will be four more years of drifting deadlock." He continued, "In the last month I have met no one, not a single person, enthusiastic about the Presidential campaign. We are inconsistent, uncertain and unreliable."

Newt closed the memo by noting, "I want to be a partner for real change. I want to work with the President to force the bureaucracy and the Democrats to support our philosophy and our values. I will continue to help the presidential campaign whenever I can. I simply don't know how to deal with the Administration's policy system. With frustration, rapidly declining patience, and dwindling enthusiasm, your friend, Newt."

While Newt was promising to be a "partner for change" Richard Darman was telling Bush that he thought Newt really wished to see the Administration fail so that it could open the door to a GOP takeover in the Congress. After the budget summit crisis both Darman and the president had mixed feelings about Newt's plans and desires. Many Republicans were as disturbed about the president's actions as he was about Newt. They thought he seemed to lack direction and were concerned about his "willingness to be rolled by the Democrats."[45]

In May, before Bill Clinton was nominated, Newt sent a memo to the president seeking to alert him to the danger of losing the election. Entitled "Leadership in the Cultural Civil War" the memo listed six points. The first bluntly warned, "Your Presidency is in real trouble." The second stated, "Only your personal leadership can turn things around." He suggested a plan of action. "You must define the five to seven principles which will shape policy choices for your staff and your allies and which will rally most Americans." Also, "You must choose three public policy arenas in which to fight for change and dramatize the public stake in the outcome." He ended by stating, "You must reorient your staff to stay on offense in implementing your five to seven

---

[45] Darman, *Who's In Control*, Chap. 13.

principles in a way that arouses the popular culture's 70 percent plus to help your side of the struggles."[46]

This memo—like so many others Newt sent to the White House—was read and ignored, or just ignored. He sent so many memos that the president's Press Secretary, Marlin Fitzwater, began making sport of them at press conferences. Newt, still wanting to help, was able to work with Calio and had some input into the speech-writing team. He and Calio worked on a request from Bush that Newt suggest ways the president might strengthen his ability to communicate his message to the American people. He sent a lengthy memo on this plan to Bush on 5 June. It stated that "people want action, not speeches, change not promises." He said Bush was going to be judged on what he did in this administration, not what he promised in the next. He called for action and outlined how it could be achieved, but to no avail.

After the Clinton/Gore ticket was determined at the Democratic convention many Republicans were pleased because they thought the American people would not vote for "a lying, adulterous draft dodger," and thought George Bush would pull it off after all. Newt, however, understood quickly the power Clinton possessed as a campaigner and warned against it. During the Labor Day recess he warned the GOP faithful back home that "Bill Clinton is one of the greatest campaigners I've seen. Don't take him for granted." Newt was especially concerned about Perot's candidacy because it could take away GOP voters and turn the election to Clinton.

While home he shared his concern with his staff and those close to him. While not wanting to appear disloyal he warned that, "We could lose this thing if we aren't careful." He not only sent memos to Bush, he also sought them from those who might have something to offer that would help. Among others, he asked Professor Don Wagner, a WGC political scientist, and Steely to put together a memo on how Bush might improve the campaign. The resulting 7 September memo in its twelve points screamed out for leadership and action. The memo cited aimlessness in the administration and a commitment to do little more than become re-elected. The president seemed to think he should be president again because he would deal with whatever happened better than his opponent. The memo argued that Bush appeared to have no

---

[46] Gingrich Papers, Election 1992 Folder, Bush Documents.

direction, goals or ambitions about what he wanted to accomplish in his second term except to wait and see what happened and then deal with it.

Newt was as concerned about Perot as he was Clinton. In the end he just could not believe people would vote in large numbers for Clinton. He warned in yet another memo, "A forty-five percent Perot, thirty percent Bush, twenty-five percent Clinton race was very plausible." Perot's presence in the race complicated matters. Which way would the conservative Democrats break? How many Republicans would turn on Bush and vote for Perot—or yet, as a protest, for Clinton? Bush was in drift and seen as out of touch. Vice President Quayle sought to establish some direction via the values issue but with little success.

Many Republicans felt as Election Day neared that the man sworn in as president on 20 January 1993 would not be George Bush. Frank Gregorsky and some other Republicans even went so far as to vote for Clinton/Gore out of protest against Bush. If he were reelected, they stated, it would only make the people more distrustful of and disgusted with the GOP and keep the Democrats in control for another decade. Clinton, they reasoned, would make things so bad that it would pave the way for a decade of Republican restoration and rule. While Newt opposed this view, they turned out to be more right than wrong and certainly had reason to feel justified after the 1994 Republican revolution.

Many from the Bush team considered Newt's work and advice helpful while others were almost willing to blame the 1992 defeat on him alone. Many of the latter thought he was divisive and disloyal. One of the interesting attributes about Newt is the way he is able to maintain loyalty from friends and colleagues who have worked with him and have suffered personal or career disappointment at his hands. His career is rife with examples. Kip Carter was fired by Newt in the spring of 1979 and yet worked for his reelection in 1980 only to break totally after the election. Carlyle Gregory ran Newt's 1978 winning campaign and expected to be offered the administrative assistant in the Washington office. He not only did not win the position but was notified, by Newt, of that reality in what was, to him, a humiliating manner. Yet he continued to be supportive of Newt's efforts from a lesser position on the staff and when he moved over to the NRCC. The man who was appointed to the AA position, Bob Weed, gave it up, temporarily he thought, to run Newt's 1980 reelection campaign only to win and then be told he could not go back to the AA job. The much liked and respected Guy Scull left Washington to run the 1982 campaign only to suffer the slings and arrows of outrageous fortune visited on most of Newt's campaign managers. Following the successful effort in 1982 he made the decision to end his political career but still remains loyal and supportive of Newt and his efforts and still thinks of himself as part of the team.

Some, like Chip Kahn, who trashed Newt in a very negative interview in *Mother Jones*, remain supportive. Catherine Brock, who was demoted from district administrator following the close 1990 election, remains loyal and supportive. Gary Crook, who replaced Brock as DA, was disappointed not to be asked to continue his position in 1993 when Newt moved to his new district. He continues to be supportive both personally and politically, as do a host of other former staffers.

It was not just staff who were disappointed and yet remained supportive of the vision and the objectives, if not of Newt personally. Representative John Rhodes resigned his position as minority leader due, in part, to Newt's activities. He nevertheless remains supportive of the goals and has little to say that is negative about Newt. Former Representative Vin Weber, who was involved in the bank scandal as a result of Newt's insistence that the list of members be inclusive, remains publicly and privately a friend. Representative Steve Gundersen, a moderate, gay member who was part of the Whip organization resigned in protest from that group and is at odds with Newt and the more conservative leadership over what he considers their anti-gay agenda. Still, he considers Newt a friend and remains supportive of much of what he is trying to achieve.

What is it about Newt that inspires loyalty and support from some who might be expected to oppose him when other former staffers, colleagues and supporters have been all too ready to trash him at every opportunity? Some might be supportive because their political or career fortunes are tied to his. Others, however, have little or nothing to gain personally from continued friendship and support. What motivates them?

The case of Randy Evans might be instructive. Evans had interned with Newt in his Washington office and lived in Newt's home while there. He finished college at West Georgia, graduated from the

University of Georgia Law School and moved to Cobb County to start practicing law. Within the year he wanted to see how he could be helpful to Newt and the GOP. He was asked to move to Douglas County and build a Republican Party there. He and his wife, Susan, moved closer to their parents in Douglas County.

Working closely with Newt's organization, Evans built the county party from nothing, became GOP district chairman, spending large amounts of his own time and money in the process, and worked in Newt's 1986 and 1988 campaigns as political director and helped the district party grow. He worked with the state GOP by holding candidate workshops and recruiting candidates as part of Newt's local plan to elect Republicans and then aid them in the election process. Evans was one of the most successful volunteers ever associated with the Gingrich organization.

While he was extremely valuable to Newt he also presented problems. Evans had a large ego and insisted on getting credit for works accomplished. Some in the state GOP saw this as Evans setting the stage for his own future candidacy for state or federal office and resented it. Some did not want to do the work but wanted the credit. They felt he was too young, too pushy, and not part of the team—their team.

The year 1988 was when Pat Robertson moved to organize his troops toward recruiting delegates for the Republican Convention in New Orleans. This caused tensions within the Georgia GOP as those from the Christian Coalition sought to pack county and district conventions to gain control of the state convention which picked delegates. Evans, who had operational control of the district convention, sided with "the team" and Newt. Many coalition delegates were thrown out. This caused serious problems for Evans as he took the heat from coalition members who were his and Newt's friends and supporters.

It was obvious that at the state convention in Albany, Georgia, Newt would be pulled by both sides and put in a no-win situation. He had strong supporters on both sides. Colleagues worked to hide Newt from the delegates except for the times he was to address the convention. Newt was isolated in a motel away from the delegates and refused to let anyone know where he was. This action was viewed by the state party regulars, "the team," as base treachery and betrayal confirming their suspicions about Evans. They saw him as brash, pushy, ego driven, overly ambitions and as something of a threat to some of their own ambitions.

As a feud developed between Evans and the party leadership Newt was put in the middle. When George Bush was elected and patronage positions were open Evans asked for Newt's support for the US Attorney's position in Atlanta. While Newt did support Evans he was blocked in Washington by party leaders. Newt probably could have forced the appointment but weighed the cost of such a move and decided against it. Evans, and many Newt staffers, were crushed. They thought Evans had earned the appointment and were not concerned about his youth and inexperience. The White House was concerned about those issues and about going against staunch Bush supporters and party officials. The cost would have been too high. Newt had been part of the "team" since the early 1970s and had made and would make his own sacrifices for their advancement. To go against them now after their candidate, Bush, had just won did not make sense to him. Some lesser position was sought for Evans but nothing worked out.

Even though he was seriously disappointed Evans continued to support Newt and to be a loyal friend. "Newt is like family and I believe in what he is doing," he told me. In a later conversation with me about the Evans situation Newt noted wistfully that brilliant people are hard to work with and sometimes it is easier to work with smart people who can follow instructions and not present the problems created by genius.[47]

"Newt is like family," is how some describe their relationship with him. "Like a brother," is frequently used to describe the relationship by Catherine Brock, Daryl Conner, Steve Hanser, Chip Kahn, Linda Kemp, Laurie James and by Evans. While having Newt as a "brother" is sometimes frustrating it is also often exhilarating. It is a very personal relationship and not easily broken. Those in that relationship find it difficult to recognize the Newt they know when they read the attacks in the press and watch as his opponents seek to demonize him.

Others who do not feel a "family" or personal relationship are committed to Newt's vision of America and want to be part of the team leading the "crusade" to help make the country what it can be. They share the vision of the conservative opportunity society replacing the

---

[47] Randy Evans Interview, 16 September 1995.

liberal welfare state and think, in spite of his faults, that Newt is the best person to lead the team in achieving that vision.

12

THE BEST OF TIMES

On 20 January 1993 William Jefferson Clinton took the oath of office for president of the United States. Newt Gingrich, the clear leader of the House Republicans and spokesman for the activist wing of the party, was ready. These two men, their actions, speeches, personal lives, and interaction would fascinate Washington and the country for the next six years.

It is difficult not to notice the comparisons made of the two men. They are contemporaries. Both were born into the lower middle class and were from broken homes. Neither had a father in their early years and sought father figures early on. Both men are bright and were popular in school, each taking a leadership role in his school. Private higher education was the choice of both men and each earned a doctorate, Gingrich in history and Clinton in law. Both studied abroad, Gingrich in Belgium and France, and Clinton in Great Britain. Both traveled widely in Europe during their school years. Both men were college teachers. Neither served in the military.

Both Gingrich and Clinton married strong-willed women who served, at least in part, as mother figures. Both men had problems in their marriages. Both became involved in politics early and developed political ambitions by the time they entered college. Both men lost early races for Congress and both were gifted campaigners who approached the campaign train in a similar manner. Each man has been accused of ethics problems and sexual improprieties. They are two of the most investigated men in Washington. Both were successful in politics, Gingrich taking the legislative route and Clinton the executive. Both men have reached their stated goals, speaker and president respectively, and are the subject of unrelieved press attacks. Both invite attacks due to their propensity for making statements they should have left unsaid and both are very open with the press in explaining their actions and positions, certain that once the press hears their side of an argument they will understand. Both are almost always disappointed when the press fails to understand their position. They both have a natural curiosity about almost everything, both immerse their lives in politics.

Gingrich was excited. Being in the opposition, with a Democrat in the White House, freed him from having to defend or explain administration policies with which he disagreed. He was quick to define his credo: "I will cooperate but not compromise." He was willing to work "within the parameters of our principles." Cooperating meant that Newt and his people would be brought in by the administration at the beginning to work to shape legislation. It did not mean the Democrats would draw up the bills and demand that the Republicans sign on or be accused of being "uncooperative." It did not mean that he expected to replace the House Democrats, who were the majority, but rather hoped the Republicans would be included at the start of any legislation that was truly serious and on which there was the need for bipartisan support. He did not expect to be consulted on every bill, but on those where the Democrats went it alone, he made it clear that there should be no presumption of support from him or his troops. Bringing the Republicans in only at the end of the process and demanding support under pain of being called partisan and uncooperative would not work. Newt was willing to give support to the new President but he was also ready to offer criticism.

Newt was not surprised when problems arose concerning some of Clinton's nominees. He was critical of the Zoe Baird nomination for attorney general because she had employed an illegal alien as a housekeeper and, as attorney general, would have to prosecute others for the same crime. Other nominees had similar problems or had potential tax problems that would be troublesome. When the new president proposed to drop the ban on gays in the military Newt was at first somewhat ambivalent. His sister, Candace, was gay. He had known and worked with gays most of his professional life. He had no problem working with an openly gay colleague, Ara Dostourian, in the history department at West Georgia College. One of his close allies in Congress, Representative Steve Gunderson, was gay.

Newt thought President Truman's integrating the armed forces was the right thing to do and was not against making changes in the military that reflected social policy as long as it did not compromise the mission of the military. He wanted to hear what military leaders thought. He talked with the Joint Chiefs of Staff and following their recommendation, opposed the plan to lift the ban. His support of the military view on the gay issue received strong grass-roots support. He worked actively to expand that support as part of his plan, expressed following the Crested Butte meeting in 1989, to recruit a citizen army of supporters who would work for conservative change in their cities and states and enlist them in the struggle to change the country.

His close ally and friend, Jeff Eisenach, had supplied a phrase for President Bush's last State of the Union address, "If we can change the world, we can change America." Newt believed this. Another friend, Owen Roberts, was critical of our objective in Somalia. He thought the idea of nation building in that country, or any country, was unworkable. Was it possible to accomplish such a task in any country? In discussing this with Newt they realized the fact that we were not doing such a good job of nation building here at home. "If we can't teach it here at home, how can we teach it abroad?" said Newt.

Newt's talk with Roberts was the stimulus for his college course on Renewing American Civilization. The course was part of a grass-roots approach to reach into every part of America with his ideas of a future America and how to bring it about. In addition to sounding the alarm warning of the country's decay, he wanted to provide a road map of how to achieve "the great city on the hill" envisioned by Ronald Reagan.

In addition to the course Newt also worked with GOPAC to send out almost 10,000 audio tapes to local candidates and others to help awaken a spirit in conservative candidates that would be infectious and lead to the recruiting of even more candidates — somewhat similar to a baseball farm system. Quality candidates who were proud of their country and sincerely believed America's greatness lay in the future would be the foot soldiers in the conservative revolution. He also gave lectures and speeches to almost any audience who would listen. Many in those audiences would comment that he seemed to be angry as he described what the current system is doing to a generation of young people. They were perceptive. He was very angry.

"It is impossible to maintain civilization with twelve-year-olds having babies, fifteen-year-olds killing each other, seventeen-year-olds dying of AIDS and eighteen-year-olds receiving diplomas they cannot read." This Gingrich mantra was used in most of his speeches and picked up by many other candidates as the truth of it resonated across the country. As we hear story after story of the unspeakable way so many of our children are treated most of us respond with emotion and sadness thinking someone should do something. Newt had moved beyond tears, though he had shed his share, and even beyond anger. He was at the point where taking action meant he had to be personally involved.

Gingrich was often criticized as outrageous when he linked particularly horrible crimes to what he saw as a liberal system that had encouraged the decay of values and patterns of behavior that ordered society in the past. That was fine with him. He felt someone had to say the obvious. He had no interest in apologizing. "The defenders of the status quo should be ashamed of themselves. The current system has trapped and ruined a whole generation while claiming to be compassionate. The burden of proof is not on the people who want to change welfare. It is on those who would defend a system that has clearly failed at incalculable human cost," he said.[1]

There are two models at the core of what he does. One is vision, strategy, projects and tactics. The other model is a processing model of listen, learn, help and lead. He lives this, with varying degrees of commitment, and is often heard asking, "what's the vision," "what did we learn" and "how can I [you] help?" Toward the end of 1994 he told Weston Kosova, in an interview for *The New Republic*, "I believe there are five parallel transformations that are unavoidable if we are going to be a healthy society."[2]

He then launched into another of his lists so prized by professors: "The first [transformation] is from a second-wave mechanical bureaucratic model to a third wave information model. The second, you have to move from a national economy to a world economy model...creating local jobs through world sales. And that requires

---

[1] Newt Gingrich, *To Renew America*, p. 72.
[2] *The New Republic*, 7 November 1994, pp. 28-33.

rethinking litigation, regulation, taxation, welfare, education, health and the structure of government. Third, the transformation from a welfare state to an opportunity society, because the Great Society experiment has now failed totally and is destroying human beings. Fourth, you've got to replace the counter-culture and elites with a revitalization of American culture and American civilization. Fifth, you have to assist in the transition from a professional politician class to a citizen activist leader system."

"All five of those have to occur in parallel," Gingrich warns, "because if they don't all five happen, we don't make the successful transition into twenty-first century America."[3]

Vision, strategy, projects, tactics. One of Newt's major projects on the road to a revitalized America was the Renewing American Civilization course (RAC). Conceived as a response to questions raised about our place in the world, the course began to be a serious possibility in the spring of 1993. Dr. Tim Mescon, dean of the business school at Kennesaw State College in Newt's district, opened discussions with Newt about offering a course that would be taught on the Kennesaw campus and televised nation-wide to reach a maximum audience.

The idea was for Mescon to take care of details on campus, students, exams, term papers, etc. and Dr. Jeff Eisenach, through the newly formed Progress and Freedom Foundation, would take care of the fund-raising necessary to televise the course via the National Empowerment Television satellite channel. Nancy Desmond was brought on board to coordinate and oversee course content. Newt's role would be to develop twenty hours of lecture, give the lectures, meet with the students to answer questions, and preside at a wrap-up session at the end of the course. The course would be held on Saturday mornings so as not to interfere with Newt's work in Congress.

During the late spring and summer of 1993 Newt met with a number of people to kick around ideas for the course. He already had a vision of the course and its structure but wanted to meet with classroom teachers to flesh out the ten lectures and make sure the content was accurate, non-partisan, and interesting. He also wanted to make sure that it would convey a vision of what America had been in the past and could be again. It would be from a conservative point of view,

---

[3] Ibid.

explained to the students at the start, because he thought most college students already had enough liberal interpretation of the world in their other college classes.

Newt's experience as a professor had taught him that each event can be taught, accurately and truthfully, from a number of perspectives depending on the belief structure of the professor. Thomas Jefferson could be taught as a guiding genius who inspired a new nation or as a selfish, rakish slaveholder who forced himself on a young slave girl. The Declaration of Independence could be an inspirational document or one exhibiting the hypocrisy of the founding fathers. Andrew Jackson would be a heroic man of the people who encouraged mass democracy and founded the Democratic Party or a crude and violent frontiersman who should be remembered for persecuting the Indians. Lincoln, judged by many as our greatest president, could be the great emancipator who held the union together, or as an awkward buffoon who covered up his wife's crimes. It could be said he only freed the slaves in order to win the war, and that he violated the Constitution multiple times in his prosecution of that great endeavor. Franklin D. Roosevelt would be one of our greatest presidents who offered hope and opportunity at a moment of despair in our history and skillfully guided us through the great depression and the most destructive war in world history. He could also be viewed as a philandering husband, a manipulative politician, and a liar of the first order who knowingly led the American people into a war all the while telling them he would do just the opposite.

Newt, like his classroom colleagues, thought most students were getting the more cynical view rather than the more positive approach. Dr. Wagner, Honors Director at West Georgia College, spoke about a bright honors student coming to him and asking, "Why was the U.S. so bent on getting into a war with Japan in World War II just to establish American imperialism in Asia?" "Where did you hear this?" he was asked. "My American history teacher told us that." "Did he tell you about Pearl Harbor?" asked Wagner. "Yeah, that was one of the battles that Japan won." World War II was seen by that professor as an attempt by the colonial powers to preserve their empires and America's role was an unjust one which sought to destroy Japan's civilized way of life and replace it with the American version of greed and capitalism. If one ignores reality and is carefully selective with the facts it is possible to make a case for that point of view. Newt, and his advisors, wanted to make sure the other side was presented.

While Gingrich, Hanser, Eisenach, Desmond, and a series of specialists spent days selecting the right illustrations and brain-storming, Eisenach worked to make sure the financing was on schedule. Financing a course of this sort was a somewhat new undertaking and part of Jeff's job was to be sure that all his efforts fell within legal guidelines. While the financial efforts were creative they were also legal, he said, and felt sure they could withstand any critical test from Newt's opponents and the ever-watchful press.

When Gingrich was asked if the course skirted the edge of what was legal, he told the *New York Times*, the course "goes right up to the edge. What's the beef? Doesn't go over the edge, doesn't break any law, isn't wrong. It's aggressive; it's entrepreneurial; it's risk-taking."[4] The press attitude seemed to be, "well, it might not be illegal but it has the appearance of illegality" and that bothered them. The press's attitude did not bother Gingrich. It was Gingrich's experience that most everything he did bothered some of the media almost all the time.

The course had the approval of Kennesaw's president, Dr. Betty Siegel, and had been cleared with the chancellor of the University System of Georgia. As it began to draw criticism the president began to reconsider her support and the Board of Regents, all of them Democrats, one of whom was the chairman of the Georgia Democratic Party, decided to restrict courses taught by politicians. This decision forced Gingrich to move it to Reinhardt College, a small private school in the north Georgia mountains.

The course goal, according to Eisenach, was "to train by April 1996, 200,000+ citizens into a model for replacing the welfare state and reforming our government." The course's purpose really bothered those committed to maintaining the status quo. Renewing American Civilization was offered three times. It was improved each time it was taught and then put on videotape for further distribution. It was offered at Kennesaw in the fall of 1993 and at Reinhardt in the winters of 1994 and 1995. It was offered by satellite on over sixty college and university campuses throughout the country as "an alternative to the multicultural

---

[4] *New York Times*, 20 February 1995.

approach" taught on so many campuses and was picked up by hundreds of individuals and small groups from one coast to the other.

Some educators found fault with the course because it did not include liberal opinions, though Newt did talk about them and use them as bad examples. Others were bothered by his positive reference to companies who had donated money to the course. His old opponent, David Worley, called it just another of Gingrich's "scams." His 1994 opponent, former Congressman Ben Jones, used it to file charges of ethics violations against Gingrich.

Other educators had different opinions. Dr. David King from the John F. Kennedy School of Government at Harvard said it might not be to everyone's liking but it was "clearly more than a partisan screed." He continued, "The course is not polished, it is repetitive, it's not muddled and it's not partisan. It touts conservative ideas, but those ideas are never explicitly linked to the Republican Party."[5] Professor David Samuels from Princeton observed, "What historians might find surprising is that it is also the product of a first-rate mind. Like his fellow professor turned politician, Daniel Patrick Moynihan, Gingrich has a scholar's range of interest and references."[6]

While Gingrich was interested in the opinions of other historians, he was more concerned about the reaction of the students who took the course and they were overwhelmingly favorable in their responses as to its value. Favorable too, were those who attended conferences such as the one sponsored by the Progress and Freedom Foundation on "The Future of American Civilization" featuring Malcolm Forbes, Jr., George Gilder, and Gingrich. The message was getting out through tapes, speeches and over C-SPAN. Gingrich could feel the tide turning. He was in his element.

The plan now called for Newt and the Republicans in the House to attack the president and the Democrats head on. After his own leadership in the House deserted him President Clinton turned to Gingrich and the GOP members to help him pass the North American Free Trade Association bill (NAFTA). This bill had its roots in the Bush administration and was something Gingrich thought would help the country. He was included in the planning and in discussions leading the administration to modify some of its more objectionable provisions.

---

[5] Ibid.
[6] Ibid.

That, he noted, is what he meant by cooperation, not compromise. The administration learned they could work with Newt if there were common interests. He would not oppose just for the sake of opposition. This stance did not mean, he explained, that they could expect cooperation on everything. Cooperation was a two-way street.

Gingrich had opposed the president's economic package and led the Republicans against it in a unanimous vote. It still passed. It did not matter. The party was starting to unify and turn directions after the 1992 elections when they had lost the White House. They had begun the session outnumbered 178 to 256 and faced a Democrat in the White House. Many were depressed. They had yet to understand the ineptness of the Clinton team. Gingrich's job was to pull them together and give them a spirit of unity in opposition. If they could not change the outcome of legislation, they could change the way the public viewed that legislation and the party pushing it through.

President Clinton presented the Republicans with a cornucopia of opportunity for opposition. The administration budget plan called for $241 billion in tax increases, a rise of 4.3 percent in gas taxes and a lifting of the top income tax rate from 31 percent to 36 percent. It would be the largest tax increase in recent memory. The crime bill placed restrictions on guns and allowed federal money for hiring police but also prevented neighborhoods from being warned of child molesters in their midst. It further limited the death penalty and generally placed more emphasis on multiple plans for crime prevention rather than for the punishment of crime. The massive health care bill threatened to further bureaucratize health care and move it toward a socialized medicine approach. There were also questions on Bosnia, Somalia and Haiti in the foreign policy field and on trade with Japan in the international economic area.

On another level, the new president faced problems with the FBI's leadership, the use of federal force in the assault on a religious sect in Waco, Texas, and serious questions about the role of the president and the First Lady concerning land deals and investments back home in Arkansas known as the Whitewater deal. Added to this was the question of irregularities concerning the White House travel office and the suicide of a high White House aide and close friend of the Clinton's, Vince Foster, and the questions of causality surrounding his death and the resulting charges of cover-up directed toward the White House.

As he expressed on *Face the Nation*, Gingrich thought "the 1992 election had sent a signal that the American people wanted change."[7] The change they wanted, he said, was a move toward a balanced budget and the end to politics as usual in the simmering House Post Office scandal that eventually forced the resignation of the postmaster and the indictment of senior Democrats such as Representative Dan Rostenkowski. Gingrich, while appearing on the *Capitol Gang* television program noted that there should be no cover-up of the post office investigation but there should also not be a rush to judgment on Rostenkowski until the investigation was completed. He also noted that this was yet another instance of House corruption resulting from forty years of Democratic dominance of the House.

During Clinton's first two years in office Gingrich kept a relatively low profile insofar as criticism of the Whitewater scandal and the Vince Foster affair were concerned. He thought, and said publicly, that those two issues were better not judged until investigating authorities had completed their work. When pressed, he would insist that both should be thoroughly investigated by outside authorities and Congress but no conclusions should be drawn before the reports were out.

He did wonder privately, and occasionally publicly, how an administration with so many of its people under indictment could claim to be honest and open. Still, he did not lead an attack against the Clintons on that basis in spite of heavy pressure to do so. For someone who is viewed as being much too open and "running off at the mouth," he kept very quiet about some of the rumors, some absolutely scurrilous, swirling around the president and the First Lady.

Newt was concerned about the events prompting Foster's death as they touched on public policy. Appearing on CNN's the *Capitol Gang*, he noted that it was a personal tragedy not only for the Foster family but also for the Clintons who had lost a close friend. Nevertheless, he noted, "When you have a person that high up in the system and something like that happens there is an absolute obligation to look into it." He went on to say that if the evidence proved to be of a personal rather than of a public policy nature then it should be sealed and not made part of the public record. "There should be some measure of personal privacy even for politicians."[8] This view probably came as

---

[7] Face The Nation, 23 October 1994.
[8] The Capitol Gang, 24 July 1993.

much from his own experience as from any conviction of fairness he might have held.

He did voice criticism of the president's handling of foreign policy, especially in Haiti and Somalia where he thought we had little concept of mission and less concept of when we would complete it and return home. The deaths of dozens of American soldiers in Somalia angered him because he thought it resulted from inept and amateurish policies. The death of any young American serving his country is a cause for sadness. When that death comes as the result of a poorly thought out mission that lacked the necessary equipment then that is a cause for anger. Gingrich was not shy about making his feelings known.

Many thought that the real fights came on the House floor over the president's budget, health care, and the crime bill. The budget bill, called by some the largest tax increase in the history of the country, did more than raise taxes. It also applied them retroactively. Gingrich called on the public to write or call their representative to tell him or her how they felt about this tax increase and its retroactive application. He also called the Rush Limbaugh radio show and personally urged a citizen's protest. Supported by Limbaugh and dozens of other talk show hosts across the country, Gingrich's request was answered as mail piled up on congressional desks and switchboards on Capitol Hill were jammed. Talk radio had come into its own and was flexing its muscle. The Democrats declared that the calls and letters were incited by a mob psychology encouraged by right-wing talk show hosts like Limbaugh and pretended not to take it seriously. It was serious, however, and was a clear sign that a new mood was abroad in the land, a mood strong enough to almost defeat the budget bill. One casualty was Democratic Congressman Buddy Darden from Georgia. Believing he had to support the tax increase for his district, he supported it and was beaten in the Republican tide of 1994.

Many representatives were subjected to pressure from the president and the leadership. They were told that a defeat for Clinton would fatally wound his presidency and many received calls personally from Clinton. The most famous was freshman Representative Marjory Mazolli Mizvinsky who, at first said she would vote against the bill due to the overwhelming feeling of the people back home only to be talked into it during a personal call from the president and pressure from the leadership. The Republicans sang good-bye to her as she walked the aisle to cast an affirmative vote for the bill. She too lost in the next election.

Newt did begin speaking out on the tax bill. He not only called the Limbaugh show but appeared on talk and news shows whenever he could arrange it and made speeches across the country denouncing the bill as another example of Democratic big spending unchecked by the White House. To Newt, Clinton was not the moderate New Democrat he had promised during the campaign but just another old liberal Democrat who campaigned as a moderate/conservative. "The American people have established the belief that their government is their fiscal enemy," he said.

Possibly Newt's greatest contribution was to hold the GOP members together in unified opposition to the tax bill. Not a single Republican vote was cast for the president's budget and enough Democrats joined the Republicans to allow it to pass by just one vote. Even though they lost the vote and the bill passed, they felt strength in unity and had a weapon for the next election to use against those Democrats who had supported the president.

Newt also supported another fiscally responsible measure introduced by Representative Tim Penny, a Democrat from Minnesota, and Representative Jim Nussle, a Republican from Iowa. They urged Congress to actually come up with the money, through spending cuts, before voting flood relief for the disastrous floods of 1993. They were for flood relief but thought Congress should pay for it by cutting funds in another area rather than simply borrow the money as was the usual custom. In addition, Newt and Michel asked Representative John Kasich, from Ohio, the ranking member on the Budget Committee, to come up with a Republican budget that cut taxes rather than raised them. Kasich, who was only 30 when elected to Congress in 1982, showed why many consider him one of the brightest and most capable of the next generation of leaders. He put together a solid budget that gave the GOP a platform and enabled them to be for something rather than just being against the Democrats.

These Midwesterners, with their reputation for good common sense, helped focus the public as well as the Congress on the difference between the two parties. The Democrats were doing their best to raise taxes and increase government spending. The Republicans were trying to cut taxes and spending. Their work, supported by the GOP leadership and talk show hosts across the nation, was in large measure, responsible for the nationalization of the 1994 election. For a change Tip O'Neill's dictum that "all politics is local" was proven wrong.

Newt also began a practice he would continue when he became speaker. In the process of enlisting allies to help fight for fiscal responsibility, he let it be known that lobbyists and special-interest groups should withhold any support from the Democrats and from the president's bills. He said he "could not understand why any group would support Democratic proposals designed to work against them."

The word was passed openly that if the lobbyists expected to win the battle and be part of the winning team, they needed to come to terms with the program and support it with their money and their influence. When the US Chamber of Commerce, an old GOP ally, issued a statement praising some points of the Clinton State of the Union Address, Newt voiced his displeasure and contacted 100 House GOP members who were to be honored by the Chamber of Commerce at a banquet in July. He wrote that he understood why the award was important to the members but encouraged them to boycott the banquet because, "it is equally important that we do not act as props for an organization that has opposed us in our fight against the higher taxes of the president's budget." Only a dozen or so members showed up for the event and afterward the president of the Chamber of Commerce wrote a letter opposing Clinton's plan no matter what form it might take.

By adopting this hard-nose approach to special-interest groups, pioneered earlier by the Democrat's Tony Coelho, Newt was able to increase the support, and the war chest, for the Republican's 1994 effort and decrease, in part, the aid given to Democrats. The traditional lobbyist idea that you have to give something to both sides was answered by Newt with, "No, you don't." Furthermore, the implication was that if you do give to the other side be sure it will be noted and remembered.

The president's health care package was probably the most dangerous bill for the Republicans to oppose. Almost everyone in the country thought something needed to be done about the runaway cost of health care. The problem was that there were so many special interest groups involved that almost any action taken would be bound to step on someone's toes. Doctors, hospitals, nursing homes, pharmaceutical companies and the home health care industry all had lobbyists and money to make sure they did not feel the sting of the reformists' whip. The most powerful of these special interest groups was the multi-million member American Association of Retired Persons (AARP).

The AARP was sometimes called the "third rail" of politics: if one touched it one died. They had their own magazine with one of the largest circulation rates in the nation as well as their own insurance program and drugs by mail operation. They had money. More than that, they had votes. If it appears that a politician might simply be thinking about making changes in social security or Medicare they could turn out AARP members against that candidate and possibly cost them the election. At least that is what passed for common wisdom at the time.

Gingrich had become concerned about the growing crisis in social security back in 1986 and had been stung when he proposed rethinking the system and at the same time protecting those under the current system. His opponents accused him of wanting to "destroy" social security and leave the elderly without the financial support they had come to expect in their retirement years. Newt knew that while this tactic typically wasused by the Democrats during election years, it still resonated with the elderly who were not sure who to believe and therefore played it safe and voted against the Republicans. He thought something had to be done to change this.

Medicare and Medicaid are similar issues with the elderly. Medicare comes into play exactly when people are at their most helpless. They know the huge cost of medical services can pauperize them or cause them not to receive needed treatment if they are left to their own resources. While most Americans know they personally can not pay for quality medical care if surgery or extended hospital or nursing home care is required, they still want the care. If they can not afford it they reason someone else should pay for it. The only practical way to do this is for the government to shoulder the burden. Politicians know that to move away from this model is to court disaster.

By the early 1990s it was becoming clear that Medicare as well as Social Security costs were taking an ever-larger bite of the federal budget. Unless they were reorganized and reformed to make them more cost effective taxes would have to be raised on a yearly basis to avoid a total breakdown of the current system. Newt thought most people could not afford huge tax increases nor should they be subjected to such state confiscation of their hard-earned wages. Such a tax would fall equally heavy on the middle as well as the upper class. Gingrich and the Republicans, along with many conservative Democrats, knew something had to change if people are going to take care of their parents and grandparents and still keep the country fiscally sound. Where and how to make changes was one big problem. Selling it to the public was the other.

Newt decided to try and obtain some independent information on the broad subject of health care. He asked his old advisor, Steve Hanser, to put together a small group to look at the problems. The dean of the school of business at West Georgia College, Dr. David Hovey, was asked to help and present the business view. Dr. Brenda Fitzgerald, a practicing gynecologist, was selected to look at the problem from a medical point of view. Their goal was to identify the problems so they could be addressed. After working for two years they made some suggestions toward dealing with the problems but the major impact they had was to inform Newt of the current issues in the health care debate.

The health care panel, Hanser, Hovey, and Fitzgerald, held hearings around the old sixth district and looked into every aspect of health care and its delivery system. They looked into what people wanted and what they were getting. They talked to ambulance drivers, lawyers, nurses, dentists, former patients, medical specialists, wellness experts and dozens of others in the field as well as surgeons, researchers, administrators and family practitioners. They read widely in the field, discussed numerous reports from specialists and looked at a variety of programs run by others around the world and at home. By the time the administration presented its health care plan Newt thought he knew enough to ask questions and offer some suggestions. The problem for Newt was that this health care plan was not NAFTA and it belonged to the First Lady and her corps of 500 experts, few of whom had any firsthand knowledge of the health care field and its complexities. He was not invited to their party.

After holding hearings around the country, Hillary Rodham Clinton took her group into secret, closed-door sessions that produced a very complex 1,342 page bill. It was finally introduced to Congress in November. Newt pronounced it "culturally alien to America" consisting of "1,300 pages of red tape." His basic thrust was to drive home the idea that it would take health care choices out of the hands of the patients and put them in those of government bureaucrats. It would bring government control of health care to America, he told the people back home in numerous town hall meetings dealing with the issue.

Newt noted that the Democrats wanted to move us toward the kind of system we were advising Russia, and other countries formerly dominated by communism, to reject. It would, he said, force many out of business if employers were required to supply health insurance for all employees. The African-American owner of Godfather's Pizza challenged the president on this issue during a televised town hall meeting. Clinton told him to "raise the price of pizzas." A young woman who worked for an insurance company asked Mrs. Clinton what would happen to all those in the insurance field if the Clinton plan were adopted. "You're a smart girl; you'll find something," she was told. The President and the Democrats were finding health care to be just as large a problem for them as for the Republicans.

Seeking to keep the pressure on the Democrats the GOP came out with its own health care plan. The Republican plan would have allowed portability for workers, contained insurance costs, allowed a series of choices for the insured and avoided forcing businesses to provide health care for all their workers. Newt co-sponsored the bill. There was no hope of passing the bill but it played well when compared with the Clinton bill.

One theme the Republicans developed early on was to deny that there was a health care crisis, but rather a financial crisis in paying for health care itself. Indeed, they pointed out, thousands came from around the world to take advantage of the health care offered in the US. The Clinton plan, they said, would benefit the 15 percent of those Americans who had no health insurance at the expense of the 85 percent who were covered in one way or another. Why should the 85 percent have their health delivery compromised to benefit the 15 percent, they asked. There had to be a better way than turning health care over to the guys who run the US Postal Service.

In July Newt appeared on *Good Morning America* with Janice Castro, author of *The American Way of Health*. She made the point that people are frightened because when they look at the president's plan, or the GOP one for that matter, they think "it'll cost them a lot and they are going to have to give up something." They were not very concerned about managed health care because seven out of ten were already in HMOs and two-thirds of all doctors were associated with some form of HMO. Both Castro and Newt thought preventive programs were very helpful. Newt noted that "we are living longer and now technology is keeping us alive longer. This is bound to raise health care cost." Still, Newt thought by such methods as malpractice reform, medical savings accounts and comprehensive preventive care, we might keep the cost down. He said he thought managed care would be acceptable as long as people had choices. They did not want to be sent to only one doctor or one hospital.[9]

At this point the various health related interest groups entered the picture in force. Together they spent around $120 million to oppose the Clinton plan. Most of this was spent in direct mail and radio and television advertising. The most effective was probably the Health Insurance Association of America's television ad featuring "Harry and Louise." This fictional couple worried about various aspects of the Clinton plan in different ads and ended each with, "there's got to be a better way."

The Republicans opposed any amendments calculated to make the plan slightly more acceptable because it was the total bill they were interested in killing. If it was changed in part the result could have been that individual Members could be lured away one by one with minimal overall change. In addition, the Democrats were finding that defending the plan something of a burden in an election year and Newt wanted to make certain that continued.

Clinton had promised he would have a health care bill to Congress in the first 100 days. It took almost a year and then was produced by questionable, later ruled illegal, methods. Once the bill reached Congress the president was still unable to pass it even though the Democrats controlled the House and Senate by comfortable margins. It gave the impression to many voters that the president and the Democratic Party were incapable of governing. As Newt saw it, this impression should be reinforced and carried into the November elections in 1994. No GOP member supported the bill in the House and only one Republican Senator voted for it, Senator Jim Jeffords of

---

[9] See also Gingrich speech to the American Hospital Assoc., C-SPAN, 30 January 1995.

Vermont. By September the Democrats declared it dead insofar as the 103rd Congress was concerned.

Gingrich understood that the voters were tired of politics as usual and wanted to know what candidates were for and not just what they were against. Whenever possible the Republicans responded with bills of their own, or amendments to bills, to have a position of their own which could be advocated once they were back home.

The administration's crime bill was a good example of one where Republican participation helped modify the bill. It was also one where Newt did not maintain unanimous or almost unanimous GOP support. The president and the House leadership figured no conservative could vote against a crime bill that provided more money for hiring policemen. Newt surprised them. He sought to paint it as a liberal measure which practically protected criminals and poured millions into things like midnight basketball to keep kids off the streets. He argued that programs were already in place to take care of that and that money should be spent keeping real, dangerous criminals off the street instead of simply processing them and putting them back on the streets.

Gingrich and Conference Chairman Dick Armey led the fight. One approach was to point out how the Democrats, through unfair use of parliamentary maneuvers, would pass bad liberal legislation and keep good Republican amendments and bills bottled up in committees refusing to even allow them to come to a vote. The use of the "closed rule" was particularly useful to the Democrats and repugnant to the GOP. At a news conference in August 1994, Representative Armey said, "The Democrats don't have ideas in step with America and therefore they are using their control over parliamentary procedures to stop any exposure of competing ideas." He described the crime bill as a "pig in a poke" and said the Republicans had only been allowed to see it two hours before they were asked to vote on it.[10]

The polls were favorable toward the Republicans at the time the news conference was held and the press, noting how much Armey and Gingrich complained about Democratic parliamentary procedures, asked Newt if he would allow "open rules" if he were to be placed in charge. In other words, would he gain a new appreciation for the "closed rule" if he were running the show? He said he "would not put

---

10 C-SPAN, 18 August 1994.

up with nuisance amendments but would substantive ones." He said they would probably work longer hours and be more open but with few "open rules." High-handed approaches used by committee chairmen such as Representative Sam Gibbons, Representative Henry Gonzales and Representative Jack Brooks were exposed on C-SPAN and in the media, giving resonance to the complaints the Republicans were voicing.

As the 104th Congress opened and the parties had now switched positions with the Democrats in the minority, it was interesting to see the role reversal on procedure. One of the most blatant chairmen, Gibbons on Ways and Means, was now reduced to blustering and arm waving while he called Representative Bill Archer, the new chairman, a fascist. He declared: "I fought against people like you in Europe." Archer was using the tactics Gibbons had used when he was chairman. Republicans who had suffered under Gibbons now enjoyed, and indeed looked forward to his daily antics. The Democratic Party song, "Happy Days are Here Again," had been replaced with a plaintive whine and it was a joy for Republicans to watch after being in the minority for forty years.[11]

Because of the relatively liberal nature of the crime bill the Republicans, under Gingrich's leadership, were able to stop it on a procedural vote on the rule. Enough Democrats, fearful of charges of liberal coddling of criminals and wasteful spending, voted with the Republicans to cause the Democratic leadership to back off and regroup.

This time the president was willing to deal and some of the more moderate Republicans were interested. Eleven agreed to talk to Clinton about working together to make the bill more acceptable. Some in the GOP Conference viewed them as traitors but Newt, mindful of his role as Whip for the whole party and not just the conservatives, assigned crime staffers to serve as technical advisors to the eleven and personally accompanied them to a White House meeting with Clinton.

As a result of their efforts and Newt's assistance, the president renegotiated the crime bill, making changes that upset many of the more liberal element in his own party and reduced the cost by three billion dollars. The bill passed this time with forty-six GOP votes made possible by the changes wrung from the President by the moderates.

---

[11] C-SPAN coverage of committee meetings in the first three months of 1995 show the frustration.

Sixty-four Democrats voted against the bill putting the margin of passage at forty-one votes.

Because it was so close, and the GOP votes provided the margin of victory for Clinton as they had in the NAFTA vote, some Republicans sought to discipline the eleven and some the other thirty-five who signed on in the final vote. Newt opposed this decision and knew that if the party was to be successful in taking over the House in 1995 they would have to all work under the "big tent" concept. While he personally opposed the bill, and voted against it on final passage, he tried to be helpful to the eleven and as a result had a bill that moved from being "terrible" to "bad." Speaking on the floor during the final passage vote he defended the eleven for doing what they felt they had to do and also noted that it was still a bad bill that had been presented at the last minute. Holding up a copy of the bill itself, with all the changes written on separate sheets of paper and sticking out of the document, he complained no one had really had time to study the revised document and asked that it be defeated.

The White House had now seen two Newts, the reasonable parliamentary leader willing to work to pass needed legislation and the partisan guerrilla leader determined to do what was necessary to stop them. Had they gone back to his earlier statement about cooperating but not compromising they would have had a better understanding of which was which.

In October 1993 Bob Michel had announced that he would not run for re-election. By this time Newt had for all intents and purposes become the de facto leader of House Republicans. Everyone respected Michel and his position. He was consulted on all important decisions and functioned as the leader. This aggressive style of politics, however, was not to his taste and it became apparent that Newt was the person to whom most Republicans turned for leadership and guidance.

Earlier in the year, in a conversation with key advisors back in the district, Newt was asked if he would be ready to challenge Michel for the leadership position following the 1994 elections. "Yes," he said, "I will if necessary but I hope and think that won't be necessary. I think he'll retire." "Will you have any serious opposition within the Conference?" he was asked. "I don't think so," he replied, "I think we've lined up our support and it shouldn't be a problem."

In an interview with Morton Kondracke in December he said, "I intend to lead. I'm never going to worry about the size of my margin as long as I'm the leader. We're going the 20 hours a day it takes. We're going to be a modern revolutionary party that really wants to replace the welfare state and get back to common sense so everything I'm going to be near is going to move that way. It is going to be a wild couple of years." He clearly expected to win the leadership or, if lucky, the speakership.

Upon hearing of Michel's announcement Newt moved quickly, as he had done in seeking support for the Whip position, to lock up votes for either Minority Leader or for Speaker. By the fall of 1993 it was becoming apparent that the speakership was a long shot but not out of the question. In less than a week Newt announced that he had enough votes to replace Michel whichever position came open. To shouts of "Newt! Newt! Newt!" he said he represented "a new generation of conservatives" who "must replace the welfare state with an opportunity society."[12] While the election was over a year away Newt had set the stage for restructuring the House after the GOP sweep in November of 1994. Bob Michel was now thinking more about retirement and Newt moved more and more into the public eye as the leader of House Republicans. He was in charge. In combination with Haley Barbour, Republican national chairman, Newt began devising the strategy that would result in the most spectacular off-year electoral victory in the twentieth century. He was becoming what *Time* magazine would call "the pre-eminent political leader in America."

All the polls showed there was profound discontent across America. The talk shows reflected it. The Perot supporters exhibited it in the 1992 election as did many Republicans who had refused to vote for George Bush. Newt hoped to corral this discontent and transform it into resurgent idealism that would be reflected in the platform of Republican candidates who would "offer hope and opportunity" instead of negativism and disappointment with their political and cultural leaders.

The polls also showed that most Americans were dissatisfied with their president. He was becoming such a liability that most Democratic candidates did not want him campaigning in their districts. Gingrich

---

12 Warner & Berley, *Newt Gingrich*, pp. 168-169.

moved toward asserting himself as Clinton's opposite number, the man with whom he had to deal. Following the crime bill's passage he sent a message to the president and the Democratic leadership: "My message back to the Democratic leadership in the House and the White House is going to be 'you want to avoid this kind of train wreck, you're going to call us in at the beginning of a bill and you're going to have conferences that are honest and you're going to share the report language with us and we're going to do this thing with dignity. And if you don't, every chance I get to wreck the train I'm going to wreck it. And then when you get tired of looking stupid in public we'll talk.'" Few understood at that time that the president was, as Newt would later call him, "the best counter-puncher I've ever seen." A year and a half later he would use his spin machine during the budget fight to make sure he was not the one to look stupid when he convinced the public that the Republicans were not only the stupid ones but mean in the bargain. Newt's plan had always worked when Democratic congressmen were doing it to Republican presidents so why would it not work now?

When asked why he had not worked to kill the crime bill Newt said, "I managed the battlefield we had, with the forces we had, to maximize our opportunity." The same could be said of his management of the campaign of 1994. In January 1994 he tasked Frank Luntz, a bright GOP pollster who had worked for Perot in 1992, to conduct focus groups every ten days. He wanted to stay in close touch with what voters were thinking and be sure the Republicans shared that thinking.[13]

Newt became busier than usual. He traveled in 125 congressional districts around the country campaigning for GOP candidates. He gave interviews and appeared on television whenever possible, endlessly reciting his double mantra: "It is impossible to maintain a civilization with twelve-year-olds having babies, fifteen-year-olds killing each other, seventeen-year-olds dying of AIDS, and eighteen-year-olds receiving diplomas they can't read. If we are not careful, our children could inherit a dark and bloody planet in the 21st century."

In addition to campaigning for candidates he helped the RNCC and individual campaigns raise money at each opportunity. He could nor-

---

[13] Ibid., p. 176.

mally raise between $10,000 and $100,000 whenever he spoke to crowds willing to pay to hear the probable new Speaker of the House. According to Representative Bill Paxton, chairman of the Republican National Campaign Committee, Newt raised at least $3,000,000 for the Republican coffers.

Looking back to the capitol steps event in 1980 he decided that was the sort of dramatic event to capture the public's attention and allow them to focus on the difference between the two parties. The question was then what should they do on the steps. After discussing it with a number of people Newt huddled with his advisors and they came up with the idea of a contract they would make with the voters. Some critics say the contract was the product of pollsters but that is not entirely accurate. Nine out of ten of the points in the contract were reflected in the polls but were not creatures of the polls. The ideas in the contract were present in most of Newt's earlier campaigns. "On core values Newt is probably more consistent than any politician I know," reported the columnist Dick Williams. The focus groups did not give him the ideas, what they did was to help ensure the wording would resonate with the voters.[14]

In early September Newt met at the Capitol Hill Club with Republican intellectuals who were somewhat skeptical of the contract and viewed it as a gimmick. Chief among those present were Bill Kristol, president of the Project for a Republican Future and *Wall Street Journal* editor Robert L. Bartley, whose paper had been very helpful in pointing out problems in the Clinton administration and with the Democrats generally. By the end of the meeting, though not completely convinced, they had signed on to the concept.

On 27 September Gingrich hosted over 300 Republican candidates who would sign the contract and make it part of their own campaigns. The contract was called "revolutionary" by Newt and the GOP leaders and was to be the centerpiece of a strategy to nationalize the elections of 1994. It was not revolutionary in the traditional or historical sense of the word in that there was no attempt to overthrow or change the form of government but rather an attempt to redirect that government in both a political and social sense. It seemed revolutionary to both parties because of the entrenched nature of the liberal welfare state.

---

[14] Dick Williams speech to Carrollton Lions Club, 6 July 1995. See also Williams, *Newt*, pp. 121-122.

Gingrich understood that the liberals were not consciously trying to enslave people in poverty and hopelessness. They were not attempting to destroy the energy and desire of people to lift themselves and their families out of the quagmire of poor education, joblessness and despair. Liberals from Lyndon Johnson to Hillary Clinton wanted a better life for these people, indeed for all the American people. He never questioned that desire. The problem was that their efforts, however well intentioned, to have government solve all the problems had not worked and indeed had the opposite effect.

On more than one occasion, Newt had defended the approach of the liberals as an honest one, with historical precedent. "Ron Dellums, Dick Gephardt and Pat Schroeder are sincere in trying to achieve their view of a better America. They are just wrong." It was clear to him that their model had failed after a fifty-year experiment. It was now time for a new approach. The contract was a start.

The American people were tired of politics as usual. They knew, even if the liberals did not, that it was time for a change. It was time the politicians played straight with them and did not promise one thing and do another as had been the case with Carter, Clinton, and so many other politicians. In the signing ceremony Newt said, "The point is to say to the American people: We want you to hold us accountable." The question then became "accountable for what?"[15]

Luntz's focus groups had confirmed Newt's feelings about what the people wanted and helped Newt and his advisors phrased them accurately. The ten points were not new. All had been included, in one form or another, in most of Newt's previous campaigns—most going back to the 1970s campaigns. What the focus groups did was to help Newt, Armey and their allies, frame the ten points in a clear and positive way, in clear language, so people could relate to the objective of each point. Thus the first, a balanced budget, line-item veto bill, became "The Fiscal Responsibility Act." The other nine were:

> The Taking Back Our Streets Act
> The Personal Responsibility Act
> The Family Reinforcement Act
> The American Dream Restoration Act

---

[15] C-SPAN, 27 September 1994.

The National Security Restoration Act
The Senior Citizens Fairness Act
The Job Creation and Wage Enhancement Act
The Common Sense Legal Reform Act
The Citizen Legislature Act

Understanding the impact of ceremony the Republicans made sure the contract event was properly choreographed. Red, white and blue colors were the order of the day. Flags, bunting, and a band playing the marches of America's greatest composer, John Phillip Sousa, were everywhere along with the proper signs and posters. Racial, regional, gender and ideological balance was observed in the selection of speakers and the whole ceremony had a feeling of a cross between an old-fashioned tent revival and a Fourth of July celebration.

In an article in the *New Yorker*, Michael Kelley described the event as one where over 300 congressmen and would-be congressmen came to the Capitol, "in order to rail against it, as if they were the Free Silverites or Dust Bowl farmers come to smite the corruption of Washington."[16] Kelley captured the feelings and intent of millions of Americans who were represented by those 300 plus candidates that day. They were there to change the future for the better and with the confidence of a reformed sinner and the zeal of a former smoker they honestly believed they would be able to do the job.

As they met in the Capitol prior to the ceremony Newt and the key leaders surrounding him were clearly aware of the historical importance of the event. With the British parliamentary system in mind, they were ready to pledge a platform that they fully intended to carry out if the people gave them the majority they were requesting. This contention was more than a promise; it was viewed as a contract because the voters had to carry out their part of the bargain. They had to elect enough Republicans to accomplish the task. As Winston Churchill said to his Washington ally in the dark days of World War II before America entered the war, "Give us the tools and we will finish the fight." After the ceremony, carried live on C-SPAN, and viewed across the nation that evening on the nightly news, Newt and his team spread out across the nation to work to achieve the goal of a Republican majority. They

---

16 Michael Kelley, *The New Yorker*, 24 October 1994, pp. 42-53.

began that evening with a very successful fund-raiser in Washington that earned in $500,000.

The Democrats carped about the contract being one on America instead of with America and were quickly bogged down analyzing cost items. The Republicans focused on their promise to bring change and taunted the Democrats with challenges to make their own contract outlining their priorities — such as "more spending, bigger government, more bureaucrats, etc."

Every item in the contract had received over 60 percent support in the focus groups and in polls. Newt was perfectly happy to compare Republican promises with any the Democrats might make. While many voters might not understand the complexities of federal budgeting they did understand that the Democrats had made promises for over twenty years that they had not kept. The people, he thought, were ready to turn to people who would take their promises seriously and try to keep them. It was time to test the theory at home, back in Georgia.

Newt did not have serious opposition in the primary in 1994 and paid scant attention to that campaign except to be home enough to establish his interest and concern for the sixth district of Georgia. His campaign was a national one that was applied to his local district. The national themes were used but presented to his constituents in terms of how they impacted on Georgia and the sixth district. He was able to do this in the new district because of its make-up. New people were moving in daily and understood that national affairs impacted directly on them and their pocketbooks. They wanted a congressman who would operate on a broader scale. The old district still had the image in mind of a congressman who spent time with them, at home, in their stores, barbershops and restaurants — not one flying all over the country. Newt's old colleague at WGC, Floyd Hoskins, had sent him a memo dated 28 January 1988 warning about this perception and quoting some of Newt's supporters, or former supporters. "He has done nothing in Washington that has been of benefit to Carroll County," declared one irate constituent. Still another stated, "He doesn't see you, he sees himself as a national figure, and I hope that he is defeated." Hoskins listed seven who felt this way and expressed his concerns about the situation.[17] Newt's theory was that people across the country had

---

[17] Floyd Hoskins, Memo to Gingrich via Steely, 28 January 1988. Biography folder ch. 12, MSC, Gingrich Papers.

basically the same concerns, worries, hopes and ideas—with local application. This theory worked with the people of the new district. Clinton and the Democrats in Congress were the targets with little attention being paid to his opponent—former Congressman Ben Jones.

Jones had been defeated in the 1992 Democratic primary after serving two terms in Congress. He was an extremely likeable fellow who had been a television actor on the "Dukes of Hazzard" where he played a relatively uneducated country mechanic more interested in truck maintenance than political philosophy. The opposite was true of the real Ben Jones. He attended the University of North Carolina and was a bright, practicing liberal. His liberal voting record endeared him to few of the Democratic leaders in the Georgia legislature. However, little interest was shown in protecting his turf while considerable concern was evident in districts drawn for more conservative Democrats.

Jones moved into Newt's district in order to run against him. One had the impression that he knew he could not win but disliked Newt and figured he could make as much money running against him as he could being a talk show host on a local station and have a lot more fun. The campaign against Newt certainly seemed to be fun for Jones. He made the most outrageous charges, some left over from previous campaigns by Worley, Clark and Center. He had a bloodhound to "track Newt down" as Newt flew around the country helping raise money and garner votes for Republican candidates.

The Democrats, who put less money into the campaign than might be expected, hoped to tie Newt down in Georgia answering Jones' charges and defending himself. They were supported in their efforts by the press, local and national, at each opportunity. The *Atlanta Constitution*, known for its liberal attitude and political correctness even on the obituary page, gave him unrelieved, unshirted hell. Indeed, Gaylord bought an ad in that paper in order to see something positive about Newt in the paper.

Jeanne Cummings, a smart, energetic reporter for the *Atlanta Constitution* who had covered the reapportionment session and now worked in the paper's Washington bureau, wrote comparison articles in August on Jones and Gingrich. They were printed side-by-side. The article on Jones pictured him as the underdog and dwelled mainly on charges he was making against Gingrich. It ended with a quote from

Newt describing Ben as "a very interesting, personable, liberal Democrat." The Gingrich article featured quotes from constituents attending the town hall meetings and a Jones campaign worker. The best any of them offered is one man whose son attended West Georgia College saying, "I've admired him through the years, but sometimes he gets a little to controversial for me, but I guess that's necessary."[18]

Jones financed his campaign through local donations and a national fund-raising drive targeting liberal organizations and Democratic stalwarts that offered an opportunity for the donors to strike a blow against the hated Gingrich. Jones was successful in raising considerably more money outside the sixth district than at home. Interestingly enough, so was Newt. When it came to fund-raising Jones was unable to match Newt's organization.

The national campaign was also working. By late August the polls were showing a strong Republican tide in both state and national elections. If one wanted to talk to Newt about anything but congressional business one usually had to fly with him and talk on the airplane between campaign stops. One supporter met him before daybreak, had breakfast in Charlestown, lunch in Omaha, and dinner in Peoria, and finally returned to Atlanta's Charlie Brown Airport in the wee hours of the morning.

As Hanser and Gingrich boarded a plane in the early morning of 14 September Newt asked Gaylord, "Well, Joe, are you planning for Leader or Speaker?" "You'd better plan for Speaker because that's what it's going to be," was the reply. Gaylord's certainty startled them. "You're sure?" "Yep," Gaylord replied. He then started in Maine and described the status of every GOP race, state by state, district by district, without notes, all across the country from Maine to Hawaii. Gaylord estimated that, at minimum, the GOP would pick up thrity-five seats and that, with a handful of conservative Democrats, would give them a working majority on the floor on many issues. Gaylord's maximum estimate was a gain of fifty-three seats. He missed the final vote by one. The GOP received fifty-two new seats in November.[19]

With all the hoopla attendant the signing of the Contract for America, most people still knew nothing about it. When the president and the Democrats decided they had been given a gift with which to

---

18 Jeanne Cummings, *Atlanta Constitution*, 27 August 1994.
19 Joe Gaylord Interview, 21 April 1995.

direct attention away from Clinton and commenced to attack it and Newt, the Republicans were "overjoyed." Tony Blankley, Newt's press secretary, remembers being surprised when a White House reporter called for a response from Newt concerning the Democrats' upcoming full-scale attack. The dapper Blankley, son of one of Winston Churchill's accountants, a child prodigy, who was both a violinist and child actor, a prosecuting attorney, White House official under President Reagan and now press secretary for Newt,"[20] was delighted because this question indicated that the contract would be the subject of all the Sunday political talk shows. Newt could not hope to buy that kind of publicity.

Blankley had come to work for Newt in 1990 and was included in almost everything. Newt wanted him, as well as Dan Meyer, his chief of staff, and Hanser to know his thinking and plans. Gingrich used a Reagan model of cross-zoning for his staff so that Blankley was in on policy planning as well as press. "He thought we could handle the press questions better if we knew what the strategy was from the beginning," remembers Tony.[21]

This approach paid off handsomely. Planning was begun immediately toward a Republican sweep. Meyer was put in charge of putting together a plan for how Newt, as speaker, would staff his office and make appointments to House committees. There had to be a plan for selecting chairmen. What role would the loyal activists play? How did the large class of expected freshmen fit into the model? Was it time to punish enemies and reward friends? How much should seniority count?

Committee memberships were pretty much set but placement of freshmen and selection of chairmen were critical decisions that would help or hurt the carrying out of the contract agenda. Meyer's work was designed to prepare Newt for discussions with key members that would take place after the election as they worked as a team to plan for the changes from minority to majority status. "The book" would be consulted often in the days to come as Newt met with Representative Jim Nussle, his agent for the transition, Armey, Walker and a series of other key leaders.[22]

October was spent campaigning, both in Georgia and across the country, and in planning for a Republican take-over. Newt traveled

---

[20] C-SPAN Interview with Fred Barnes, 11 September 1995.

[21] Tony Blankley Interview, 11 November 1995.

[22] Dan Meyer Interview, 22 September 1995.

across the sixth district, sometimes in an English double-decker bus. As he spoke at barbecues he assumed the mantle of speaker and extolled the virtues of the power of the speaker's office. He explained what being speaker could mean for Georgia and the district as well as what a GOP take-over would mean for the country as it began the process of reversing the welfare state.

Newt and Marianne spent time shopping and casually moving around the district, which was relatively small and compact, going to movies, and dining out. It became apparent to the hundreds of constituents they saw that they were comfortable and belonged there. They were more than Washington politicians, they were neighbors. The image of Newt as an interloper, cultivated by his opponents, was a thing of the past.

The Democrats' attacks on Newt and on the contract did nothing to change the outcome of the election but they did paint Gingrich in a very negative light in many people's eyes. The people were also negative toward President Clinton. Newt won with 64 percent of the vote, the first time he had broken 60 percent. The GOP won fifty-two new seats, a switch from 256 Democrats to 178 GOP to 230 GOP to 204 Democrats. Democratic switches to the Republicans would put the Democrats below 200 for the first time in half a century.

Election night for "the happy warrior," as he was called by Michael Barone, was a victory party from the start. The only question was how big the win would be. "Speaker Gingrich" blue and white bumper stickers were being handed out. In addition to his family, Newt had invited key GOP leaders who had contributed to this victory such as Guy Vander Jagt, Pierre Dupont and Bo Callaway. Some of Georgia's GOP congressmen like Mac Collins and John Linder attended as did newly elected Republicans like Bob Barr. Old supporters from the former sixth district joined in and fought for room in the ballroom with a phalanx of media people.

This was clearly Newt Gingrich's victory—not just in Georgia but across the nation. He had started with nothing but an idea that he could make a difference. He was not the product of any political machine. He made the machine. He did not have large financial resources behind him at the start, but raised it along the way. He had to change the state and national party to make it capable of winning such a sweeping victory. He inherited no big team; he built it. Through energy, willpower and strategic political savvy he put together and directed one of the most stunning electoral victories in the history of American politics.

Vander Jagt, Dupont, and Callaway acted like new fathers, bursting with pride at Newt's accomplishment and clearly relishing their roles in the victory. Old supporters felt much the same, congratulating each other and waiting on Newt's next appearance. Gingrich was in a quiet room making phone calls to check on other candidates and setting up the next step in the transition, thanking key national campaign leaders, old colleagues like Walker and Weber and sharing the credit and the joy with them.

Gaylord and his staff were holed up with John Duncan, the 1994 campaign manager, in a boiler room atmosphere counting victories. Newt sought Gaylord out when the magnitude of the victory became apparent—not a single GOP loss nation wide. Even GOP governors were winning. "This is your victory, Joe. It could not have happened without you," Newt quietly told Gaylord.

When later asked about Newt's role in their partnership Gaylord responded, "He is the most remarkable person I know. He has incredible energy and is a natural born optimist. He never lost heart that we wouldn't do it [gain a majority]." Gaylord went on, "He is wonderful at keeping other people up around him and is never short of an idea of how to solve a problem....He understands what he is trying to do. He gets up and does it every day. He does it with incredible enthusiasm. After he's solved a problem in his own mind he has to think himself through what he's trying to get done and then he is very cheerful about doing the work."[23] When asked about how they won in 1994, Gaylord said, "He [Newt] amassed enormous resources from the party. He had a message. Message and resources."

While savoring the victory, Newt was also thinking ahead. So was his brother, Randy McPhearson. He said, "The whole family is proud of him. He beat the odds, everyone was against him." When asked if criticism of Newt bothers him he responded, "It hurts at times. I get offended. Newt attacks on ideology but they attack him personally." McPhearson worried about his brother. He explained, as a cop, that security is important. "There are nuts out there. He's challenged their

---

[23] Joe Gaylord interview, 21 April 1995.

way of life or viewpoint." McPhearson used the *Newsweek* article that appeared shortly before the election as an example. Present for the interview with Newt, he thought the reporter came in looking for a fight: liberal versus conservative. "They kept arguing the whole time and would ask the same question many different ways seeking a predetermined answer. This was a predetermined hatchet job they wanted to do on Newt, GOPAC and everything else."[24]

The media had launched an attack on Gingrich that was to be constant and negative for the next six months. In December and January it was pack journalism at its worse. At one point so many reporters were in the halls of the West Georgia College history department that they were running into each other. One, from the *New York Post*, after interviewing me for an hour, said in disgust, "You haven't given me anything I can use. I need dirt. We'll pay for it." C-SPAN and the Arts & Entertainment people seemed to be the only ones not looking for dirt to bolster their personal attacks on the new Speaker. Newt and those close to him knew press attacks would be forthcoming and thought they were prepared. Gingrich professed he "was shocked at the depth and intensity of the attacks." He was prepared for them to be negative, he was not prepared for the meanness and viciousness involved.

Newt and Representative Dick Gephardt had a good working relationship as the new year came around. Newt had hoped that the election would lead the Democrats to turn more conservative and be willing to work with the Republicans during 1995 to settle issues that were of mutual interest, and there were a number of such issues. On the last night before going home in October, they stood in the halls of a quiet and almost deserted Capitol and talked about their futures. They agreed they would both probably be speakers at some point and expressed a desire to work together whenever possible. Newt liked and respected Gephardt and thought those feeling were shared. He honestly believed some cooperation might be possible—at least for the first year. 1996 was an election year and he was realistic enough to know that there was little hope of cooperation in an election year. It became clear after the election that Gephardt's expectation at the time was that he would be speaker and Newt would cooperate with him. The idea that

---

[24] Randy McPherson interview, 9 November 1994.

he would have to cooperate with Speaker Gingrich was as foreign as the Chinese language to him.

The press, almost as if they were defending their very way of life, attacked Gingrich from every quarter. Dick Williams, a journalist who had worked for the *Atlanta Constitution* and knew all about biased journalism, said that he thought Newt was "the most unfairly covered politician of our lifetime."[25] Calling him "the grinch who stole Christmas" from the Democrats, and themselves as well, the press did story after story on the hardships faced by Democrats. Members and staff, who would no longer be in the majority, smaller space, smaller staffs, less prestige and power, were all listed as the consequence of being a minority. Reading the articles one would think the Democrats had a lifetime guarantee on a majority and it was somehow unfair to expect them to make the shift.

Seeing Newt's success at using the "define your opponent tactic" the Democrats decided to take a note from his book and work to define him in such a way that only his mother could like him. "Mean-spirited" and "extremist" were the most frequently used adjectives in the effort to demonize him. His success at their expense really upset them. The shock of the loss in November was not absorbed for months. His very presence was a reminder of what had been and who took it away. The Democrats decided to strike back. He became the most investigated man in the Capitol. He had even had his own special prosecutor and was still standing. The Democrats just knew that he must have done something they could use against him and if he had not he would at some point. Florida Democrat Harry Johnston told his Palm Beach audience early in 1995, "He's smart and extremely dangerous." In an article in *The Miami Herald*, he is quoted as saying, "The guy thinks he's invincible...We're going to stay on his back until one [a special prosecutor] is done."[26] These, incidentally, are the same people who will scream "unfair" later when President Clinton is being investigated. One of the stories that is illustrative of their feelings toward Newt is about a Democratic meeting where Minority Leader Gephardt suggested that maybe they should back off and that Newt was his own worst enemy. "Not while I'm alive," supposedly growled Minority Whip David Bonier. As Republicans used the one-minute speeches

---

[25] Dick Williams speech to Carrollton Lions Club, 6 July 1995.
[26] Rep. Harry Johnson in the *Miami Herald*, 21 February 1995.

starting the legislative day to talk about the contract the Democrats responded with a series of personal attacks on Newt. They seemed to think that if they could cut off the dragon's head then the beast devouring them would die.

Despite the opposition, Newt and his team had prepared as well as they could. By the end of the year most of the chairmen had been selected in a process designed to have the best man in the slot rather than on a seniority or personal loyalty basis. A good example was the Rules Committee chairman, Representative Gerald Solomon. Solomon, who had come to the House with Newt in 1979, was not a supporter and had given serious consideration to opposing him when Newt sought to replace Michel. Some wanted Newt to make an example of him to be sure everyone understood they had better support Newt in the future, but Newt refused.

A similar situation had arisen a decade earlier in the Georgia House of Representatives. Tom Murphy had faced a challenge for speaker, had won anyway and after subjecting his opponent to a brief period in the wilderness, had brought him back into the leadership. Surprised and grateful, no one gave Murphy more loyalty that that former opponent. Newt had watched Murphy's approach and was impressed. Now he was in a similar situation. Solomon was clearly the person to handle this most important committee...one that had to be responsive to the leadership and especially to the Speaker. Solomon, a former Marine, made sure that Newt knew he remembered the Marine motto, "*Semper Fidelis*," always faithful.

Tom Murphy had commented that Newt would do himself in by talking too much. With a full time Democratic team working to find something they could use to attack Newt many thought he would pull in his horns to avoid making Murphy's prediction come true. At a planning session in 1989 Eddie Mahe had told Newt he needed to be "very sensitive to the brilliant ideas you get behind the podium."[27] Six years later his friends still worried about his habit of thinking out loud before the thought was refined.

Newt's speaking habits aside, the House was working at a break-neck pace. The speed and long hours had caused Representative Barney Frank to comment that "When they [the GOP] talked about

---

[27] Gingrich Papers, Steely Papers, folder on Gingrich biography, ch. 13, "Notes On 24 March 1989 Planning Session.

family values I didn't realize they were talking about the Addams family." Newt and the leadership kept the pace moving. At the end of the hundred days the contract had been completed and all ten points had been brought up for votes and all but one, term limits, had been passed. "Promises made, promises kept" became the watchword of the House Republicans. Newt asked for and received time on national television to talk to the nation about what had been accomplished and what could be expected. He talked about changing the welfare state and opening up the opportunity society to help America renew herself. Others, friends and foes, talked about Newt.

His book deal with a $4.5 million advance stirred attention for months. The status of his marriage, his relationship to GOPAC and other parts of "Newt Inc." were the subject of detailed scrutiny. Speculation on whether he would run for the presidency was the subject of conversation and debate for most of 1995. The talk, unfortunately, was about almost everything except the real, genuine accomplishments made in the halls of Congress.

At the end of November 1995 in a news conference held in Newt's Marietta office he announced he would not be running for president. After the conference ended, Newt called President Clinton. He appeared relaxed and confident talking to the president of the United States. Listening to one side of the conversation one could see how much each man was manipulating the other. Each knew they were being manipulated and understood exactly what was going on but they went along with it because it served their own purposes. From all appearances, these two working together could own Washington.

13

UNRAVELING

In his first year as Speaker Newt began on the cover of *Time* magazine identified as the "King of the Hill."[1] He ended the year selected as their Man of the Year.[2] During this year he became the heroic figure he had pictured himself being on the ship coming back from Europe as a young teenager. He led his troops in bringing about an historic power shift from Washington to the states. He transformed the speakership into an "unprecedented instrument of personal and political power" and the House of Representatives from a "weak, discredited institution into a humming legislative engine that could tow the Senate and the White House behind it."[3]

The year 1995 was the year that the believers in big government as the solution for all problems began to see the power they had amassed in Washington over the last half-century begin to come unraveled. President Clinton would note in his State of the Union Address that, "the time for big government is over." Newt, equating big government with liberalism, went a step further, perhaps precipitously, stating "The age of liberalism is over, and millions upon millions of ordinary Americans are in effect calling on us to figure out how to replace it without too much disruption."[4] He wanted to transform government from one of liberal largess wherein the federal government is the

---

[1] *Time* (9 January 1995): pp. 23-32.

[2] *Time* (25 December 1995): Cover and pp. 48-99.

[3] Ibid 50-58.

[4] Newt Gingrich, *Lessons Learned the Hard Way* (NY: Harper Collins, 1998) 40.

machine to solve all problems to one based on the COS model of conservative opportunity with individuals, and governments closer to them, acting as the problem solvers.

The new speaker had a number of things going for him. Momentum was in his favor. The GOP had just won fifty-two House seats giving them a small majority. They had also won twelve governorships and eight Senate seats without suffering the loss of a single Republican incumbent. Party unity seemed solid. He had been able to hold the Republican members together during the 1994 budget fight. Not a single GOP Member voted for the president's budget. Though they lost the battle, they were strengthened by the unity they showed. Nineteen ninety-five would be a test year to see if Gingrich could inspire that unity throughout the year—especially after the passage of the Contract during the first 100 days. He also had public opinion with him during the first weeks of the new Congress. His unfavorable ratings were only at twenty-nine percent after repeated unfavorable coverage by the media culminating in a description of him as the "Grinch who stole Christmas" from the Democrats.

In addition to party unity and public support, Newt thought he had arrived at an understanding with the White House that would allow them to work together to pass legislation on which they were in general agreement during the first year of the new session. No one expected harmony or excessive cooperation during an election year. Newt's willingness to help with NAFTA, when Clinton could not get the more liberal and pro-labor union members of his own party to support it, seemed to Gingrich to be a strong signal to the White House. He had also criticized the "scandal-based politics" surrounding the president after Paula Jones filed her sexual harassment charges.

"I think we have gone way overboard as a society in, on the one hand, wanting the deepest prurient interest in every public person's life, and, on the other hand, tolerating levels of behavior that are grotesque....We have become a very weird and, in some ways, sick culture. I think this is a society that is destroying the institution of the presidency as an important symbol binding us together.

"Republicans who were screaming about Anita Hill are hardly in a position to turn now and run around brandishing Paula Jones. Ninety-five percent of Republican energy should go into creating a series of reform proposals and communicating those reform proposals. The country is so exhausted by the politics of destruction that it is eager for someone who says we have serious problems and who focuses on serious solutions, even if they are controversial."[5]

As the new year approached it seemed to Newt that it would be the best year of his life. Much would be attempted and much accomplished. Few suspected what that year would bring. Party unity began to be shaky following the 100 days. His unfavorables rose to 56 percent and the relationship with the White House began to sour.[6] Some of this deterioration he could control but some parts were out of his hands. Four very negative and very personal events started the slide. The Rupert Murdoch $4.5 million book deal, the mini-crisis over the newly appointed House Historian, the Clinton=McGoverniks article and, most embarrassing, the Connie Chung ambush report, were negatives that might have been avoided.

After the 1994 election Newt had signed a contract with HarperCollins Publishing Company to do a multi-book deal carrying a hefty advance. Newt's literary agent had put his book package on the table and heavy bidding resulted with HarperCollins coming up with the winning bid of $4.5 million. The numbers by themselves raised eyebrows and even some of his supporters wondered if he was trying to "cash in" on his new status as speaker. While there was nothing illegal about the contract, it got reporters and his Democratic enemies wondering if there was more to this transaction than first met the eye. It came out that Newt had met with Rupert Murdoch, the owner of HarperCollins, on 28 November 1994 and had discussed regulatory problems concerning another arm of his media empire, the new Fox television network. Gingrich was sympathetic to Murdoch, whom he viewed as a major conservative ally, with or without a book contract, and would have tried to be helpful even if they had never met. Try as they might, the anti-Gingrich crowd failed to come up with any evidence that Murdoch instructed HarperCollins to do the deal with Newt or that HarperCollins had even asked Murdoch's opinion on the subject. Accusations and charges swirled through most of December. Newt, fearful that his motives might be challenged and that this could impact on the Contract with America agenda, decided to bring the

5 Scott Shepard, "Gingrich Raps Scandal-Based Politics," *The Atlanta Journal*, 19 May 1994, B5.

6 *Time*, 25 December 1995, 56.

controversy to an end. On 30 December he announced that he would only accept $1.00 as an advance and let the books earn what they could on the open market. His advisors were split on this decision. Hanser thought he would be criticized by his enemies no matter what he did. Take the money, write the books and move on with the agenda was his advice. Others agreed with Newt that it would get in the way of the agenda and should be taken off the table. This was a costly decision because his agent wanted her percentage figured from the $4.5 million and not the $1.00. Her cost and fees for co-writer, fact-checker and book tour expenses took up most of the $1.2 million earned by the book.[7]

A second event that deflected from the agenda came when Democrats leveled charges against his newly appointed House Historian, Christina Jeffrey. In 1987 Jeffrey served on a confidential US Department of Education review panel for a course on the Holocaust. In what she referred to as a "mocking remark" she noted in her review of the course that it "lacked balance because it did not include the Nazi [or Klan] perspective." Her confidential comments were leaked to the press and she was accused of anti-Semitism. Jeffrey was not an anti-Semite nor a racist. She was defended against these accusations by the Anti-Defamation League and other Jewish organizations. The Department of Education issued a belated letter of apology over a year later.

Newt's enemies ignored the facts and used the incident to attack him through this incident. On 10 January Democratic Representatives Charles Schumer, Maxine Waters, and Barney Frank repeated the accusations on the floor of the House and argued that they made her unfit to serve as House Historian. Newt, concerned to keep the focus on the Contract With America agenda, removed her from her position rather than have the Democratic spin machine take her comments and focus attention on them rather than the agenda he wanted to advance. Jeffrey was hurt and angry at the attack. "...Newt's enemies unfairly and dishonestly attacked me. In a reckless act of cruelty reminiscent of the McCarthy era, Congressman Charles Schumer (D-NY) denounced me as "an affront to [his] constituents who survived the Holocaust." Jeffrey was also upset with Gingrich who, she felt, had capitulated to the Democrats much too quickly and had cost her reputation and over

---

[7] John K. Wilson, *Newt Gingrich: Capitol Crimes and Misdemeanors* (Monroe ME: Common Courage Press, 1996) 29-31.

$30,000 in relocation costs. As far as she was concerned Newt should have defended her instead of firing her and later included him and his press secretary, Tony Blankley, in her slander suit.[8]

His hope for a working relationship with the president was also endangered by a comment he made election night. He spent a good deal of time giving "carefully thought-out and responsible" interviews to the media concerning what might be expected from him and the GOP majority once Congress convened in 1995. Around 2:30 A.M. he took a walk around the convention complex with two reporters from the *Washington Post* and the *New York Times* who wanted to get an "inside take" on his views. He let down his guard. He later commented, "any conservative who does not keep in mind at all times that the press has a natural inclination to lean left and favor the Democrats is not paying attention to reality." After a series of questions about his intentions and agenda they asked why he thought President Clinton's policies had been so badly repudiated by the American people as they elected a GOP congress earlier in the evening. He said, "…it seemed to me that the Clintons having worked as McGovern activists in their student days was a legitimate clue to their real beliefs, and that these beliefs were also being reflected in a number of the president's appointments." The next morning both papers focused their stories on his "McGovern" related comments rather than his agenda ideas. "There went all my effort to reach out and establish a good working relationship with the president."[9]

Newt was not the only Gingrich getting into trouble with the press. After the November election CBS-Television had arranged for reporter Connie Chung to interview Newt's parents in their home in Harrisburg for a show that would be aired after Congress returned in January. Chung and her team spent the better part of the day being friendly with the Gingrichs and winning their trust. Colonel Gingrich, usually reserved in contact with strangers, warmed up to the point that he baked the CBS team a cake. It was understood that much of what was being taped would not be used in the featured segment of Chung's show and an easy informality developed. Late in the interview Chung

---

[8] Jeanne Cummings, "Fired House Historian Fights Back," *The Atlanta Constitution*, A3, 15 May 1996; Jeanne Cummings, "Gingrich Named in Slander Suit," C2 *The Atlanta Constitution*, 17 May 1996.

[9] Gingrich, *Lessons Learned*, 35-36.

asked Kit Gingrich what her son thought of the First Lady. Kit replied that she would rather not say. Chung insisted, "Why don't you just whisper it to me, just between you and me." Kit shielded her mouth, leaned forward and said, " He thinks she's a bitch." Newt was notified of this by Tony Blankley early the morning of his swearing-in when CBS began airing promos of the show featuring Kit's unfortunate comment. Newt and his mother apologized to Mrs. Clinton who was gracious in accepting the apology and inviting Kit to tea at the White House. Though the event was smoothed over it had, no doubt, left a tear in the fabric of the relationship Newt was trying to develop with the president. Newt knew how he would have felt if the president had said that about Marianne.[10]

Other events were developing that were beyond his control. The Democrats were still in shock and denial over the outcome of the election. Their world had changed and they were striking out at the man they held responsible for their misery. In what could be described as a mean-spirited frenzy they filed over 100 ethics charges against the new speaker and viciously attacked him from every possible venue. The unprincipled attacks by Schumer, Waters and Frank on Jeffrey were part of a daily series of one-minute speeches Democrats gave each morning at the start of each business day. They were coordinated and led by the Minority Whip, Representative David Bonior. Bonior and his team met regularly to find new ways to slash at Gingrich and attempt to destroy his authority, influence and reputation. Having watched Newt's efforts against the Democrats over the past decade, and having learned his lessons well, they adopted his attack approach in spades and turned it on him. They saw Newt as unprincipled, unethical and worst of all, victorious. They were determined to do all in their power to bring him down. Bonier, Waters, John Lewis, Pat Schroeder and Henry Waxman became regulars on the attack and were joined by various other Democrats as the situation warranted. The hostility engendered by these tactics precluded any comity that might have led to bipartisan cooperation. There was nothing Newt could have done—short of resignation—that would have changed this unhappy situation.

There was also little Newt could have done about the approach the media took toward him and his agenda. Newt's success meant a loss for

---

[10] Ibid., 39-40.

the liberal agenda and the big government approach. The liberal world was crumbling and the media was not happy. In addition, many in the media, print and electronic, were now playing the "gotcha" game. Newt played directly into their hands. Gingrich likes reporters and news people. He believed, against all evidence, that if he could just explain his agenda they would see the merit of it and report it fairly. Gotcha journalism quickly took over as the reporters looked for a slip on his part and often baited and prodded until they got one. CNN carried the briefings live and there was little room for Newt to make a mistake without it being front-page news. Newt remembers that "our press briefings turned out to be an ongoing headache. They got to be little more than a game of 'pin the tail on the speaker.'"[11] It was not long before they ended the daily briefings, much to the dismay of the reporters.

In spite of all this Newt and his lieutenants attempted to remain focused and move resolutely through the Contract agenda attempting to get all ten items up for votes during the first 100 days of the 104th session. They were amazingly successful but success did not come without preparation. The Republicans knew they would have fights with the Democrats during preliminary skirmishing on each bill but they thought they would carry a number of Democrats on the final vote for almost all the items on the contract. They reasoned that the items were simply too popular to vote against on final passage. The problem would come in organization and the ability to move bills quickly through the House in spite of expected Democratic attempts to delay and side-track them in the process.

The contract itself was not a political public-relations effort as much as a basic training document. It guaranteed that from Election Day through early April, that the House Republican party would have to behave in a deviant manner from what it would normally be expected to do. The theory being that if you could get them through the first 100 days being deviant, that the deviancy would become normal," Gingrich said. Implementing ideas he had picked up from working with TRADOC (US Army Training and Doctrine Command) concerning small group management, he had decided that taking a normal approach for the first 100 days would lead to normal, undirected

---

[11] Ibid., 37.

behavior so familiar to Congress. A unifying challenge and goal had to be applied. For instance, tax cutting was a given but how much and at what price? Knowing the cuts would upset many people, including some supporters, he had to offer a greater goal than just the cuts themselves. What would be worth the pain? This goal led to his adopting the balanced budget by 2002 as the over-arching goal. This goal was, to Republicans and most Americans, large enough to make the suffering worthwhile.[12]

The most critical problem was House organization and Newt's being able to control it. A good deal of planning for reorganization had been done even before the election when Newt and Gaylord realized they would have a majority. Newt's able chief of staff, Dan Meyer, had been working on committee recommendations since October in an effort to make sure that Newt and the leadership team would not be blind-sided. It appeared that the South was once again dominating the House in leadership positions. Of the six major party positions, five were held by people from the South. Haley Barbour (MS) was RNC Chairman and Representative John Linder (GA) was the new NRCC Chairman. Gingrich (GA) was the new Speaker, Dick Armey (TX) Majority Leader and Tom Delay (TX) the new Majority Whip. Only the Conference Chairman, John Boehner (OH) was not from a state in the old Confederacy.[13]

Regional balance, although a factor, was not a major consideration for Gingrich, but competency was one. He made a point of letting people know that appointments would not be made on seniority alone. He wanted people who "would bring a level of aggressiveness and risk taking that we would need in these very important positions." Part of this aggressiveness was to eliminate some of the committees that no longer were needed and to reorganize or rename others and shift their focus to make them more functional and responsive. The aim was "to rethink the entire size and structure of the Congress." Representative David Dreier (CA) chaired a task force to consider what should be done

---

[12] Damon Chappie, "General Gingrich's Battle Plan," *Roll Call*, 42:5 (30 September 1996): 26.

[13] Jon Meacham, "A Defiant South Secedes Again," *Newsweek* (16 January 1995): 20-21

in this regard. Following their recommendations three committees disappeared and most were reorganized in one way or another.[14]

While competency remained the main consideration for leadership, others were added. In addition to regionalism and seniority, gender and loyalty were also considerations. Newt, a strong believer in the equality of women, made sure they were represented in the leadership. Two were made chairmen. Jan Meyer (KS) chaired the Small Business Committee and Nancy Johnson (CT) chaired the Ethics Committee. Two more were now in the new leadership. Susan Molinari (NY) was conference vice-chairman and Barbara Vucanovich (NV) became the conference secretary. In addition, Robin Carle was appointed clerk of the house and Cheryl Lau was made house counsel. Nancy Desmond as appointed chief of staff over his district office in Georgia and his congressional office in Washington. Never before in any other Congress had women been as well represented in power positions within the House.

Pennsylvania was best represented, holding four seats at the chairman's table. New York, Kansas, and Texas each had two seats and only five came from the south (two from Texas and one each from Arkansas, South Carolina and Louisiana). While Newt worked within the leadership in selecting chairmen, four key positions were his choice and he received support from the leadership. Solomon on Rules, Livingston on Appropriations, Bliley on Commerce, and Hyde on Justice were all more or less hand picked. All but Solomon were advanced over more senior members. In addition, a number of spaces on key committees were reserved for junior members to get them quickly involved in the process of the House and to make sure they had representation in decision making. Newt wanted to make sure they were heard and not just seen. He was surprised at the positive reaction to the new appointments even though he had talked of "reform from the ground up" for months.[15]

There were those who talked of a Republican Revolution but in truth it was planned as a reform not a revolution. Newt understood that while he had a majority it was a small one that he hoped to increase in the 1996 elections. He also knew that he was dealing with a short time

---

[14] Newt Gingrich, *To Renew America*, 121-122.
[15] Ibid.

frame and a total lack of experience in carrying out the majority's role in the legislative process. He studied the subject and read everything he thought might help him. He talked to a variety of people who had some successful experience in motivating people and running large groups or corporations. He talked to former Prime Minister Margaret Thatcher and football coach Joe Paterno as well as numerous CEOs and academics experts on the process.

Newt was attempting two apparently contradictory goals at the same time. He wanted to increase the efficiency and the effectiveness of the congressional leadership. He also wanted to democratize the function of the Congress by getting younger members into the decision making system immediately without the normal wait for seniority and being assigned to the less advantageous committees. Before now no freshman would have been assigned to the Appropriations, Ways and Means, or Budget Committees. These assignments gave the freshmen much more power and impact than in earlier years. At the same time he wanted to bypass, as much as possible, the logjams so prevalent in the committee system.[16]

In the end he came up with a structure that he and his team thought was right for that group at that time. The committees were only part of the structure. There was also a superstructure that many thought was even more important than the committees themselves. The use of task forces and special ad hoc committees was seen by Newt as a way to get around the slow moving committee structure at a time when the committees had their hands full with reform agendas naturally assigned to them. A task force was of short duration dealing with a specific subject or problem. It was cheaper than a committee because it used staff from other areas. It could also be controlled better because Newt would appoint its members. Under the old system committee chairmen would have fought what they would have seen as turf grabbing but these new chairmen were Newt's and they understood that he was in the process of creating precedent rather than following it. The result was the most centralized House in living memory and one that was subject to the speaker's control more than most.

---

[16]Steve Hanser, interview by author, 2 November 1998, Gingrich Papers, State University of West Georgia Archives, Carrollton.

First came a special executive advisory committee made up of the elected leadership of the conference. They would be Newt's sounding board and advisory group on a day to day basis. While any member could come see the speaker most would find it useful to make suggestions or ask questions through one of these members as a simple matter of efficiency. The first task force was Representative Nussle's group that dealt with the transition. Another was Representative Dreier's task force that studied House organization and made recommendations about change. Both of these committees were of short duration, reported directly to Newt and by extension to the leadership group and ceased to exist once their jobs were done. There was no chance for empire building and they were effective. An example of an ad hoc committee was the bipartisan Committee on the Family, chaired by Representative Frank Wolf. Wives, including Marianne Gingrich, participated in the work of this committee and made a series of recommendations that were designed to make Congress more family friendly. Shorter vote times, getting out by 3:00 P.M. on Fridays so members could catch planes home and limiting the first 100 day session to ninety-three days to have the recess coordinate with the public school's spring recess. This particular committee actually was bipartisan because it was in the interest of all members to work out these details and everyone benefited as a result of their recommendations.[17]

The new task forces and ad hoc committees created more efficiency and more effectiveness but with it came a certain amount of friction. It allowed some to exercise influence and at times create disruption simply by the fact of their position. The same sort of disruption also came on the regular committees. Much of this was due to the fact that this new large freshman class came with strong personalities and had not served an apprenticeship in their state legislatures or even on municipal councils. They were new to politics and were ideologically committed very strongly to certain legislative agendas such as budget reduction and term limits, social issues such as abortion and prayer in schools, and personal agendas that covered the spectrum. They did not see themselves as legislators but rather as spokesmen for their particular issues and had little interest in compromise and the legislative process except as it would facilitate the passage of their agenda. They were not

---

[17] Gingrich, *America*, 122-123.

worried about defeat at the polls, usually a check on extremist positions, and were ready and willing to go home and resume their non-political lives. Many took the attitude that if they compromised with the liberal Democrats then they were no better than the Democrats. They did not come to Washington to act like Democrats. Better they should let the Democrats run it than be coerced into supporting something in which they did not believe. What Newt faced was new strong personalities with strong agenda item commitments with new positions of power and influence untempered by experience in the legislative process. As Steve Hanser noted, "a certain amount of tension and friction was implicit in that combination."[18]

In spite of the shrill protest Democrats exhibited in committee meetings some Democrats were not totally displeased with the changes Speaker Gingrich had wrought. They were comforted as they watched Newt trying to deal with his unruly brood of freshmen. Their leaders appreciated the changes Newt had made and anticipated the day when they would return to power and benefit from those changes. Hanser tells of having lunch with a scholar researching the speakership and listening to his account of a meeting he had with Minority Leader Gephardt and his staff. "They were drooling at the power they thought the new Speaker Gephardt and they were going to have after the election of 1996."[19] Their problem was to make sure they returned to power. The first step in that process was to match and surpass the actions of the freshmen in making life unpleasant for Newt.

Coming to terms with their loss of power was not easy for the Democrats. They had expected the Republicans to make gains in the 1994 elections but taking the House was totally unexpected. The experience was repeated day after day and week after week as they experienced the reality of their loss. Many ranking members still thought of themselves as chairmen and committee meetings were extremely frustrating for them as they realized they had little or no control over what passed or what was kept from passing. Their staffs were cut severely and their office space considerably more limited.

Many Democrats, especially staff, had the impression, or maybe the hope, that Gingrich would not take away all their positions and perks.

---

[18] Hanser, interview, 1998.
[19] Ibid.

After all they had been there for forty years and were the experts in their fields of interest. Of course he would use their expertise, they thought. So wedded to being in the majority they thought he would come in and try to work with them instead of the other way around. In point of fact, when compared to the treatment Republicans had received under the three previous speakers, they were treated much better than they had treated the Republicans but everything is so very relative. They were not used to being in the minority and had no experience in that arena. Any treatment short of equality was viewed as shockingly unfair. When one is psychologically unprepared for it defeat offers little perspective.[20]

The Republicans had prepared for opposition from the start. Training sessions were held by Representatives Solomon on possible problems with the rules, by Walker on floor tactics and DeLay on holding the majority together. They held practice sessions on the floor during December with GOP Members playing the roles of expected Democratic adversaries such as Minority Leader Gephardt, Barney Frank and David Bonior. They tried to anticipate any possible problem and to prepare for it. Newt hoped to set the tone for bipartisan action in his acceptance speech. "I tried to rise to the occasion in my speech, wanting very much to reach out to the whole House and not be just a partisan Republican leader."[21] His speech was designed to reach out to all Americans and was generous in its praise of Democratic accomplishments such as its leadership in the New Deal and the Civil Rights battles and ended with a hope that bipartisan action would accomplish much for the American people.[22]

The Democrats and the press appreciated the speech but semantics got in the way. The concept Newt had concerning "bipartisan" action was somewhat different from that of the Minority. He had the view that it meant that both parties would work together from the start in crafting legislation. The GOP would, for example, introduce parts of the Contract with America agenda. Democrats would then meet with them to work to make it more to their liking and some compromises would result with the majority still having things pretty much their way. To the Democrats forty years of arrogant domination of the House had led

---

[20] Ibid.

[21] Gingrich, *To Renew America*, 126.

[22] *Congressional Record*, 104th Congress, 1st Session, 1995, 109:2.

them to expect that "bipartisan" meant the Republicans would agree with them with little or no compromise. The idea that they would compromise with a GOP position was unacceptable. Anything short of agreement with the Democratic position was viewed as blatantly partisan on the part of the GOP. If they wanted to be bipartisan then they should agree with the Democrats. By March 1995 this position was in place and has remained the touchstone of their policy ever since. A good example is the impeachment trial of President Clinton in 1998-1999. Anytime the Republicans agreed to a Democratic request or demand that was viewed as bipartisan. Anything less was viewed as partisan. The idea that complete unity on the part of the Democrats would be viewed as partisan was unacceptable. Only unity on the part of the Republicans could be viewed as partisan. It is a tribute to the Democrats' public relations experts that the press and public, to an amazing degree, accept this interpretation as an accurate view of the situation.

Newt was successful at first in holding the Republican team together. He and his leadership team pled with the freshmen and the moderate wing of the party that unity was essential to get through the 100 days and pass the contract. Any sizable opposition to the contract by Republicans was unthinkable and endangered any future legislation favored by individuals. Their majority was too small and defections, even small ones, could create havoc. Those with ideological concerns were told that their turn would come and that now was the time for Contract passage. They were advised to be patient. This worked because they already supported the items in the contract. They were willing to compromise to the extent of allowing these items to come up before their special interest with the assurance that their concerns would be attended to in the near future once this was out of the way.

They began working on passing the contract on 5 January. Gingrich thought of this operation as a single package with ten items, finally worked out as thirty-one bills. He viewed himself much like a CEO of a corporation, or as the chairman of the board. Armey, the Majority Leader, was to be the chief operating officer and, with his fellow Texan, Tom DeLay, would make sure that everyone stayed in line to support the package and deal with Democratic opposition.[23] On opening day

---

[23] Gingrich, *America*, 127.

they passed the Shays' Act which required all laws that apply to the rest of the country also to apply equally to Congress. They began the process of conducting an outside audit of all congressional accounts for waste, fraud and abuse and they cut congressional staffs and reduced the number of committees. That was the opening act and now it was time for the main attraction.

The Republicans introduced ten bills at the end of a very long opening day. They promised that each would be debated and voted on within the 100 days. They included bills on term limits; welfare reform emphasizing work and family; a balanced budget amendment and a line item veto. A common sense litigation reform bill targeting malpractice, product liability, and strike law firms was included. Also pushed was an effective anti-violent crime bill with a limit on death penalty appeals, honest sentencing for violent crimes, and adequate prison space for violent offenders to serve full sentences. An economic growth act reshaping taxation (a cut in the capital gains tax) and regulation (including unfunded mandates and risk assessment) to encourage job creation and higher take home pay was included. In addition, a pro-family bill eliminating the marriage penalty in income tax and Social Security and adding earned income tax credits was introduced along with three other bills to be reported and voted on in the first 100 days.[24] The three bills carrying the strongest public support when expressed in general terms were the ones for welfare reform, a balanced budget and for term limits. They would also be the most difficult to pass once the specifics saw the light of day.

Getting a term limits bill out of committee was a challenge in itself. The limiting of terms would require a constitutional amendment and was thus assigned to the Judiciary Committee whose chair was Henry Hyde, an open opponent of limiting terms. By direct appeal to his principle and party loyalty Newt was able to get Hyde to push the bill through committee with the understanding that neither he nor any other member would be pressured to vote for it on final passage. The promise of the contract called for getting it to a vote so everyone would go on record as being for or against it. In the past many had said they would have voted for it had it ever been brought to the floor for a vote.

---

[24] *Contract With America: A Program for Accountability,* 1994 Campaign folder. Gingrich Papers.

This would at least require them to put their vote where their mouth was, or explain why they voted to oppose it. The contract did not promise passage of any of the items, only a vote on each of them. As it turned out, many amendments were offered to the bill. Some would have set the limit at six years and others at twelve years. Six-year intervals were generally preferred because that is the term of a US Senator and they wanted House and Senate to be under the same limit. Others were concerned about what to do with incumbents. One line of thought was that if they had already reached the term limit they should resign or not stand for reelection. Others felt that was too harsh and would guarantee defeat for the bill. Instead they wanted to exempt incumbents completely or at least grandfather them in so that their calendar would start at the next election. Newt favored the twelve year bill with the time starting at the next election for incumbents. In the end the bill did get reported out of committee and was voted on by the House. It failed but most members could take some cover behind the fact that they had voted for at least one of the substitutes or amendments and could go home claiming they voted for term limits.

Numerous Republicans had reservations about the term limits bill and were not especially vigorous in their efforts to pass it. They were more supportive of the balanced budget bill. Newt's old ally, Senator Mack Mattingly, had proposed a balanced budget amendment in the early 1980s during the Reagan years. Gingrich had advocated such a bill throughout his career starting in 1974 with his first campaign for Congress. On the first day of the session the House had passed, 429-0, the Congressional Accountability Act that was designed to make Congress live under the same laws it imposed on the general public. Some wags argued that they were already doing that concerning the budget and thus reform was not needed. They said Congress was borrowing and charging like all other Americans. The polls showed that most Americans wanted Congress to live within their budget as most of them attempted to do.

The new majority party faced a test even before it passed the balanced budget amendment. Commitments in Haiti, Africa and the Balkans were going to require some new appropriation to cover their costs. In addition, major flooding in the Midwest and California needed new expenditures to cover unbudgeted costs as did other emergencies. The problem was where to get the money. Normally Congress would just ignore the budget limit and pass the appropriations. Not this time. The leadership team did not want to begin their watch by violating one of their major points in the contract. Such an act would give the media a wonderful opportunity to demonstrate that the Republicans were no better than their predecessors when they had to make hard decisions. The new Appropriations Committee chairman, Bob Livingston, decided to lead the way by opting for recisions rather than tax increases or increasing the debt. He and his team were able to find $17 billion in spending cuts that would cover the appropriations and still have money left over. His stopping by Newt's office late in the day with the news of the unexpected amount was a major high point of the 100 days for the new speaker and the leadership team.

Equally important as Livingston's finding the money for recisions was House passage of those bills with significant Democratic support. Not only that but the Senate passed an almost equal amount by a 99-0 vote and the president signed the bill. A year earlier almost no one would have given a bill with that amount of cuts a chance of even getting out of the House much less being signed into law. President Clinton was now talking of the era of big government being over, real cuts were being made in current budgets and the discussion of a balanced budget was now when and how it would be done, not if it could be done. Some thought the Washington world had been turned on its head.

One of the heroes of this new world was the indefatigable chairman of the Budget Committee, John Kasich. Gingrich often described Kasich as "a younger brother" with whom he has a close personal as well as professional relationship. If the amendment were to pass the budget committee would have to demonstrate that a balanced budget was possible without causing extreme disruption to American society. Kasich loved the challenge. It had been his passion since he had been in Washington. He found the money to do it with a combination of cutting spending and projecting growth in tax income. Because of his personality and believability he was able to sell it to his committee, including most Democrats, and to the House. The press, with its usual skepticism, resisted at first but later bought in to his figures. President Clinton and the left wing of the Democratic Party, dominant among House Democrats, resisted, argued and negotiated until most agreed, including Clinton, that it might be possible to balance it by 2002...in seven years. Many thought that even if it passed it would be quickly undermined by the desire to spend in the future. The lack of growth in social spending would be too great they predicted and too much pain would result. Interestingly enough, with constant pressure from Gingrich and the Republican majority to keep costs down and the income brought in by the tax increase of 1994 there was a $2.6 trillion overage, over eleven years, projected in January 1999. It had been balanced in under four years and the debate had shifted to whether to use the excess for tax reduction or fund new social programs.[25] None of these changes would have been possible if the Republicans had not dominated the Congress and kept the pressure on Clinton and his allies.

During the 100 days Newt was able to use his influence almost without restraint. He was the man who had brought about the majority. He was viewed by the party as a Moses of sorts and few were ready to challenge his ideas or request. This attitude was helpful when he was asking for support from moderate and right wing conservatives in the GOP coalition, especially during the debate on the welfare reform bill when the question was raised of potential abortions resulting from a cut-off of money if a welfare recipient had more children. Some had serious reservations but when faced with a solid Democratic front against the bill, they decided to listen to Newt and vote for the bill rather than join the Democrats in defeating a major part of the contract.[26]

The Christian Coalition, a major part of the GOP victory in November, thought they should be rewarded by having their agenda included in the 100 days. Newt was able to convince them to hold off by persuasion, horse trading and a promise to bring their issues to a vote at a later date during the session. They "agreed not to include school prayer, abortion, or any other powerfully divisive issues in the contract in exchange for the tax break for families."[27] Moderates, like Nancy Johnson, appreciated the way Newt had worked with them while Whip and thought they owed him something and did not want to undercut him because to do so would also, in the end, undercut their own influence as well.

---

[25] CNN news report, 29 January 1999.

[26] Gingrich, *To Renew America*, 131-135.

[27] Ibid., 135.

All during 1995 Gingrich was in the process of holding together a coalition within the party. Regular party members, the moderates, the new ideologically driven freshmen and non-congressional party leaders such as Paul Weyrich and GOP Chairman Haley Barbour all were players in the coalition. It was thought that Newt was possibly the only one who could hold this group together. Maintaining unity was important because of the small vote margin they held in the House. The president was, at the same time, trying to hold together his own coalition and the left wing Democrats were not making it easy. As long as he had followed a leftist agenda, as in 1993-1994, there was amazing unity. As Clinton began to move to the middle and then, oftentimes, right of center he found his Democratic coalition in jeopardy. A good example was when he wanted to pass the NAFTA agreements and the House Democratic leadership, Representatives Gephardt and Bonior left him in favor of their labor union roots. He had to turn to Newt and the Republicans for help. The president and the anti-president, as Newt had become, were both having problems with the fringes within their respective parties. Clinton had put together a coalition from the left that Bush could not touch. "He had surprised Republican free-traders by enlisting most of the large environmental groups."[28] Gingrich was involved in a similar process from the right in order to help bring about Medicare reform.

Frank Gregorsky argues that Clinton and Gingrich were practicing the art of "transactional politics" in that they were "developing a new set of tools for riding herd on their respective partisan coalitions. I call it transactional leadership, a sort of 'share the risk' public deal-making that emulates the norms of private life." Each was willing to carry the load for their supporters but expected more than PAC money, petitions and buses on election day. They expected change and cooperative effort to make the changes necessary to solve the major problems facing us at the end of the century.[29] Had they had the ability to move toward each other and work together they might have energized and revolutionized the Washington political structure. Neither, however, was capable of such movement and an opportunity was lost. Newt had hoped for a

---

[28] Frank Gregorsky, "Gingrich, Clinton and the New Transactional Politics," *Renewing American Civilization*, 1:9 (Oct./Nov. 1995): 1 (A tabloid published by the Progress & Freedom Foundation.).

[29] Ibid., p. 8.

center-right coalition. "He really thought that it was possible to have a center-right effective majority carrying through very meaningful reform in that first year and a half following the 1994 election."[30] All the hope and good will in the world, however, could not counter the fury of the Democrats' left wing. Not only were they defeated in the election and removed from power and position but if Gingrich was successful the ideological world at the core of their belief system would be destroyed. The welfare state was under attack. They saw themselves in the trenches and were not about to surrender without a serious fight.

Part of the reason Newt had received support from special interest groups in the 100 days was that he had let them sit at the table and have input. He even went so far as to have some of their lobbyists help write the bills. He promised their turn would come and worked for things dear to their hearts like capital gains reductions, tax cuts, a freeze on new government regulations and a hold on unfunded mandates to the state and local governments. These commitments got him in trouble with the press and the public at the same time that they were strengthening his base and holding his coalition together.

The Democrats had long had big labor and the National Education Association sitting at their tax writing table. This practice was commonly accepted. Having lobbyists from business interests there was something else again. The economic agenda of cutting taxes, especially capital gains taxes, left Newt open to the charge that he was cutting taxes for his rich friends, who had helped write the legislation, and paying for it on the backs of the poor, sick and elderly and especially on the backs of the children. He was getting the full treatment from the Democrats each morning during the one minute speeches and their leaders and the press were going full bore with stories on hungry children, suffering families and cruel orphanages. In addition, the Democrats continued to file new ethics charges against Newt. On 26 January, his old opponent Ben Jones filed charges regarding the November book deal. Almost a month later Representatives Pat Schroeder, Cynthia McKinney and Harry Johnston filed charges concerning his college class. On 27 July Newt testified before the Ethics Committee hoping to put all this behind him...at least for the present, but that was not realistic. The Democrats were putting too much

---

[30] Hanser, interview, 1998.

pressure on the Committee and getting the press to respond by pressuring GOP Members back home in their districts. ON 6 December an outside counsel was appointed and a week later five Democrats filed charges concerning GOPAC and his campaign.[31]

Despite all of this, Newt was able to achieve much of his agenda. "Without so much as a decent burial he has killed the old order of politics," said *Time* magazine.[32] It certainly appeared that he had. No administration of theirs should have been talking balanced budget and a break on entitlement spending and yet Clinton was doing just that. If they could not resurrect the old order at least they could destroy the head of the new order and do what they could to turn it around.

On the evening of 7 April 1995, after finishing the work of the contract, Newt asked for and received time from the networks and C-SPAN for a national address. Speaking from his office in the Capitol he outlined the successful passage of the items in the contract and noted, "While we've done a lot, this contract has never been about curing all the ills of the nation. One hundred days cannot overturn the neglect of decades. The contract's purpose has been to show that change is possible, that even in Washington you can do what you say you're going to do." He called for a bipartisan effort that "must totally remake the federal government—to change the very way it thinks, the way it does business, the way it treats its citizens. Government is not the end it is the means." He told his audience that government, like business, should become more efficient. "We sincerely believe we can reduce spending and at the same time make government better," he said. Newt talked about the legacy for our children. He wanted to get rid of debt for them, make society more livable and recognize the moral and economic failure of the current methods of government. He said they should create a "better future with more opportunities for our children." He wanted to work together to make not just a better government but a better America and to set up "a truly compassionate government [that] would replace the welfare state with opportunity." He listed future goals as reforming welfare and the IRS. He wanted government to use technology better, to work to make health care and Social Security more secure for all Americans, and to return power to the states. He closed by

---

[31] *Atlanta Journal-Constitution*, 7 November 1998.
[32] *Time*, 25 November 1995, 54.

observing, "We as a people have the natural ability to respond to change. That is what we do best when the government is not in the way." He ended by calling on the people for help and offering to help establish a national dialogue to find better ways to solve problems.[33] The speech got excellent reviews. Newt still had hopes, even at that late date, that he could work with Clinton and the Democrats to bring about the passage of some of the items he had listed.

The budget fight and the numerous spending bills dominated most of the business of the House after the 100 days. There was not excessive opposition to the early bills but as the months wore on the Democrats were emboldened to fight and some Republicans were getting tired of having Newt press them to compromise in the interest of unity and were beginning to chafe at their loss of independence. Majority Leader Armey referred to it as "greater good fatigue."[34]

Luckily, the August recess arrived at about the same time as the fatigue. When the members went home they found a strong support for their efforts. At town hall meetings and speeches given to various community groups Newt was congratulated time and again for the 100 days achievement and for the leadership he provided. He heard the same thing as he moved around the country giving speeches and helping raise money for the GOP and his colleagues. As he went around the country on his book tour for *To Renew America* he was stopped in airports by strangers who wanted to give him a pat on the back and encouraged at signings to "keep it up." Other members reported similar experiences. These reports were encouraging and restored some of Newt's "greater good" leverage. The fact remained, however, that some Republican members had yet to have their agenda placed on the front burner.

Newt was still confident as Congress returned from the Labor Day recess. The budget battle lay ahead and he felt confident that he could win it. Remembering Clinton's unpopularity in November and secure in the knowledge that presidents cave in rather than shut down the government when presented with unpleasant budgets, at least GOP presidents did; Newt thought he was in the driver's seat.

---

[33] C-SPAN, 7 July 1995. See also original of Gingrich speech in UWG Archives, "National Speech" folder.

[34] Ibid., 58.

A number of events would derail Newt's hopes. The ethics charges had brought on an outside counsel and that made both Newt and his troops nervous. The Democrats and the labor unions had decided to begin the 1996 campaign early and the labor unions started running ads, most directed at Gingrich personally, that were designed to picture the Republicans and Newt as mean spirited and hard hearted. The object was to drive down the positive poll numbers and obscure any achievement the GOP might trumpet. The press went along with this approach frequently doing support stories on the ads. Newt upset many of his supporters when, speaking before a congressional hearing on campaign finance reform, he advocated more not less money for campaigns. He made himself look petty by whining about being made to exit Air Force One from the rear when returning from Prime Minister Rabin's funeral and he totally forgot that Clinton is full of surprises and earned the sobriquet "the come-back kid."

Gingrich had been charged with numerous ethics violations ever since he led the charge against Speaker Wright. In and of themselves they did not bother him because they were on their face clearly desperate attempts to find something somewhere that might stick and give the Democrats a shot at him. This attitude changed with the charges about Newt using GOPAC to help fund his college course taught at Kennesaw State back in Georgia. These were picked up by the press and taken seriously. A full time legal staff was hired to deal with it. Newt Inc., had grown so large and was involved on so many fronts that even Newt could not be absolutely sure that every point had been covered. He believed everything was fine, but knew he should be certain.

While these ethical questions were being raised the unions were running their ads and the Democrats in the House, now joined by the White House team, were keeping up their regular game of demonization. The president, who had been used in the 1994 campaign as the bad guy by the Republicans as they morphed Democratic candidates into Clinton, was not at all squeamish about using the same tactic against Gingrich. It was widely believed that the president's negatives in November 1994 helped bring down the Democrats. Now they would do the same to the Republicans by using Newt as their foil. The ads were not run nation-wide but were targeted where they could do the most damage. The White House contributed by bringing in their first team public relations experts. "The Master of Spin," Mike McCurry had replaced Dee Dee Myers as White House Press Secretary. James Carville, Paul Begala, and George Stephanopoulos had run the operation during the 1992 campaign as spokesmen for both spin and damage control. Stephanopoulos remained as special counsel, not press secretary. Myers, though loyal, had not proven to be first team and so McCurry was brought over from the State Department, partially at the First Lady's urging, to take over the propaganda machine. Working with the new White House Chief of Staff, Leon Panetta, he soon had the spin machine humming. Over the next two years he would be joined by Lanny Davis, Rahm Emanuel, John Podesta, Don Baer and Ann Lewis. They were the "small collection of loyalists who worked relentlessly at presenting the boss in a favorable light and deflecting the scandal questions that seemed constantly to nip at his heels."[35] This team was quickly acknowledged to be the best at spin. Reagan's team had been good, especially at setting up an event and drawing media coverage. They were not, however, in the same league with Clinton's team when it came to spin. Much of their work was targeted at Speaker Gingrich.

Both Clinton and Gingrich were being questioned by the press about finances and fund raising. In addition, Newt and the Republicans were accused, as the *Washington Post* noted, of "cashing in on the Revolution." The pressure exerted by Gingrich, DeLay (GOP Whip), and Bill Paxton (NRCC) to raise money for GOP candidates for the 1996 campaign was drawing complaints and attention. Newt thought groups who had an interest in keeping the Republicans in power, such as the Chamber of Commerce and the various lobbying firms representing conservative causes and commercial interests, should only support the GOP. Giving money to the Democrats or hiring Democratic lobbyists would only be counterproductive. This ran against the usual practice of firms giving to both parties with a larger amount usually going to the party in power. Understanding the importance of money in politics, Newt sought to cut off as much as possible from the Democrats. "If you want to play in our revolution, you have to live by our rules," said

---

[35] Howard Kurtz, *Spin Cycle: Inside the Clinton Propaganda Machine.* (NY: The Free Press, 1998) xxiii-xxiv.

Newt.[36] This brought about much grumbling and accusations of high-handed pressure tactics being exercised by the Republicans. It also made it easier for the press to criticize both parties for being overzealous in fundraising and for the White House and the DNC to note they were guilty of doing nothing more than the Republicans. Likewise, the ethics charges against Newt led the public to believe that both parties were guilty of politics as usual and that something needed to be done to clean it up.

Newt and President Clinton had met in Claremont, New Hampshire on 11 June and shook hands over a deal proposed by a local citizen to create a nonpartisan commission to reform the system of campaign financing. The event received prominent coverage and lifted expectations. Both wanted to make changes but neither was willing to put his party at a financial disadvantage with an election coming up in just over a year.[37] The president, a few weeks after the handshake, sent a letter to Newt that he also released to the press. It proposed an eight member bipartisan commission, copying the military base closing commission, with the president and Congress legally bound to accept or reject their recommendations in full. Newt responded by labeling the letter "a cheap political trick." It was his understanding that he and the White House would work out the arrangements and logistics privately. He thought Clinton had broken their agreement by unilaterally writing and releasing the letter and was furious at having been tricked by the president and boxed in publicly with the press on this issue. The spin had begun; the president wanted change and Newt was standing in the way. In July Clinton mentioned it in his Saturday radio address and called on Newt to honor his commitment. On 22 July he called the citizen who had suggested the commission to "report on its progress." Frank MacConnell was recuperating from a cancer operation and was pleased to hear that the president was working on the problem. This news was also released to the press. What the White House did not release was a chiding MacConnell gave Clinton about White House fundraising. "I told him that I was so disappointed about the selling of the president," reported MacConnell to reporters. On 4 August the president held a press conference in the Oval Office expressing again

---

[36] Howard Kurtz, "Cashing in on the Revolution," *Washington Post*, national weekly edition, (4-10 December 1995) 6-8.

[37] *Atlanta Journal*, 12 June 1995.

his desire for the appointment of the commission. Picking at Newt he said, "All he has to do is to do what he said he'd do when he shook hands with me. Let's set up a commission."[38]

Newt was thinking about campaign finance reform but was approaching it from another direction. His ideas were made public in November when he testified before a House panel that was holding hearings on campaign finance reform. It was a dramatic setting. Newt entered the room alone with only a couple of pages of statistical notes. He opened with a grabber. "I think, candidly, there are grave threats to the survival of American freedom and self-government," he said. He called for a "very profound overhaul of our political system" including lobbying, campaigns, political parties, incumbency, the nature of Washington and the impact of the information age. He said campaigns might need more money not less if they truly were meant to inform the people. He called on them to bypass current reform bills that he thought were inadequate and to form a bipartisan commission to study the whole democratic system from top to bottom. He lectured on the misuse of foreign money and the alienation and isolation Americans feel. He ended with a warning of the fate of Greece and Rome when their civic life fell into disrepair and concluded with a reading list "because this is not a new problem. This problem of how do you organize power so people can be free has happened over a very long period of time."[39]

Much of what Newt said at the hearing was bypassed by the press in favor of a focus on his call for more money. Having not seen the entire statement many, supporters and opponents, were left shaking their heads with wonder. Everyone else was calling for less, not more money to flow into campaigns. What was he thinking? Forgetting that the sound bite and the quick quote get the coverage he had sought to take a serious approach to the problem. Many of his supporters, moderates and some of the freshmen, were upset with the more rather than less approach and also because he had not warned them first. He should have alerted his troops so they could provide support for his position but his speech caught them cold and they were not happy about it. Neither were the liberals. *Washington Post* columnist Mary

---

38 *The Washington Post*, national weekly edition, 10-16 June 1996, 23-24.

39 *The Washington Post*, 10 November 1995, F4.

McCrory viewed Clinton's efforts as sincere and thought Newt "made a farce of it." "He suggested that too little money is spent on campaigns," she wrote.[40]

McCrory continued by describing the impact the attacks on Gingrich were having around the country. "Washington is mesmerized by Gingrich, fixated on his chunky, white-thatched figure. The country, however, is not. *Washington Post* reporters deployed through swing districts from coast to coast came back with notebooks full of negatives—like "blow-hard" and "loudmouth." What strikes Washington as masterful looks like bullying beyond the Beltway."[41] Loudmouth bully was the image the Democrats sought to project and were successful in doing so. Reading the daily polls they would build on this every chance they got.

Everything since the 100 days was warm-up. Now came the main event, the budget. The White House spin team was at top form. It was not that the press did not know it was a spin war—they knew but were unwilling to point out the factual inaccuracies and distortions put forth by the Democrats. Even the conservative *Washington Times* headlined "Gingrich needs budget deal to regain lead in spin wars." They referred to Newt in the article following as "the driving force behind two partial shutdowns of the federal government" who "risks being portrayed as the grumpy Republican leader who stole everybody's Christmas for partisan advantage."[42]

Newt and Senator Bob Dole, the Senate Majority Leader, were counting on the fact that no President wanted to be responsible for shutting down the government by vetoing a budget bill. Reading the polls, however, Bill Clinton knew the public was suspicious of Gingrich and in an act of marvelous political jujitsu was able to flip the responsibility for shutting down the government back on Congress, back on the Republicans, and back on Newt. Steve Hanser, remembering the budget fight, said, "The president of the United States has real intrinsic powers. If you do not have a large enough majority to overturn presidential vetoes you can not carry out any

---

[40] Ibid., 12 November 1995, C1.

[41] Ibid.

[42] *The Washington Times* national weekly edition [vol. 2, issue 51, 25-31 December 1995]: 9

legislative program without his consent much less cooperation. You just can not do it. We discovered that."[43]

Leon Panetta began the attack by accusing Gingrich of "holding a gun to the president's head" and threatening to "shut down the government" if they did not get their tax cuts to help the rich and cut spending that would help the young, the old, the poor and the needy. This, following on the heels of the Union ads already being run, continued the depiction of Newt as the bully trying to push around the president who was only trying to help people. It was at this point, at the end of the budget struggle, that the major mistake was made by Newt and the Republicans. "[W]e seriously underestimated the effect of the attack dog tactics of the White House awarded by the friendly press," remembered Hanser. They "were brutally directed and effective and not aimed at the Republican Party or even the Republican majority but specifically at the Speaker."[44]

Hanser said that a clear decision was made not to waste resources responding to the personal attacks on Newt. "It was his feeling that the purpose of the campaign was not primarily to destroy Newt Gingrich the individual, but to regain control of Congress." Gingrich was more interested in holding and possibly expanding the gains made in 1994. "Maintaining those seats was absolutely vital and all of our resources, it was decided had to be used to do that to maintain the majority. If Newt personally took a beating it was thought that it would not be that serious or difficult to reverse. Point of fact, it was that serious and very difficult to reverse."[45]

During the struggle Newt did not understand the vulnerability of his position. He thought that if he could get the president away from the House Democrats he could still work out something with him. The effect Clinton had on him was remarkable. Newt described meetings he and Senator Dole had with the president where it seemed they had reached a compromise on sections of the budget. After leaving the White House and returning to the Capitol they would find out that McCurry, or some Clinton spokesman, would be announcing the results of the meeting and they would not be what they had agreed on at all. The press would then turn to Newt and Dole and if they disagreed with

---

[43] Hanser, interview, 2 November 1998.

[44] Ibid.

[45] Ibid.

the White House statement the press would ask why they were breaking the agreement. Newt's frustration at such situations was evident: "...I don't know how to deal with someone who systematically lies to you...what can you believe, when can you trust him?....When you're with him you just want to believe him." The situation deteriorated so much that a cartoonist drew cartoons showing the president sitting in the Oval Office with Newt as a sheepdog at his feet getting his back scratched[46]. The freshmen talked of never letting Newt meet with Clinton by himself because of what he might give up.

While visiting with Newt, who had just ended a meeting on the budget with the House leadership, a call came from the White House agreeing to a meeting. Newt told Dan Meyer that he would go but that he did not want any congressional Democrats at the meeting. He said Meyer should relay that to the White House. He thought something might be accomplished if the Democratic congressional team could be kept away because they always objected to compromises he suggested. He felt it was a waste of time if they were there to insist on a more liberal agenda. I was surprised. Newt could not tell the president whom to invite to a meeting at the White House. To do so only made him look petty when the president refused, as he surely would. Newt would then go in spite of his demands being rejected or not go and be branded as unwilling to negotiate.

There were other problems. A week earlier Newt had accompanied the president as part of a congressional delegation to Israel for the funeral of Prime Minister Yitzhak Rabin. They were deep into the budget struggle by then. Newt and Senator Dole thought there would be plenty of time on the way over or back for the president to get with them to talk quietly about the budget. As it turned out the president had no interest in doing that and preferred to play hearts instead. Disappointed, the speaker and the Majority Leader viewed this as a missed opportunity. Clinton only came back to their section of the airplane for a brief exchange of polite conversation and a photo. Dole had worked with every president since Lyndon Johnson and knew that none of them would have passed up such an occasion. They thought Clinton had purposely avoided meeting with them. This feeling was

---

[46]   MacNelly, Editorial Cartoons, *Chicago Tribune*, (Chicago IL), 29 September 1997, A24.

magnified when they were required to exit from the rear of the plane while the president exited from the front where the television cameras were located.

Both Dole and Gingrich were upset at this treatment feeling it was not only a slap at them but at their offices as well. Gingrich's press secretary, Tony Blankley, had begun the process of getting the press to focus on how petty the president was to pull such a stunt when Newt, to Blankley's horror, took the matter into his own hands at a televised news conference.

A week or so after the Rabin flight Newt was the guest at the Sperling Breakfast answering press questions. The budget fight was the main topic. Newt hoped to explain the difficulties in working with the White House and their Democratic allies in Congress. "I was trying to explain how hard it is to do business with the Clinton Administration and why, fatefully, we had in the end been prepared to let funding for the government lapse in order to force a confrontation over the balanced budget."[47] He said the president said he wanted an agreement but his party was running utterly dishonest ads about the issue. Clinton professed to want an agreement but sent over negotiators who only wanted to argue ideology. It was hard to take him seriously when his words and actions did not match.

"Let me give you an example of how hard it is to understand this president," he said. Noting that his press secretary had warned him not to do this and with Tony in the room vigorously shaking his head side to side, Newt launched into what the press called a whine about his and Dole's treatment on Air Force One. "If he was genuinely interested in reaching an agreement with us...why didn't he discuss one with us when we were only a few feet away on an airplane? If he wanted to indicate his seriousness about working with us, why did he leave the plane by himself and make us go out the back way?" Newt went on to describe Clinton's behavior as selfish and self-destructive. The last adjective could certainly be used to describe Newt's own actions at that particular moment. Gingrich later described this encounter as one where he had been acting as a "foolish professor, delivering a free-wheeling lecture full of careless and unguarded statements to a press

---

[47] Gingrich, *Lessons Learned*, 44-45.

corps that was looking for a sensational angle."[48] The Democrats accepted the resulting press as a gift and had a field day with it. Georgia House Speaker Tom Murphy, Newt's old foe, had predicted that Gingrich's mouth would do him in. That prediction seemed to be coming true at that moment.

Numerous newspapers headlined the idea that Newt had shut down the government because he was upset with his treatment on Air Force One. The most effective was the *New York Daily News* which ran a banner headline on page one that read "Crybaby" in large letters with a cartoon of Newt as a baby with his bottle, in diapers, throwing a tantrum.[49] One by one the Democrats marched to the well of the House to denounce the speaker for being willing to make government employees suffer because of some personal slight. Mounted beside them, on an easel, was a large blow-up of the *Daily News* front page. Mercifully, the GOP majority forced the removal of the prop but the damage had been done. Gingrich took a pounding, as did the Republicans. The president indicated that had he known how upset Newt was he would have remedied it and Mike McCurry, giggling, said that maybe Newt would be mollified if they sent him some of the little M&Ms in the packets with the presidential seal on them.

Gingrich had wanted to make the point that it was difficult to work with a White House that was not serious and preferred to play games rather than deal realistically with the budget problem. The example of his and Dole's treatment at the hands of a callous president was meant to show how Clinton had passed up an opportunity to negotiate the budget in spite of his comments about how much he wanted to reach an agreement with the congressional leaders. It was meant to show the press how petty Clinton was but instead backfired, as Tony Blankley knew it would, and instead demonstrated, as the press saw it, Newt's own pettiness. "All because I didn't know when to keep my mouth shut," remembered Newt.[50]

A more serious problem impacting on the negotiations was the willingness of the president and his team to lie repeatedly and fail to negotiate in good faith. By the end of 1995 there probably were not many people in America who were not aware of the president's

---

[48] Ibid.

[49] *New York Daily News*, (New York NY), 16 November 1995, p. 1.

[50] Gingrich, *Lessons Learned*, 46.

propensity for handling the truth in a rude manner. Yet again and again the Republicans walked into negotiations with him and his team ready to rely on what they were told in the belief that they would keep their word. Each time, however, they thought that this is different. Surely they will be serious and truthful about the budget. Because it affected so many people it was inconceivable that they would not take it seriously. The truth was that Clinton, Panetta, and their team did take it seriously. Lying and dealing in half-truths were seen as weapons or tactics to be used to get what you wanted in the negotiations. Gingrich, being a historian, should have seen that he was in audition for the role of British Prime Minister Neville Chamberlain in his dealings with the Germans during the period leading up to the Second World War. Chamberlain negotiated in good faith and did all he could to avoid war. In the end, however, the German government and their press blamed him for being the one who wanted war.

Jeffrey Nesbit, in an article in the *Washington Times*, chronicles the problems faced in dealing with the White House team in an article entitled, "White House Dishonesty Stalls Talks on Balanced Budget." For those who take government serious their cavalier attitude was breathtaking. "Lies and cheats. That essentially, was what Republicans in Congress were thinking of the president's budget-negotiating team last week." He then reports a series of acts of bad faith and outright lies committed by Alice Rivlin and Leon Panetta and George Stephanopoulos. In an exchange between Senator Pete Domenici and Panetta he reports, "Mr. Panetta looked the two Republican budget negotiators in the eye, and lied." Faced with Panetta's unwillingness to deal honestly Domenici and his team walked out. No actual negotiations had begun. "White House aide George Stephanopoulos emerged from the room and immediately found the TV crews staked out near S-207, 'The Republicans are demanding huge cuts in Medicare and Medicaid before they'll even negotiate,' Mr. Stephanopoulos lied. Of course the Republicans had done no such thing. They hadn't even begun negotiations, much less demanded that there be huge cuts before starting the talks. But no matter. Whatever plays. Image wins over policy any day."[51]

The problem for the Republicans, and Clinton knew it, was that Bill Clinton was president and they had no alternative but to deal with him.

---

[51] Washington *Times* 25 December 1995, 12.

They were wary in their dealing with him and cautious in accepting his word but to refuse to work with him was impractical. The president had been the clear winner in the budget negotiations and in the public mind. Gingrich, after masterminding some of the greatest change in government since 1933, was viewed by the public as a whining bully and a generally unpleasant person. The Democratic spin had worked. On the positive side, Newt had absorbed most of the hits personally and the GOP Congress had come through the year relatively unscathed. The objectives of passing serious legislation in 1996 and getting his majority reelected for the first time in over a half century was still a possibility.

An editorial article entitled, "In Defense of Newt Gingrich," said a reelected majority was a probability. The article opened with a paragraph listing his achievements. "The Speaker of the House finds himself in an almost unprecedented position these days. Without changing his views, his strategies, or his tactics one iota from his triumphant first hundred days; while holding fast to the principles that helped elect the first House Republican majority in four decades; and with a record of relentless legislative achievement that has, in just one year's time, made him the most remarkable legislative leader in the second half of the twentieth century, Newt Gingrich has become widely unpopular. This is not the way things are supposed to work in Washington." The article chronicles the dishonest Democratic assault on Newt pointing out that the charges made on ethics and policy are petty and in areas where both parties, in the past, have made missteps. It asks the question, "Why then Newt?" when so many others have done the same thing. "Because it's not about GOPAC; it's about the Republican revolution." Why was he criticized about his book deal when it was not illegal? "Because it's not about the book deal; it's about the Republican revolution." The article ends with a hope that united GOP support for Newt and his efforts will lead to the "transformation of American politics and public policy" to which the GOP says they are committed.[52]

The hope for unified support was a vain one. Now that the contract was behind them both the freshmen and the moderates felt freer to exercise their option of differing with the speaker. This development

---

[52] Fred Barnes, "In Defense of Newt Gingrich," *The Weekly Standard,* (New York NY) 25 December 1995, 11-12.

was made easier by the humiliation of the budget fight loss and some of Gingrich's public statements. They had their own self interested agendas and thought that Newt might be getting in the way. "The revolution to restore confidence in government transcends Newt Gingrich. He may have gotten the movement started; he may have been the engineer who got the train rolling," said freshmen David Weldon, "but now the train doesn't need him to run down the tracks. It's more powerful than him."[53] "We remain independent and suspicious of the entire leadership," added freshman Joe Scarborough.

The moderates, whom Newt worked so hard to include in the process, now found that their agenda on social issues and environmental issues differed from those of the conservatives and frequently stood in the way of working out compromises that Gingrich was brokering. In addition, they had concerns about the multitude of ethics charges being brought against Newt. The Democrats were able to play on these concerns by attacks on the moderates where it hurt the most—back home in their districts. They were called lackeys of the speaker and accused of covering for him and put in the position of having to at least say they would make no judgment until the facts were in. This accusation allowed the Democrats to announce that even the Republicans had questions about the speaker's ethics and to use GOP quotes in their denunciations attacks. The moderate under the most pressure was Nancy Johnson, chair of the Ethics Committee. Through the skillful use of committee leaks, when she could not respond without violating the committee rules, and attacks on her in her district the Democrats forced her to take a defensive posture and almost cost her the 1996 election.

The Democrats were also ready to continue their attacks. Everyone had expected Representative Bonior to keep pressing. He was a true believer, a genuine liberal who thought Newt and his actions were doing damage to the nation. His world was at risk and he was fighting back. He neither asked for nor gave any quarter in the struggle. Gingrich and his allies had not expected that members of his own state delegation would lead in the attacks. Representatives John Lewis and Cynthia McKinney had been critical since his Whip days but now took leadership positions in the assault following the advice of the *New*

---

[53] Ibid., 16.

Republic's opinion column that all pretense of fairness should be dropped and that liberals should concentrate on simply destroying Gingrich.[54] The Georgia delegation contained eight Republicans and three Democrats. Their personal attacks on Newt, such as McKinney's description of the speaker as "a little piglet...rolling around in a filthy ditch," made it almost impossible to maintain a good working relationship within the delegation. This tension between the parties was not only in the delegation but was also reflected throughout most of the House membership.[55]

For their part, the White House had learned two lessons. First, the Republicans, especially Newt, were punchy about the shutdown and the publicity beating they took as a result. They had claimed they were now in charge and the president was glad to let them have that title when he could use it to his advantage. Clinton and Dick Morris, his advisor, had planned the shutdown since August and it had worked beautifully in November when the trap was sprung. Secondly, they had learned that the president could handle Gingrich. On a personal one-to-one level, they assumed, the president would never lose. Between the president's ability to manipulate Newt and Newt's own proclivity to say and do things that would get him in trouble, the White House felt sure it could go into the 1996 session with confidence and an assurance that they need not be on the defensive—that was the role they ascribed to the Republicans. "A year ago he [Newt] was battling Clinton for number one politician. Now he's on the defensive hoping to spoil a Democratic counterrevolution," said *Time* in its annual "10 Most Powerful People" profile. Newt is listed number ten.[56]

One lesson Newt learned was he needed a lower profile. During the first months of 1996 he tried to stay out of the limelight, not wholly successfully, and to present a kinder and gentler image to the public. He would be speaker in the more traditional sense of a legislative director instead of a party spokesman. He would play to his natural love for animals and children and present a "warm and fuzzy" image instead of the serious, angry one that enabled Democrats to picture him as hard hearted and mean spirited. It was, after all, a presidential

---

[54] *The New Republic*, 19 December 1994, TRB opinion column.

[55] Erika Niedowski, "Members Swap Epithets," *The Hill*, [Washington, DC] 11 December 1996, 4.

[56] *Time*,17 June 1996, 83.

election year and Senate Majority Leader Bob Dole, the probable GOP nominee, and RNC Chairman Haley Barbour were perfectly capable of being the party spokesmen. He appeared on late night talk shows to display the more personal, relaxed Newt. This effort produced mixed reviews such as the time he was handed a struggling pig on the Jay Leno show. After talking about how he loved animals he was seen holding the baby pig at arms length in order to attempt to keep his suit clean because he had another event to attend after his television appearance. It was awkward and came off as his being uncomfortable with animals. He got somewhat better results from visits to schools but these were not widely disseminated.

Perhaps his best performance came on Sunday evening 29 September during a PBS debate among the four party leaders in Congress. He and new Majority Leader Trent Lott faced House Minority Leader Richard Gephardt and Senate Minority Leader Tom Daschle. The Democrats earned points when they pointed out the cost of the government shutdowns in 1995 but the audience responded favorably as Newt discussed the problems with education and the drug problem. He argued that the bureaucracy forced on the school systems by the government and the unions was sapping resources that could go to the students and teachers directly. Taking a leaf from the Democratic play book, he used individual and personal examples of waste in the Washington, DC school system pointing out that the $9,000/pupil being spent on the system at that time could pay the teachers $90,000/year if the bureaucracy were cut in half. Newt also tied the drug problem to foreign policy when he noted that the "first foreign policy priority should be to stop drugs coming into the United States."[57]

The pollster Frank Luntz conducted a focus group watching the debate. He noted that the mixed group of Democrats, Republicans and independents thought Newt had gained the most ground in the debate. Gingrich had entered the debate behind all the participants in public esteem but emerged ahead in the estimation of the focus group. "He was calm, collected, and intelligent. He played the educator...I think this could be a new Newt," reported Luntz. While Newt and Lott took some hits for the shutdown, Luntz said, overall, that the focus group indicated that "Gingrich's vision and substance is superior. The only

---

[57] Morton M. Kondracke, "A New Newt?" *Roll Call*, 3 October 1996, 8.

question is whether his style will let people hear his substance." The author of the article covering this event, Morton Kondracke, responded to Luntz's hope, "Not likely." He pointed out that Gingrich can project sweet reason or uncontrolled anger and frustration as he lashes out to the press blaming them and the Democrats in a whining, finger-pointing manner that does not set well with the public. He went on to note that women, especially, respond negatively to the "hot" Newt and while the public appreciates Newt's work and accomplishments with the 104th Congress, they do not appreciate him personally. "If Luntz's claim is correct and the general public determines that Gingrich's vision and substance are better than his Democratic foes', then the only question is whether his style will allow voters to hear what he is saying. So far, the answer is no."[58]

The problem was that at a time when Newt should be providing a vision for the America seen by the Republicans he was instead practicing a "Dare to be Dull" strategy. "He in fact has evolved into one of the most effective Speakers in modern times," noted David Brooks in his article on "What Happened to Newt Gingrich?"[59] In retrospect, to have taken this weapon from the GOP arsenal was foolhardy at best. Had he been able to ignore the personal attacks and focus on the vision as he did in the congressional debate the Republicans might have come out better in November. The attacks and the battering, over 80,000 union sponsored ads, did take their toll. He kept his head down until the summer when Senator Dole formally left Congress and began to lead the charge. Dole, like Bush before him, failed to project any clear vision during his campaign. His campaign staff was fearful of Newt's public involvement in the campaign because they thought it might further weaken public support and they did what they could to keep him in the background. In addition, they underestimated the president's political skills and they overestimated the willingness of the American people to develop the same level of indignation with Clinton's behavior that they held. Instead of getting mad at Clinton and the Democrats they focused their resentment on the Republicans for shoving it in their faces.

---

[58] Ibid.

[59] David Brooks, "What Happened to Newt Gingrich?" *The Weekly Standard*, 21 October 1996, 20.

Newt continued his speaking to GOP groups where he was always well received. He also was able to focus more on the legislative side of his job as Speaker. His greatest success in the legislative area during 1996 came from serving as a brake on the president and his liberal allies. He had hoped to continue his work on tax cuts, decrease the bureaucracy in size and authority, solve the Medicare problem, continue cutting waste in the appropriations bills and move toward the balanced budget. He was, however, still licking his wounds from the public opinion drubbing over the shutdown and hesitant to give the president another opening to do it again. Clinton, knowing his veto was a trump card, was able to deal with Newt and the Senate leaders from a position of strength and regain some of what he had lost in 1995, especially in the spending areas.

As Congress moved through the summer of 1996 toward a September adjournment so Congressmen could go home and campaign internal reforms were many but the big, national changes so hoped for were not in sight. Newt and his allies could point to symbolic, but real internal reforms. They had cut out ice deliveries to congressional offices and saved $500,000. The ice bucket became the symbol of their reform and Newt and other candidates carried it with them throughout the fall campaign. They also passed bills revoking pensions for members con- victed of a federal felony, one turning the House post office over to the US Postal Service and also banished legislative service organizations and their staffs. They cut the number of committees and their staffs. They privatized parking lots, shoe shines and haircuts. They also provided for the introduction of new computer technology for themselves and the Library of Congress through the "THOMAS" system.[60]

While success came on the internal level of reforming and reorganizing, and was largely supported by the Democrats, the bigger visionary programs on the national level were not addressed or fell short of the mark insofar as the Republicans were concerned. By the summer of 1996 it was clear, even to the freshmen, that a cautious Senate and a veto-wielding president were going to force a slow down of the GOP agenda. Both welfare reform and domestic spending reductions were achieved but not as the Republican agenda had

---

[60] *Roll Call*, 30 September 1996, 22.

envisioned. Still they were accomplishments. Looking back two years neither would have been possible. Change had come even though compromises were made toward the end of the session in order to get out of Washington to campaign. The president, in another brilliant example of political jujitsu, was now taking credit for the balanced budget, welfare reform and spending reductions. It confused and infuriated the Republicans to see Clinton taking credit for programs he had opposed but still they had been passed. The reforms were more appreciated by the GOP moderates than the conservatives and even Senator Daschle noted that if the Democrats took over in 1997 they would change little or nothing done in the 104th Congress. House Minority Leader Gephardt noted, "We're all New Democrats now."[61] The 104th had redirected government toward the conservative side and the President and his party seemed to be accepting it, though grudgingly.

There were Democrats, however, who firmly rejected the New Democrat label. Representative Bonior would go to his grave an old fashioned, union-supporting liberal and there were others who joined him. The Democratic mantra showcased in the union sponsored ads was their battle cry. "Republicans were taking food from children's mouths by cutting school lunches. The tax cut favored the rich. Newt and the rest were greasing the skids for big business by making lawsuits harder to file."[62] It was deceitful for them to picture Newt and the Republicans as being against children and victims of predatory business interests and for the very rich. It was unfair and untrue but it did have an impact.

By the end of summer Newt was focusing on the November election and the ethics charges filed against him. Some criticized him and the House leadership for compromising to get an end to the session by the end of September. They saw this as a short-term gain and a betrayal of his promise at the start of the 104th Congress to work with the president and the Democrats but not to compromise.[63] Gingrich did not see it that way. Faced with thousands of negative ads and what he considered unfair tactics such as what he called the "Mediscare" assault by the Democrats, he thought it critical that his Republicans get on the

---

[61] *The Weekly Standard*, 18 November 1996, 11-13 & 26-29.

[62] Ibid. 26.

[63] *Atlanta Journal/Constitution*, 17 November 1996, H4.

campaign trail and fight back. Their challengers were getting free shots at home while they were tied up in Washington. He considered it critical that the Republicans retain control of the 105th Congress. To do this they had to get on the road and the session had to end for that to happen. Some compromises now would, he thought, pay off later and were not too high a price to pay.

Like the president, Newt read the polls. He understood that as long as the GOP was viewed as the materialistic party only interested in deregulation, low-interest rates, tax cutting, supportive of corporations and anti-poor, they would lose. They could not be, in essence, the party without a heart viewed by the public as wanting to tear down the social safety net.[64] The "House Republican National Strategic Plan for 1996" recognized this reality. Their goal was to keep control of the House and add sixteen seats. They also wanted to elect a GOP president and add to their majorities in the Senate and on the state level. They noted that the president would probably win if it was a close election and that they would almost certainly lose if the election was "one of personalities and pure politics." Emphasis was on the choices "for the future of you and your family." They noted that the Democrats "will use fear and ruthlessly attack us as extremists" and "will have no regard for the truth and will replace facts with brazen assertions and bland repetition." They admitted, "we got locked into a struggle with Clinton, the left and the news media—so we became negative, embattled, defined by our opponents and too political."[65]

Newt and the leadership team developed five themes for the campaign:

1. The 1996 election is a choice between two very different teams, two different sets of values, two different goals, and two different futures for you and your family. It is a choice between America and Washington.
2. A compassionate America vs. a well meaning, but failed effort to create a compassionate bureaucracy.

---

[64] John B. Judis, "The Republican Splintering," *New Republic*, 19 August 1996, 34.

[65] "1996 Campaign folder," Republican Conference working paper, Gingrich Papers.

3. We are working toward common sense solutions that are outside the mainstream only to those in Washington.
4. The failing Clinton economy.
5. Renewing America's greatness requires integrity in our leaders. We need a president with integrity who can provide real, consistent leadership.

It was clear that the GOP knew they needed to present themselves as a compassionate party providing common sense solutions. They also knew the Democrats' strategy for attacking them. The difficulty came in putting knowledge into practice. Could Dole, Gingrich and the RNC sell this package to the American people? Could they overcome the politics of personality that the Democrats were sure to play? Newt felt fairly good about holding on to Congress but was less sure of taking the White House. The momentum at that moment was in Clinton's corner and the Republicans were hoping the Republican Convention to be held in San Diego in August would break his momentum and start theirs.

Leading to the convention the NRCC, RNC, the state parties and the GOP leadership joined in a positive ad campaign that would run in twenty-three states and thirty-five congressional districts. "The ads will focus on the accomplishments of the Republican Congress, highlighting our promises kept and our real common sense solutions to the nation's problems." They billed themselves as the "Common Sense Congress" and the "most significant congress in a generation." They stressed ways their legislation had worked to make life better in meaningful ways.[66]

Preaching the big tent approach to party unity Gingrich addressed the GOP House members in an open letter as they prepared to go to the convention. "We remain committed to an opportunity society, based on a smaller, more effective government," he began as he then listed the 104th Congress' accomplishments such as welfare reform, a balanced budget bill, modernization of sixty-year old telecommunications laws, the end of Depression-era farm subsidies and the guarantee of portable health insurance regardless of pre-conditions. More needed to be done. "We need a sincere effort to end illegal drug use and violent crime," which he saw as major family issues. He called for stemming illegal

---

[66] Ibid., "NRCC Majority Memo", Gingrich Papers, 23 July 1996.

immigration and strengthening English as a common language. "Welcoming people who abide by our laws and contribute to our economy is the American way; rewarding those who are here illegally is the wrong way." He noted that "this is a twofold challenge: economic and cultural." Resources diverted to illegal immigrants should be used to help the legal immigrants and native-born citizens. Culturally, "it is critical that all immigrants become Americans in the fullest sense of the word." In addition, "We must reform welfare to require work. Americans have demanded welfare reform not just because people on welfare may be abusing the system but, more importantly, because the system abuses people—particularly our children—trapped in poverty."[67]

Gingrich ended his open letter with a visionary hope. "The Republican mission is a clear one: Our goal is to wake up on a Monday morning when not one child has been hurt anywhere in America. It is a Monday morning when every American adult either has a job, is creating a job or is studying to acquire the skills to get a job," he wrote. "It is an America where every child goes to a school that works, where the drug dealers are gone, the children are safe, and violence is minimal." Falling back on the Reagan theme of what was once in romantic memory may be again, he envisioned "It's an America many of you grew up in—unafraid to leave your door open, take a walk at night or sit on your front porch. Our dream is to reestablish that America and to do whatever it takes so that every child of every ethnic background in every community can pursue happiness."[68]

Newt arrived in San Diego early. Though chairman of the convention, his role was pared down to a five minute speech because his enemies were more anxious to use his image than were his friends. Still, he remained one of the most influential and popular leaders within the party. He attended a "Salute to Newt" party on Saturday night, 10 August attended by thousands and held at the San Diego Zoo, a favorite of his. On the previous Tuesday, 6 August, he met with the managers of the Platform Committee who were frustrated and tired and were facing a public relations disaster over the abortion plank. The committee was split with strong feelings on both sides. He calmed them

---

[67] The Washington Post, 12 August 1996, 21.

[68] Ibid.

and suggested that they look at their options. Newt also assisted them in writing a speech for the next day.

The next morning, as Jeanne Cummings of the *Atlanta Constitution*, tells it, "Gingrich strutted into the platform committee." Though they were preoccupied with the abortion question, "It took him no time to change the subject and hit his stride. His arms were flying. His voice boomed off the auditorium walls. "The news media," he cried; glaring at the long row of startled reporters, "that's the real enemy! They are trying to divide us!" His audience responded. "The platform committee members were euphoric. They are party activists, the core; they love it when Gingrich lets it rip," she wrote. "Their delight was so pure they didn't even mind the rest of the message, which was directed squarely at them: Settle the abortion fight, Gingrich said. Stop whining or bragging about it, and for heaven's sake stop running to every camera to talk about it."[69] By the end of the day the question was settled and a public relations disaster averted. "Without Gingrich's help we would have blown the platform committee," recalled Weber.

What Cummings did not mention in her article was Newt's challenge to the media to cover the split in the Democratic Party as aggressively as they covered the one in the GOP. He read from a David Broder column printed that morning noting the division in the Democratic Party. He challenged the press to ask Gephardt and Daschle about their opposition to the president's support for the welfare reform bill and listed a number of points of contention within Democratic ranks. He noted that both sides of the abortion question were represented in the platform speeches at the convention, emphasizing the failure of the Democrats to allow any pro-life speaker at their convention. He pointed out that the Republicans were a united party when compared to the Democrats and advised the platform committee members to "smile our way through interviews, it'll drive them [the press] nuts." He had complied with Weber's request and left a committee clapping and stomping and more agreeable to working out a compromise.[70]

Newt's media availability was more limited than usual but he was personally all over the place. He even welcomed a group of motor-

---

[69] *The Atlanta Journal/Constitution*, 11 September 1996, A13.

[70] C-SPAN Platform Committee coverage, 8 August 1996.

cyclists, led by Senator Ben Nighthorse Campbell, who came to help raise money for charity and lobby for a law outlawing forced wearing of helmets when biking. He posed on a Harley, though he did not ride it, and appeared on *Nightline* as something of a cheerleader for the Dole-Kemp ticket seeking to explain the tepid response among many Republicans for the Dole candidacy. His own rather pedestrian speech to the convention was best remembered for its shortness and its example of beach volleyball as an example of what is great in America. As chairman of the convention he presided over the voting for the presidential and vice-presidential candidates in a business-like manner offering little red meat to the faithful. He was keeping a low profile and making sure that he did not compete with Dole for the spotlight.

Gingrich continued to travel the country to help raise money for Republican candidates but also had to pay attention to his own campaign back home in Georgia. Though he felt confident of reelection he had to take his opponent seriously. Michael Coles was a self-made millionaire who had made his fortune selling cookies in malls. He was established in the sixth district and had donated a considerable amount of money to Kennesaw State University where they named the school of business for him. The business building bearing his name was the location for Newt's college course on Renewing American Civilization. Coles had the personal money to compete with Newt on television and was determined to run an aggressive campaign. He put well over $1 million of his own money into his campaign and launched "the heaviest barrage of paid advertising he [Newt] has had to endure in his career."[71] Coles ultimately raised over $2.3 million, most of it from his own checkbook and political action committees outside the district. Gingrich countered by raising over $3.6 million including a large portion from Georgia sources.[72]

Gingrich's campaign was focused on the accomplishments of the 104th Congress and his ability to deliver for the folks back home. He could take their ideas and wishes to Washington and turn them into laws. He could take care of keeping the local Lockheed aircraft factory operating. "He kept his promises. He forced Congress to live by the same laws as all Americans. Sponsored the first balanced budget in a

[71] *Roll Call*, 21 October 1996, 10.
[72] *Atlanta Journal/Constitution*, 3 November 1996, H5.

generation," emphasized his ads.[73] Coles, using the attacks of previous Gingrich opponents, accused the Speaker of being out of touch with the people back home and blamed him for the budget shut-down. He pictured Newt as the ultimate insider politician and himself as a local businessman with deep roots in the community. He described himself as a conservative Democrat interested in a balanced budget and regulatory reform. "I'll be a congressman more interested in listening to your voice than hearing my own," he promised.[74]

Gingrich pulled out all the stops. He spent more time campaigning at home and agreed to debate Coles on the Bill Nigut *Georgia Week in Review* program on Georgia Public Television. During the debate Newt pitched this race as a struggle over control of Congress. "Congress is a team sport. There is a liberal team and there is a conservative team. The people he [Coles] would put in power are liberals." Using a time tested tactic, he then asked Coles again how he would vote for president. "This is a guy who wants to run on his cookies, not his beliefs." Because Dole's popularity in the sixth district was ahead of Gingrich's, Coles refused to answer. Calling for bipartisanship Coles said, "What we've got to do is stop playing this game [partisan bickering] and this is a game that Mr. Gingrich has created." He stressed his local roots and again blamed Newt for the budget shut-down. Both men seemed satisfied with their performances though not much in the way of issues was discussed.[75]

During the last weekend of the campaign Newt and his supporters again filled three British double-decker busses for a tour of the district. The press, local, national and international, was in attendance as Newt traveled around three counties, spoke at five rallies and numerous short stops to hand out campaign materials and knock on doors in subdivisions and eat barbecue. He also brought in House Budget Chairman John Kasich, a popular Republican on both sides of the aisle to help cheerlead and raise money. Noting the polls indicated that his support was soft with women, even GOP women, Representative Susan Molinari came down to lend her support. The same weekend Coles was campaigning at craft fairs with little press and no major celebrities. According to Jeanne Cummings, "The difference in the company the

---

[73] Ibid., 2 October 1996, C2.
[74] Ibid., 3 November 1996, H5.
[75] Ibid., 26 October 1996. A1 & C2.

two men kept Saturday illustrates the choice being offered to voters in the 6th Congressional District. It is between the chief Republican revolutionary in Washington and a local representative who says he is willing to work between the partisan trenches in Congress."[76] Michael Coles could not have said it better.

An old foe had once told Newt that if he wanted to see something good about himself in his paper then he had better take out an ad. Feeling that he was getting less than a fair shake from the Atlanta newspapers, Newt decided to take out his own full page ad in both papers the day before the election. Bold type addressed the readers, "To The Readers Of *The Atlanta Journal-Constitution*" "We thought you might like to read for yourself what another newspaper in the sixth district has to say about the reelection of Speaker Newt Gingrich." He then reproduced the endorsement given him by the *Marietta Daily Journal* on 27 October entitled "Newt Deserves Another Term." "As House speaker, Representative Gingrich gives Cobb County and Georgia a guaranteed voice in the direction our country is traveling and in how our taxes are spent. His clout, already substantial, would continue to grow if he is given another term in Congress and again is voted Speaker by his GOP peers. His 1994 victory affirmed Cobb's status as the center of the Republican universe. With the retirement of long-serving US Senator Sam Nunn, it is more vital than ever that someone of Gingrich's stature be reelected to safeguard the interests of our state and county." The bottom of the page carried Newt's campaign slogan, "Listening to us, working with us to lead America."[77]

The voters of the sixth district reflected the advice given by their newspaper. The polls shortly before the election showed the race at 55-45 percent favoring Newt. Faced with labor's massive ad campaign which targeted him and the Democrat ads, making him their number one target, and being faced with the largest ad campaign against him in his career, Newt directed all his resources towards his campaign. He felt like he would win.

Newt had hoped to inspire and participate in a "great debate" that would be the hallmark of campaign 1996. The debate would have offered the alternatives of the welfare state and the opportunity society.

---

[76] Ibid. 13 November 1996, A1.
[77] Ibid. 4 November 1996, B10.

No debate occurred, however. Because of his low standing in the polls Newt was sidelined in the national campaign and relegated to fund-raising, which he did well, raising almost $100 million for the party and its candidates.[78] Realizing that the Republicans would not take the White House he focused his concern on keeping control of the House and winning his own election. Election night, speaking to his supporters in the early part of the evening he was optimistic about the outcome, telling the crowd, "It will be the first time in sixty-eight years that a Republican majority was reelected to the US House so it will truly be a historic moment." But he was worried on a personal level. He told the gathering of supporters at the Cobb Galleria ballroom that his father, Bob Gingrich, was in the hospital in Harrisburg with lung cancer and asked for their prayers. In spite of his remarkable ability to compartmentalize it was clear that his father was on his mind that night. His mother, at Bob's insistence, had come to Georgia to be with her son but clearly had her mind on Harrisburg as she sat quietly looking into space for much of the evening.

In the "war room" Joe Gaylord, Rich Galen and Dan Meyer sat behind the table talking on the phones and gathering election results as they watched races around the country. Gaylord said he was not worried about Newt's race but the many staffers scurrying about clearly had that uppermost in their minds. They were the soldiers in the campaign and though they thought he would win, they were concerned about the margin. They wanted a significant margin for Newt. Newt's race was decided fairly early in the evening when he was declared the winner with what would be a 57 percent-43 percent margin. Not the tremendous margin his supporters had hoped for, but a comfortable one given the forces marshaled against him.

As the evening wore on even Gaylord showed concern. One Republican after another began to lose as the results came in from around the country. At one point Newt came into the room and asked for the results in the Nancy Johnson race in Connecticut. She, as chairman of the Ethics Committee handling the charges against Newt, had been targeted by the Democrats. "She's up by 3,000 at this point," Gaylord reported. Her race was a roller coaster one, however, with the result not being decided until a recount. "She really has paid a price for

---

[78] Ibid. 3 November 1996, H5.

that job," whispered Newt under his breath. He was concerned about his fellow Georgia Republicans and showed evident pleasure as, one by one, their reelection was passed on to him. Georgia started the evening with eight GOP House Members and kept them all, including his close ally, Representative John Linder whom he would soon appoint to head the NRCC. Gaylord was right to be concerned. The GOP would ultimately lose eighteen members with a net loss of nine leaving them with a 225-207 balance in the House. At 11:28 P.M. CNN called Congress for the GOP and relief and cheers filled the room. Handshakes all around. When asked how he felt now, Newt responded with a big smile, "great, but I'll feel better when Joe tells me." That assurance took somewhat longer but finally Gaylord reassured him that the California vote was in and they had retained control. Newt moved quickly, followed by his key aides, to proclaim victory to his supporters waiting in the ballroom and to talk to his mom about how he wished his father was there.

Newt and the party had survived 1996. The historic reelection for control of Congress was now an accomplished fact. The Speaker had been in the trenches, had been singed by the blast and smelled the powder. Dead political bodies lay around him but the GOP had retained control of the House for the first time since the start of the Great Depression and they had done it with his leadership. If anyone had earned a rest it was Newt. As he began to think about the 105th Congress he summed it up. "Yes, I'm a little more battered than I was two years ago. Yes, it's been harder than I would have guessed. Yes, I made some mistakes. On the other hand, I was in 130 districts. I helped re-elect an awful lot of very important members and elect some brand new freshmen. Think how bad it would be if I was here tonight as a defeated one-time speaker continuing the Republican tradition of losing control."[79] Little did he know that he was facing losing control, not only of the speakership but of his own members whom he had just led to a historic victory.

---

[79] *Roll Call*, 12 November 1996, 16.

14

THE FRUSTRATING
105ᵀᴴ CONGRESS

Nineteen ninety-six had been a rough year but the continuation of the GOP majority in both houses of Congress had made the rough spots seem more bearable. Even as Gingrich phoned his leadership election night to offer and receive congratulations some in his party were focusing on the losses and blaming him for them. By this time the party had broken into at least five major factions with subgroups in each of the five[1]. The Republicans were beginning to look like a 1930s European multiparty political system incapable of governing itself. Each faction was resentful and suspicious of the others and inclined to oppose a compromise. Generally unhappy with Newt's leadership and low popularity in the polls, some seized on his ethics problems as a means of removing him from the Speaker's office.

Adopting the saying that 'it's not personal, it's politics,' an old moderate colleague and ally, Representative Chris Shays announced less than a week after the election that he would not vote to reelect Gingrich as speaker unless the Ethics Committee's outside counsel's report was made public before the scheduled vote on 7 January. He would vote to nominate Newt for re-election but noted "Newt Gingrich is hated!" Representative Steve Largent agreed. The Republican columnist, Kate O'Beirne went further, writing in the *National Review* that Newt should step aside until the ethics matter was cleared up. She suggested that Representative Henry Hyde could take over the

---

[1] *US News & World Report* (9 November 1996): 41-43.

speakership until Gingrich had dealt with his problems.[2] At the same time Senator Charles Grassley attacked Newt for using military aides to explain organizational structure to his leadership. "There is simply no legitimate role for the armed forces in politics in the United States of America. Period!" he said.[3]

While Shays and Largent said they would not vote for Newt until the ethics report was out and O'Beirne asked him to step aside temporarily, others went further. Representative Peter King, a sophomore from New York, called for Newt to step aside for at least a year or "until he has rehabilitated himself." On 11 November he announced that even if Newt stayed Speaker those upset with him intended to curtail his power and said that possibly as many as twenty GOP members would join him in opposition to Newt. If they voted against Newt or failed to vote this would be enough to give the speakership to Gephardt and the Democrats. The next day the Majority Whip, Tom Delay, spoke out. "I don't know their motives, but it seems very selfish and they're playing right into the hands of the liberal Democratic leadership and the liberal media. It's very distracting at a time when we need to be preparing for the next Congress. It's very disappointing that any of them would even talk about this." Representative John Shadegg noted their logic would mean that Bill Clinton should not be sworn in until all the charges against him were resolved. Newt announced that he had no intention of stepping down.[4]

The Democrats were delighted. After trying to get rid of him by almost any means possible over the last decade he had just beaten them once more in the 1996 elections and held on to a Republican majority for the first time in over sixty years. They had taken some satisfaction in lowering the GOP numbers in the House and a lot in the reelection of President Clinton. They were not happy about another two years under Republican rule in Congress and concerned about the split in their own party over fast track legislation. The *Washington Post* referred to the Democrats as surveying "the carnage left behind" in the wake of that vote.[5] Then the unexpected happened. At the moment of triumph Newt's own troops had turned on him. Unlike the GOP dissidents,

---

[2] *Roll Call*, (11 November 1996): 1 & 26.

[3] Ibid., 1 & 25.

[4] *The Hill*, 13 November 1996, 1.

[5] *The Washington Post* weekly edition, (24 November 1996): 12.

Democrats understood political loyalty. Though puzzled by the action of the dissidents, the Democrats were pleased to see their nemesis being savaged by his own people and used the GOP attacks on Gingrich to buttress their own assaults on the speaker.

When Newt's 1994 opponent, Ben Jones, filed ethics charges concerning the financing of Newt's Renewing American Civilization course at Kennesaw State College during the campaign Newt and his staff took it only somewhat seriously. So many charges had been filed and dismissed that this attempt seemed like just one more nuisance charge filed in a campaign to get press for his opponent and cast doubt on Newt's candidacy. His staff and lawyers had looked at it to be sure it was within legal guidelines and he felt confident there was no problem. Acting with an abundance of caution, he ordered his staff to prepare a response to the charge for the Ethics Committee. This response, sent to the committee on 10 October, was factually accurate and described the involvement of GOPAC in the organization and financing of the course. On 8 November the election sent a GOP majority to Congress for the first time since 1952.

The 1994 election angered and frustrated the Democrats. They established "The Project" which was "a coordinated, calculated effort that would culminate in the political destruction of Newt Gingrich." The *New Republic*'s TRB (editors's opinion column) called for Newt to be "beaten to a pulp" and Newt's nemesis, Representative David Bonior, coordinated efforts with the ranking Democrat, Representative Jim McDermott, on the Ethics Committee to do anything necessary to turn the committee into a partisan political tool to remove Gingrich and punish him for what he had done to them. Bonior began calling for a special counsel to investigate Newt in December 1994 and the committee indicated interest in the IRS implications of GOPAC's involvement in the Kennesaw course.

Two letters of response were prepared by Newt's attorney's answering the charges filed by Jones. The first was dated 8 December 1994 and the second 27 March 1995. Both had inaccuracies regarding GOPAC and were at odds with Newt's staff response filed 4 October 1994. The unresearched and almost cavalier response presented in the two letters became the cross upon which the Democrats hoped to crucify Gingrich. Newt and his staff, busy getting a new legislative session off the ground, did not catch the contradictions and inaccuracies and signed the letters. "I blame myself," said Hanser, "we all read the letters before they were sent and didn't catch it."[6]

In December 1995 the Ethics Committee dismissed all the charges but one, the GOPAC inaccuracies. They also decided to hire a special counsel to investigate that charge and in addition passed it on to the IRS. The IRS would keep it under active investigation for over three years allowing the Democrats to use that investigation to castigate Newt for tax violations. They would conclude their inquiry three months after Newt decided to resign from Congress and after the 1996 and 1998 elections. Their conclusion was that Newt and GOPAC had not violated tax laws and were innocent of the charges.[7] To some of Newt's supporters this showed the politicization of the IRS that had been seen in the Justice Department and the FBI during the Clinton years. Interestingly, in February 1996, Judge Louis Oberdorfer dismissed a case against GOPAC brought by the Federal Election Commission. The next month forged documents concerning GOPAC fundraising and spending on congressional candidates were sent to *Roll Call* in the obvious hope that they would print them and help discredit the Speaker.

The situation in early 1996 had not looked that bad to Newt. He thought the documents sent over to the Ethics Committee would handle the problem. In March they dropped more charges. The Democrats were filing charges on a regular basis hoping that something somewhere would stick. The special counsel, James Cole, submitted a partial report to the Committee following his investigations over the summer. This report was leaked to the press and the Democrats began asking for it to be made public. On 6 June, in a rare moment of relaxation on the Speaker's balcony, Newt admitted there were a lot of problems but still looked at his own situation with confidence. No one seemed confident about Dole's chances in the November election, but Newt said anything was possible in politics and "[i]f Dole does not win then I'll go for it in 2000," he said.[8]

---

[6] Steve Hanser, audio tape interview by the author, 2 November 1998. Gingrich Papers, State University of West Georgia Archives, Carrollton.

[7] *The Atlanta Journal*, (Atlanta GA), 4 February 1999, A6

[8] Election 1996 folder, Steely notes, 6 June 1996. Gingrich Papers, State University of West Georgia Archives, Carrollton.

While Gingrich was blamed by the press for the shutdown and refused to point fingers, some of his staff and other GOP members were insistent that the blame should be shared with Senator Dole. "By November 1995 we had completely redefined what was possible in the area in Washington," said Arne. "My thought was always that at that point the deal worker, Bob Dole, would see the final connections. That would make a deal possible. In the end Dole was not a master deal maker. In fact Dole had been very unimaginative. His approach, most of the time, was to hang out and let everybody wear out until it became kind of obvious where things are going to end up. He was no better at reading Clinton than Newt even though he had been around a lot longer and done a lot of deals. In some ways I fault him more than Newt because I thought at that point the endgame was more his than Newt's."[9]

Newt clearly thought a lot had been accomplished and that his dream of turning Washington politics around from an assumed liberal position to a more conservative one had been partially accomplished. The drive toward big government had been slowed and there was hope for the balanced budget amendment. There were reasons to be optimistic. The untrue leak by the Democrats in September that the special counsel had a final report finding him guilty of tax violations was the first step in denting that optimism. Representative Bonior accused him of engaging "in a pattern of tax fraud" and his henchman, Representative John Lewis, said he was "engaged in a massive tax fraud scheme." There was no final report and the question of tax fraud had been turned over to the IRS.

The demands for the committee to make public the report would be a major fixture in Democratic press opportunities throughout the campaign and after. The election returned a Republican majority on 5 November and Newt was faced with some of his own colleagues turning on him. Newt's mood had changed from that of the summer. He had been told of his father's lung cancer on 8 October and he and Marianne had visited Bob Gingrich in the hospital on 10 November. Even for a man who specializes in compartmentalization this was a heavy load. Facing a father's death and colleagues' betrayal was

---

[9]Arne Christensen, interview by author, tape recording, 13 November 1998, Gingrich Papers, University of West Georgia Archives, Carrollton.

enough to push him to the edge of melancholy. His innate energy carried him through a mobilization of his loyal supporters within the GOP conference to reassure his nomination. That was achieved, without opposition, on 20 November, the day his father died. The funeral was held two days later.

Three weeks after a somber Thanksgiving, 13 December, the real blow fell. Christensen said he was talking with Newt as he took a fax from the Ethics Committee. Newt read it, looked up and said, "You know, this could hardly be worse. I may have to resign." Arne describes him as "shaken."[10] The fax was a draft of the statement of alleged violations. His spirits were lifted later in the day when his friend, Representative John Linder called. Linder met with Newt and told him that he had talked to Representative Steve Schiff, a member of the subcommittee, and would stand by him. He thought the statement would have to be confronted but that it did not mean the end of his career. Schiff and Representative Porter Goss, the other Republican on the subcommittee, also stood by Newt and encouraged him.

The leaks about a supposed final report had alerted Newt to a potentially serious problem. He quickly discovered the inconsistencies in his three letters to the committee. His October 1994 letter was accurate concerning GOPAC's role in the college course. The ones prepared by his lawyers (December 1994 and March 1995) and signed by him contained inaccuracies. Newt, on advice from his staff, decided to get some outside counsel. "Newt and his staff became concerned that the lawyers representing him may have made mistakes that the committee was focusing on—I specialized in lawyer ethics and he wanted somebody to look at it from the ethics standpoint," remembered Randy Evans.[11] Evans, an old and close ally from back home, had advised Newt on the Jim Wright ethics filings and had served as political advisor to his campaign until 1992 when Newt moved to the new sixth district. Since that time Evans had gone on to earn a national reputation as a responsible litigator. In addition, Evans' friendship and loyalty were unquestioned.

In addition to Evans Gingrich hired former Congressman Ed Bethune who had an office in Washington. Evans flew up from Atlanta,

---

10 Ibid.

11 Randy Evans, interview by author, on videotape, 21 September 1998, Gingrich Papers.

met with Bethune and his staff, and they concluded that he had serious problems. "The letters were on their face inconsistent with the attachments. A phrase in the letter said GOPAC had no involvement when the attachments referred to GOPAC seventy or eighty times." "The problem was we had lawyers advising him on what he should do based on the mistakes they had made. There was a direct conflict because their interests were completely different from his interests. His interest was to not defend the letters and say they were wrong then turn to his lawyers and say what they had prepared was inaccurate."[12] Newt "was deeply disappointed and he felt betrayed. He had given them [his legal team] his confidence. He had taken a lot of extraordinary steps. He had voluntarily relinquished the lawyer/client privilege. He ordered his staff to totally cooperate, answer all questions," and was completely open. What he got for this "was a deliberate policy of destruction. It was not a fair process," remembered Hanser.[13]

Before Bethune and Evans got too involved the Ethics Committee fax arrived on 13 December and events moved rapidly. Evans brought in his "swat team" from Arnall, Golden and Gregory in Atlanta and set up shop in a suite in Bethune's office. "At that point we had two choices, either litigate it and it would be a litigated matter at the time of the vote for the Speaker in January 1997 or we could do something else. We were balancing two issues. Newt was really concerned about the cost to the institution. There was no question that any further proceedings would've been a political bloodbath," Evans said. This would likely have produced partisan gridlock for the first months of the new session. A second concern was the cost to Newt. "He had to consider what he was prepared to do. There were certain parameters. He was not going to agree to a fine. That would've indicated some personal gain or advantage and there was none. If they'd insisted on a fine we would have litigated."[14] They felt certain they had not violated tax law but the problem of the two inaccurate letters persisted.

At this point the special counsel, Jim Cole, contacted Evans and indicated that he was willing to talk with him about possibilities. No report had been finalized nor made public and both Cole and Evans

---

[12] Ibid.

[13] Hanser, interview, 1998

[14] Evans, interview, 1998.

were ready to talk. Evans considered the fax of the draft of alleged violations to be "an open offer for a plea bargain. Between 13 December, which was a Friday, until 21 December there was constant negotiation first of all between Evans and Cole and ultimately between Evans and the Committee members as to what they were willing to have Newt agree to," remembered Christensen.[15] "It was a very rapidly moving process, we worked on it constantly," agreed Evans. "I told Newt point blank that if we tried the case we would prevail. I had no doubt of that." Still, that was not in his best interest and Evans worked with Cole and the committee to come up with a compromise they could all embrace. "We finally agreed to say he should have consulted with lawyers more in putting together the college course and the lawyers he had hired to assist him with the ethics violations charges submitted two letters that were inaccurate, incomplete documents." As a result of these negotiations the ethics subcommittee issued a statement of alleged violations on 21 December and Newt issued a statement admitting the violations. From his point of view it was an admission of a careless but serious error in reporting. It was a mistake and not a purposeful attempt to mislead the committee as was indicated by the October 1994 letter and the attachments to the other two letters.

Mistake or not, after hundreds and hundreds of ethics charges one had finally drawn blood and while it might not be overly serious the Democrats and the press had a point with which to attack Newt. Bonior, "the lead hyena in the howling partisan pack"[16] had a field day. The *Atlanta Constitution* editorialized that Newt was guilty of "more than a minor violation of tax law" and their cartoonist, Mike Luckovich, drew Newt pointing to "Newt's Contract With America II" and checking off the top nine items. The items were "lied, ignored tax laws, blamed others, whined, conspired, abused power, attempted cover-up, misrepresented, and sullied Congress." The tenth item, "resigned" was not checked off.[17] His old nemesis Tom Teepen proclaimed, "Gingrich explores new depths."[18]

---

[15] Christensen, interview, 1998.

[16] Richard Matthews, *The Atlanta Journal/Constitution* (Atlanta GA), 14 December 1996, A10.

[17] *The Atlanta Journal/Constitution* ,(Atlanta GA) 12 December 1996, A10.

[18] *The Atlanta Journal/Constitution*, (Atlanta GA) 29 December 1996, G3.

The problem now for Newt and his supporters was how to deal with the media knowing that the Democrats would be in full howl on all the weekend talk shows. The hope was, as explained by Conference Chairman Representative John Boehner, "that over the next ten days or so that the Ethics Committee can meet and resolve this issue and bring it to the floor on opening day and get it behind us."[19] Newt was under a gag order regarding his discussions with the committee but had to say something to his troops. "Ed Bethune was specifically authorized to prepare talking points which were submitted to the independent counsel who edited them." These were the talking points discussed in a leadership conference call that was taped by a Florida couple who turned their tape over to Democrats in Washington who used it to accuse Newt of violating the rules with his call.[20]

Newt's admission that there were inaccuracies in his response letters stirred some of the Republicans to raise again the question of voting for Newt for Speaker. Linder and the leadership team took the lead in defending him. "We were on a wild ride from the 21ˢᵗ of December until January 7ᵗʰ when we had to get enough votes to allow Newt to be elected Speaker. Paxon was great. We did conference calls every day. It was an ongoing operation. Just amazing how it worked," remembered Christensen.[21] On New Year's Eve Representatives Goss and Schiff issued a letter endorsing Newt for reelection as speaker. Their support, as members of the ethics subcommittee, ended any serious resistance from the Republicans. Representatives Armey, DeLay, and Boehner all went on talk shows to defend Newt as did Paxon, Molinari, Dunn, Dennis Hastert, Sue Myrick, and Bob Ney. Newt also got strong support from fellow Georgians Bob Barr and Mac Collins in addition to Linder.[22]

In addition to worrying about his mother, holding his own troops in line and defending himself in the media, Newt was concerned about the committee's next step, deciding on a penalty, and also about the legislative agenda for the 105th Congress. Evans was responsible for dealing with the committee and, in effect, negotiating a penalty. Gingrich refused to pay a fine but would agree to reimburse the

---

[19] Ibid, 12 December 1996, A3.

[20] Evans, interview, 1998.

[21]Christensen, interview, 1998.

[22] *The Hill*, 22 January 1997, 14.

committee for cost incurred because of the inaccuracies in his letters. A public-reprimand by the full House and the payment of the reimbursement was agreed upon as a proper and acceptable punishment. There was considerable discussion of how much money Newt would pay. "The reason that number [$300,000] was picked was that it would be paid for in campaign funds. It was never the idea that it would come from his personal funds. If personal then it would have been ten, twenty, or $30,000. Everyone on the committee understood that and discussed it," said Evans. The committee accepted it and when it was voted on in the House the two Democratic members of the subcommittee immediately demanded that it be paid out of personal funds, "knowing full well that we'd negotiated based on the idea that it wouldn't be paid out of Newt's personal funds."[23]

Newt was angry and frustrated feeling there seemed to be a double standard; one for him and one for the Democrats. Minority Leader Gephardt had committed an offense similar to Newt's letters of inaccuracy and had been allowed by the committee to make the necessary changes to set it right. He was open and forthcoming in his dealings with the committee while the president and his team were stonewalling and showing incredibly forgetful memories in their dealings with Congressional committees. He had maintained a professional approach to Ethics Committee Chairman Johnson and the Democrats had put incredible pressure on her within the committee and back home in her district almost causing her to lose her race. He had followed committee rules in discussing committee actions and had been accused of violating them while the ranking member of the committee leaked untruths about Newt and went so far as to possibly commit a criminal act with his use of the tape sent to him by loyal Democrats in Florida.

Newt did not react well to this seemingly unfair treatment. "He was disappointed in the system. Every time we did something they would change the rules. There was a great deal of frustration and pain. The process was hurtful and designed to cause pain. They wanted to inflict pain and I think that at the point where he agreed to pay for it out of his personal funds they understood they had inflicted pain and to some

---

[23] Evans, interview, 1998.

extent the beast had been satisfied. Their appetite for retribution had been temporarily quenched," reflected Evans.[24]

At the hearing before the full committee in the Rayburn Building on 17 January 1997, special counsel Jim Cole presented his findings. He admitted the course Newt taught at Kennesaw State met the test for IRS approval as an educational course (501c3) but indicated that the spirit might have been violated by partisan motives in setting up the course. While critical of the lawyers who prepared the two "inaccurate, incomplete and unreliable" letters Cole nevertheless held Gingrich responsible because they were, after all, his letters. Noting Newt's prior agreement to the recommendation he offered, he asked for "a reprimand and $300,000 toward the cost of the investigations."[25]

Evans and Bethune represented Newt, who was not present at the hearing. Evans, while not challenging Cole's presentation, pointed out that the approach to fundraising used by Newt and GOPAC was neither new nor unusual. Half the US senators and almost a third of the sitting Congressmen had similar approaches. Indeed, the IRS provided for it as an example in the field manual for its agents. Evans pointed out that there were no charges of illegality or gain of any sort. He said Newt was taking it seriously and that is why he had agreed to the $300,000 reimbursement.

Following the Cole and Evans presentations the committee members asked questions and made statements for the record. GOP committee member Lamar Smith protested the money payment saying that he thought it was out of proportion to the infraction, was a double standard designed to punish Newt more than other members and set a bad precedent for future ethics violations. When the vote was taken it was seven in support of the Cole recommendation and one, Smith, opposed. The committee recommendation then was passed on to the full House.

Representative Boehner put out a three-page fact sheet on House Republican Conference letterhead to aid Republicans as they talked to their constituents over the weekend before the House vote. "All of us can expect a lot of hot rhetoric and gross exaggeration in the next few days as we move toward the conclusion of the speaker's ethics case," wrote Boehner. "Please keep these major talking points in mind as you

---

[24] Ibid.

[25] The best coverage of the complete committee hearing is provided by the C-SPAN cameras.

prepare your speeches, discussions and media interviews." The document noted that the no tax law violations were found and that experienced tax lawyers, including the committee's own counsel, had advised him that it was legal. It pointed out that the committee had found no intent to mislead on Newt's part, no tax law violations, and indeed no violations of any law. It ended by making a pitch for a quick closure to the case and warned, "Any further harassment by the Democrats will be seen as attempting to prolong this process solely for partisan purposes."[26]

The Democrats did indeed use the occasion to attack Newt and seemed bothered that Republicans were defending him. One of the subcommittee members, Representative Nancy Pelosi, toned down her usually harsh rhetoric but pointed out that Newt had violated ethics laws "not because of a comedy of errors but because he thought he could get away with it." Special counsel Cole said in his presentation to the committee that Newt had a history of pushing organizational fundraising to the edge. Representative Charles Rangel reminded all who would listen that "Their Speaker pleaded guilty and said he either recklessly or intentionally lied."[27]

When the full House met on 21 January to receive the committee's report and vote on its recommendations the level of passion was toned down some and a more conciliatory approach was in evidence on both sides. At his moment of triumph Representative Bonior sat quietly with hands folded never rising to speak. Gingrich was not on the floor. Most members seemed ready to move to a quick vote and get on with other business. The Democratic speakers reminded the members of Newt's admitted guilt while most Republican members talked of being pleased to see it all ending in an agreed upon recommendation. There were a couple of exceptions. Representative Lamar Smith, the only 'no' vote on the committee, spoke briefly and said he thought it was too harsh a punishment. "Do *you* want to be judged by the same standard that we are judging the speaker today?" he asked the House. The GOP Whip, Representative Tom DeLay, made a plea: "Let's stop using the ethics process for political vendettas." He said he thought a double standard was being applied to the Speaker and pointed out that since 1989 over

---

[26] John Boehner, "House Republican Conference Talking Points," 17 January 1997; Gingrich Papers.

[27] *The Hill*, 1-2 February 1997.

500 ethics charges had been filed against Newt. Of those 500, none ever came to the floor. "He's being charged today because during the process he happened to screw up. We have abused the process," he said. The microscope Newt had been under for so long "had not exposed corruption or lawlessness or personal profit." DeLay reminded and, like Speaker Jim Wright, asked for an end to the cannibalization.[28]

"House SPANKS Speaker, 395 – 28" headlined *The Hill* the day after the vote. "Behind-Scenes Deal Quells Partisanship" and "Chastened Newt Seeks New Start" read other front-page articles.[29] The last two acts to the ethics drama were played out later. On tax day, 15 April, Newt, with Marianne's strong support, made the decision to pay the $300,000 reimbursement out of personal funds instead of from his campaign fund. As Newt's old opponent, Ben Jones, crowed, "I cooked Newt's Goose,"[30] the Democrats objected to Newt borrowing the money from a bank wanting it to come from his savings or salary. Senator Dole suggested that he guarantee or loan the money to Newt who would then pay him back at agreed upon intervals. In the discussion that followed Evans, taking notes for the legal papers necessary in such a transaction, asked about repayment to Dole's heirs in case of his death. The senator replied quickly that they should designate Senator Strom Thurmond to act as executor "because he will outlive us all."[31] Newt ended up not borrowing the money but the guarantee allowed him to pay the money to Congress in installments.

The final act did not come for over two years. The Ethics Committee had turned the question of GOPAC and the Progress and Freedom Foundation's involvement in funding the college course over to the IRS. The courts had already cleared GOPAC when, a month after Newt stepped down as speaker, 2 February 1999, the IRS issued their ruling. The audit letter they issued cleared Newt, the Progress and Freedom Foundation and the Kennesaw State University Foundation of any illegalities. "After an intensive, 3 1/2 year audit, the IRS has concluded that Gingrich and the foundation violated no tax laws, that the foundation did not intervene on behalf of candidates for the Republican

---

[28] C-SPAN, 21 January 1997. Complete coverage provided by C-SPAN's cameras.

[29] *The Hill*, 22 January 1997, 1.

[30] *The Washington Post*, (Washington DC), 3 February 1997, 21.

[31] Randy Evans, interview, 1998.

Party, and that the course itself was strictly educational in content and was not biased toward particular politicians or a particular party." The report continued, "The course taught principles from American civilization that could be used by each American in everyday life, whether the person is a welfare recipient, the head of a large corporation or a politician. Gingrich, a victim of the politics of personal destruction, correctly proclaimed this ruling a full and complete vindication."[32]

Everyone took a deep breath and attempted to move on. The Republicans, and Newt, were particularly anxious to move on the legislative front, pass popular bills and get them on the front pages instead of articles about ethics. They also wanted Newt out of the news. Whether they supported Newt or not there was resentment and unease about having to do so every time new charges are made. They also had their own ambitions and leadership expectations and were somewhat resentful of Newt's strong leadership during the 104th Congress. Some did not like him personally. When votes were being rounded up for the floor vote on the Speaker in early January, Evans told him that the specific ethics violations were not the problem but that he, Newt, was the problem. "The members don't like you and don't support you. They will turn on you. It is not ethics but you personally. The question we need to answer before the vote on Speaker is are you the person to be speaker?"[33] That question was answered to Newt's satisfaction and he and his supporters were able to make the case that he was the best person to be speaker. The personal animosity was still there and this made the support thin and shaky. Had there been another strong candidate for Speaker on the scene Newt would have been in serious trouble.

As it was, the chairmen saw this as an opportunity to strengthen their positions at Newt's expense and got him to agree to a reorganization of the leadership structure. The SAG, or Speaker's Advisory Group, would be disbanded and their power would now flow to the committee chairmen. Representatives Susan Molinari and Jennifer Dunn were appointed to the expanded steering committee and a representative from the moderate Lunch Bunch and the Conservative Action Team were also added to the leadership. In addition, a new

---

[32] *New York Post*, 5 February 1999, 32. An editorial entitled "Partisan Lies."

[33] Randy Evans interview, 10-10-97. Telephone interview notes in Evans folder. Steely Papers.

communications director would be appointed to replace the departing Tony Blankley and Leigh Ann Pusey. The new director would work out of the Speaker's office but would coordinate all communications from the entire leadership.[34]

Newt hoped he could now work with the Democratic leaders, or at least some of them, to get legislation of common interest passed. When he appeared on the Reverend Jesse Jackson show, *Equal Time* shortly after being reelected Speaker he indicated his desire to work with the Black Congressional Caucus. He was willing to hold regular meetings with them in the Speaker's office and had talked to Representative Maxine Waters and Representative Charles Rangel about programs to help fight drugs and rebuild the inner city.[35] He also indicated his desire to help the poor in the nation's capital. In a December speech to the Heritage Foundation he had "urged Republicans not to fixate on White House scandals but to make saving the poor of the US capital a top priority for the next two years."[36] In February, at Representative J. C. Watts's urging, he agreed to go slow on bringing a bill to ban affirmative action to the floor. He said, "the national debate on whether the preferences are still needed should play out first."[37] Some of his colleagues and supporters inside and outside Congress were critical of his opening the door to Jackson and the Black Caucus. They thought Jackson, Maxine Waters and John Lewis were not his friends and would only use him. They also did not want him to go slow on affirmative action. His friend Bill Bennett said he "should stop trying to curry favor with Jesse Jackson and other black liberals or give up his Republican leadership post."[38] Reading this as an attempt to develop a "new Newt" they did not understand that working with African-Americans was not new to Gingrich. His concerns about their community and a desire to bring them into the mainstream of American life had been a part of his politics, and indeed his belief system, for over twenty years. At a town hall meeting back home on 15 February, he argued "that Republicans need to build bridges to the minority community and

---

[34] *The Hill*, 20 November 1996, pp. 1 & 19.

[35] *Equal Time*, CNN 12 January 1997.

[36] *The Atlanta Journal*, 4 December 1996.

[37] Ibid., 14 February 1997, B1.

[38] *The Atlanta Journal*, 6 February 1997, A10.

urban America as part of their effort to become the majority party in the country."[39]

Reacting to criticism from the *Weekly Standard* Newt defined himself as a member of the Jeffersonian wing of the Federalist party. "That wing believed in a constitution, but also it believed that the constitution should be limited in its scope and reach," he wrote. "The founding fathers deliberately designed a system that dispersed power" and they would have to work with the Senate and the president if they were to get things done. The old idea of two years earlier that compromise was to be rejected was now revisited. Cooperation was now the idea. Newt argued that this had been his idea all along when he talked of cooperation but not compromise.[40] He observed that what he had experienced in 1996 was that when the Democrats got their way that was considered bipartisan cooperation. When they did not that was considered partisanship. Compromise only ran one way to the Democrats and he hoped to change that in 1997.

The approach to affirmative action was not the only issue moving slowly. During the first two months of 1997 the House was scheduled to be in session only fifteen days, four in January and eleven in February. The main items on the agenda for Newt and the leadership were passage of a balanced budget, welfare reform, the fight against drugs and targeted tax cuts. Passing a balanced budget bill in both Houses and getting it signed by the president was critical. They had come close in the 104th Congress and this seemed a good issue on which to test presidential cooperation. It was popular with the people and Clinton lived by the polls—most of the time. Welfare reform was being successfully pioneered by the states and public opinion was building for it too. There was room to work with Clinton on this issue. Everyone was for fighting drugs. How it was to be done and how much it would cost were the difficult issues. Targeted tax cuts were fine with both sides but they differed on the targets. Maybe they could even do something about Medicare. Getting off to a slow start and allowing time for people to work together might prove more profitable than the hectic pace of the 100 days.

---

[39] *The Washington Post*, 24 February 1997, 10.
[40] *The Weekly Standard*, 23 December 1996, 6.

The Republicans, who differed widely about their agenda, thought one needed to be agreed on. "We need to spend less time examining our navels and more time examining our agenda," said one. "I'm certainly concerned that the Williamsburg retreat needs to focus more on the actual agenda and the issues," noted GOP Representative Ernest Istook.[41] The problem was that in the 104th Newt drove the agenda by will and force of personality. He was the strategist who had brought the revolution and his troops followed him. Two years of troubles, attacks and missteps had taken their toll. Blind following was not the order of the day anymore. Faith was lacking in his judgment and his management ability.

By the end of February it was evident that Newt was more focused on self-renewal than on leading the majority in the House. "The disarray among House Republicans has been evident in recent weeks. They mustered fewer votes for term limits than they did two years ago. They saw forty-four of their colleagues defect to help President Clinton win release of foreign aid for family planning groups. They also could not push a constitutional amendment to balance the budget out of the Judiciary Committee, "even though it is a cornerstone of their agenda," reported the *Washington Post*.[42] The newspaper predicted that if Newt could not regain his confidence and that of the House GOP then he might not make it through the year as Speaker. As summer approached Newt did get his self-confidence but was not able to pull the party into the unified machine it had been during the first 100 days.

Party factionalism was probably most evident in the emergency relief bill designed to aid the victims of the Red River flooding in the spring of 1997. The flood was substantial with whole towns in North Dakota and Minnesota being wiped out by the deluge. There was bipartisan support for the relief effort and the president was ready to sign it. In a classic example of overplaying their hand and underestimating the enemy the Republicans managed to turn this humanitarian effort into a public relations disaster.

Because President Clinton wanted the bill the Republicans thought they might tack on an item or two that he did not want and still have him sign it. They figured it would look bad for him if he did not sign a

---

[41] *The Hill*, 29 January 1997, 16.
[42] *The Washington Post*, 24 February 1997, 10.

relief bill. One would have thought that they would have remembered his veto leading to the shutdown less than two years before. He vetoed it but was able, in the press and the public mind, to blame the Republicans for the shutdown.

One faction of the party wanted to add a provision to the spending bill, officially a supplemental appropriations bill, that would require the Census Bureau to use actual enumeration of the population as required by the Constitution. Noting that actual enumeration always resulted in millions not being counted for one reason or another, the Democrats wanted to replace that method altogether and substitute instead statistical adjustments or projections. Large urban areas, the usual victims of an undercount, would have benefited greatly by the statistical approach. The Democrats thought this would help them count more people who were most likely to be their voters. This would be especially helpful to them when the lines would be drawn for the legislative reapportionment resulting from the 2000 census.

The Republicans were not sold on this idea. First, it would threaten their number of seats in both congress and in state legislatures. Second, with political appointees doing the statistical analysis there would be room for all manner of corruption. Given their experience with the Clinton-Gore administration's willingness to use government agencies for partisan political purposes they could anticipate similar behavior in the census count. Third, it was unconstitutional. The Constitution specifically required that the census be taken by actual enumeration. No ghosts and no guessing was allowed. The Republicans felt they were on the high ground on this issue, defense of the Constitution versus partisan tinkering with the census.

A second issue, pushed hard by a group of Republican senators, was passage of a continuing resolution to keep the government running at the previous year's level in case of a presidential veto of the budget. This would make sure there was no shutdown of the government the next time the budget came up for signing. It would also take away a great weapon from the president's arsenal of anti-GOP weapons. Having been through the unpleasantness of being blamed for the last shutdown many Republican House members agreed with the senators on that issue.

The Republican leadership looked at both issues and approved adding them to the supplemental spending bill. Newt and the other leaders thought this would work because they were convinced Clinton wanted and would sign the bill, even with the additions. It had originated as a bill to provide additional funds for US peacekeeping troops in Bosnia and the floor relief was tacked on as a needed addition. "We were walking ourselves, not for the first time, to the edge of a political precipice," remembered Newt. He explained, "One of our greatest weaknesses has been to undertake things one at a time, without giving enough consideration to what comes next."[43]

One looks back and wonders how Newt and the leadership could have failed to remember what Clinton did to them last time. How could they not have understood that the census restrictions and the continuing resolution were as politically important to him as was the money for Bosnia and the flood? Though some would argue with his observation, Newt explained, "It's not that we were stupid, it's that we were simply too focused on our own intentions and not sufficiently mindful of our opponents. Somehow...we talked ourselves into believing that the Democrats could be bluffed into acting according to our scenario."[44]

"Among our several miscalculations, in some ways the most dangerous of all, was to underrate the communications prowess of William Jefferson Clinton. Give the man a victim, and he can bring a lump to your throat and a tear to your eye. And if you add to that the opportunity to charge the Republican Congress with some villainy or other, he will positively go into overdrive."[45] The master of political spin was going to tell the American people that Newt and his henchmen were playing politics, for partisan political advantage, with money needed for our troops in the field and for devastated flood victims who had nowhere else to turn. There would be interviews with these victims and stories of their suffering on the nightly news. The president would "feel their suffering" and be saddened by the partisan Republicans' efforts to deny them the help they so desperately needed.

Representative Bob Livingston, chairman of the Appropriations Committee and his counterpart in the Senate, Pete Domenici, did everything they could to make them understand that it would not play out the way they thought. Clinton had a long history of vetoes both as a governor and as president. The road they were taking would lead to

---

[43] Newt Gingrich, *Lessons Learned the Hard Way*, pp. 140-141.

[44] Ibid., pp. 144-145.

[45] Ibid., 146.

"defeat and major embarrassment," they were warned. Domenici must have thought he was playing with amateurs as Livingston shouted, screamed, beat his fist on the table and angrily warned of the disaster that lay ahead.

Why did not Newt, Armey and the rest listen to the warnings they were being given? "We House Republicans had gotten into the habit of trying to will things to happen. This time the Republican party, however weary and bruised and gun-shy some of its House members had become, would nevertheless continue to be dominated by those of us who still believed unconditionally in the power of the will. We outlasted our more sober and calculating colleagues in setting the stage for the supplemental appropriations fight," wrote Newt.[46]

The leadership was divided on the bill. Some wanted no additions but one that was clean and took care of the troops in Bosnia and the flood victims period. Some wanted only one addition, the census or the continuing resolution and not the other. Others wanted both added. In addition some members wanted the total amount cut back because they thought it was too extravagant. Others were not bothered about the amount but wanted to know where the money was coming from and to put its source in the bill in order to make sure the president was not coming up with another budget buster.

It all played out as Livingston said it would. The president made his points. The nightly news paraded sad flood victims wondering why they were not being helped and showed brave American soldiers doing their duty in faraway Bosnia. Gingrich and his crew tried to explain the census problem and show why the continuing resolution was important. Victims and soldiers always win over political talking heads. This led to more frustration among the GOP members. Heated debates broke out again and again. It got so bad that the Speaker finally acted decisively. "I simply overruled my associates," he said. He dropped both additions to the bill and said it should be passed with the amount the president requested. In the end they gained nothing but bad publicity and gave Clinton the opportunity to look presidential and statesmanlike.

"Newt did not realize how exhausted he was, and how exhausted we were and he had really lost some moral authority that would take some time to regain," remembers Christensen. Arne went on to de-

---

[46] Ibid.

scribe the confusion and lack of leadership in the Republican conference. "If there was not proper leadership in the conference then it tended to walk around disorganized. So what had happened was disillusion in the leadership."[47] Even those in the leadership, Armey, DeLay, Boehner and Paxon, were concerned enough that the rebellious freshmen and anti-Newt faction thought they had their support in a move to make a change and remove Gingrich.

Newt had angered and puzzled many of his supporters in a number of ways. His embracing of Jesse Jackson, his suggestion that a balanced budget might take precedence over a tax cut and his decision to cut his losses and agree to the president's relief bill without even telling the leadership what he was doing did nothing to maintain their support. When the vote came for the bill the leadership led a planned demonstration of opposition to Newt by voting against the bill. "Disaster Bill Disaster Engulfs House GOP" read the headlines. One of the more rebellious sophomores, Lindsey Graham, noted they were "no longer willing to turn our fate over to the leadership. We're no longer like children."[48]

Having announced that they were no longer "like children," the small group of renegades who wanted to oust Newt, continued to act like unruly teenagers. An anonymous letter was circulated to GOP House members calling for a vote of confidence in Newt's leadership. Citing Gingrich's mistakes the letter concluded, "We cannot sustain such blunders any further." Plotting sessions were begun, the first on 17 June, to decide on a course of action and build support for that action.[49] "House GOP Rebels Meet on Newt's Fate," read the headlines in the next day's *The Hill*. The article spoke as much about the rebels' meetings with Armey as they did about the meeting itself. Clearly the majority leader was less than supportive of his Speaker and the rebels had the impression that he was open to working with them though no specific actions were taken at that point. The rest of the leadership was also taking note of the anti-Newt activity and wondering how serious it was and what role, if any, they should play in it.

"I think there are some who believe we could have a better leader. I think there are people who get disgruntled. But I doubt if you could

---

[47]Christensen, interview, 1998.

[48] *Roll Call*, 42:48 (16 June 1997): 1.

[49] *The Atlanta Journal*, 17 June 1997.

find eight people who'd be willing to sit in a room and agree on replacing me," said Newt.[50] He was wrong. DeLay was concerned that Newt had not told the leadership about his decision on the disaster bill. He was also upset that after they conspired to vote against him and embarrassed him by publicly rejecting his leadership on that disaster vote he responded by acting as if nothing had happened. They wondered if he cared enough anymore to do what it took to lead. "You know, a month ago I voted against [Newt] and brought the ruler down. We met in Newt's office and he did not even get mad. He did not even care about what I had done," Delay told Christensen.[51]

On 9 July the leadership met. Armey said he had "Newt fatigue" and was "not willing to clean up after another one of his messes." Boehner joined in, "We all know Newt is finished. It's just a question of when." DeLay and Paxon were supportive of that tone. The next day the four met in Paxon's office. It was decided to contact the renegades and see how serious they were about removing Newt. DeLay was chosen to meet secretly with them and see how far they were willing to go and to assess their strength. Meeting in Representative Lindsay Graham's office, the renegades posed the idea of using the motion to vacate the chair as a method of removing Newt without having to go through the GOP conference. Knowing they could not get the conference to remove Newt they thought they might work with the Democrats to do it on the House floor.[52] DeLay left the meeting thinking the renegades were serious and they left thinking they had the full support of Armey, DeLay, Boehner and Paxon. DeLay returned to the other three meeting in Paxon's office where they plotted until after 2:00 A.M. About this time Representative Chris Shays, a moderate who had raised questions about the ethics problems faced by Newt at the first of the year, was approached by the renegades to join them. He refused to join and instead went to Newt with news of the plotting going on around him.

Later, after reflection and in hindsight, Newt was philosophical about the coup. At the time it happened he was hurt and angry. He

---

[50] Ibid., 27 June 1997.

[51] Christensen interview, 13 November 1998

[52] *The Hill*, 16 July 1997. Sandy Hume's summary sketch of the coup attempt is an excellent look at poor judgment and ambition being overcome by ineptness on the part of the leadership.

had never really trusted DeLay, who ironically turned out to be the most honest of the bunch. Paxon was like a younger brother and held his total trust though Evans and Rachel Robinson, Newt's personal assistant, warned him of Paxon early on. "I knew in three minutes that Paxon was disloyal," said Evans. They saw Paxon as devious and ambitious to the point that he would betray Newt if it would advance him. Lacking personal advantage, he would keep his wagon hitched to Newt as he did in the December/January Speakers fight. "DeLay is not smart enough or ambitious enough to [plan a coup] on his own," said Evans. Still, "Newt did not respect him enough [and]...he is a very, very, good whip" and deserved that respect.[53] Armey and Boehner had suffered numerous slights from Newt and both were ambitious men. Having been tested in the nastiness of academic politics Armey knew how to play the game and few on Newt's staff were surprised to hear he was involved in the coup attempt. He must have been upset when Newt urged Livingston to stay on and possibly become the next speaker. Armey viewed himself, as majority leader, as the heir apparent. If Newt's removal was in the cards then there was no reason why he should not benefit. Newt was angry with Boehner and DeLay. He was hurt to find out that Armey and Paxon were involved. He and Marianne had been close to both men and their wives. They thought of Paxon and his wife, Representative Susan Molinari, as part of their extended family and their betrayal cut deep.

On Friday morning, 11 July, the four leaders met in Armey's office. During the time between the two meetings Armey found out that the renegades did not have him in mind for speaker. Indeed, they had approached Paxon the last time they challenged Newt. Paxon also was starting to think of himself as the Speaker. Armey covered himself by sending a staff assistant to inform Christensen of what was going on without admitting that Armey was involved. Newt already knew what was happening but not from his "loyal lieutenants." He called an emergency meeting of the leadership early that afternoon and listened to their tales of how they were not encouraging revolt but just meeting with the renegades to see what they were doing and how far they would go. The renegades were meeting in Representative Steve Largent's office and discovering the change of heart on the part of the

---

[53] Evans, interview, 1997.

leadership they were assured backed them only last night. They sent over five representatives to meet with Armey and the others and were told they would not receive backing for their coup attempt, which would never have been taken seriously without the support and encouragement of the leadership. Only a couple of years earlier these men were part of a respected and formidable partnership that was changing America. Now they were part of the sad mentality that seemed to be overtaking their party. A year later the Democrats would have their turn as their party followed in lock step to defend Bill Clinton and serious men like Senator Byrd and Representative Gephardt explained why that was acceptable. For now, however, it was the turn of the Republicans.

Working through hurt, disappointment and anger, Newt understood that it was up to him to stoically bear the emotional burden of betrayal. After venting to his staff he scheduled a "get it off your chest" meeting with the leadership and the renegades. Armey called the renegades "irresponsible and immoral." In turn, they felt betrayed by the leadership calling them "spineless, directionless, craven opportunists who tried to push the troops up the hill but ran at the sight of the first musket." The renegades thought the meeting might lead to improved efforts at communication but did not give up the idea of getting rid of Gingrich. They would just have to be better prepared next time. Speaking in tones David Bonior would envy, one remarked, "When we move against Gingrich, we'll have the gun so far down his throat that there will be no way he'll survive."[54] For the time being, however, they would have to live with the fact that he had once again survived the plotters, was still speaker, and there was no other option but to deal with him.

The next Wednesday, 23 July, Newt called a meeting of the entire conference to have a "truth-telling" session and get it all behind them. "Gingrich forgives prodigal Republicans," wrote Jeanne Cummings about the meeting she describes as "true confessions: The GOP conference recalled an AA meeting or an old-time revival." Each leader in turn spoke to the conference and all but DeLay sought to lay the blame on the renegades and distance themselves from the rebels as best

---

[54] *The Hill*, 16 June 1997, 25.

they could.[55] When Newt spoke he began by reading from the book of Romans. "Remember this was at a time when he was trying to wrap up the balanced budget. There was a lot hanging in the balance and then all of a sudden something happened that threatened to blow it all up. He made clear that he did not want to have retribution. He wanted to stay focused on the issues and in the end he quoted from Romans 12. He basically was willing to ignore what had happened. He is far more generous than I," remembered Christensen.[56] Sonny Bono told a story of an embarrassing incident and said he thought it "was God's way of telling me to forget the past and move on." Newt took the advice and, in retrospect, described the events of the coup attempt as "growing pains in the coming-of-age of a new and very different kind of party. I call it the entrepreneurial party."[57]

Newt was the first to say sincerely that it was time to move on. Still, the members' betrayal hurt. A year later *The Hill* reported in a story entitled "Newt Still Grieves Over Aborted Coup" that Newt felt betrayed. "Those were people I campaigned for. In many cases I got them their committee assignments. I tried to give them the widest possible scope for their talents. I had listened to them, I had met with them. And then you realize that in the end somehow it just wasn't working. It was really, probably the deepest, purest sense of grief that I have had," he said. He talked about feeling the pain of "raw rejection" and how it felt to realize that "a significant number of my friends" were upset enough with him to risk losing the majority in order to remove him. He could forgive but forgetting would be more difficult.[58]

Given the confusion of the ethics struggle and the attempted coups it is a wonder that Newt and the team were able to accomplish anything by the August recess. To the surprise of many the work on the budget was coming to fruition as was the work on Medicare and the tax cuts. The impact of the coup attempt changed the way Newt dealt with his own troops more than it did the way he worked to move needed legislation. He continued to use compromise and give and take to get part of what his troops wanted rather than following the previously unsuccessful way of confrontation. Many were critical of his working

---

[55] *Atlanta Constitution*, 27 June 1997, A4.
[56] Christensen, interview, 1998.
[57] Gingrich, *Lessons Learned the Hard Way*, 163-164.
[58] The Hill, 15 July 1998, pp. 1 & 36.

with the president, some to the point of drawing cartoons of him, and sometimes Senator Lott, as lap dogs to Clinton. Nevertheless, he thought the rest of the year was a productive period. "We continued to make progress as we cut the bureaucratic red tape that was wound around the Food and Drug Administration and so accelerated the much needed distribution of new drugs and new medical technologies," he wrote. "We also launched the universally applauded campaign to overhaul the Internal Revenue Service, along with a nationwide debate about sweeping tax reform."[59] Nineteen ninety-seven was turning out to be a year not only of trials and tribulations but also one of minor triumphs and one major one, the balanced budget amendment. Other observers agreed. In a commentary column in *US News & World Report* Michael Lind suggested that "judging from history, the GOP woes are growing pains, not death throes."[60]

During the recess Newt decided to spend some time on travel and on working on his image. He took time out to go to Montana to dig dinosaur bones and relax with his friend, paleontologist Jack Horner. He also appeared on the Jay Leno show, visited New Hampshire, spoke to veterans groups and helped raise money for a few colleagues and helped build houses for Habitat for Humanity. "A new, improved Newt," editorialized the *Atlanta Constitution*. "Newt the Revolutionary has become Newt the Statesman. Newt the Right-wing Warrior has become Newt the Moderate. The change in his tone and rhetoric is startling." While his old adversary, the *Constitution*, felt sure that it would not last, they nevertheless thought "there's reason to hope."[61]

Presidents in trouble at home have long found that foreign travel helps their image. During the earlier spring break Newt experienced that phenomenon himself on a trip to China. During his years in Congress he had infrequently traveled abroad though he had made some trips when he thought they were policy related. In most cases he sought the information he needed when foreign leaders visited the US or by dispatching his friend and aide, Dr. Steve Hanser, to go in his stead and meet with foreign officials. Hanser's relationship to the speaker was much like that of Harry Hopkins to Franklin Roosevelt. In sessions with Newt prior to leaving on a fact finding trip, Hanser would

---

[59] Ibid. 163.

[60] *US News and World Reports*, 4 August 1997, 28.

[61] The *Atlanta Constitution*, 29 August 1997, A18.

ascertain what information was needed and what message Newt wanted to convey. It was clear that Hanser had Newt's trust and they dealt openly with him. Slovakia, Egypt, Israel, Turkey, and China were some of the countries where Hanser traveled for Newt. His trip to China was especially helpful in preparing Newt for his own journey there in March 1997. Both men were careful not to give anyone the impression that there were two American policies. While understanding clearly that the president and the State Department spoke for American foreign policy Newt thought that there was a constitutional role for the legislative branch to play, especially as related to legislators in other countries.

In March Newt led a congressional delegation on a five nation trip to Asia with the Peoples Republic of China being the centerpiece of the visit. The trip took place within days of Vice President Al Gore's official visit to China. Following the administration's policy, Gore had avoided any critical statements regarding China's behavior toward Taiwan or concerning human rights violations. He had, instead, focused on what might be called China's growing partnership with the US concerning space and business. Gingrich, on the other hand, used the opportunity to "goad China toward change." Speaking at a high-level reception 28 March in Beijing he prodded the Chinese leaders "on a series of sensitive issues, from human rights and the balance of trade to Hong Kong and Taiwanese autonomy."[62] He and his group delivered a list of political prisoners they requested be released and discussed the need for greater religious freedom. At a later meeting vice premier Zhu Rongji raised the issue of Chinese involvement in US elections and denied any such involvement. Newt, who did not dispute Zhu's assertions, noted "there were apparently renegades who were violating both our law and their government" and requested Chinese help in the investigations. He also received assurances from the Chinese that they intended to preserve Hong Kong's capitalist way of life because it was their lifeline to the west.[63]

While speaking to students at the Chinese Foreign Affairs College Newt continued his blunt talk. "China's leadership needs to understand that political freedom must accompany economic freedom," he said, and

---

[62] *The Atlanta Journal*, 29 March 1997, A6.
[63] Ibid.

"we do not see our insistence on freedom — as an inappropriate intrusion into another country's internal affairs. We see it as the greatest gift we can offer the world."[64] In later meetings with the Chinese leaders Newt wanted to make sure there was no misunderstanding about America's commitment to defend Taiwan. Historians have pointed to a misunderstanding about the US commitment to defend Korea as a cause of the Korean war. Newt wanted to avoid any such confusion: "I said firmly, 'We want you to understand, we will defend Taiwan. Period...'" The Chinese did not dispute Newt's contention and assured him that China had no intention of attacking Taiwan. The press favorably compared Newt's "startling bluntness" in talking with the Chinese with the cautious approach taken by the vice president.[65]

Leaving China he traveled to Japan where he spent two days meeting with Prime Minister Ryutaro Hashimoto and Japanese officials and business leaders. Trade issues and concerns over the heavy concentration of US troops on Okinawa were the main topic of discussion. The Japanese were also anxious to hear Gingrich's impressions of his China visit and of his stop in South Korea prior to the visit to Beijing. Leaving Tokyo the group stopped off briefly in Taiwan for a largely symbolic meeting with President Lee Teng-hui where Newt, in private conversations, reaffirmed America's commitment to Taiwan's defense but also urged caution and expressed US interest in China and Taiwan reaching a peaceful solution to their problem.[66]

Arriving back in the US on 2 April Newt enjoyed the best press coverage he had had in over a year. As the obsequious Representative Paxon observed, "This trip is a very positive step forward for our party and for our Speaker. It played to his strengths. It helped many of our members have a clearer understanding of the strengths of the speaker and his ability to articulate the philosophical direction of our party and our country." While his performance in Asia received good reviews his critics, inside and outside the party, and the press quickly returned to a domestic agenda focusing on when he would pay his $300,000 repayment and on the party's failure to develop a strong and aggressive legislative agenda.[67]

---

64 Ibid., 30 March 1997, A6.

65 Ibid., 31 March 1997, A6.

66 *Washington Times* weekly edition, 13 April 1997, 15.

67 Ibid., 1.

The speaker's other foreign trip came in December when he and Marianne flew to London as guest of ARCO Oil Company and spoke at their annual meeting. Their three-day trip was a mixture of business and pleasure. He met with Secretary of Defense William Cohen to discuss US policy toward Bosnia and Iraq, with former Secretary of State Henry Kissinger for an overview of current European policies and with Betty Boothroyd, the Speaker of the House of Commons. He and Marianne also took time for sightseeing. The couple visited the London Zoo, toured Westminster Abbey and had lunch with historian Martin Gilbert, the Churchill biographer.[68] Much was made by the Democrats and the press of their flying over on the Concorde and staying at the upscale Claridges Hotel, the site of the ARCO meeting, as well as the fact that ARCO paid his expenses. [69]

He also had the opportunity to visit with his good friend former Prime Minister Margaret Thatcher. As chairwoman of the Institute of US Studies at the University of London, she had invited him to speak to that group at Lincoln Inn, an ornate medieval hall for London lawyers. Thatcher became Prime Minister just as Newt was entering Congress and he had developed a tremendous admiration for her and her policies. She had long believed, and stated publicly, that America was selling herself short and was too timid in exercising leadership based on its historic agenda of freedom. She encouraged Gingrich to run for president because she thought he was the only politician, in either party, who was capable of running a campaign of hope and opportunity much like the 1980 Reagan campaign.

In Newt's speech, he laid out "a conservative agenda for the new century" calling for "strong US leadership abroad based on sweeping reforms at home." He said the US "must lead." He thought America needed to accept that and "behave accordingly." To Newt that meant that America must learn to lead better, listen better, avoid being a bully and not be dictatorial. He noted that the US already has the technological capacity. To complement that capacity, he said, "we have to have litigation reform, education reform, regulation reform and taxation reform."[70]

---

[68] *The Atlanta Journal*, 5 December 1997, C7.

[69] *The Atlanta Constitution*, 7 January 1998, A3. "Gingrich got ritzy trip thanks to oil company."

[70] Ibid., 6 December 1997, C7.

Most of the reforms he mentioned in England were part of the original Contract with America, but with a different presentation. Newt was working to moderate his public statements and make them sound less angry and threatening. He had called one of his heroes, Coach Joe Paterno, for some advice on leadership and team building back in July after the coup attempt. Paterno told him to slow down, listen better to his troops and his enemies and focus on what was important. He decided to pay attention to the more day to day activities of the House and focus on specific legislation. He personally took over the negotiations with the White House on the balanced budget and tax cuts and later focused on the census problem and blocking aid for international family planning programs that would support or encourage abortion. He listened better. "He's less likely to immediately fire back with an argumentative response. He thinks more before responding," noted one senior House Republican.[71] He also began to lose weight, ultimately losing thirty pounds, and get more sleep and exercise.

The budget deal came in August with both sides gaining something from the compromise. The bipartisan nature of the agreement was accompanied by a photo opportunity as Clinton, Gore and Gingrich joined in a White House announcement. The House also approved an $80 billion multi-year tax cut but saw it go under when the Senate failed to even call it for a vote. He worked with the White House to try to get fast track authority for the president and Most Favored Nation status for China. Though fast track was defeated, largely by the president's own party, Most Favored Nation status was granted to China. Despite some losses, Newt was reclaiming his statesman-like appearance. He avoided being caught by hot issues. He stayed away from his colleague Bob Barr's impeachment petition as his fellow Georgian attempted to remove Clinton. Newt, as speaker, needed to work with the president and as Speaker he thought he needed to stay above the fray in this context. In any case others needed to lead that fight.

Newt did move to reconcile the international family planning programs and accepted health care entitlements for children as part of his "let's get what we can now and the rest later" approach. He helped

---

[71] *The Washington Post*, 15 November 1997, A1.

block the administration's desire for a national testing program for school children and worked to repackage the school voucher program. The Democrats were successful in selling the vouchers as a plan by the GOP to harm public education so he decided to regroup and drop the voucher idea and instead work to provide privately funded scholarships for children caught in dangerous or unproductive schools. He was also successful in working a compromise to let Central American refugees stay in the US and to enable others to get permanent resident status without leaving the country. The latter compromise worked well as a first step to help bring Hispanics back into the GOP. At the end of a hard day of campaigning in four states in twenty-four hours, where he raised over $300,000 for candidates, he landed in Miami where Hispanic immigrants hailed him as a hero. "Hispanics Love Newt" and "The Nicaraguan people will remember you now and always with love" signs and banners greeted him as he came to Little Havana to speak for Representative Lincoln Diaz-Balart.[72]

As the year moved to a close the polls showed that 69 percent of those polled thought the Congress was doing an average or above average job and Newt's personal approval rating began to improve a little. He hit a low in July with just 18 percent approval and now that was up to 24 percent. While the numbers were still not good for Newt they were improvement enough for the press to again start asking about when he would make a decision about running for President in 2000. He told them he and Marianne would make that decision by Labor Day 1999.[73] Representatives John Boehner and Ray LaHood thought his leadership had improved and even one of the renegades, Lindsey Graham, was more sympathetic to his situation: "I'm trying to put myself in his shoes a bit, with all that he's got to deal with I need to be more sensitive to that."[74] In fact, his stewardship of the office had changed enough to allow his Georgia critic, Representative John Lewis, to say, "I think he [Newt] tried in his own way to be a little more accommodating"[75] and to drop his hostility to Newt long enough to suggest that they might have joint book signings.[76]

---

72 *The Atlanta Journal*, 16 November 1997, A8.

73 *Roll Call*, 43:44 (15 December 1997): 6.

74 *The Washington Post*, 15 November 1997, A4.

75 *The Atlanta Journal*, 16 November 1997, A12.

76 Ibid. 25 December 1997, A3.

Gingrich began 1998 with two broad agendas, one political and the other legislative. Newt's political agenda was to raise the money necessary and develop a campaign plan sufficient to guarantee a Republican win in the off-year elections. Keeping the House in GOP hands was the overriding priority. The return of a Democratic majority would, in Newt's opinion, almost certainly result in a renewed tax and spend program of big government so desired by the liberal leadership of the House. Historically, the party not in the White House gained seats during the off-year elections. Newt wanted to make sure 1998 did not break that precedent. Starting on 9 January he began a fourteen day, seventeen state fundraising tour for the party and for individual candidates. He used the tour to preview parts of his legislative agenda, a war on drugs and reform of the IRS. He proposed, after visiting Hollywood, a one-year job suspension for actors and athletes found to use drugs. He also "suggested taking a third of the employees from the Internal Revenue Service and making them drug enforcement agents and erecting a triple fence at key border areas to keep out smugglers." He focused on education problems. In Columbia, South Carolina he proposed their legislature enact legislation requiring that "all fourth-graders be able to read and write and that all contracts for teachers and administrators be rendered null and void if their school routinely falls in the lower fifth on standardized tests." "Focus on the children, not the teachers union, not the principal," he said. "We will be startled at how rapidly our worst schools improve."[77]

Newt had tested this agenda on 3 January at a planning session at his campaign headquarters with state GOP leaders and key supporters. He had talked with his congressional leadership and they wanted to keep the revolution going instead of having it slow down. The agenda was reflective of the contract and was in a way, a second contract. The speaker defined the struggle, not just for 1998 but for 2000 as well. "We want a people centered society and they [the liberals] want a government centered society." He told his supporters he had seen something when, in December 1995, he had been in budget nego-tiations. "When you get down to the core and there ain't nobody else watching, this is who they really are. They are basically committed to big government. They distrust the American people and they believe

---

[77] The *Atlanta Constitution*, 23 January 1998, A4.

in coercion." The Democrats operated on the idea that government knows what is best for the American people. If the people disagree then it is in the best interest of the country that they be made to do what is right. He used the California anti-smoking restrictions as an example of what he meant.[78]

Gingrich thought that if the Republicans could explain this agenda to the American people it would increase turnout at the 1998 and 2000 elections. It needed to be short, simple and vital. He put forth a four point agenda. (1) "We must have a drug free safe America for our children." He advised a World War II type all-out approach designed to guarantee victory. (2) "We should put kids first and advocate lifetime learning." He stressed his commitment to public schools but noted that "some schools are destroying kids." (3) "We should rethink retirement and set up the best and safest system possible, one that you control instead of the government." This would include a good health care delivery system. (4) "We must determine how much government, at all levels, can take out of our income." He suggested twenty-five percent as the proper amount and said the IRS would have to be reformed. The group carried on a spirited discussion of his four points and all stressed the presentation would be critical. Most people would agree with the basic four points. Implementation was the problem and the people had to be satisfied that it would be helpful and not hurtful as the Democrats were bound to claim. The GOP had been stung too often by the claims of attacks on social security and the class warfare assaults by the Democrats.[79]

Newt tested the ideas two days later in a speech to the Cobb County, Georgia Chamber of Commerce. He brought Representatives Bob Barr and Mac Collins along for support and to meet with local leaders. He began by noting the accomplishments of the Republican Congress. In January 1995 a $320 billion deficit was projected. In January 1998 a $32 billion surplus was projected and there had just been twelve months of surplus for the first time in decades. He wondered if this would have been possible if the Democrats had controlled Congress. He called for a national, bipartisan program of adult discussion on where we are going and how we are going to get there. He talked of progress on the

---

[78] 3 January 1998 videotape of planning meeting. UWG Archives, Gingrich Papers.

[79] Ibid.

domestic front in the fight against diabetes and the quick availability of experimental drugs. He praised the Drug Free Community Act and went through the four points of the agenda, which he called Goals for a Generation, to generally good applause. When asked what he would do with the surplus he said they should secure the Social Security and transportation trust funds first. Then some should be used to give a small tax cut each year to get down to the twenty-five percent level advocated in the agenda. When asked about Bosnia and Iraq he was in general support of the president noting that whatever we do we do not want to re-ignite a war there. A congressional delegation had gone over with Clinton and came back with the recommendation that we keep troops on scene to prevent a renewal of the fighting. He was critical of Saddam and said we had to stop him from getting chemical, biological and nuclear weapons of mass destruction. He had no doubt Iraq would use them if they had them. The agenda was a success and the audience was positive in its support.[80]

The agenda, or vision, Newt introduced to the Cobb Chamber sought to reassure Americans that Social Security would be safe while at the same time protecting everyone's retirement system. He wanted to look at the entire retirement package, not just Social Security. He wanted to rethink a system of retirement that would ensure increased rates of returns. He suggested each congressional district should set up retirement commissions to look into the problem noting, "There's no crisis, but there's a long, steady problem unless we invent a better model." Observing that the baby boomers and the generation X kids do not believe Social Security will be there for them, he said, "We can avoid generational warfare if we have a dialogue about creating the best retirement system in the world."[81]

Getting the surplus was critical to all the other projections, especially if tax cuts and saving Social Security were to be accomplished. "I believe unequivocally that our first goal should be to get to surplus and in peace time to stay in surplus. I don't think we should do anything that threatens getting to surplus." He thought we should wait until we have the surplus to spend it, as the Democrats wanted, or to cut taxes, as the GOP wanted.[82] He had already seen how new spending

---

[80] C-SPAN, Cobb Co. Chamber of Commerce meeting, 5 January 1998.

[81] *The Atlanta Journal*, 5 January 1998, 1.

[82] Ibid.

requirements could destroy a budget if one were not careful. The floods and natural disasters took their toll on a budget that had not planned for them as did foreign involvements such as sending American troops to Haiti, Bosnia, Macedonia, Somalia and a half dozen other places needing peacekeepers. While Newt generally supported the president in questions dealing with NATO and situations where US troops were already involved, he was disturbed by the administration's reactive position on most issues. The US seemed to have no plan or program and most of all, no consistency or predictability unless it was one of talking big and then backing down. The president seemed to have serious problems with when and where to use force and this was most disturbing to Newt.

Once his tour was over Newt had to sell his agenda to congress and begin the process of filling-in the specifics. He had avoided partisan attacks while on his travels around the country in the hope that the Democrats would join him in trying to find the answer to part of that agenda. The difficulty was that they started from quite different assumptions about how the solution would develop and whether the answers could be found in government or in the private sector...or a combination. Two things intervened to make that task more difficult. The sexual dalliance Clinton had with a young White House intern, Monica Lewinsky, broke in the media and it seemed briefly that he might have to resign. Within days of the Lewinsky affair's becoming public, Chairman Dan Burton, of the Government Reform and Oversight Committee, issued a subpoena to the First Lady. It called for documents on the "Filegate" affair related to her discussions with attorneys in the past year concerning the unauthorized White House collecting of FBI background files in 1993-1994. Neither event was likely to inspire the president or the First Lady to work with the Republicans but rather tended to put them in a bunker mode or defensive posture.[83]

The Clintons were not the only ones with problems. Keeping peace in his own official family also took some of Newt's time. Ever since the coup attempt in 1997 members of the House leadership had been watching their backs or plotting how to move up. Anticipating trouble, Newt had suggested that all House leaders pledge loyalty to each other to keep the team together. He declared his support for all his team and

---

[83] *The Hill*, 11 February 1998, 1.

Dick Armey seconded the idea stating that, "neutrality equals hostility." Some of the leadership team, however, thought the other members of the conference might see it as a self-serving attempt to "shut out any challenges." "This is a blatant attempt to exclude Bill Paxon from leadership—nothing more, nothing less," noted a Republican aide. Paxon, who "has all the markings of a man steadily plotting his return to the leadership," had been working inside the conference and around the country to develop support for himself as either Majority Leader or Speaker, depending on how things broke.[84] Of course, Newt's own plans regarding his future fueled part of the positioning going on at the time. Was he, or was he not going to run for the presidency in 2000? If he left that would open everything. While he said he would be speaker until 2003, his high profile, rise in the polls and travels around the country seemed to indicate that he was at least considering a run.

Paxon was challenging Armey for the leader's position and now House Appropriations chairman, Robert Livingston, was openly challenging Armey for the speakership in case Newt should step down. The team had been elected just over a month earlier and now they were positioning for an election that was almost two years away. The Republican renegades who had challenged Newt during the coup now wanted him to stay out of the struggle between Paxon and Armey. The irrepressible Lindsay Graham gave his usual warnings and David McIntosh, the Indiana renegade and new leader of the confrontational conservatives who still had ideas of removing Newt, echoed them.[85] The fruit basket turnover was now dropping down to chairmanships. Representative Bill Young declared publicly that he wanted to replace Representative Bob Livingston at Appropriations if he stepped down or moved up.

Newt was upset and irritated at all the choosing up of sides. The Democrats were in some disarray over the President and a lack of direction. The GOP had just won control of the Congress for two terms in a row for the first time in seventy years and had had a great 1997 by sweeping the special elections of that year. They held the mayor's offices of both New York and Los Angeles and a majority of the

---

[84] Ibid., 14 January 1998, 1.

[85] The *Washington Times*, 15 March 1998, 3 and *Roll Call* (12 February 1998): 1.

governorships. He thought that should have been enough to hold them together and gain him some respect. He did all he could to make it clear that he intended to stay as Speaker. He dealt with the renegades by coming out for Armey against Paxon saying that he wanted to keep his team together and could not remain neutral in that struggle. His cause was helped somewhat by Paxon's unexpected announcement that he would not seek reelection to the House. Following his wife's example in leaving congress Paxon left the renegades without a champion. They still had DeLay but his ambition was not sufficient to stir revolt.

By the end of February Gingrich, who was trying to work with the renegades, was of less interest than Clinton. Clinton, in fact, was disturbing the renegades. It seemed that every time the Republicans came up with a new initiative the president would hijack it and claim it as his own if it had any popular appeal. In addition, he had, in their minds, done everything he could do to disgrace the presidency both legally and illegally. He had become a running joke on the late night television shows and had gone from one scandal to another. The Republicans could clearly see what was happening and felt certain that if the American people just knew, just paid attention, they would also agree that he had to be removed. The problem was that poll after poll showed the president stronger and stronger with each new revelation. It seemed to them that the more he did wrong the more the people loved him. It was infuriating and led one Republican to comment, "Can you imagine how popular he'd be if he'd slept with sheep? He'd be over 100 percent."[86]

The renegades were not the only ones taking notice of a possible impeachment. News reports indicated that independent counsel Kenneth Starr was considering sending Congress evidence that might lead to impeachment procedures against the president. Gingrich, who was still trying to work with Clinton, was not anxious to get caught in that quagmire. He had been cautious in his public statements and had advocated the same caution among his colleagues. Privately, he was befuddled. He had watched his own poll numbers nose-dive over relatively mild incidents that were overplayed by the Democrats. By comparison, Clinton's sins were on a much larger scale and over a longer period of time and still his numbers were high. The public

---

[86] *The Hill*, 4 February 1998, 6.

seemed not to be willing to punish him for any of his indiscretions. If punishment was to come it would have to come from Congress.

The first week in February Newt met with several committee chairmen and some of the leadership to discuss the possibility of Clinton's impeachment. They did not want to be caught short if and when Starr handed them the case. Moving as quietly as possible behind the scenes Newt selected Henry Hyde and the House Judiciary Committee as the team to deal with the problem. He cautioned that he had no inside information that evidence was forthcoming but that they should be ready to move if it arrived. He told the group that he would dip into the reserve fund, then at $4.4 million, to fund staff and investigators. Both Newt and the leadership sought to avoid the partisan label that was sure to come as soon as an inquiry began. Both Newt and Hyde had avoided supporting Representative Bob Barr's call for impeachment hearings but now it was time to prepare for that possibility.[87]

As word leaked out about the preliminary impeachment planning the Democrats quickly responded. They began by calling the reserve fund, used to support oversight and investigator committee cost, a slush fund and questioning the motives of the Republicans and denouncing any investigation as partisan. They also began looking at the personal lives of the Republicans and wondering publicly who were they to cast the first stone. The lead Democrat on the Judiciary Committee, John Conyers, began criticism of Starr and his team for leaking information regarding the president and demanded an investigation into the leaks.[88]

The speaker tried to keep focused on legislation and the agenda and off the scandals. He was critical of Clinton but not on the sex scandals. He was "incensed" by the president's treatment of Prime Minister Benjamin Netanyahu of Israel pointing out that the White House was treating the communist Chinese better than the only democracy in the middle east.[89] He questioned the president's request for funding for the International Monetary Fund because of its poor record in the past and the possibility of some of the money being used for supporting abortion programs. "I'm not prepared today to indicate support for the funding

---

[87] *Roll Call* (4 February 1998): 1.

[88] *The Hill*, 4 February 1998, 3.

[89] The *Atlanta Constitution*, 21 January 1998, A3.

in the absence of having hearings that are thorough and timely."[90] He attacked the administration's drug policy as a "hodgepodge of half-steps and half-truths." Calling the president's plan "the definition of failure," he recommended they follow one based on the successful policy followed by Mayor Rudolph Guiliani in New York and reaffirmed his commitment to the anti-drug recommendations that came out of his discussions concerning the goals for a generation agenda.[91] He continued the struggle on census sampling and sought reconciliation with some of his old enemies like John Lewis. Lewis invited Newt to tour a photo exposition on the 1965 Selma march. As they viewed the pictures and talked quietly together Newt commented, "Even when we were in our most partisan and ideologically difficult periods, I don't remember ever seeing John where there wasn't a sense of personal respect even when we were fighting pretty hard about things. I don't have it in me not to admire him." Lewis responded, "I've known him for a long time. I have never, ever had any ill feelings of malice toward him. He's my friend, he's my brother."[92] This was the same "brother" he had attacked so harshly on the House floor that the House voted to silence him. People were amazed.

While Newt was insisting that he would be speaker until 2003 he was nevertheless keeping his options open. He made fundraising trips to Iowa and New Hampshire. He kept his promise to religious conservatives and brought up the school prayer amendment. He took positive steps toward Hispanics by sponsoring a bill allowing Puerto Rico to choose its future, possibly opening the door to statehood. "It was an effort to soften our edge with those voters," said fellow Georgian Representative Jack Kingston.[93] At the same time Newt supported the English only official language bill. He supported tax cuts but not as large as some in the conference wanted. While having some questions he was generally supportive of the president's policy on Iraq. By trying to keep all his options open he upset the renegades and some of his supporters who thought he was too far in front of his troops. Kingston noted that many Republicans were having problems with the use of military force in the Persian Gulf. "I just didn't want the leadership to

---

[90] *The Hill*, 25 February 1998, 28.
[91] *The Atlanta Journal*, 15 February 1998, A3.
[92] Ibid., 13 February 1998, A3.
[93] Ibid., 13 February 1998, A3.

cram a resolution of support down our throats," he said. "Few Republicans say so openly, but they worry that Gingrich's reported interest in the presidency may be driving his 1998 legislative agenda in a direction many in the party would like to avoid, namely the center."[94]

The dissatisfaction exhibited in Washington was also evident back home in the sixth district. At home, as in Washington, there were "pure" Republicans who would rather Newt be true to their cause even if it meant losing the majority. The chairman of the Cherokee County GOP gave up his party office in order to work against Newt and show that he was not a real conservative. A group of Cobb County businessmen began an active search for a replacement. They were encouraged by Speaker Foley's defeat at the polls in the state of Washington and sought to duplicate it in Georgia. They thought Newt was foolish for befriending his enemies, like Jesse Jackson and John Lewis, and had compromised too much with President Clinton. They were also bothered by his assertion that no anti-abortion litmus test should be applied to candidates. While there was little chance of defeating Gingrich, who had a sixty-eight percent approval rating in the district, they could become an irritant and needed to be dealt with. The Cobb County Commission chairman, Bill Byrne, said that it would be foolish to replace the speaker for a newcomer and if that happened the district would be the loser. He and other party leaders were at work to "head off a challenge."[95] While he was not fearful of a challenge he did pay attention and get his campaigners at FONG to become more active and to schedule him into more public events in the district.

He had been active in saving the big Lockheed aircraft plant in Marietta and a number of military bases in Georgia from the base closing ax. He had worked to help solve the regional water problem, pressured the city of Atlanta to clean up its waste dumping into the Chattahoochee River, urging Governor Miller to take over waste water plants if necessary, and to make a park of the river above Atlanta. He "brought home the bacon" for highways and sponsored a high speed rail line between Atlanta and Chattanooga, Tennessee that would become part of a regional system linking Tennessee, South Carolina,

---

[94] Ibid., 7 March 1998, A3.

[95] Ibid., 24 January 1998, 24. See also Mark Sherman, "Counsel's Results Could Be Gingrich's Hot Potato," *Atlanta Journal*, 20 March 1998, A3.

Georgia and Florida. He had worked to help redevelop downtown Atlanta by making a federal building out of Rich's, an old, historic department store and to bring federal money to the colleges and universities in the area. He was very active in a series of charitable activities such as the diabetes foundation, programs for the handicapped and Habitat for Humanity. He was doing all he needed to do at home.

One area that upset his GOP critics was his handling of foreign policy questions. In most cases Gingrich tried to support the president because he thought the country should speak with one voice when it came to foreign policy. The suspicion many had regarding Clinton was that he was using foreign policy and military action to distract from his domestic difficulties. This "wag the dog" policy, added to the lack of any consistent direction in foreign policy, was a cause for serious concern by the speaker. US policy concerning China, Iraq, Israel, Palestine, Ireland, Bosnia and Kosovo were all areas of disagreement between the White House and Congress.

The area of least disagreement was Ireland. President Clinton had worked for a number of years to help bring an end to the discord in Northern Ireland and had some success. Peace in Ireland was welcomed by both parties but there was some feeling that it was too one sided. Newt, whose mother was of Irish heritage, a Daugherty, took a keen interest in the Irish problem. He was careful not to take sides but to treat all visiting Irish dignitaries with equal attention. During the second week of August he led a twenty-eight person delegation to Ireland. He talked with Clinton who thought the trip would be helpful and who was himself going to Ireland three weeks later. "We wanted to communicate strongly that there is bipartisan support from both the legislative as well as the executive branch," Newt said. While there he and the other Congressmen met with representatives from Sinn Fein, the IRA, the Ulster Unionists and Irish Catholics as well as the elected leaders of Ireland. "Our message again and again is very simple: the agreement [the Good Friday accord] is there, it's clear, it needs to be implemented." He said he knew it would be difficult for the pro-Irish republican and pro-British Unionists to support the agreement and avoid violence because extremists on both sides would try to break it. The delegation joined together to help Habit for Humanity, Newt's favorite charity, build a house in Belfast. Some young Irish boys hung around shadowing them as they worked. At the end of the day Newt posed with the boys telling the reporters, "Our visit is really about these boys' future." He also visited the ancestral castle of the O'Doughertys noting, "it was far more emotional than I would have imagined."[96]

While the Irish trip was supportive of Clinton's policy, his visit to Israel was just the opposite. In January Newt had criticized the president for being unrealistic in its demands on Israel and for favoring the Palestinians. "It is totally wrong for some American, sitting in the security of the White House, to prejudge the passion and concerns of the elected prime minister of the only democracy in the region," he said. His impression was that the administration was asking the Israelis to give up some of their security and trust the Palestinians who had a poor record of keeping their word given in previous agreements.[97] He continued this line of thought on 19 May: "When I see an American diplomat suggest to Israeli generals that our understanding of their security needs on the West Bank is better than their under-standing — I'm looking at somebody who's been in fancy hotels too long and out of touch with reality. Israel's right of self-determination has to be defended at all costs, even against the best intentions of some of Israel's friends, including the United States."[98] A week later Newt led a delegation, including Minority Leader Gephardt, to Jerusalem to celebrate Israel's fiftieth anniversary. Meetings were held with Prime Minister Netanyahu, his opponent Ariel Sharon and with Yasser Arafat. Newt, whom Arafat accused of being "the baby of the Isreali lobby in the United States," said he thought the State Department was, and had been, pro-Arab and that it was pressuring the Israelis to give up security for promises. He suggested that the US might consider a $1 billion request to pay for security needs incurred by giving up land to the Palestinians. He said he wanted Arafat to understand that he could not use the US to unrealistically pressure Israel.[99] His meeting with the Palestinian was correct and polite. Newt explained that he wanted to have peace for the entire area and not just for the Jews but that fair

---

[96] *The Atlanta Journal*, 7 August 1998, A3; 12 March 1998, A3; 13 March 1998, A15.

[97] Ibid., 21 January 1998, A3.

[98] *The Washington Times*, national edition, 25 May 1998, 3.

[99] *The Atlanta Journal*, 25 May 1998, A7 and 26 May 1998, A3.

treatment was needed on both sides. Arafat agreed but thought it was the Jews who were not being fair, but he did not press the point.

Newt's outspoken comments caused something of a furor. A State Department spokesman said, "If true, those would be rather stunning comments that would undermine the efforts we're trying to make to advance America's national interest." His recognition of Jerusalem as "the united and eternal capital of Israel" also upset the State Department, though Clinton had signed legislation to that effect. The Democrats expressed concern that he was undermining US policy and his old enemy, the *Atlanta Constitution*, weighed in with an editorial writing that he had undercut Clinton's effort to bring peace by giving "a remarkably destructive speech" to the Israeli parliament. Noting his criticism of 1984 legislation regarding Nicaragua as "dangerous, unpatriotic and unconstitutional," they suggested "The Gingrich of fourteen years ago, his head as yet unmuddled by the scent of power, was in many ways far wiser than the man making headlines today."[100] Some American Jews also expressed concern. A group of 248 American Jews signed a letter saying they thought the efforts by Gingrich, and Gephardt, were hurting the peace process. They were accused of "pandering to the right wing among Jewish people." Robert Goodkind, one of those who initiated the letter, said, "I have been deeply bothered by the effort of the Republicans and some Democrats to use the peace process in a partisan way to advance their own particular interest."[101] Clinton certainly did not see this congressional visit as helpful but both Gingrich and Gephardt defended their actions as reasonable and needed.

A student of modern European history, Gingrich was concerned about the resurgence of socialism in western Europe. The main problem was whether the economies of those countries could sustain the level of benefits and entitlements without economic growth. In addition, he was concerned about the euro, the new European currency, and the probability of its fueling economic crisis in Europe. He had not seen sufficient determination on the part of socialist governments to make hard decisions. He said their leaders "are gambling that as the pressures of that monetary system are brought to bear on the weakest

---

[100] Ibid., 27 May 1998, A1 and *The Atlanta Constitution*, 27 May 1998, A10.
[101] The Hill, 17 June 1998, 3.

parts of their economy, they will somehow find the political will to solve their structural economic problems. If they are right, this will turn out to be a *deus ex machina* of remarkable power." He thought they were approaching it from the wrong direction noting that the US had adopted a single currency only after it had clearly established a single national economy. He pointed out that the US had created more jobs in the last two months of 1997 than had been created in Europe in ten years and suggested that the United Kingdom might want to join NAFTA instead of the European Union.[102]

The real foreign problem Gingrich had with the administration was its approach to China. While Newt agreed on keeping China as a most favored nation trading partner, he was concerned about the seeming inability of Clinton or Gore to criticize the Chinese government for anything. It became quite clear that China was obtaining illegal missile technology from America and the administration was very careful in dealing with the issue. A Congressional Research Service report detailed twenty-one possible Chinese violations of restrictions on transferring missile technology, chemicals or atomic materials to Pakistan and Iran since 1992. The administration applied sanctions in only two cases.[103]

Matters came to a head when India successfully conducted their own nuclear test in May. The administration quickly talked of applying sanctions to India but many, including Newt, wondered if the administration's willingness to give missile technology to China might not have forced India's hand on testing. India pleaded that she had a right to protect herself when her neighbors were obtaining nuclear arms. Noting the administration's action that allowed American companies to provide the Chinese expertise to improve their ballistic missile systems, Gingrich said, "The president seems perfectly comfortable waiving the sale of missile secrets to the Chinese. If the actions of the Clinton Administration are even indirectly responsible for spurring India's nuclear detonations, this would be a very serious matter." What really upset Newt was the possibility that Clinton and Gore had gone easy on the Chinese because of illegal foreign contributions to the Democrats in the 1996 elections. It was clear that they had gone to extraordinary

---

[102] *The Washington Times*, national edition, 27 April 1998, 24.
[103] *The Atlanta Journal*, 14 May 1998, A10.

lengths to avoid turning over documents to a Senate investigating committee and almost everyone involved had convenient lapses of memory or, as in the case of Chinese nationals, fled the country.[104] The polls showed that most people thought the administration did take illegal money from the Chinese for technology. The late night television shows made jokes about it regularly and even the cartoonists raised the question. Newt, like so many, thought "What is the country coming to when people joke about the President selling secrets to the Communists?"

While it was a joke to talk show hosts and cartoonists it was dead serious to Gingrich. The *New York Times* reported that satellite technology with military applications had been sold to the Chinese. The information came from administration documents withheld from Congress. Even the Democrats seemed concerned. Senators Joe Biden, Daniel Patrick Moynihan and Bob Kerrey all thought it was serious. Senator Biden said, "It bothers me, quite frankly; this is serious stuff, and it should be pursued." Gingrich, after conferring with the House leadership, decided to appoint a select panel to investigate the matter. "This is a national security matter," he said. "[Reports] of the Chinese military's effort to infiltrate the American political system are so serious that they require the legislative branch to get at the facts immediately."[105] He said the committee would investigate "everything to do with Indonesia and China. It's such a big list. I think this president has to prove that he was not influenced by the Chinese, that he did not give them military secrets and that the United States has not been undermined for campaign money." He announced that he would appoint Representative Chris Cox to head the five Republican and three Democrat panel. While agreeing that the matter needed investigating,. Gephardt protested the appointment of a special committee saying that there were enough standing committees to take care of the problem. Nevertheless the committee was appointed and almost immediately ran into the same problem other committees had faced when dealing with the White House, stonewalling and convenient lapses of memory. Almost everyone but Attorney General Janet Reno saw something was wrong here but getting to it would not be easy. In March 1999 it was

---

[104] Ibid.

[105] *The Washington Times*, national edition, 25 May 1998, 3.

revealed that the Chinese had received top secret information from our nuclear facility at Los Alamos and the administration knew about it but covered it up until after the 1998 elections.

Knowing it and proving *quid pro quo* were two different matters.

Chinagate, as it quickly came to be called, was only part of what needed investigating. For three months Newt said little about Starr's investigation of the president. Toward the end of April, however, it became clear that the Democrats intended to do all they could to protect the president. Representative Henry Waxman, the ranking Democrat on the House Government Reform and Oversight Committee, led all his colleagues in a vote to deny immunity to four witnesses who were about to testify about Democratic fund-raising problems. This decision effectively prevented their testimony after the Justice Department had agreed to give them immunity. "The time has come to draw a line in the sand," said Newt. Newt went on to tell reporters that they intended to get to the bottom of the scandal concerning illegal contributions from Indonesia and China even if they had to tie it to International Monetary Fund funding for Indonesia.[106]

On a western fundraising trip he said the White House is about to "sink all of us in a sea of cynicism. The American people deserve to know the truth, and to say no one is above the law is the minimum duty of the speaker of the House." He suggested that Secret Service agents should testify if it is about lawbreaking commenting, "We are being forced inch-by-inch to break through the stone wall and the cover-up by the White House." The president's press secretary, Mike McCurry responded, "As soon as he comes back to his senses, we'll do business" and wondered if this might not just be Newt playing to the right wing of his party to insure his base. He later corrected himself and said the White House would do business with the speaker. There was too much to do indicating that Clinton would continue to do the business of the country even if Newt was playing politics.[107]

Having been the subject of the politics of personal destruction, Newt warned his colleagues on the Hyde Committee that they "lack the staff to go head-to-head with Democrats and their vicious attack machine." He wondered if they were ready to handle an investigation of this

---

[106] *The Atlanta Journal*, 30 April 1998, A4.

[107] Ibid., 29 April 1998, A3 and 3 May 1998, A3.

magnitude and said each of the GOP leaders should be "prepared for the Democrats to dig through their personal garbage. Democrats will sully reputations, dig into our pasts, and destroy people. Part of our responsibility is being prepared for that and being ready to respond." Already Chairman Burton and Majority Leader Armey had come under attack for past transgressions.[108]

"I'm just sick of the Democrats spinning everything," said Newt. "But the American people are not going to be denied the truth by a bunch of cover-up Democrats in Washington. I believe most Democrats in the country want the truth. It's only the Washington Democrats that are being sucked up into cover-up and corruption." The problem for Newt and the Republicans was that most Americans already knew the truth, wanted the president to stay in office anyway, and did not want the Republicans to bring out all the sordid details. The 19-0 vote by Waxman and his colleagues to deny immunity to witnesses who might have damaging testimony against the Democrats angered Newt. The American people, however, responded to Democratic spin and considered the Republicans as the partisan participants and took a "so what" attitude toward the 19-0 vote. He had just written, in his new book, *Lessons Learned the Hard Way*, that a major mistake was underestimating Clinton and the White House when it came to spin.[109]

Chairman Burton did not help matters by releasing part of the Lewinsky testimony and withholding some sections that appeared favorable to the president. Newt was furious. This gave the Democrats something else to focus the people's attention on besides the president's conduct. He chastised Burton before the conference and said he should be embarrassed to have been so sloppy.[110] He also began to focus more on the Starr report and the investigation Hyde and his committee would conduct to determine if there was sufficient evidence to warrant an impeachment trial.

Gingrich continued to be noncommittal concerning the president's guilt or innocence and urged his GOP colleagues to do the same. Hyde echoed that by saying, "It is our constitutional duty to provide a fair, full and independent review of these facts in their proper context."

---

[108] *Roll Call* (23 April 1998): 1.

[109] *The Washington Times*, national edition, 4 May 1998, 3 and *The Atlanta Journal*, 5 May 1998, A17.

[110] *The Atlanta Journal*, 6 May 1998, A10; *Roll Call*, (7 May 1998): 1.

Newt did tell a Heritage Foundation audience though, "We have the spectacle in Washington today of the president frankly as defendant-in-chief."[111] While critical of the tactics and spin used by the White House, Newt continued to withhold public judgment regarding the president's guilt or innocence. He said he thought "only a pattern of felonies and not a single human mistake should constitute grounds for an impeachment inquiry. You cannot render any judgment until you have given the president a chance to respond and given the Judiciary Committee a chance to do its job." He insisted on doing it by the book. When the White House and the Democrats sought to short-circuit the process through a censure resolution he responded, "For anybody to talk about doing anything before we finish the investigative process simply puts the cart before the horse. We need to proceed in an orderly and fair manner." He said, "This is not political, it's not partisan. This is constitutional." Hyde agreed, "The decision about cutting a deal is very, very premature."[112] Sticking with the process, however, was going to cost the Republicans in November.

The possible mishandling of the impeachment process was not the only problem facing the GOP in November. The party was in the process of balkanizing itself as each special interest demanded that it not only be heard but that its agenda be put forth. The Christian right thought they had been taken for granted much too often. Allegiance was pledged to their agenda, prayer in school, anti-abortion legislation, anti-gay and pro-family bills, abolition of the National Endowment of the Arts, etc., but once Republicans were elected they pursued an agenda of lowering taxes, balancing the budget and regulatory reform. In addition, the cultural conservatives felt the party did not give proper support to their candidates while asking for their support for mainstream candidates. Senate Majority Leader Lott and Speaker Gingrich were criticized for failing to challenge Clinton. "What we see is Clinton, Gingrich, and Lott appear to be together on most issues," Eagle Forum's Phyllis Schafly said. James Dobson and Gary Bauer, spokesmen for the cultural conservatives, met with the GOP leaders, including Gingrich, but were not mollified. They seemed to have little interest in voting for Republicans who, in their opinion, were little

---

[111] *The Atlanta Journal*, 19 August 1998, A4 and 7 June 1998, A3.

[112] Ibid., 24 August 1998, A7; 13 September 1998, C4; 23 September 1998, A1 and A14.

better than the Democrats. Indeed, the situation was serious enough that it threatened the elections in November as the *Washington Post* noted in a article entitled, "The GOP IS Coming Apart at the Seams." If the Christian Coalition decided to sit on their hands the results could be disastrous and cost the GOP the House.[113]

To complicate matters, if the GOP pushed the religious right's agenda too rigorously they ran the risk of alienating business and corporate backers who provided much of the funding for the party and for individual candidates. The businessmen were interested in trade. Ethical and religious amendments to trade bills, such as anti-abortion amendments, would, they thought, endanger that trade. The hostile treatment the tobacco industry received also bothered them as they wondered who was next.[114]

Added to this disturbing mix was the problem of the "new and improved" renegade group who had sparked the coup attempt of 1997. They were a little more mature, had learned "to cut deals without cutting principles" and were better able to manipulate legislation. They seemed less interested in falling on their swords, especially since their numbers had dwindled after the 1996 elections, and in trying to obtain unachievable goals all at one time. Legislation that gave them part of what they wanted now and the rest later was no longer anathema to them. Because the GOP majority was only twenty-two seats they were able to have much of their agenda included by threatening a bloc vote and by occasionally allying with the moderates. They had attempted a coup once, voted against the leadership on critical issues on more than one occasion and had no problem with public criticism of Newt and his leadership team. Representative Livingston now had their support for speaker instead of Armey or Paxon. They were a constant and unapologetic burr under the speaker's saddle.[115]

Another burr was the moderate group of Republicans who were described as "people who tend to hold up their issues as being more important than the principles that 95 percent [of the GOP conference] are for." They represented liberal or mostly Democratic districts, and with some frequency, voted with the Democrats against the leadership, sometimes on critical votes. With only an eleven-seat margin their

---

[113] *The Washington Post*, national edition, 6 April 1998, 13.

[114] Ibid., 22 June 1998, 10.

[115] Ibid., 13 April 1998, 13.

defection had cost the Republicans several pieces of legislation including the Paycheck Protection Act, the Fairness for Small Business Act and two anti-affirmative action amendments. Some, like Chairman Jim Leach, had even voted against Gingrich for Speaker. Newt was reluctant to discipline a member for voting his conscience or the interest of his district. He also knew he could not let this continue if he was to be an effective leader. It was time to take another lesson from his old enemy, Georgia's Speaker Tom Murphy, and make sure those who opposed you on vital issues knew there was a price to pay.[116]

Representative Robert Ehrlich, a Gingrich loyalist, led a group that met with the speaker to insist that those who "routinely buck the leadership on key votes" be punished for their actions. While none thought that a member should be forced to go against his or her conscience they should not expect to be rewarded for that behavior. If they held leadership positions, such as chairmanships of committees or subcommittees then they should be removed. Plum assignments should be withheld from those not in those positions. How could anyone expect to lead if they are voting against the interest of the majority of those they are leading? They also wanted to set conference rules to discourage members from signing discharge petitions. Newt too was concerned about the number of Republicans who had joined the Democrats in signing discharge petitions to force campaign reform bills to a vote. Newt and the leadership saw these bills as favoring labor unions at the expense of business groups and individual PACS and wanted reform to cover labor as well as business. A vote against the bills would be seen as a vote against reform so they were reluctant to let them come to the floor for a vote preferring to wait for a bill covering all groups. Leaders, like DeLay, as well as rank and file members, questioned Gingrich's resolve to do something about the problem. "These guys get plum committee assignments, and then they screw the [conference] on these key votes," they reminded Newt. "The question is, will the Speaker do something about it?" One staff member, expressing his boss' frustration, said, "We are losing our definition as a party because we can't pass things that are philosophically easy votes, like the Paycheck Protection Act and the small business bill. Something must be done."[117]

---

[116] *Roll Call*, (25 May 1998): 1.
[117] Ibid.

Newt understood and appreciated the concerns of the Ehrlich group. He shared their views on the subject. The problem was that he really believed in the right of members to vote their consciences and was loath to appear to be punishing someone for doing just that. He was also concerned about his image as a mean-spirited bully forcing people to do things his way. The Democrats had disciplined members for decades but he knew they would be quick to condemn him for the same behavior. Transportation chairman Shuster had used highway funding to reward his friends and punish his foes thus creating turmoil within the conference and the leadership. If Newt went with the Ehrlich group he would be viewed as doing the same on a larger scale. His public image was important but more important was his effectiveness as the Speaker. Ehrlich came to see him on 18 June and brought with him a petition demanding that high-ranking GOP members who vote with the Democrats on certain votes be punished. Newt signed the petition and within twenty-four hours it had over 100 other signatures. This confirmed his intent to create a formal system to punish Republicans who opposed the leadership on key votes. Gephardt and the Democrats were preparing to file discharge petitions to force votes on their health care, tobacco and minimum wage bills. It was time to make sure Republicans understood the cost of embarrassing the leadership and the party on key votes that might weaken them in November's elections.[118]

The elections were clearly on Newt's mind. He had formulated his "goals for a generation" agenda as the engine to carry the GOP through November. He worked to change his own personal image so it would not be a millstone around the party's neck nor his own if he decided to enter the presidential race. After his harsh comments concerning the president and the Democrats in April his pollsters, Linda DiVall and Frank Luntz, warned him that the politics of anger was out and his attacks were not going over well with the public. He immediately shifted and soften his rhetoric and was introduced to Stanford University students as the "kindlier, gentler, thinner Newt."[119] A few days later he spoke to the New Hampshire legislature in what he

---

[118] Ibid., 22 June 1998, 1.

[119] Rebecca Carr, "Gingrich Softens Rhetoric..." A3, *The Atlanta Journal*, 2 May 1998, and Judy Holland, "Gingrich's Angry Tone," *The Atlanta Journal*, 15 May 1998, B3.

considered a gentler tone. He avoided the president's sexual indiscretions and focused on the future of America. At one point, however, he was critical of the uncooperative attitude of the White House and mentioned specifically the Webb Hubble case and the possibility of payoffs to prevent harmful testimony. The New Hampshire Democrats criticized him for "descending into the muck" and walked out *en masse*. The thinner Newt was there but the kindlier, gentler one was not in evidence according to the Democrats. He quickly understood that any criticism of the White House or any of the Democratic scandals would result in attacks on him from the Democrats.[120]

While he understood that the excess of corruption and scandal produced by the White House and Democrats offered an opportunity for the GOP to take the moral high ground he was not sure how to do it. He vowed to mention the Democratic scandals, not the Clinton sexual ones, at every opportunity to try to tie scandal and Democrats together just as the Democrats had linked Republican and Depression, via Hoover, for two generations. Democrats were just as determined that the Clinton/Gore scandals would not rub off on the party to the GOP's advantage. First, they condemned the president's sexual escapades as shameful and quickly noted that they did not rise to the level of impeachment. Second, they said Clinton only did what any man would do in lying about sex and sought to focus the public mind on sex and personal behavior instead of genuine corruption. "If you had been in Clinton's situation what would you have done?" they asked. "Do you want people looking into your sex life and making it public?" Third, they investigated the personal lives of the Republican leaders and those calling for investigations or impeachment and made public any indiscretion in an attempt to make them look no better than the president when it came to this kind of behavior. "Everyone does it," they said. Finally, they campaigned to picture the special prosecutor, Starr, and the Republicans as holier than thou extremists who had gone too far, were mean-spirited and wanted to hurt children and the elderly while they gave tax breaks to their rich supporters. While noting that it was spin and largely untrue, the press still reported it with a straight face and mostly unchallenged. Gingrich and the Republicans did not

---

[120] Ibid., 8 May 1998, A3.

have a chance against this well-oiled spin machine backed by the president's unrivaled ability to sway public opinion. Newt understood what was coming; he had warned his colleagues to get prepared for it, but was unable to stop it. When faced with a league of Democratic scandals they would find at least one Republican one, trumpet it and declare that everyone was guilty of bipartisan corruption and reform was needed. The problem they said, as they sought to deflect the spotlight, was that they could not get the greedy Republicans to agree to reform.

By September Newt had begun to actively focus on the election. He had hoped to make his "goals for a generation" the centerpiece of a national debate on the election. The Democrats had little interest in helping him on this venture. If the problems facing Social Security, Medicare and retirement programs were solved they would be deprived of a time-tested weapon against the Republicans. The Republican pollster, Luntz, had warned in May that attacking the president on moral grounds was acceptable but it had to be done more with sadness, in subdued tones, rather than in negatively angry tones which are likely to communicate extremist impressions to the electorate. The ideal campaign would be to campaign on issues and the GOP record and avoid making Clinton's character a campaign theme. Character could be mentioned, but not as the major theme. A moral approach would almost certainly be interpreted as a personal, mean-spirited attack on his private sex life and this, the pollster warned, was a loser for the GOP.[121] The problem was how to balance character and issues. To many cultural conservatives the president's character *was* an issue. The polls showed most Americans did not agree.

By the end of the summer many Republicans were worried about the possibility of losing the House. Some GOP strategists warned that only the base vote of each party turned out in off-year elections. If history was any example that meant that Newt and his team should work to turn out their base vote and not be too concerned about moderates and independents. The key, they said, was to excite the core conservatives and get them to turn out. Newt understood this message. Failure to turn out conservative supporters had, to a large degree, caused Senator Mack Mattingly to lose his close election to a liberal

---

[121] *The Hill*, 20 May 1998, 15.

Democrat in Georgia in 1986. Newt himself had experienced this in 1990 when he came very close to losing to David Worley. Other strategists said that this was a year of close elections and many key swing contests. In that situation the moderates and liberals were important and a partisan, ideological campaign designed to turn out the faithful would turn off the moderates who would then turn to the Democrats.[122]

In June Ken Rudin was predicting "a historic Dem pickup, but the GOP will keep control."[123] A few weeks later Dick Morris wrote that the "Republicans will expand their margins in both Houses in November."[124] Newt's personal expert, Joe Gaylord, who had predicted the 1994 victory district by district, agreed with Morris and said it could go as high as a thirty seat pickup in the House. The Democrats were nervous and privately hoped to hold down the number of new GOP seats, hardly thinking they had a chance to actually gain seats. Newt understood this. History and everything he was hearing and reading seemed to justify that outcome. He had no serious thought about the Republicans actually losing seats. His challenge, as he saw it, was to maximize the number of seats that would be added. How could he balance the moral character question with a presentation of the issues that would appeal to both the moderates and independents and at the same time appeal to the Republican base to be sure they would turn out?

He had worked hard at raising money for the party for a year and the coffers were filling up. In the last eighteen months he had raised $4.8 million and spent almost that much in his national campaign to elect more Republicans. He was pleased that almost 70 percent of that money came from contributions of less than $200 because that meant that they would probably turn out to vote. The Democrats, on the other hand, almost reversed those numbers with around 60 percent of their donations coming from big givers.[125] He could raise the money to put the ads on television. The problem was what message those ads would convey. In June the House voted to scrap the tax code, a popular anti-IRS issue almost everywhere Newt went. He was working on women's

---

[122] *Roll Call*, (7 May 1998): 8.

[123] *The Hill*, 17 June 1998, 29

[124] Ibid., 22 July 1998, 14.

[125] *The Atlanta Journal*, 10 June 1998, C2 and 18 July 1998, A7.

issues by making sure women were well represented in the leadership of the GOP conference and by supporting one of those leaders, Conference Secretary Deborah Pryce (OH), when she founded VIEW PAC to aid female GOP candidates regardless of ideology. He also asked her to oversee the House's tobacco and childcare bills. He and the leadership were listening to women on how to better communicate with women. GOP efforts to involve women even impacted on the Democratic women. Representative Louise Slaughter commented, "The party's [Democrat] taken the women's vote for granted. When you look at the Republicans, in comparison, it's really astounding."[126] He was openly courting Hispanics through legislative action and personal appearances. "Gingrich Pledges Open Door to Hispanic-American Voters," read the headlines as he appeared at the annual meeting of the League of United Latin American Citizens.[127] J. C. Watts was doing what he could to help with the African-American vote.

The Democrats were doing all they could to counter Gingrich's efforts. They clearly had decided to turn out their base vote in large numbers and hoped that would make the difference. They were able to use GOP positions on affirmative action and welfare legislation to paint the Republicans as anti-black and, in some cases, as out-and-out racists. They used the English-only bills, especially in California, as well as voter concern about illegal immigration that was exploding at the time, to appeal to the Hispanics. They worked organized labor hoping for the kind of result they got from the unions in 1996. Most of all they stuck to their old agenda of picturing the Republicans as anti-Social Security, pro-HMO and against the patients, and against public education. GOP candidates were pictured as mean-spirited politicians who were only interested in taking care of the wealthy and the corporations at the expense of "the people." Along with the old tried and true came an increased effort to turn out their voters on election day.

To counter an anticipated ad blitz by the labor unions, the Republican leaders devised a plan, called "Operation Breakout," to "blanket as many as fifty to sixty battleground districts with issue advocacy television ads touting the GOP's success in balancing the budget, cutting taxes and reforming welfare." They priced the

---

[126] Ibid., 30 April 1998, B9.
[127] Ibid., 28 June 1998, B1 and 2 July 1998, A6.

campaign at $37 million and expected that this would make the difference in November. It also included a "new communications regime and a legislative agenda that caters specifically to the Republican financial contributors off Capitol Hill." Polls had found that the GOP message on key issues like education and the budget was more popular than expected in the competitive districts and the leaders decided to maximize communicating that message.[128]

As the fall campaign approached Newt felt confident. He predicted GOP victories in Georgia on almost every level and carried that message as he moved around the country campaigning for Republican House candidates. President Clinton had just televised a speech about his relationship with Monica Lewinsky and the news was full of his grand jury testimony. How could the country not understand now that this was about perjury and cover-up and not about just sex? That made the impeachment hearings seem a little less risky. The targeted issue ads were ready to run and the money was coming in. Gingrich felt good. He even decided to make minor history of a sort. Wearing blue jeans and an open-necked pin-striped shirt he positioned himself and decided to set a world record in shaking hands and having his picture made with guests at a free reception in Vashon Island, Washington. Working at 700 photos an hour he spent five hours shaking hands and ended up with 3,609 hands shaken and pictures taken. He and the local Republicans hoped to have a new category entered in the *Guinness Book of Records*. He did make *Ripley's Believe It or Not!* the next month along with a giant seventy-two pound cantaloupe.

Newt did find some time to spend back in the sixth district campaigning for his own job. His opponent was a lawyer, Gary Pelphrey, who had graduated from the US Naval Academy and received the nickname "Bats." He had run for the seat in 1996 but had been defeated in the primary. This time he had no primary opposition. The two candidates differed on almost every issue. Newt avoided or deflected questions about the president's Monica problem and tried to stick to the issues. His volunteer newsletter, "The NEWTletter" emphasized the GOP record. "Newt lays out the choices for this November," it read. "When we became a majority in 1995, the projected deficit for the next eleven years was three trillion, one

---

[128] *Roll Call*, (23 July 1998): 1.

hundred billion dollars. But we reformed welfare, saved Medicare without raising taxes, balanced the budget, enacted entitlement reforms, cut $100 million in domestic discretionary spending, and cut taxes, causing economic growth." It went on, "Because of this, in three and a half short years, we have changed the direction of government so that the projection now is that we will have a one trillion, six hundred billion dollar surplus. Democrats fought us every step of the way, because they are committed to higher taxes and bigger government."[129] The 1998 effort was basically his standard us versus them campaign. Newt had a $3 million budget whereas Pelphrey had only raised $9,000 by mid-October. He hoped for free media coverage but with Newt spending little time campaigning in the district there was little for the press to cover. "I'm entitled to coverage," he argued. "But I've got a screwy name like 'Bats' and people say, 'It's some crazy guy.'"[130] As Gingrich traveled the district on his regular English double-decker bus tour the weekend before the election all looked well. He had big turnouts wherever he went and his polls showed him up 70 percent-30 percent. He knew he would win big but was concerned about the number of seats the GOP would take as they increased their margin. The budget struggle in Washington in September and October had focused his mind on the need to get as many as possible.

The Republicans had feared the president might try to find some reason to shut-down the government again and blame it on them. They also thought that they needed more time back in their districts to campaign and less time in Washington arguing with Clinton. Knowing this, the president was able to keep raising objections and offering new suggestions and demands until they were willing to give in on a good deal just to be able to get out of Washington and start campaigning. Lott and Gingrich "again proved themselves no match for the political adroitness of President Clinton, as the 105th Congress staggered to the finish line a mere two weeks before Election Day," was the verdict of an editorial in *The Hill* newspaper. In truth, the president received more than the Republicans wanted to give but much less than he had desired. "I think the Republicans bought Clinton off a lot more cheaply [than Reagan had]," wrote Donald Lambro, an observer friendly to the

---

[129] "The NEWTletter," Oct. 1998, 1. UWG Archives, Gingrich Papers, 1998 campaign folder.

[130] *The Atlanta Journal*, 13 October 1998, B2.

GOP. The president's strategy, he said, was to keep them in Washington "fighting over spending issues that appealed to the Democrat's base." Had they played his game and stayed and fought, as the GOP renegades demanded, it "would have played into his hands, undermining the GOP election strategy, energizing his party and distracting the nation and the media." Having the press the last two weeks before the election talking about the Republicans fighting to the last to get tax cuts for their rich friends and working to hurt the children and the elderly while the brave Democratic President stood up to them would have been disastrous. Lambro thought Newt made the right decision by going home to campaign to boost their numbers and have a stronger base to confront the White House in the 106th Congress.[131] Gingrich and Lott were willing to pay a small ransom to stay on message and go home.

As the campaign entered the home stretch, Newt and the leadership approved a $10 million ad campaign focusing on the president's character. While the ad was a soft one it nevertheless changed the focus from issues to character. Many feel this was Gingrich's major mistake in the campaign. Still, Starr had presented his findings to Congress and there were going to be hearings. The polls showed that people wanted to avoid those hearings and just have Congress go for a quick censure of Clinton and then get on with their regular business. It seemed important to let them know this was about the Constitution and not about sex. The House could not just walk away from their responsibilities. In addition, if they tried to avoid impeachment hearings the GOP base would react negatively.

Newt and Lott were already under fire from many rank and file members for not providing a campaign message that had impact. They had spent a lot of money on issue ads and nothing seemed to be sticking. The Republicans were going home without "a salient set of arguments to aid them in their reelection bids." McIntosh, the renegade leader, criticized "the communications meltdown" and was joined by the leader of the GOP "Theme Team," Georgia's Jack Kingston. The coastal Georgian, a rising star among the non-extremist conservatives, complained, "We've been told [the same thing] for six months and the rank-and-file members are still wondering what the hell we're going to

---

131 *The Hill*, 21 October 1998, 10; *The Atlanta Journal*, 23 October 1998, A14.

say." The opportunity seemed so ripe. The Democrats had no real message except to attack Republicans and accuse them of being mean and unreasonable and wanting to persecute Clinton in direct contradiction of the wishes of the American people. Why could not the Republicans have a clear message that they could all get behind? Many complained that the failure to communicate was not just with the public. They argued that the leadership had also failed to communicate with the members about the compromises being made in the budget talks with Clinton. They ended up being presented with a forty-pound document no one had a chance to read before they were required to vote. Complaints were bipartisan with even Chairman Livingston expressing dissatisfaction. "To say I'm not happy is pretty accurate," he said. "I believe we have to pass this bill and go home. But do I have to be enthusiastic about it? No," he whined. The rank-and-file wanted to get out and go home. They just did not want to pay the price it took to get them there.[132]

The renegades did not even want to go home. They were ready to fall on their swords rather than to sell out to Clinton by compromising on the spending increases he demanded. The idea of removing the leadership reared its festering head again. They did not like the pork in the budget and were embittered at the way it was done and upset over what they considered a sellout. Still, sophomores like Steve Largent, Ray LaHood and Lindsey Graham understood that the election results would hold the key to any leadership changes. If the GOP won big, as predicted, then it would be hard to argue for change. If, on the other hand, there were losses or only modest gains then leadership changes made sense.[133]

During the final weeks of the campaign the Democrats ran a series of directed, hard-core, negative ads designed to demonize the Republican candidates. Using ads targeting blacks they said, "When you don't vote, you let another church explode. When you don't vote, you allow another cross to burn... another assault wound on a brother or sister." Also, "Martin Luther King had a dream for all children... Don't let Republicans take away that dream." A week before the election new ads were introduced claiming, "Republicans have made removing the

---

[132] *Roll Call,* (19 October 1998): 1 and The Hill, 221 October 1998, 1.

[133] *The Atlanta Journal,* 30 October 1998, A1; 3 November 1998, A3.

president from office their top priority. They want to waste millions of our tax dollars on endless investigations." It continued, "Newt Gingrich is so obsessed with investigating President Clinton that he ordered his henchmen to spend $10 million in special interest money to air these vicious, venal and vitriolic ads." The *Washington Times* noted that "vicious, venal and vitriolic" described the Democratic ads especially when compared to the rather tame GOP ones.[134]

Newt, having approved the character ads, personally stayed away from discussing the House's impeachment hearings, mentioning them only when criticizing the media for over emphasizing the scandal and asking them to focus more on the issues. Visiting twenty states in a pre-election blitz the week before the election Newt tried to talk issues and boast about Republican accomplishments during the 104th and 105th Congresses. The polls said people were unhappy about the impeachment inquiry and the Democrat's attack ads were having some impact. Many Democratic state parties sought to play the race card in efforts to turn out their voters. By tying burning churches and crosses to the Republicans they hoped to motivate their voters to go to the polls. Red flags should have been flying for Gingrich and the GOP but they continued to feel confident of victory. "If everything breaks against us, my guess is we'll be about plus-ten. If everything breaks for us, we'll be much closer to plus-forty," Newt said.[135]

The election experts tended to agree right up to election day. Dick Morris was putting the GOP gains in the House at thirty seats while most were more cautious as they reacted to internal polls that showed some slippage. NRCC chairman, John Linder, predicted a ten to fifteen seat gain while GOP pollster Kellyanne Fitzpatrick was even more optimistic.[136]

As crowds began to gather at the Cobb Galleria for Newt's victory celebration on 3 November, everyone was in high spirits. They not only thought Newt would win his election but that Republicans would gain seats in both houses of Congress and on the state level as well. The war room was filled with key players and excited campaign staffers. Grover Norquist, Representative John Linder, Representative Mac Collins, Arne Christensen, Steve Hanser, Rachel Robinson, John

---

[134] *The Washington Times* national edition, 2 November 1998, 23.

[135] *The Atlanta Journal*, 23 October 1998, A3; 27 October 1998, A18.

[136] *The Hill*, 21 October 1998, 19.

Duncan, Christina Martin and a host of others close to Newt were in high spirits. Joe Gaylord estimated the GOP would gain twenty or more seats in the House. One group of staffers, headed by Scott Rials, Newt's Georgia campaign manager, were tracking the vote in the sixth district. Another, headed by Rich Galen, Gaylord's right arm, watched the national results. Each would give Gaylord and Newt up to the minute results from Georgia and around the nation. A feeling of satisfied expectation filled the room.

As results started coming in Rials' team was excited and pleased with the results of their efforts. They would win with a 71-29 percent victory. They thought this was exceptional because Newt had spent little time in the district. Their pleasure, however, was short-lived as national results began to come in. By 9:00 P.M. it was clear that the GOP had lost the Senate races in New York and North Carolina and close House seats were going to the Democrats who were up two seats by ten minutes later. Gingrich huddled with Christensen and Gaylord in serious conversation trying to figure out what was happening. Linder, looking ashen, watched the results, his mind clearly on the impeachment hearings. "God help us if the American people vote to save Bill Clinton," he whispered almost to himself. To Linder it was incomprehensible. What could the voters be thinking?

Newt's personal returns came in early. He won by a landslide and about 9:45 P.M. went down to the ballroom where the victory celebration was taking place. With him was Marianne, his family and key staffers wearing war room tags around their necks, which read in bold letters, "America's Victory." He gave a victory speech thanking his staff and the hundreds of volunteers gathered there for all their efforts on his behalf. He pointed out that the evening was still early, encouraged everyone to hang around and have a good time and said he would be back later with more news.

Back in the war room Newt conferred with his advisors. It was clearly time to restructure the message he was to give the public. By 10:30 P.M. it was clear that the Republicans would not pick up any appreciable number of seats and were fighting to hold their own. Linder was back looking at the returns and clearly agitated. "My God, my God, we may lose the House," he moaned.

Newt, Linder, Armey and the rest of the leadership quickly claimed victory pointing out that this was the first time since 1928 that

Republicans were elected to three straight majorities and the last Republican Speaker to serve three consecutive terms was Nicholas Longworth in 1925. The loss of five seats to the Democrats and the failure to make any gains in the Senate was blamed on the press for their focus on the Monica scandal instead of on the issues. Getting their second wind, they promised an aggressive agenda that would seek significant tax cuts and long-term reform of Social Security.[137]

No one was buying it. A drop from 228 to 223 seats was not a victory. Debacle and disaster were the most frequently used terms to describe the Republican showing. The GOP leadership team began working the phones early Wednesday morning. Conference calls abounded. Chris Shays said, "We need some changes in our leadership." James Dobson, leader of the cultural conservatives, said the loss came from not following the conservative agenda and moderate Constance Morella called for a move to the center. Gingrich pointed to the landslide victories provided by GOP governors who had built diverse coalitions as a model for the future for congressional candidates. Whatever the cause of the losses, Newt took the blame. "I'm Speaker, so I'll take responsibility," he told a news conference Wednesday. When asked about challengers to his job he described them as "people who would in fact take the party to a narrower base with fewer members." He and Linder said they both expected to stay in their jobs.

Wednesday was spent getting a list together of the members and their phone numbers for Newt to call asking for support for speaker. Christensen thought that day looked pretty good as he put together the calling list. He was not listening to Newt's calls. Gingrich was picking up the distress among the rank and file. Chairman Livingston put it to him directly and suggested that he should think about resigning. He also indicated that he might run against him if he did not resign. Livingston, whom Newt had talked out of leaving Congress, followed the call with a faxed list of demands that would have emasculated Gingrich as Speaker.[138] Fellow Georgians Bob Barr and John Linder indicated reservations about supporting him. Newt indicated he would allow the NRCC chairmanship to be decided by vote rather than appointment and this assertion was resented by Linder. A minor flap

---

[137] *The Atlanta Journal*, 4 November 1998, D10.
[138] *Roll Call* (11 November 1998): 22.

resulted as Linder and Newt sought to retain their jobs. Henry Hyde refused to endorse Newt at a press conference and new Congresswoman Mary Bono reminded him that he had told her that sometimes one had to sacrifice for the good of the party. "What I have to say to you is the hardest thing I've ever had to say to anybody except my kids. I suggest that it is time for you to search your soul....I'm sorry I can't give you a yes."[139]

By Wednesday evening Newt and Marianne began to consider his giving up the speakership as an option. The thought had flashed through his mind on Tuesday evening but had been banished because the Republicans still held the majority, small though it was. It had been difficult with 228 and should not be that much more difficult with five less. The calls Wednesday began to make him question whether it was going to be worth it. He went to bed Wednesday night still planning to run for Speaker but after talking to his close advisors, Marianne, Hanser and Gaylord and a few others, he began to give it serious thought. While angered by Livingston's list of demands he was also saddened to see what was happening to the party. It was clear to him that he could not remain as a shadow Speaker with others, principally the chairmen, calling the shots. McIntosh and the radicals were sure to make demands as their price for voting for him as would the moderates. The religious right would be knocking with their demands. The party was fragmenting to the point that he did not think he could bring about reconciliation and a sense of unity. Each bill would not only require struggling with the Democrats but with multiple groups within his own party.

Newt and Marianne began to talk seriously about resignation on Thursday. If he gave up the speakership he thought it would be futile and divisive to remain in a lesser position. It would not be fair to the new speaker nor to the party because his very presence would be divisive and used by some to attempt to undermine the new man. The staff and his allies, along with Newt himself, were still making calls asking for support throughout the day Thursday. Friday morning came with seemingly enough votes to give Newt the nomination. Representative Dennis Hastert (IL), the chief deputy Republican whip,

---

[139] *The Atlanta Journal*, 23 November 1998, A11 and Christensen, interview, 1998.

who had been making calls for Gingrich, told him that he had enough votes to get the nomination but he was worried about the ten or so radicals who had announced they would not vote for Newt under any circumstance when the whole House met to choose a speaker in January. If they kept their word they could possibly give the speakership to Dick Gephardt even though the Democrats were in a minority. Hastert thought they could probably be forced by the use of House rules to support Newt but that in itself would bring on a bloodletting within the GOP conference.[140]

Meeting with his advisors Friday morning at his Marietta office, Newt told them they had talked about resignation. Marianne, according to Hanser, "was still thinking about it" but Newt "gave the impression that he had moved to the point that he'd have to be talked out of it." He gave Hanser and Gaylord some alternatives but "more or less wrote off all but resignation."[141] Key staffers Nancy Desmond and Lula Davenport sensed something was wrong by the way Marianne was acting. Meeting privately with them she confirmed that Newt would probably step down. Desmond asked him, "Do you have the votes to remain as speaker?" He responded, "Yes, but why would I want to?" The decision had been made.

Gingrich first called his old friends from the Hill, Vin Weber and Bob Walker. He told his Georgia staff and around 6:00 P.M. called his Washington staffs to tell them the news. He then set up a conference call with key members who had supported him. "I think, for the future of the party, it makes a lot more sense for me not to be a candidate for Speaker. We have to get the bitterness out...It is clear that as long as I'm around, that won't happen. I have always put the party ahead of my own ambition." Representative Joe Barton (TX) asked him to at least remain in Congress but Newt told him that would not work because his presence "would just overshadow whoever my successor is." He felt sure the district would elect a Republican to replace him. Representative Fred Upton (MI) commented on the sadness of the occasion and RNC chairman, Jim Nicholson, told him, "On behalf of all the Republicans all over America — thank you — and Godspeed and good luck."[142] He then told the press.

---

[140] *The Atlanta Journal*, 7 November 1998, A8.

[141] Steve Hanser interview, 11 November 1998.

[142] *The Atlanta Journal*, 7 November 1998, 1.

Gingrich returned to Washington on 9 November. When he arrived at the Capitol a large crowd had gathered on the steps to welcome him back. He and Marianne were met by his combined staffs, former staffers, and close associates. Well over 200 applauded him, told him they were proud of him and proud to have worked for him and hugged him, Marianne and each other in an emotional display of their support. He spent a good part of the afternoon with Marianne, Ken Duberstein, Gaylord, Hanser and Martin working on the speech he was scheduled to give at a scheduled GOPAC function for their major donors and staff. That night he spoke to GOPAC contributors to ovation after ovation. By this time it was clear that Bob Livingston was the choice to replace Newt. His anger and hurt at Livingston's list of demands had passed and, in front of his GOPAC supporters, he publicly embraced the man he thought would replace him. He had genuine affection and respect for his Appropriations Chairman and wanted to do what he could to help him make the transition. The next day he met with Livingston to brief him on the job and answer questions the new man might have. He made sure his staff was helpful to Livingston's staff and Marianne took Livingston's wife to lunch.[143]

The next day, Veterans Day, calls came in all day from present and former cabinet members, Cohen, Rubin and Berger from the Clinton administration and Jim Baker from the Reagan and Bush cabinet. They wished him well and asked him to stay in touch. Jim Baker was especially helpful with tax advice and suggestions about speaking engagements after Newt left office. Dick Armey came by around noon for a short visit and Gingrich spent part of the afternoon asking members to give him support for reelection as leader. Calls offering jobs began to come in. Newt was careful and turned down some lucrative offers because he thought they were not interesting or because they were just not right for him. He asked three questions; what did they want him to do, what would be success, and how would they reward success? His mind was on the future and what direction his life would take. He knew he wanted to continue to be useful to the party and to do all he could to guarantee the success of the GOP majority but at this moment he was still searching to find the most effective way to achieve that goal.

---

[143] Ibid., 15 November 1998, A12.

On Saturday, 12 December, Newt held his final town hall meeting at Walton High School in Cobb County. The auditorium was filled with current supporters and those from his old district as well. He told a standing room only crowd he had gone to Congress twenty years ago "with goals of cutting taxes, balancing the federal budget, reforming welfare, defeating the Soviet empire and establishing a Republican majority in the House. By 1998, we had accomplished every major goal." He explained why he had stepped down. "As long as I was speaker, I was the excuse. The fact is that I was the excuse for Clinton—For the Republicans who didn't want to learn how to be the majority—For the news media that doesn't want to think about the issues and just wants to cover stories. I don't think you can have two head coaches," he said, explaining why he was leaving congress as well as the speakership. "We're leaving public office, but we're not leaving public life." Following the speech he was thanked by one after another for personal services he had rendered them. One thanked him for help with the IRS and for supporting the "innocent spouse" law. Another brought her wheelchair bound son on stage to thank him and tearfully praise him as a "compassionate champion for the disabled" and triggered a sustained standing ovation when she said, "There is not another leader in the world today of his caliber." One after another they came to the microphones to praise and thank him and to suggest ways he could still be helpful until, after the meeting had run an hour overtime, he finally called it to a halt. He thanked them all for their prayers and support over the years because it was their support that made possible his work in Washington. He left the meeting to another standing ovation and began preparations for the next phase of his remarkable life.[144]

He submitted his resignation letter to Governor Zell Miller effective 3 January 1999.

---

[144] Ibid., 13 November 1998, F5

15

CONCLUSION:
LOOKING TO THE FUTURE

An Interview with Newt Gingrich

After stepping down from Congress Newt became a senior fellow at the American Enterprise Institute in Washington, D.C. and a distinguished visiting fellow at the Hoover institute at Stanford University in Palo Alto, CA. He also is the host of a nationally syndicated daily radio show, *The Age of Possibilities*. He is CEO of The Gingrich Group, an Atlanta-based communications and management firm and heads FONGPAC, designed to help and encourage conservative candidates. He is a member of the Senior Advisory Board of the Secretary of Defense's National Security Study Group and is on the Board of the Juvenile Diabetes Foundation.

I met with Newt on 7 May 1999 at his former campaign headquarters in Roswell, Georgia, where he and Marianne were helping sort items for moving as they closed down that office. Both seemed relaxed and friendly and showed no sign of the separation and divorce action that was to take place a few days later. I had requested an interview to talk with him about his plans after leaving the Speaker's office. I was most interested in which issues he would focus on in his work at AEI and Hoover and in the direction his work at The Gingrich Group would take. The interview that follows answers those questions.

Steely: How are you doing since you left the speakership?

Gingrich: You know this is almost exactly six months since we decided to stepdown. I couldn't help but think that when I first met you twenty-nine years ago, I was just beginning a new career as a college teacher. Then you were with me when I first decided to run for Congress. You were with me through two defeats and victory, and then at first, we began talking about becoming a majority after sixteen long years of work. Then the "Contract With America," four years as Speaker, five years as the leader of the party. In a sense, I see this as another transition period, moving toward an interesting, positive, constructive future. Just as I saw a role in teaching and helping young people have a better future, I saw a role in serving my district in the Congress and I saw a role in helping lead the Conservative movement. I think that the opportunity to continue to be a server, to have a public life, even if not in public office, is still very great. I'm working on a number of projects in that direction. I started with the idea that I just have a deep personal need to be involved in public service. Some of it may have come out of my stepfather's career in the U.S. army, and the notion of duty, honor, country is the West Point slogan. I think I'm happiest if have things that are positive and are helpful.

What I'm doing is focusing, first of all, on learning. Because I don't see how in an age of dramatic change you can do anything positive if you don't spend a lot of time learning. I'm a student one day a month at Georgia Tech. I'm a student a half day a month at the Center for Disease Control. I find about a third of my time is spent in meetings where I'm learning and reading. I'm putting special emphasis on Palo Alto and Silicon Valley and the emerging information revolution. I'm going to be a fellow at the Hoover Institution looking at science, individual opportunities, society, and the public policy. I'm active in looking at opportunities in better health policy, and better environmental policy at the American Enterprise Institute. I'm looking at the U.S. role in leading the world and how we improve our ability to be a leader, also at the American Enterprise Institute. In addition, I have a firm called the Gingrich Group that is working on solving, on strategic planning, strategic analysis, and a special emphasis on health issues. We're working with Price-Waterhouse, with Fleissman Hiller, several private firms that have hired me to do consulting. Intellectually, we stay very active.

I'm also giving speeches and Gingrich Enterprises is the firm which handles the speech making side. Finally, we still have a political action committee, which is focused on a couple of key issues: How to create a younger generation to stand in the gap and the opportunity they have in keeping their right to invest part of their social security taxes in a personal social security account. We've tried to establish a tax cap of twenty-five per cent so that nobody would pay more than twenty-five per cent of income in total taxation: federal, state, and local combined. That would include a provision that everybody at all levels of income would not pay more than twenty-five per cent on the grounds that in a free society in peace time, if you work all of Monday and part of Tuesday for the government, that should be all you're really asked to do. (voices continue and getting louder) It's wrong in peace time for the government take more than that amount of your time. You should be allowed to use the rest of your time if you use DeTocqueville's vision of a voluntary society. I think it's very important that people have the take home pay and free time to be active as volunteers and be active in raising their families.

In addition to all those things, we're working on one of the opportunities available in the information revolution which Alvin Toffler called the third wave. The idea being you grew from a hunting and gathering society to agriculture, from agriculture to industry, and now we're going from industry to sub-industry. We broadly characterize this as an information age, I'm not sure what the right term is because there are so many parts to it, bio-technology, MGM project, all the other kinds of parts of the scientific revolution. Those are creating opportunities in health, in the environment, in learning, in rethinking the legal system, and rethinking how government works. Both the political action committee and my speech making came into the consulting work we're doing. We're trying to look at what are the opportunities inherent in all these new technologies? How do we make the transition to have these technologies lead to actually better services for citizens and better services for consumers? I'm staying surprisingly busy. I don't think I would have ever thought six months ago that I would be as busy as I am now.

Steely: I've noticed all of the different areas you've mentioned are domestic areas. There is so much you've been involved in earlier in the foreign policy field and diplomatic area. Do you plan on continuing any of that? Or can you do that since you're not an elected official?

Gingrich: I can have influence but not power. I think ideas really matter. I think practically if you don't have ideas, you don't know what you are using for your power for anyway. So both in my role at the American Enterprise Institute where one of my topics is U.S. Leadership in the World and in my role in the political action committee, we're emphasizing US leadership role in the world as one of our criteria. Finally, I'm on a National Strategic Study Group which I helped set up. It's a pentagon-civilian task force, led by Warren Rudman and by Gary Hart, which is looking at the [year] 2025, trying to assess our national security needs and then trying to assess the level of change we need in order to make those needs effective. I'm going to retain an active interest.

   I'm really studying four areas: globalization and the whole rise of the modern world in terms of CNN, international finance, monetary systems, the environment, military power, economic competition, etc. So globalization is one topic, the second is the scientific revolution, the third is the natural world, both in the sense of the environment and in the sense that humans are, in fact, organic, natural beings. And then the fourth area I'm looking at is American exceptionalism, the set of values, principles, and culture which has enabled us to be both the most prosperous and the most integrated society in the history of the world. To try to codify what are the principles which allow people to be free, safe, and prosperous. Can that be developed either into a course, or into a presentation on the internet that could be made available worldwide to any young person who is interested in what should their country be doing, how they can be more prosperous, and how they can be safer and freer? My guess is that three to five years out from now, I'll teach a course like that.

I'm going to be in Israel later on this year at a conference. I'm being honored by the Knesset for my role in public policy. I will probably be in Europe. I may well be in Latin America, and I'll probably be in Asia before the year is up. I think I'm going to retain an active interest in the world at large. My Ph.D. is in European history, and as an army brat, I grew up with a sense that the US is a leader in the world. I think I'll probably stay interested in both domestic and international relations.

Steely: Since leaving office, have you maintained much contact with the people who are still there?

Gingrich:No, I've deliberately backed out for a couple of reasons. One is I thought psychologically you've got to give Denny Hastert time to grow and give the leadership a chance to get use to working on their own. I think its very bad when you have former leader looking over their shoulder or being too close. The second is that under US law, it is a criminal violation for me to lobby at any point during this year. I don't want to take any risk given my relationship with the Clinton administration. I'd just as soon not have the Justice department have any excuse to make any claims. So, I've been very, very cautious. I return phone calls from friends who call me who are members, but I don't initiate any phone calls.

Steely: Talking about the Clinton administration, I noted in the paper the other day, one of the comments they made was they wouldn't be having as much trouble with Congress if you were still Speaker, so maybe they meant—I know you don't want to comment on that—but maybe they miss you over there, after all. (laughing)

Gingrich:I got a lot of calls from people, like Bob Rubin, Sandy Berger, and chief of staff, Erskine Boles, and others during the period immediately after my stepping down. And they all indicated that they appreciated the fact that I consistently tried to deal with foreign policy on a bipartisan basis. I do feel pretty strongly that you only get one president at a time, you only get one foreign policy at a time. Congress can shape foreign policy, but Congress should not attempt to compete in terms of leadership in a foreign policy role. It's practically impossible, that's why the founding fathers designed it so that Congress has enormous weight domestically, but the president is clearly the leader on foreign policy and military affairs.

Steely: Kevin Kelly's new book *New Rules for the New Economy* talks about a lot more than the economy and opens the door to the concept of using the net, using connections in almost every area. We're actually watching that happen now on CNN and other places, fax machines, e-mail, and the conflict that's going on in Kosovo at the moment. You mentioned doing some work in foreign policy, or at least keeping that door open. Do you anticipate using a lot of technology in these world forums, and that sort of thing?

Gingrich:I think one of the reasons we're going a little slowly right now is I want it to be an internet based system. I've spent a fair amount of time of getting better at e-mail, chat rooms, and bulletin boards, and surfing the net. Because I really think it's very important to recognize that in the information age, the process of the entire electronic system is going to be at the center of how we operate. I think that it is (phone ringing) extremely important that new start up companies start with the idea that you are part a of the world wide internet system, and that the internet system really has a very different set of objective requirements than the way we've operated in the past. One of them is that the minute you're on the net, you're actually on a world wide system. The people can randomly find you from anywhere. In a sense, it's the difference between a magnet and broadcasting. The magnets draw to them, broadcasting is pushing out. I'm trying to understand Kevin Kelly's book which I recommend that everyone buy. It's a good starting point. There's another earlier book, called *Out of Control*, which is intellectually fascinating. To give an example of what I'm not doing, I had lunch with Kevin last Monday when I was in Palo Alto at Hoover. I talked about ideas and pursuing things, how to understand what's happening in Palo Alto. But I do think that the information age will create enormous new opportunities, but they will require people to learn a set of new rules, and new principles, and new ways of thinking, because the internet does in fact function very differently than more traditional systems.

Steely: Are you pretty comfortable with the use of the internet yourself, now? You say you are starting to learn this.

Gingrich: I'd say I'm semi-comfortable. I'm comfortable doing e-mail. I'm very comfortable working on computers. I've written five books on computers, so I think I have some facility there. I am moderately comfortable working with the net, looking up movie times or, even if in San Francisco looking up places to have dinner. I'm not yet as fast as I'd like to be using the internet, in terms of the web. We're really at the baby stage of learning how to run really efficient chat rooms and really efficient team effort. I think it's going to take six months to two years to really get to the level I'd like to be at.

Steely: There's no question that the internet can be used to help develop public policy.

Gingrich: The net is to the next generation, what printing was in 1454 to Gutenberg. It is a profound breakthrough that changes the equation of how people operate and I think it is extraordinarily important.

Steely: You spent a good portion of your life getting to a place where you could influence public policy. Does this stepping back mean that you're going to be out of politics now, elected politics, and work from the outside? Are you leaving that open, or what?

Gingrich:I'd be very surprised if I run for office. There are circumstances in which the governorship or the presidency might be interesting, but it is a very hard business. It's a business I've spent forty years in. It involves a tremendous amount of conflict. I'm very surprised at how comfortable I am not being in it. I think if you had asked me six months ago, knowing each other for almost thirty years, I would have been surprised that I have so many interests that are non-political that I could spend six or seven days in a row, and never think about it. I spent a long period where I'd read the headlines in the top half of the paper that shows in the box. And unless one is compelling, that's it. I've checked off the news for the day. I don't think I could have imagined six months ago how happy I am being in free enterprise, and how comfortable I am being a teacher again, and focusing on learning, and focusing on making an intellectual contribution, rather than a contribution in terms of direct power.

Steely: The most obvious place to try to influence public policy in the near future would be to do it during the presidential campaigns coming up in 2000. I know you're not getting behind any particular person at this moment. Do you have an agenda that you would like to have presented?

Gingrich:I think we are building an agenda. Put in things like the right to have a personal social security savings account so you have a better return on your investment, and you would have the social security actuaries tell us we've allowed you to invest even as little as two per cent of your social security tax that would create so much more wealth, by making it private, that you would actually end up saving the social security system without a tax increase or a benefit cut. I think probably the number we'll recommend is five percentage points, in which case, virtually everybody would retire as millionaires. That's just a very different model, much closer to the Chilean model of saving or the Singapore model. That's a big policy. I'd argue that we'd have to be for that if we're going to make the next generation successful.

I think this twenty-five per cent tax cap is an area where I'm probably going to write every Republican county convention and urge them to adopt the idea of twenty-five per cent tax cap, and the idea that governments at all levels, state, federal, and local should be using privatization as the way of lowering the size of government. There are many things that people want done. I'm not against them getting them done. I think we can get them done better, faster, and with better technology by privatizing. There are issues that I'm adamantly in favor of, the United States playing a leadership role in the world. I would oppose a Republican nominee who's an isolationist. I think that's impossible in the modern world.

Steely: Domestic front. Right now, we're just a couple of weeks away from the murders that took place in Colorado. We have two young boys who killed several of their classmates. I've noticed in the *Weekly Standard* that Bill Kristol has written a long, two page editorial praising Al Gore, which was somewhat of a surprise, because Gore seems, he says, to have tapped into the feeling that that event generated. He is now in the process of talking more about God and religion and family, than anyone would have ever have thought six weeks ago. You did not mention earlier on when you were listing the things you were concerned about, that particular area religion and the family. I know that's been a concern of yours ever since I've known you. How do you feel about that now?

Gingrich: I think you can notice this in a lot of my speeches. You can't understand America's founding without understanding the role the founding fathers put in terms of God. Yesterday I took two coins, one which was given to me in Chicago the night before last. I was sharing with the audience that the nature of the meaning of these two coins. This is a fifty kopek coin from the Soviet Union, given to me by a Jewish refugee. This was issued in 1967 and has Lenin on it. It was the celebration of fifty years of success for the Soviet Empire. This is a US dollar given to me by Congressman Duke Cunningham, who is our first naval Ace in Vietnam. This is a dollar that had been given to him. This is an

Eisenhower dollar that says, "In God We Trust." I made the point yesterday that it's interesting to me that the fifty kopek piece celebrating the fiftieth anniversary of the Soviet Empire, is actually now celebrating a failed ideology that has collapsed, and that the notion of a spiritually based society is still there in America, and the two coins. I then used this to introduce Margaret Thatcher at a prayer breakfast, and made the point that the two people most responsible for the defeat of the Soviet Empire were Ronald Reagan and Margaret Thatcher.

I also think you have to look at, and this is a challenge where Tipper Gore was on the edge of something and then backed off a few years ago. You can't describe what's happening to young people today without taking into account two primary realties. The first is that popular culture—from Nintendo games to MTV to Hollywood—is essentially so destructive now that to argue that kids can play games where they kill six thousand people in a weekend, or to argue that watching night after night of violence on television has no impact is crazy. Nobody believes that. We are saturated in violence today. I think that it shouldn't shock us that that has had some impact on coarsening all of our society, which developed into vulgarity. I think that has a direct impact. I'm a fan of Bill Bennett's in that sense. The next time Gore goes to a fundraiser in California, it would be nice if he would talk about God and religion to the crowd that's raising the money for him because those are the people who have done more than any other single group to provide the vivid images of death and violence. The same is true with tobacco. It always amused me that this administration talks about tobacco when Julia Roberts must have smoked three packs in "My Best Friend's Wedding" and then to suggest that Leonardo DiCaprio's smoking has no impact or that you don't understand why thirteen year old girls think smoking is cool, I think is to miss the whole point. I think violence is very similar.

The other point I'd make about adolescence is that it is a nineteenth century world bourgeois that has failed. You cannot afford to have young males idle at thirteen, fourteen, and fifteen years of age. They have to bond with adults. If you allow them to be isolated and surrounded by thirteen, fourteen, and fifteen year olds, they are inevitably going to be more violent. That's part of what I mean about seeing human beings as organic beings. Young males have a natural propensity toward violence and hostility, and unless it is socialized out of them, it is very dangerous. The idea that you can let your child spend the entire summer doing nothing but hang out with equally young, equally immature, equally testosterone driven adolescents and not have a bad outcome is just going against the core nature of society, of the natural world. I think you have too much social science that started with the idea that we're rational beings and not enough social science that started with a deep understanding of the ethology of vertebrates and the ethology of living organisms, and the nature of primates. And then said, "Given these realities, you'd better take these things into account." We'll have three or four weeks of people playing games about what happened in Colorado, which is a great tragedy, but nobody will be honest and direct about the two major changes. You've got to change adolescents, and you have got to take head on the culture of violence that is at the heart of the MTV/Hollywood environment.

Steely: Part of the problem some people have pointed to is the role of young black men in society, a high percentage of those who have had some type of problem with our criminal justice system. They've either been arrested, in jail, or victimized.

Gingrich:There's no question that the deepest problem in American society is the combination of the culture of poverty with racism. Unless we're prepared to address it head on, how do you replace the culture of poverty with the opportunity for prosperity? How do you reach out to reintegrate people who are alienated from America, who eventually are going to have some kind of very painful explosion? The tragedy in most of our major cities is young black males having a greater likelihood of going to jail than going to college. I think this is something which, despite the president's banal talk about race, nobody has taken seriously head on the level of remediation, and the level of acculturation that should be underway and that's one of the things I'm going to be working on.

Steely: One of things you did work on when you were speaker and before that was trying to bring about some change inside Washington, D. C. I remember you early on as a whip talking about how it was almost criminal that the city of Washington was in the shape it was in with us being the capital of the world, so to speak, and having a city as a capital that the people were not safe to walk the streets in. Talk for a minute, if you would, about your efforts and why they didn't work?

Gingrich:First of all, they have worked to some extent. Washington is a safer city today. It has job growth for the first time in many years. The reform bills we passed changed the city government. It is now out of bankruptcy. The new mayor is a reform mayor who's trying really hard. Symbolically and very important was the snowstorm this winter. He was in the cab. He was out with the people cleaning up, in the cab of the truck, cleaning up the snow. A totally different tone, he's not quite Rudy Giuliani, but he's making a difference in the quality of life for these people in DC. There is no question that the effort that Ted Forcman and John Walton have launched on private scholarships for poor children — there are thousands of them in Washington — is making an impact. There's no question that the effort we made with Cellular Telephone Industries Foundation to give cell phones to schools that are too old to be rewired, has actually brought children into contact with the internet because we started with this school in downtown DC. I think we have had some type of impact. We could never get the momentum we really needed, partly because of the political power structure of Washington — it was so self-destructive. I think with the new mayor, you have a better chance to get some real things done. I think its fair to say if you look at the four years of work we did in D.C. that the city was healthier, safer, and had a slightly better educational system; it had a significantly better job growth at the end of that time than when I took over as speaker.

Steely: You've been criticized a good bit for being against public education, even though you were a product of it yourself, your children were, etc. You taught in public schools in Newnan. You've been pretty much immersed in it. Nevertheless because of your support for the equivalent of a HOPE scholarship for children to get out of there and to go into private schools, people have said you're against public education. Would you talk for a minute about what you see as the future of public education?

Gingrich: First of all, I'm for public learning. The government's providing scholarships for going to school works with public learning. I'm totally committed to universal public learning. I think every child in America ought to have the opportunity to go to a public learning center of some kind. I think the unionized, bureaucracitized, credential current system doesn't work. It doesn't work because from the schools of education on, it has the wrong standards, it has the wrong model! Credentials people don't know what they're doing. In most inner cities schools, the physics teacher doesn't know any physics, the chemistry teacher doesn't know any chemistry, the Spanish teacher cannot speak fluent Spanish. It is a tragedy. Furthermore, the Carnegie unit, grade oriented, sit for fifty minutes, what really matters is whether or not you're disciplined enough not to cause trouble. And please don't learn too fast because that will put you ahead of the state curriculum guide. That model is exactly, explicitly wrong. The state is wrong. If you want to save the public bureaucracy, then they need a total, thorough, intellectual, overhaul from the ground up. If they don't get that overhaul it ought to be replaced.

I'm for replacement with publicly financed public learning that guarantees that every child in America learns at the best rate in the world. Now if people don't want their children to learn at the best rate in the world, they can be against that. I'm surprised, that the self-interest of bureaucrats, and politicians and union bosses whose careers are tied to mediocrity accept that. I would be surprised at anybody else that really thought about twenty years of bad scores, twenty years of failed reforms, really wants to sacrifice another generation of children inside systems that guarantee they're not going to learn, not going to get to college.

Steely: Now, the thing I've learned is that public education tends to be the only business in the world where the person who is receiving the education demands that he not get what he's paid for. Don't make me read, don't make me study. Don't make me go to the library.

Gingrich:We ought to have very tough standards. We ought to expect children to do real homework. We ought to basically be very tough with the parents. Say, "Look, you bring a child into the world, you have a real obligation to help raise that child. You have a real obligation to get that child a good enough education that they are not going to be living off the rest of us." I think that requires reasserting that responsibility is the other half of rights. You can't sustain rights without responsibility. Starting sometime in the late 1950s, we drifted away from authority. When I was growing up, when you were growing up, there was a presumption that the teacher was an authority figure. There was a presumption that the students should obey the teacher. There was a presumption that the parents would automatically reinforce the teacher. That all got undermined starting with the rising suburban middle class of the late '50s, who decided their children are too precious to be disciplined. Their grandchildren are now the ones who are doing really terrible, tragic things. I'd rather have discipline. I'd rather have standards. I'd rather have the requirement to do real work than have children who degenerate into self-destruction because they are bored and they are told misleading things about their abilities.

Steely: How does religion fit into this?

Gingrich:I don't know, what is "this?" I'm not sure how you're asking the question.

Steely: Into getting children who are disciplined, children who are not violent.

Gingrich:I think that voluntary school prayer was a good thing, because it reestablished the hierarchy of authority. But I also think you cannot explain America without starting with the idea that we hold these truths to be self-evident. The word truth, in that sense, had very deep meaning. Second, that we are endowed by our Creator with certain unalienable rights. I think that to try to explain the Declaration of Independence or the founding fathers, or Washington's, or Jefferson's writings, or Lincoln's writings, without a reference to God is an impossibility. I think it is proper that our society has a sense that each of us has to approach God in our own way, and each of us has to find our definition of the happiness we're going to pursue. But we are spiritual rather than purely physical beings, and that the life of the mind and the spirit is central to physical health. There are greater values than pure hedonism; I think this is at the heart of a healthy society.

Steely: A healthy society is usually reinforced by healthy political parties. Some observers have said that 19 January 1995 was the peak for the Republican party, and for you personally. They see a kind of decline since then. When you look on the national scene, Reagan's gone, you're gone, a number of people who were viewed as leaders are no longer there. It seems to some that no one has stepped up to fill that void.

Gingrich:No one can fill the void until the presidential nomination. Then we'll find out whether or not the nominee can fill the void. It's impossible. You know I've spent sixteen years preparing for a majority. Reagan was a national figure who had spent fourteen years — you could argue sixteen years if you go back to '64 — preparing to be president. You don't fill that kind of a vacuum just by saying, "Gee, we need somebody." If the presidential nominee is a clear enough, strong enough, and effective enough leader, they'll fill the vaccum. If they're not, they won't fill the void. You can make a pretty good argument that nobody has really changed the Democratic party since Franklin Delano Roosevelt, that even people who were pretty strong, like Lyndon Johnson, in the end were strong within a system they inherited, and Jimmy Carter, in part crippled his presidency by trying to change the Democratic party. Clinton ended the Democratic party's domination by sticking with the old party and has, at least in terms of his personal style, been much more centrist than the Democratic party. But I say that because I think it's a big mistake to look at personal fame, or personal achievement which is very rare and confuse it with institutional health. The Republican party has a majority in the House for the third time. That is something it has not achieved since 1926. The Republican party has a majority in the senate, and I don't know of anyone who thinks they're going to lose it next year. The Republican party has thirty-one governors. The Democrats have seventeen. There are two Independents. The two biggest cities in America, New York and Los Angeles, have Republican mayors. Now, I'm amazed that we're at a point that we're the strongest we've been since the 1920s, and people routinely assume we're the ones who are in trouble. Why is that we have thirty-one governors, and the Democrats have but seventeen, and we need to rethink what we're doing? We have the Speaker of the House, they have a Minority Leader, we have the majority of the senate, they have a Minority Leader, and *we* should rethink what we're doing? It seems to me that in fact that we need to calmly and methodically stick to our real values, favor limited government, lower taxes, maintain strong defense, be for the implementation of information age policy, offer a personal social security savings account, offer real practical, bold, and dramatic efforts to help poor people in the inner city and learn to communicate in Spanish, and learn to communicate in African-America media, starting with Black Entertainment Network. If we do those things, the odds are we'll be the dominant party for the next thirty to fifty years.

Steely: For many years, the Republican party was home to Latinos when they came to America. Some say that's changing now because of the various rules that tried to be passed in California and elsewhere, dealing with English as the only language and restrictions on immigration. How do you feel about that?

Gingrich:Reardon got seventy per cent of the Latino vote in the reelections as mayor. George W. Bush carried the Latino vote to be reelected as governor. Jeb Bush carried the Latino vote to become the governor of Florida. Christy Whitman carried the Latino vote to be reelected as governor of New Jersey. We had a bad year in California. There's no question that we need to work hard to be more effective in reaching out to the Hispanic communities. But if George W. Bush is our nominee, and you had to choose between George W. and Al Gore, my hunch is that George W. would do better in California than Gore.

I do think we have to learn to be better at outreach, but that's been a Republican party problem since 1912. From the time Theodore Roosevelt and the Progressives split off, we have been too isolated and too insular a party, and too focused on who we already have and not willing to open our doors. That's endemic to the party. That was true in dealing with the Irish Catholics, it's true of southern whites. It's consistently been a weakness with this party since 1912. In that sense I'm delighted that George W., for example, has a web page in Spanish as well as one in English. I think that's exactly right because it communicates a sense of concern. We should reach out to every ethnic group in America and offer them better social security, lower taxes, better education, better opportunities in health, and a better chance for an economic future. My guess is that there is not a single group that we can't compete in. But the hardest group would clearly be African-American, and maybe secondly Jewish women, who are so intensely pro-choice. But even there, I think someone like George W. or Elizabeth Dole could compete much more effectively than the media thinks.

Steely: You don't think there's any serious danger in having the Hispanic community become much like the African-American community?

Gingrich: No. And I think they're a very different situation, a very different political leadership in the way they gather information. And as I said, you look at New Jersey, Texas, Florida, the Los Angeles mayor's race, you offer the right person with the right message, they're like consumers who switch brands if in fact they get a better offer. I think that the trick is for us is to be much more aggressive in reaching out in those communities. I wouldn't write off African-Americans. I think that our message of lower taxes and more take home pay are good messages along with the message that your child deserves real learning. Virtually all of the parents who applied for the scholarships in Washington were black. There's no reason why we can't reach out to every black parent who knows their child's getting cheated, and have a chance of having a much better future than people expect. But we have to be willing to go and talk to them. We have to be willing to meet. They have to know that you care before they care that you know. I don't think we do a very good job of letting them know that we care.

Steely: You're saying basically that color is not as important as the dream that a person has, and that most everyone has basically the same dream for a decent life and good education for their kids.

Gingrich: It's very straightforward. If you believe that "we hold these truths to be self-evident;" if you believe "we are all created equal;" and if you believe that we're "all endowed by our Creator with certain unalienable rights," then by definition you think every individual has a chance to dream and a chance to have a better future. It's sort of racist to imply that they don't. I actually believe every American is an American. So I think that you can appeal to every American, but you have to recognize that somebody's habit is to watch television. You know that there are big gaps now in terms of what black audiences watch and the white audiences watch. You're pretty stupid if you don't communicate with black audiences by being on the show they're on. If you know that there's a local black radio station, and you're never on it, it shouldn't surprise you that the people who listen to it never hear you. I just think we're not good enough at marketing. Marketing, in the truest sense, not selling. There's a big difference. Understanding what the market wants, talking with the market. My guess is rising young blacks who are twenty, twenty-five-years old, with a college degree who are out there earning a living, are appalled at the level of taxes they are paying and are appalled at the social security that they're paying and would love to have more take home pay and a personal savings account. But if they never hear it from us, if they never see anybody who they identify with talking about it, we shouldn't be surprised that the message doesn't get out.

Steely: Why don't you begin on a wrap-up now?

Gingrich:The whole reason I suggested doing this is that my experience with the first six months is that the adventure is continuing. And that my impact on public policy world wide may actually be greater in the next twenty years than it was in the last ten. I just want to communicate that sense of looking at the longer term, very big decisions, and that you're in a period of dramatic change and ideas are more valuable then ever.

Steely: It's like this biography that ends with you leaving the town hall meeting in Cobb County, your last town hall meeting, to a big ovation. The comment I make on it is that you're leaving this part to go to the next phase of a most remarkable life.

Gingrich:Yes, I hope that this conversation will be in the outline of some of that phase.

Steely: What you haven't said so far is your book, your next book. What's the topic of that?

Gingrich:Probably we'll do a book for early next year on the five major changes we need to make, which are: one, having a social security personal savings account; two, setting a tax cap at twenty-five per cent, eliminating the debt tax and having privatization to shrink the size of the government; three, applying new technologies to help the environment, learning the legal system, and bureaucracy so we get into more modern things; four, redesigning the strategy to reach out to the underclass in culture, to reach out to blacks in particular, reintegrate America into a truly active, truly dynamic society of individuals. Then finally designing a much better model of US leadership in the world. My goal is to write a book which is sort of an open memo for presidential candidates and for anybody who is interested in how to apply these new ideas, how to describe them. It would be where I think we need to go over the next ten years, and would be a pretty good blueprint for a more successful America.

Steely: Even though you are Republican, would you be willing to sit down with Democratic candidates, a Democratic president?

Gingrich: As an American citizen, my concern is for the future of America. I want a successful America that has economic growth and saves social security, that expands freedom, that integrates everybody back into society. That is able to, in a sophisticated way lead the world. Now government takes too much of your money, and services are too poor, and we use an industrial era model which is very expensive. We can't succeed in things like health, environment, and the law when we continue to allow an underclass to exist with people who are entirely cut off from the rest of America. We can't lead the world very effectively, because we are too clumsy and too bullying. I think that model—I mean the difference in those two worlds is pretty dramatic.

Steely: As I remember—if I remember correctly—at the beginning of the Clinton administration, you sat down with Mrs. Clinton and talked with her about what was possible in healthcare.

Gingrich: Actually, if she had followed my advice, we probably would not have become a majority. I just told her if she could pass one small reform bill a year, every year, over eight years that would be a very dramatic change, but she could never pass a very large bill. It was impossible in this society to get a truly big health bill through because it offends too many people. She promptly ignored my advice and wrote a wrote a very large bill, and got everybody mad at her. That was a major factor in our becoming a majority. So in a very real sense, if she had followed my advice–I have a standard rule: I either don't advise people or I tell them the truth as I know it. So I gave her the best advice I could give her.

Steely: What's the difference this time, they didn't follow your advice. I say they, I think she and the president both, were involved in that. And yet, on a number of issues, the NAFTA agreement and other things, you advised the president, usually him asking first. I don't know that you called him up and told him what to do. At least you talked about it, and he did follow your advice.

Gingrich:Beats me.

Steely: You had no idea why one worked and the why other one wouldn't.

Gingrich: I think in the case of health, it was her plan. She knew what she wanted to do. She'd already made her mind up and she was transactually coming around and listening purely for surface transactual reasons.

In the case of NAFTA, we were invaluable. If he didn't work with us, it couldn't pass. So, it depended on where they were, what they were doing, what was up.

Steely: On foreign policy, you almost always supported the president, didn't you? Was there any philosophy behind that or not?

Gingrich:Yes, the philosophy that unless you're egregiously stupid, you should be supportive of the president of the United States. As an army brat living in Europe, I knew how much it used to undermine our morale and infuriate us when politicians back home were not supportive of American policy overseas. I think particularly, once you put mostly young American men and women at risk, you have an absolute obligation to try to make it work and to try to help them. That was the way I always approached the administration. I was the Republican Speaker of the house, but I was also the American Speaker of the house. In foreign policy, American interests came first, not parties.

End of interview.

BIBLIOGRAPHY

Books

Barone, Michael. *The Almanac of American Politics 1990*. Washington, DC: National Journal, 1989.

Barry, John. *The Ambition and the Power*. New York: Simon & Schuster, 1989.

Cheney, Richard B. & Lynne V. Cheney. *Kings of the Hill*. New York: Simon & Schuster, 1996.

Clift, Eleanor & Tom Brazaitis. *War Without Bloodshed*. New York: Simon & Schuster, 1997.

Darman, Richard. *Who's In Control?* New York: Simon & Schuster, 1996.

Drew, Elizabeth. *Showdown: The Struggle Between the Gingrich Congress & the Clinton White House*. New York: Simon & Schuster. 1996.

D'Souza, Dinesh. *Ronald Reagan*. New York: The Free Press, 1997.

Duffy, Michael & Dan Goodgame. *Marching in Place*. New York: Simon & Schuster, 1992.

Gingrich, Newt. *Lessons Learned the Hard Way*. New York: HarperCollins, 1998.

_____. *To Renew America*. New York: HarperCollins, 1995.

_____. *Window of Opportunity: A Blueprint for the Future*. New York: Tor Publishing, 1984.

Kurtz, Howard. *Spin Cycle: Inside the Clinton Propaganda Machine*. New York: The Free Press, 1998.

Maraniss, David. *First In His Class*. New York: Simon & Schuster, 1995.

_____ & Michael Weisskopf, *"Tell Newt To Shut UP!"* New York: Simon & Schuster, 1996.

Matalin, Mary & James Carville. *All's Fair*. NY: Random House, 1994.

O'Neill, Thomas P. *Man of the House*. New York: Random House, 1987.

Roberts, James C. *The Conservative Decade*. Westport, CT: Arlington House, 1980.

Rollins, Ed. *Bare Knuckles and Back Rooms*. New York: Broadway Books, 1996.

Sabato, Larry J. & Glenn R. Simpson. *Dirty Little Secrets*. New York: Random House, 1996.

Smith, Hedrick. *The Power Game: How Washington Works.* New York: Random House, 1988.

Stewart, James B. *Blood Sport: The President and His Adversaries.* New York: Simon & Schuster, 1996.

Warner, Judith & Max Berley. *Newt Gingrich: Speaker to America.* New York: Signet, 1995.

Williams, Dick. *NEWT!: Leader of the Second American Revolution.* Marietta GA: Longstreet, 1995.

Wilson, John K. *Newt Gingrich: Capitol Crimes and Misdemeanors.* Monroe, ME: Common Courage Press, 1996.

Newspapers and Magazines

The Atlanta Constitution
The Atlanta Daily World
The Atlanta Journal
The Carroll Co. Georgian (Carrollton, GA)
The Chicago Tribune
The Clayton Daily News (Jonesboro, GA)
The Congressional Record
The Douglasville Sentinal (Douglasville, GA)
The Daily Times (Gainesville, GA)
Esquire
The Henry Weekly Advertiser (McDonough, GA)
The Hill (Washington, DC)
Hustler
Insight
Mother Jones
The Los Angeles Times
The Marietta Daily Journal (Marietta, GA)
The Miami Herald
The National Inquirer
National Review
New Republic
The New York Post
The New York Times
The New Yorker

The Newnan Times Herald (Newnan, GA)
Newsweek
Roll Call (Washington, DC)
Time
The Tulanian (New Orleans, LA)
U.S. News and World Report
Vanity Fair
The Wall Street Journal
The Washingtonian
The Washington Post
The Washington Post, weekly edition
The Washington Times
The Washington Times, weekly edition
The Weekly Standard
West Georgia Educational Development Program Newsletter (Carrollton, GA)
The West Georgia News (Carrollton, GA)
The West Georgian (WGC Campus paper, Carrollton, GA)

Interviews

Amabile, Nando
Ball, Coach Bubba
Barrow, David
Blankley, Tony
Burba, Gen. Ed
Brock, Catherine
Callaway, Howard "Bo"
Claxton, Dr. Robert
Crook, Gary
Conner, Daryl
Coverdell, Sen. Paul
Dangle, Dr. Richard
Davis, Dock
Desmond, Nancy
Duncan, John
Dupont, Gov. Pierre
Egan, Sen. Mike

Eisenach, Jeff
Evans, J. Randolph
Ferris, Melinda
Fessenden, Arthur
Flynt, Rep. John J.
Gay, Dr. Jim
Gaylord, Joe
Gibson, Dr. Chester
Gingrich, Jackie
Gingrich, Robert & Kathleen
Gingrich, Marianne
Gingrich, Speaker Newt
Gregorsky, Frank
Gregory, Carlyle
Grunden, John and Pat
Hanser, Dr. Steve
Henderson, Ed.
Hoskins, Floyd
Irvin, Rep. Robert
Jackson, Wayne
James, Laurie
Jenkins, Rep. Ed
Jocoy, Kurt
Johnson, Rep. Nancy
Kahn , Charles "Chip"
Kemp, Linda and Jim
Lamutte, Virginia
Lee, Rep. Bill
Linder, Rep. John
McPhearson, Randy
Mahe, Eddie
Martin, Dr. Mac & Carol
Mattingly, Sen. Mack
Meyer, Dan
Meyer, Gen. E.G.
Muncey, Jim
Murphy, Speaker Tom
Newbill, Sen. Sallie

O'Malley, Dr. Jim
Pafford, Pres. Ward
Patrick, Davon & Sue
Prince, Jack
Ray, Rep. Richard
Rhodes, Rep. John
Robinson, Rachel
Robinson, Steve
Roda, Tony
Roush, Chester
Ryan, Dave
Scull, Guy
Scruggs, Barbara
Starry, Gen. Donn
Swindall, Rep. Pat
Tilton, James
Todd, JoAnn
Towery, Rep. Matt
Trotter, William
Upchurch, Dr. John
Updegraft, Tracy
Van Brocklyn, Karen
Vanderjagt, Rep. Guy
Ward, Shelia
Wagner, Dr. Don
Walker, Paul
Walker, Rep. Robert
Wansley, Jeff
Watkins, Pres. Foster
Weed, Robert
Whaley, Jan

INDEX

This book is set in Book Antiqua, 10/13. The text was designed by Marc Jolley. Photographs were laid out by Jay Polk. The dust jacket and the cover were designed by Jim Burt. The book was printed by McNaughton & Gunn, Inc. of Saline, Michigan, and was bound by John H. Dekker & Sons, Inc., in Grand Rapids, Michigan.